Italy's Christian Democracy

Italy's Christian Democracy

The Catholic Encounter with Political Modernity

ROSARIO FORLENZA AND
BJØRN THOMASSEN

OXFORD
UNIVERSITY PRESS

Great Clarendon Street, Oxford, OX2 6DP,
United Kingdom

Oxford University Press is a department of the University of Oxford.
It furthers the University's objective of excellence in research, scholarship,
and education by publishing worldwide. Oxford is a registered trade mark of
Oxford University Press in the UK and in certain other countries

© Rosario Forlenza and Bjørn Thomassen 2024

The moral rights of the authors have been asserted

Published in the United States of America by Oxford University Press
198 Madison Avenue, New York, NY 10016, United States of America

British Library Cataloguing in Publication Data
Data available

Library of Congress Control Number: 2023944838

ISBN 978–0–19–885986–4

DOI: 10.1093/oso/9780198859864.001.0001

Printed and bound by
CPI Group (UK) Ltd, Croydon, CR0 4YY

Links to third party websites are provided by Oxford in good faith and
for information only. Oxford disclaims any responsibility for the materials
contained in any third party website referenced in this work.

Contents

Introduction

This book is about the encounter between Christianity and democratic politics in Italy. Although what we offer is a narrative and reassessment of a nation's political history, the relevance of what follows also has broader implications, much beyond the Italian setting. The last lines of this book were written shortly after Giorgia Meloni won the Italian elections of September 2022, and was then appointed prime minister a few weeks after. With a background in the neo-Fascist youth movement of the Movimento Sociale Italiano (MSI, Italian Social Movement), Meloni presented herself throughout the electoral campaign as "Italian, Christian and a Mother." Unlike Matteo Salvini, the leader of the League for Salvini, she did not make public use of religious objects like the rosary in her political speeches. Yet her appeal to jointly defend Italianness and Christian values against multiculturalism and left-wing political correctness that abjures everything "traditional" places her neatly within what many would identify as right-wing populism. So what is happening with religion and politics in the twenty-first century? While we cannot answer this question definitively, we believe that any search for it must take account of the long and tormented history that from the outset brought Christianity into contact with modern politics.

Contemporary social theory as well as political and cultural debates focus much on the role religion should play in public life and on how religion and secularity can, or should, coexist. In the American context, these debates fundamentally concern the public role of religion in a multicultural environment and the search for what John Rawls called an "overlapping consensus" in support of the American version of liberal democracy (Rawls 1993: 143–9). In the European context, the underpinning value of religion for modern democratic and constitutional traditions came to the fore as an object of public debate in the process of writing the European Constitution (2004). The topic was famously taken up in the momentous debate between Jürgen Habermas and the then Cardinal Joseph Ratzinger (Habermas and Ratzinger 2006). More recently, in the seemingly ever less religious West, Christian identity has become a focal point for right-wing populist parties and movements, also outside Italy. Experts and commentators are now grappling with the populist appropriation of religion, identifying (secular) "elites" or migrant groups as dangerous Others (Marzouki et al. 2016).

At the global level, the overshadowing focus during the last decades has been on Islam and its relationship with modernity and democratic political arrangements

Italy's Christian Democracy: The Catholic Encounter with Political Modernity. Rosario Forlenza and Bjørn Thomassen, Oxford University Press. © Rosario Forlenza and Bjørn Thomassen 2024. DOI: 10.1093/oso/9780198859864.003.0001

(Eickelman 2000; Eickelman and Piscatori 2004 [1996]; Keyman 2007; Rosati 2012). This emphasis was only strengthened by 9/11 and the wars that followed, and then again ten years later by the dramatic events related to the "Arab spring," which saw both secular and religious forces vying for power in (post)revolutionary settings, while Western commentators were expressing ever more concerns regarding the growing influence of Islamic currents and their political—domestic and international—intentions.

In this general scenario, there is one national case that serves as a crucial reference point for our broader reflections on religion, secular politics, and modernity: Italy, the symbolic home of the Roman Empire and birthplace of institutionalized Christianity, which developed—sometimes in contrast, sometimes in symbiosis—with and within that empire. A millennium later, Italy would furthermore become the birthplace of the European Renaissance, that historical period of intellectual, political, and artistic achievement that developed out of the search for a balance between Christian traditions and Greek philosophy and science (Szakolczai 2007). After the demise of the Renaissance, the Italian peninsula hosted some of the fiercest battles between religion and secularity in Western history. This tension continued with the formation of the modern Italian state (1861), first during the decades preceding unification, when condemning and celebratory attitudes toward the French Revolution and its radical secularity were pitted against each other in the Italian *Risorgimento*, and then from 1870 onward, when the popes' temporal power ended and Rome became the capital of Italy. The Italian state thus became an integral part of modern liberal and secular politics, coexisting in strained tension with the Vatican and institutionalized Catholicism. Italy constitutes a theoretically challenging case study of the relationship between religion and modern politics for the simple reason that the country embodied the institutional hierarchy and spiritual centrality of Christianity.

The only real comparison with this paradigmatic situation is perhaps Turkey, even if the latter abolished the caliphate in the 1920s and erased any representation of a universal, extra-territorial organization; in Italy, things developed very differently. And yet, if one disregards the enormous literature on Italian Fascism, famously defined as a "political religion" by the historian Emilio Gentile (1996), the case of Italy has never really made it to the heart of theoretical debates about religion, secularity, and modernity, nor has the country figured prominently in attempts to understand the multiple culture-specific roads toward modernity. The Italian case is worthy of attention, both because of its intrinsic importance and its comparative resonance, especially at a time when secularity is no longer the unquestioned premise of claims to political modernity. Moreover, the fact that Christian Democracy and a Catholic-inspired form of politics are currently undergoing a crisis in many national settings, as the "traditional parties" are challenged by new political movements, makes a deeper reflection on the history and presence of political Catholicism and Christian Democracy all the more urgent and relevant.

I.1 Italy, Christian Democracy, and Modernity

This book explores how Catholic ideas have framed a hermeneutics of democracy and political modernity in Italy, tracing continuities and changes in the tension between religion and secularity throughout the country's history, from the French Revolution to the current, post-secular era. In this time frame, Italian Catholic positions developed from a *radical rejection* of political modernity to a *hesitant embracement* and, finally, *critical co-articulation* of the modern democratic project. Employing more current terms taken from the wider literature on multiple modernities (Thomassen 2010), the Catholic Church and Catholicism at large moved from a position of anti- and countermodernity to one of alternative or parallel modernity.

Contrary to a purely secular reading, we wish to demonstrate that the Catholic embrace of political modernity and democracy emerged as a historically significant alternative to both Socialism and liberalism, one that reincorporated transcendence as a legitimate perspective of truth and re-anchored democracy, justice, and freedom in a religiously argued ethos. The institutionalization of Christian Democracy in the wake of World War II was fundamental in this development. The end of Christian Democracy as a party in the early 1990s did not mean the end of Catholic politics; it rather meant that Catholic "politics" would have to broaden its scope and engage with society in a multitude of ways, rather than through a single party.

The term "Catholic modernity," which will recur frequently in what follows, is not new. In the mid-1990s, Charles Taylor engaged in the question of how Catholics should relate to the culture of the modern by highlighting that a full rejection or acceptance of the secular world is incongruous with Catholicism (Taylor 1996; see also Taylor 2003). To be Catholic is to seek "universality through wholeness," and wholeness requires the respect of difference. In other words, Christianity and Catholicism cannot but manifest themselves in different forms of thought and life. Taylor's contribution to this debate is significant. However, Taylor does not really pay sufficient tribute to the long and deep historical development that gave rise to the idea of a "Catholic modernity". Moreover, Taylor's reflections remain at the philosophical level, with very little contact with concrete political developments. In this book we wish to discuss "Catholic modernity" in empirical and historical terms, examining how Catholic ideas manifested themselves in politics and effective history.

The main thrust of this book is to show how Christianity and Catholicism inspired and influenced political, social, and cultural developments in Italy in multilayered ways that still need to be accounted for and put into perspective. At the same time, the larger development that turned Catholicism into a "partner" of modernity and democracy cannot and should not be reduced to Italian or European party politics (for a comparable discussion focusing on Germany, see Mitchell 2012; see also Sigmund 1987). While part of the development we wish to trace is a mostly Italian story, the institutional development of Catholic thought was also a universalistic, extra-territorial project. By zooming in on the Italian case, our broader comparative aim is therefore also to indicate how the Italian case allows for a deeper understanding of Christian-inspired politics of relevance in other national settings and at the global level.

There is no doubt that Italy is one of those countries most often described by political commentators as "backward," hopelessly trying to "catch up" with modernity.[1] We have already challenged this approach in our previous book, *Italian Modernities* (2016). As has been argued for some decades now within the larger paradigm of multiple modernities (Eisenstadt 2000), it draws on a teleological, unilinear account of modernization processes that is analytically obfuscating and theoretically disabling. One of the inherent "tensions" (to use Eisenstadt's terminology) in modernity is exactly that between religion and secularity. This tension is a crucial variable through which one can historically account for the differentiation of pathways to modernity. The task we set ourselves in this book is to demonstrate how, in given historical periods and in the thought and political projects of concrete persons and movements, modernity became elaborated from *within*.

Approaching modernity as a more open-ended "interpretative space" (Wagner 2012), therefore, also means engaging in both the open and hidden interconnections between religion and politics, between the sacred and the secular. In his genealogical account of the secular, Asad famously argued that secularism must be viewed as something that is much more than the mere separation of religious from secular institutions of government since it presupposes *new* concepts of religion, ethics, and politics, and is closely linked to the emergence of the modern nation-state (Asad 2003: 1–2). Asad rightfully argues that the "secular" cannot be seen as the "rational" successor to "religion." Rather, the secular emerges as a multilayered historical category related to the foundational premises of democracy and modernity. However, precisely the same can and must of course be argued with respect to religion itself, which—in parallel with formations of the secular— dialectically transforms itself, accommodates new realities, and opens itself to alternative readings of the modern.

---

[1] Elements of this approach can be found in the works of social and political historians (Ginsborg 1990), social scientists (Banfield 1958), and economic historians (Rossi and Toniolo 1992, 1998).

In short, in what follows, we will reconstruct how Catholicism put its own imprint on interpretations of political modernity within Italy. By "Catholicism" we mean both positions taken by the official Catholic Church (itself an extremely layered and complex institution) as well as activities and spread of ideas coming from Catholic-inspired organizations and lay thinkers. Our focus is both on broader tendencies within Catholic thought relating to democracy and political modernity and on the more narrowly institutional and party-political context in which Catholic thought developed, especially in the second half of the twentieth century, via Christian Democracy. As we will indicate throughout, the narrative which developed was of course contested and rejected by other cultural and political forces, from liberalism to Fascism, from Socialism to Communism.

I.2 New Perspectives on Political Catholicism and Christian Democracy

Over the past decades, the study of religion and politics has blossomed. Yet, the normative debates on the appropriate place of religion in politics have often remained separate from the study of the actual practices and meanings of religion in the political sphere. This book aims to bridge this divide by focusing on the fertile, paradigmatic case of Italy to illuminate, exemplify, and challenge current empirical and normative theories of religious politics. Although Italy is a core country for Christian Democracy and political Catholicism, there simply is no comprehensive study of the topic in English-language literature. A primary aim of this book is to fill this gap.

Until the 1980s, the history of the Roman Catholic Church and Catholicism in modern Europe was mostly the exclusive right of the theologically and confessionally defined field of "church history" or "ecclesiastical history." Catholic historiography was thus sealed off from mainstream (Anglo-American) historiography, with nineteenth- and twentieth-century Catholicism seemingly acting as little more than a backward-looking footnote in the dominant narrative of secular modernity and progress (see the important review article by Blackbourn 1991). The literature on Christian Democratic parties, which dominated in much of continental Europe, was almost nonexistent. Christian Democracy was relegated to a form of conservatism—or worse, to reactionary politics and a mere weapon in the hands of the Vatican—and considered a rootless centrist party with a minor political tradition, which did not deserve the same attention as Fascism, liberalism, Communism, and other "secular" political ideologies.[2]

---

[2] There are elements of such an attitude in Bracher 1984; Hobsbawm 1994; Mazower 1999. In other works, post-World War II Christian Democracy appears mostly as a force deviating the whole of Europe from a progressive path; see Judt 2005.

However, the notable lack of interest in the histories of Catholicism and Christian Democracy has arguably been more a feature of English-language historiography than literature written in other European languages. There is certainly no shortage of French, Italian, German, or Spanish-language works on Christian Democracy and Catholic practices, ideas, and politics. Granted the importance of Catholicism and Christian Democracy in Italy, where Christian Democracy was the dominant political party from the end of World War II to 1994, Italian historical and social science literature on the topic is gigantic. Throughout the book, we will draw on this scholarship. This includes more recent works by non-Italian (primarily British and American) scholars that include discussions of Christian Democracy in Italy.

In countries like France, Spain, Germany, and Italy, as well as in Latin America and the Philippines, Catholicism has been much more than an official religion; it has been a culture, a way of life, and a reservoir of tropes, symbols, and images placed at the heart of people's world-making. For scholars working in Anglo-American democracies embedded in a Protestant culture, instead, writing about a Latin—or Mediterranean—religion has been of relatively little interest. Historians, after all, are inevitably inclined to share the assumptions and beliefs of the environment in which they live and work. Catholicism was foreign to most of the English-speaking nations except for Ireland, and it was never central to the political cultures of the United States and the United Kingdom. Moreover, the idea of Catholicism did not fit easily in the widespread vision of Europe's twentieth century, the scene of the conflict between secular ideologies and the political projects of the Left and Right (as noted by Conway 1996: 4–5).

More recently, historians have worked hard to integrate Catholicism and its institutions, beliefs, and practices into the narratives of nineteenth- and twentieth-century Europe. Historians have focused their attention on a variety of topics and themes that include, among many other things, the Catholic revival of the late nineteenth century, the Vatican's controversial role in the Third Reich and the Holocaust, the plurality of Catholic experiences and the resilience of Catholic identity vis-à-vis "the age of extremes," the intersection of Catholicism and nationalism, and the Catholic contribution to authoritarian and democratic forms of politics.[3]

Indeed, in very recent years, Christian Democracy has become an almost trendy topic in scholarly literature; historians, social scientists, and political theorists are now working to reconstruct Christian Democratic ideology and its historical development in Europe, Latin America, and the United States, covering

---

[3] See, among others, Blackbourn 1993; Anderson 1995; Buchanan and Conway 1996; Vincent 1996; Conway 1997; Gugelot 1998; Warner 2000; Byrnes 2005; Patch 2010; Porter-Szücs 2011; Houlihan 2015.

a lacunae of earlier scholarship.[4] It is become increasingly clear that Catholicism continued to function as a notable component of modern European identity and that even over the course of the twentieth century, the "secular age" par excellence, Catholicism did not retreat from the public sphere. The history of post-World War II Europe and beyond is incomplete if we fail to consider the role of Catholicism and Christian Democracy. Indeed, during the twentieth century, Catholics—challenged by secularism—expanded their field of action and turned their gaze to a wider range of issues, framing these as religious and ethical matters and claiming authority to speak out and act. The rise of Christian democratic parties and movements, especially after World War II, was a clear manifestation of this process. However, already in the aftermath of the Russian Revolution and World War I, the Catholic Church had emerged as a new political, social, and cultural power, expanding its reach beyond Rome and Europe to regions in Latin America, Africa, and Asia, and shaping the international state system (Chamedes 2013, 2019).

The historiographical move toward Christian Catholic topics has, in fact, been part of a wider "religious turn" in European and American historical studies and international affairs. From Hugh McLeod's (1981) survey *Religion and the People of Europe* onward, this "religious turn" has increasingly called into question stories of secularization, disenchantment, and modernism, providing counternarratives of the re-enchantment and re-sacralization of the world.[5] Several factors have triggered this "religious" shift: from the swooning fortune of the secularization thesis in sociological literature (Casanova 1994, 1996; Berger 1999; Stark 1999) via the insights of the "new cultural history" that emerged and developed in the 1980s and 1990s to the post-modern agenda that has encouraged scholars to include religion in their interests (as noted by Howard 2006: 157).

Thus, in recent years a number of important books have taken on the task of writing Catholicism and Christian Democracy into the history of the twentieth century (Müller 2011; Andes 2014; Moyn 2015; Fontaine 2016; Chappel 2018; Kosicki 2018; Chamedes 2019; Invernizzi Accetti 2019; see also Forlenza 2017a, 2019a). Rather than trying to fit Catholicism into what Charles Maier called the "moral narrative" of the twentieth century (Maier 2000: 826), that is, the narrative focusing on the Holocaust, its causes, and its consequences, these works try in a broader vein to take stock of the crucial contribution of Catholicism to modern European and global history. By integrating cultural studies with intellectual history and methods of social analysis, they have expanded the definition of what constitutes political behavior, putting into question instrumental and functional

[4] These include Durand 1995; Kalyvas 1996; Hanley 1994; Papini 1997; Conway 2003; Kselman and Buttigieg 2003; Mainwaring and Scully 2003; Kaiser 2004; Gehler and Kaiser 2004; Kaiser and Wohnout 2004; Van Hecke and Gerard 2004.
[5] See, for example, McLeod 1981; Howard 2003; Sheehan 2003; Thomas 2005; Cox et al. 2006; Preston 2006; Sorkin 2008; Viaene 2008; The Persistence 2010; Shah et al. 2012; Brodies 2017.

perspectives that reduce religion to a mere epiphenomenon and raising topical questions about Catholic engagement with the political, cultural, and societal spheres. We obviously stand on the shoulders of these and many other works. One humble and primary aim of this book is quite simply to offer the first comprehensive coverage of Christian politics in modern Italian history, hopefully useful for other scholars in the field. At the theoretical level, we hope to contribute to existing scholarship by stressing two interrelated aspects that we consider crucial for a better understanding of the role that Catholicism and Christian Democracy have played in the nineteenth and twentieth centuries: the political dimension of spirituality and transcendence and the transformative power of historical experiences.

I.3 Christian Democracy as Political Spirituality: Generations and the Power of Transformative Experience

Throughout this book we seek to foreground two aspects that in our view can enrich existing scholarship on Christian Democracy: the question of religious experience, transcendence, and spirituality and the power of historical events as transformative experiences. Spirituality as we invoke it here does not refer to an intimate and personal essence but rather implies a combination of culture, lived experience, and mentality, a Weberian *Weltbild* that comes to shape political activities, choices, and behavior in a given historical time.

By political spirituality, we refer to the much-contested concept introduced by Michel Foucault in the late 1970s. Foucault used this term in a series of articles written for the Italian daily *Corriere della Sera*, in which he reported on the revolutionary situation in Iran in the fall of 1978. Foucault was fiercely criticized for this and other writings on Iran (not least because of the subsequent political developments under Khomeini). Leaving aside these criticisms relating to the Iranian context, in what follows we advance the term "political spirituality" as an analytical tool to understand a transformative figuration in which political thought and action become guided by spiritual and religious inspiration. Pace Foucault, political spirituality implies a search for new foundations and a new way to establish a regime of truth and government of the self and others (Foucault 1991, 1998). We will thus not approach religion as a particular faith or a set of doctrines; rather, we will consider the practical, political, and nonreligious effects of religious worldviews, especially in times of crisis and transition.

Surely, Catholic thinkers far from always embraced democracy or democratic ideas. Indeed, the Catholic answer to the challenge of the modern—in Italy and elsewhere—often went in authoritarian and paternalist directions that took the shape of multiple political and cultural manifestations. In other words, there was nothing inevitable and smooth in the Catholics' historical move from countermodernity to an alternative modernity. In what follows, we will unravel this tortuous and complex path made of discontinuities, tensions, and conflicts, and show how transcendence, religion, and lived spirituality often played a decisive role.

It is in this vein that we invoke the concept of "transformative experiences," drawing on the work of Harald Wydra (2007: 4–8) and Arpad Szakolczai (2008). As argued by Szakolczai (2015), human experience can best be captured by invoking the notion of liminality, understood as the middle-phase in a rite of passage. Indeed, experiences that matter to human beings contain some central features recognizable from rites of passages, and their threefold structure of a rite of separation, liminality and rites of re-incorporation (drawing here on the vocabulary introduced by van Gennep 1960 (1909); see also Thomassen 2009). As stated by Szakolczai (2009: 148), "an 'experience' means that once previous certainties are removed and one enters a delicate, uncertain, malleable state, something might happen to one that alters the very core of one's being."

People who go through a rite of passage are genuinely transformed, painful as this may often be. Such an anthropologically inspired view opens up for a different approach to transition and transitology at a general level (Horvath, Thomassen, and Wydra 2015). As we apply it here in this book, it means to pay close attention to transformative experiences that altered the worldviews and self-perceptions of individuals living through a period of crisis. And the two World Wars.

Our focus on transformative experiences is closely connected with the question of generations. As we shall see, Christian Democrats in Italy eventually came to recognize themselves as belonging to three distinct generations and would throughout the twentieth century place themselves with direct reference to such a generational categorization.

The first generation was that of Luigi Sturzo (1871–1959) and Alcide De Gasperi (1881–1954), those who were already active in politics before Fascism and who were heavily marked by World War I. Evidently—and as we shall discuss in Chapters 1 and 2—there were important forerunners to their thought and activity (Giuseppe Toniolo and Romolo Murri, to name just two significant thinkers of the late nineteenth century). However, it was with the first generation that Christian Democracy became a more concrete and embodied idea, one to become institutionalized in the Partito Popolare Italiano (PPI, Italian Popular Party). The second generation was comprised of those Catholics who came to maturity during Fascism and had to develop their political views during the Fascist period, such as Giuseppe Dossetti (1913–96), Aldo Moro (1916–78), and Amintore Fanfani (1908–99). World War II resulted pivotal to their political vision of a Christian democracy. Indeed, as we shall argue (see in particular Chapter 5), World War II was a highly liminal historical period. Living through the war (for those who survived) amounted to a genuine rite of passage. This was the generation that made Christian Democracy Italy's leading political party right after World War II and put themselves forward for elections in 1948. The third generation can be defined as those who entered the ranks later in the post-war period, after the founding moments of Italian democracy, and when the political system had become at least relatively stabilized. They were too young to really having had to deal with Fascism, and therefore also had no direct, personal experience with the Resistance movement during World War II: Ciriaco De Mita (1928–2022) and Arnaldo Forlani (1925–2023) belong to this generation. There has been some discussion of a fourth generation. De Mita, for example, in his later years several times invoked the need for such a fourth generation. However, it is not a coincidence that such a fourth generation has never really established itself as a self-conscious category, and this has much to do with the fact that Catholic politics was "splintered" from the early 1990s.

In Italian historiography the term "generation" is routinely used in a merely descriptive manner: one generation follows after the other. As we use it here, it means something much more than that: it implies having gone through similar threshold experiences in moments or periods of change and transformation. Following again Harald Wydra (2018), we understand generations not only as a cohort of people linked by local proximity, age group, and temporal congruity—a purely biological and biographical dimension—but also as groups and individuals passing through historical situations of crisis where major social and political upheavals coincided with fundamental changes in consciousness and self-identification. Mannheim here talked about an "inventory of experiences" where important occurrences or proper initiations in the formative years of an individual, which then became absorbed, becoming their "natural view of the world," remain active carriers of political and cultural meanings (Mannheim 1952: 300; see again Wydra 2018: 7).

Generational experience is intimately tied to the question of political spirituality. The first generation was deeply marked by the dramatic upheavals represented by World War I, as the second generation was marked for life by their experience of Fascism, the collapse of political order in Italy and the dramatic years of World War II. For both generations the turn to a Christian Democracy was a necessary answer to cope with nothing less than a civilizational crisis, a crisis that had shattered their own worldviews. For both generations, we argue, Christian Democracy was indeed a deeper form of political spirituality that animated their more concrete actions in the political field, rooted in a deep and "humble" sense of reflexivity. This was much less the case for the third generation. They entered the ranks of the party when Christian Democracy had already become institutionalized. Not surprisingly, for the third generation, religion and spirituality would play a less direct and prominent role, both in their political action and in their view of themselves. They were quite simply more pragmatic.

It is with this approach in mind that we hope to make a conceptual contribution to existing scholarship, Italian or not. Historians and social scientists cannot simply treat Catholicism and Christian Democracy as a set of ideas, a political philosophy, or a series of practices and efforts at constructing parties and movements (as in Caciagli 2003), disregarding the content of religion and religious experience. In other words, experience matters, but so does that which Max Weber termed the religious "contents of annunciation." In his comparative analysis of *World Religions* and the rationalization processes that took place within these religions, Weber started from the premise that a religious ethic "receives its stamp, primarily, from religious sources, and, first of all, from the content of its annunciation and its promise" (Max Weber 1958: 270). Indeed, Catholic thinkers more than often took the wording of the gospel seriously. Historical analysis and interpretations remain flawed if this essential fact is not taken into consideration. From this perspective, Catholic thinkers were not "second-hand dealers" of just any text.[6] They were, in fact, existentially committed to translating the ethos of the gospel into a guiding device for individuals and political communities, with a formative impact on institutions and practices. Here, it is useful to invoke Arpad Szakolczai's notion of "reading-experiences," that is, the formative and transformative "encounters with certain works that struck a chord with personal experiences," generating an intellectual drive (Szakolczai 1998: 212).

We of course do not wish to suggest that everything can be reduced to a kind of "essential" character of Christianity and Catholicism, a position that goes against the entire Weberian framework. For Weber, specific social strata may seek to seize a religious ethic or reinterpret it according to their needs and desires. Hence, what matters is how a religious ethic becomes "seized" by historical personalities and with a "stamping effect" on subsequent historical developments (Max Weber 1958: 270; see also Forlenza and Thomassen 2016: 84–5). Our task is to reflect on Catholicism and Christian Democracy as an alternative "political spirituality" in the context of modern European history; to recognize the spiritual impulse behind politics; to pay credit to the central role played by religious factors in historical dynamics without reducing religion to an ideological factor; and to critically understand how Catholics tried to reimagine politics, culture, and society through the transformative and creative power of religion. In short, our analytical premise, pace Weber, involves a fundamental need to move beyond the traditional view of religion as anathema to modernization. It also involves a recognition that processes of rationalization, even in the political realm, must be placed within the sphere of religion, rather than outside its realm.

[6] Taking a cue from Friedrich von Hayek, Müller's book on political ideas in twentieth-century Europe focuses less on "high philosophy" and more on the thought and influence of "in-between figures," or statesmen and politician-philosophers, constitutional advisors, and bureaucrats with visions—what Hayek would define as "second-hand dealers in ideas" (Hayek 1949: 417; Müller 2011: 3).

In an even broader vein, this also means challenging the hegemonic, secular, and liberal vision of modernity, trying to capture the potential richness and deeper challenge of Catholic political modernity. In one of the most important recent works on political Catholicism, James Chappel (2018) argues that Catholics became modern when they accepted the modern split between the private sphere of religion and faith and the public sphere of politics and economics. There is an obvious element of truth in that argument. The fact that religious matters belong to the private sphere is undoubtedly a central (arguably *the* central) assumption of a secular, liberal vision of modernity. Yet, "Catholic modernity" at the same time emerged as a historically significant alternative to both Socialist and liberal visions of modernity, reincorporating transcendence as a legitimate perspective of truth and reason and re-anchoring the sphere of politics in a religiously argued ethos (on "the politics of transcendence" see again Wydra 2015: 97–124). In so doing, Catholics essentially challenged the liberal dictum that religion is confined to the private sphere *even while* accepting the fact that religion cannot stand as a truth elevated above discussion once entering that public sphere; in fact, they worked consciously to translate moral and religious values into social and political life without, of course, reducing the political to the religious (or vice versa). This was not always an easy balance to strike.

The point that must be stressed from the outset is that the most significant thinkers behind Catholic visions of modernity simply did not embrace liberal modernity, even if they accepted some of its essential features (including political pluralism). Instead, they conceptualized, from within the Catholic tradition, a "competing" modernity that was compatible with a Catholic religious vision of history and politics. From this perspective, the emergence of Christian Democracy party politics after World War II cannot therefore be explained as an act of simply putting forward liberal values once again after the disaster of Fascism, couched in a different vocabulary, as implied in the analysis offered by Müller (Müller 2011: 133–43, 2013a: 84–99, 2013b). Hence, the Catholic articulation of modernity should not simply serve as an adjustment of Catholic or European history; it must relate to a more nuanced understanding of the very discourse of "modernity" and the tension between religion and secularity as it unfolded in Europe in the twentieth century.

I.4 Methodology and Methods

The methodological framework of this book relies on the treatment of political culture, ideas, and ideologies which must be considered not simply as second-rate reflections of reality but as part of a historical process. Thus, we approach political ideas from an anthropological perspective, which we argue is necessary for the understanding of the dialectical relationship between thought and experience, following the methodology of the political theorist Eric Voegelin (1952, 1987). In short, we will examine ideas, ideologies, and politics as the symbolization of lived experience. Following again a Weberian approach, we will examine the role of religiously inspired "world images" (*Weltbild*), especially in "out-of-ordinary" moments or—adopting an anthropological language—liminal moments (Thomassen 2014a). Our focus is jointly on the institutional level of political democratization but also on the experiential dimension of politics, that is, how the constitution of a (collective and individual) political subjectivity occurs primarily through experience, especially in crucial moments of transformation, provoking fundamental changes in consciousness and political beliefs and actions.

In what follows, we will focus on the background experiences, thoughts, and action of leading Catholic politicians and activists, operating within or beyond the church. In line with our conceptual approach, we zoom in on historical periods marked by crisis and political transformation, and how these experiences generated a new state of consciousness, meanings, and symbols that shaped the political beliefs and actions of Catholics. Where possible, we will also indicate how Christian democratic ideas penetrated civil society down to the microhistories of families and personal narratives. For this purpose, we will consult not only political speeches and events related to "high politics" but also private letters and diary entries written by Italians for whom Christianity became a salient *topos* for their understanding and interpretation of politics as a lived reality and personal sacrifice.

In terms of concrete methods and sources, the book draws on newspaper articles, interviews, magazines, and a long list of documents conserved in various archives as well as autobiographical and biographical material (including letters and memoirs written by political protagonists living through moments of transition), which serve to illuminate the personal reflections of Catholic politicians and activists. Much of our argument also builds on the secondary literature on Christian Democracy. We will make due reference particularly to the extensive Italian scholarship on the topic, building on the many important contributions, with the aim to propose a more complete and more theoretically informed view of the religious dimension of political Catholicism and Christian Democracy in modern Italy.

It goes without saying that the account we put on offer cannot in any way be exhaustive. We have wished to paint the broad picture of the interrelationship between Christianity and politics throughout the last two centuries of Italian political life, with due reference also to global developments. This ambition of course comes with a price, as we cannot go into detail with all complexities in question. It is for example well known that Italy is an extremely varied country, also in terms of politics. Regional differences, also in voting patterns, are huge, and were huge also at the time of the first local and general elections after World War II (Forlenza 2008). Having ourselves both lived and worked across northern, central, and southern regions of Italy, we have indeed in earlier works tried to contribute to the regional and locality-specific dimension of Italian political history (Thomassen 2001, 2006). When we in the following speak about "Italy" and the "nation," we do so because our focus in on thinkers and activists for whom the development of a Catholic kind of politics indeed related to a national project. Yet, even when we in this book allow ourselves to generalize about "Catholic positions" or broader political tendencies in the country, we are conscious that such generalizations cannot do justice to regional differences. One of the secrets behind the triumphant entry of Christian Democracy into Italian politics after World War II was indeed the fact that the party managed to "speak to" the Italian population in a language understandable to various socioeconomic and demographic groups. This includes both men and women—even if we also will not be able to go into great detail with gender politics and the question of women's role in society (but see Chapters 2 and 8 in which we deal more with the dimension of gender). It is indeed important that the leading figures trying to establish and develop a Christian Democracy came from both the North and the South, and this—as we will indeed discuss—played quite a crucial role both for their thinking and their ability to "understand" their country.

I.5 Outline of the Book and Chapter Contents

This book explores the history of the Italian Christian Democracy and the relationship between Italian Catholic politics and political modernity and democracy from the French Revolution to the post-secular, global world of the present. It explains why the case of Italy is interesting from a historical point of view but also why it is relevant for the heated debates on politics and religion in the current global world. Although the book has a chronological structure, transversal themes discussed throughout the chapters will suggest diachronic connections with reference to the broader European and global developments against which the Italian case must be understood.

Chapter 1 ("Sanctifying Democracy") focuses on the Catholic response to the challenge of the French Revolution, the popes' condemnation of the principle of 1789, and the first emergence of lay Catholic politics. Chapter 2 ("Democratizing from Below") evaluates the impact of Pope Leo XIII's *Rerum novarum* (1891) on Catholic social, cultural, and political positions, the emergence of a full-fledged and well-organized Catholic subculture or "pillar" that was established from the inside, and the first attempts at a "Christian" democracy. Chapter 3 ("Popular Democracy") explores how the experiences of World War I were decisive for Catholic political thinkers and activists of the first generation, with the birth of the Italian Popular Party—the Italian Catholics' first sustained experiment in mass politics—by the Sicilian priest Luigi Sturzo, and then tells the story about the end of the PPI when it was outlawed by the Fascist regime in 1926. Chapter 4 ("Death and Resurrection: The Challenge of Fascism") focuses on the relationship between Catholic politics and Fascism from the late 1920s to World War II and on the new generation of Catholics who grew up in Fascist Italy. This second generation of Catholics thirsted for new cultural inspiration and engaged in an eclectic combination of cultural references—including Jacques Maritain, who became a fundamental moral and intellectual compass—and liberated Italian Catholicism from its provincialism. Chapter 5 ("Democratic Conversion") deals with the Catholic experiences of World War II and details how this experience represented a political and existential crisis, a genuine moment of liminality, that triggered the emergence of a new state of consciousness and a new political subjectivity, pushing Catholics to elaborate, through a series of documents, a rich Catholic democratic political project in clear discontinuity with their own tradition. While Chapter 6 ("Integral Democracy") covers the years 1945–8 and the emergence of Christian Democracy as the dominant party of Italian politics, Chapter 7 ("Instituting Catholic Modernity: The Writing of the Italian Constitution") more specifically examines the Catholic contribution—of a group of Catholic intellectuals and politicians known as *professorini* ("fledgling professors")—to the writing of the republican and democratic Constitution of 1948, focusing on the specific way in which the Italian citizen became symbolically coded as a "person" and not an "individual." Chapter 8 ("Consolidating Democracy") analyzes the consolidation of Christian Democracy between the late 1940s and the late 1960s. It does so by discussing the social and economic reforms implemented by the party, the reinforcement of its structure, and the governmental alliance with the Socialists (the so-called opening to the Left) that was contested by the church's hierarchy. The chapter also deals with the impact of the Second Vatican Council, in itself a global event, on Italian politics. Chapter 9 ("'The Secular Challenge") examines how the forces of secularism, consumerism, and sexual modernization as well as other societal changes deeply affected Italian political Catholicism from the late 1960s onward. While the most important and active sectors of Catholicism refused to join the party after the Council, Christian Democracy in this period was increasingly becoming a static apparatus of grey politicians of the third generation, with Aldo Moro as one of those few who attempted to steer history in a different direction in the 1970s. His attempt failed, though, as he was kidnapped and executed by the Red Brigades, a leftist terrorist group. Finally, Chapter 10 ("Orphaned Catholics") describes the demise of Christian Democracy following the end of the Cold War and the morass of corruption in which Italy had fallen; we explain how the Catholic involvement in politics became fragmented, while also focusing on the cultural project launched by the church in 1994 to reaffirm the role of Catholicism in the public sphere without the help and support of a single party, thus renewing the Catholic political and cultural identity—a development that can be traced up until today.

The concluding chapter ("The Futures of Christian Democratic Politics") situates the discussion of the Italian case within the current global context and deals with a series of larger questions of comparative relevance: what lesson, if any, can be learned from the Italian case? What is the role of religious politics and, more generally, "political spirituality" in the present, global world? Does Christian Democracy have a future? Is there any space for a "Catholic modernity" or perhaps even a "re-enchanted modernity" today? What would be its contours, in Italy and beyond? And how can we understand and assess the use of religion by new "populist" political actors making claims to Christianity in the twenty-first century?

1

Sanctifying Democracy

To understand the complex relationship between Christianity and democracy in the Italian context and the Catholic involvement in national politics even before the emergence of the unified state in 1861, hence from the very first moment Catholics participated in the process of unification (*Risorgimento*), it is necessary to understand the church's reaction to the French Revolution. Time and again, from Gregory XVI's encyclical letter *Mirari vos* to Pius IX's *Syllabus errorum* of 1864, popes condemned the ideas of 1789: democracy, progress, and the principle of national self-determination. Following the 1870 conquest of Rome by the new-born Italian state, the Vatican's *non expedit* (using the famous formula "neither elected nor electors") forced Catholics to stay out of Italian politics, at least at the national level. However, during the second half of the nineteenth century, Catholic responses to modernity at the same time started to soften. Already before the unification, the journalist and Catholic priest Davide Albertario had claimed the need to "sanctify democracy." The expression is noteworthy and signals a decisive conjunction—and evidently also the danger of fusion—of the religious and the secular, that is, of the millennial tradition of Christianity and modern politics. Albertario saw, with clarity, that democracy was not a momentous historical mistake. The church must domesticate this new political animal. Alignment rather than rejection was the strategy to follow.

Another important thinker of the nineteenth century, the Catholic philosopher Vincenzo Gioberti, similarly argued that Italy's civilizational mission as a nation was to develop a political alternative to the French Revolution anchored in spirituality and Catholic principles. In fact, after the unification and despite the official *non expedit*, Catholics across the country would participate in local elections and start to associate their political interests with those of the church. It was neither an easy battle nor a uniform movement. However, despite its heterogeneity and massive resistance coming from within and outside the church, the historical contours of an alignment that would come to shape modern politics did indeed start to emerge. Let us, in this chapter, look at some of the most significant voices in this formative period ranging from the French Revolution to the unification of Italy in 1861.

In the autumn of 1789, the Jesuit theologian and historian Francesco Maria Zaccaria warned that a "very strange revolution" was threatening "the ecclesiastical" and "the political" (Zaccaria 1790: 163; see also Pellettier 2013: 237–9).

Italy's Christian Democracy: The Catholic Encounter with Political Modernity. Rosario Forlenza and Bjørn Thomassen, Oxford University Press. © Rosario Forlenza and Bjørn Thomassen 2024. DOI: 10.1093/oso/9780198859864.003.0002

Zaccaria was writing about the religious spirit of the eighteenth century, which he considered to be negatively marked by increasing incredulity and by the fact that the church was going through a dramatic time during which many people were losing their faith. The Parisian events did not go unnoticed by this sensitive man of the church. The revolution in the political field, Zaccaria thought, could provoke sinister consequences for the church.

Opposition to the Catholic Church, considered a stronghold of the old regime, was indeed one of the animating forces behind the French Revolution. Following the Revolution, the properties of the church were nationalized, the religious orders were dissolved, and men and women of the church were forced to swear loyalty to the state. Anticlericalism was explicitly written into government policy in 1792, when the First Republic was declared. The papacy watched with dread as the Enlightenment "cult of reason" sought to replace Christianity. Instead of worshipping God, the revolutionaries worshipped Man. In 1793, the humiliation of the church reached its symbolic climax when, during the so-called "festival of Reason," the Parisian Cathedral of Notre Dame was turned into a "temple of Reason." The Christian altar was destroyed and replaced with an altar to the goddess of Liberty. The end of 1792 and the beginning of 1793, a period marked by the peak of the Terror and the execution of Louis XVI, was a time of "big fear" (Pellettier 2013: 397–415) for the church. The papacy, and Christians all over Europe, watched with anxiety as the wars of Vendée unfolded, from 1793 to 1796. As a reaction to the centralizing policies of the Republic, which involved the persecution of disobedient local clergy and the violent suppression of religious orders, Vendeans eventually took up arms against the Republicans under the banner of "The Catholic Army." Over the next three years, men, women, and children were brutally and systematically massacred, and the Catholic and monarchist peasants of the Vendée were killed in the name of the Revolution (Martin 2014).

While the papal domains in France were annexed by plebiscite, by the end of the eighteenth century, Napoleon went on to annex the Papal States in Italy and General Berthier conquered Rome, proclaiming the birth of the Roman Republic (1798). Pope Pius VI left the Vatican and died in Valence on August 29, 1799. His successor, Pius VII (1799–1823), negotiated—through the minor cleric Ercole Consalvi—a concordat with the First Consul Napoleon. The treaty did not restore the old Christian order in France, but it certainly gave the church certain guarantees. In the following years, the new pope followed a policy of cooperation with France based on mutual respect and attended Napoleon's coronation in 1804. Although the pope decided to support France's continental blockade of Great Britain, Napoleon annexed the Papal States in 1809. Pius VII was taken prisoner and exiled to Savona. The exile ended with the Concordat of Fontainebleau in 1813. Pius VII returned to Rome a few days after Napoleon abdicated, in April 1814, and soon revived the Inquisition and the Index of Condemned Books. With the Congress of Vienna, the restoration could become reality, also for the church.

Revolutionary and, subsequently, Napoleonic France had been an issue for Rome not simply from a territorial, political, and institutional viewpoint. It had been—and would continue to be—a challenge in terms of ideas and philosophy. The French Revolution had given political and cultural expression to Enlightenment anticlericalism, to atheism, and to the will to replace God with the Supreme Being and the Goddess of Reason. From a Catholic point of view, the idea of science and reason as an overcoming of religion simply had to be rejected. Truth was a product not of individual reason but of the tradition of a community as interpreted, codified, and institutionalized by the church, the indispensable mediator between God and mankind.

The French Revolution was also the "national" modern event that was decisive in giving political content to the ideas of cultural difference and popular and individual self-determination, which had initially been introduced by the Protestant Reformation. The Reformation had shattered the Catholic medieval world, the *Respublica Christiana*—the world that combined a wide normative community of Christian culture with a variegated series of overlapping jurisdictions. What emerged was a set of realms of inviolable borders controlled by secular rulers. From a Catholic point of view, the secular occupation—at once a conceptual and a territorial occupation—of the religious domain was quite problematic. The pretensions of popular autonomy and self-determination were also problematic: the twin ideas of the individual's sovereignty over himself (it was still a "he") and the sovereignty of the nation-state created through a contract (i.e. a constitution) among those individuals. The French Revolution had given political content to these pretensions, even institutionalizing them through an eponymous declaration of the "rights of Man." Its notion of popular rule was inherently anti-Catholic, as it was inherently volatile. The changing secular, political authority was incompatible with the religious control and the integralist and universal (Catholic) conceptions of society. The French Revolution was premised on the idea that hitherto separated individuals could gather together in groups and communities that supposedly expressed a national will with supreme command over human affairs. This very notion of "secularization" was, for obvious reasons, exceedingly difficult for Catholics to accept.

Rome could not but officially condemn the Revolution and its modern political project (Pellettier 2013). A limited section of the French clergy—the so-called "constitutional" clergy, such as the Abbé Henry Jean Baptiste Grégoire (1750–1831)—embraced the ideas that Christianity was a religion of liberty and fraternity, that the "rights of Man" derived from a Christian principle, and that the Revolution could blaze the trail for evangelical renewal (Goldstein Sepinwall 2005). The French "constitutional" clergy obviously rejected the separation of church and secular state, and yet they embraced—at times enthusiastically—the idea of a "republican Christianity" (Plongeron 1973: chs 3 and 4). Nothing of the sort happened in Belgium or Rhineland. However, in the northern regions of the Netherlands most of the clergy supported the party of the "patriots" who, in 1795, overthrew the old regime with the help of French soldiers and replaced it with a republic that granted all citizens equality of rights and freedom of religion. In Italy, the clergy were at best skeptical of the principles of 1789 and tried to protect and safeguard the church's rights and prerogatives. Yet, many believed that the church should remain indifferent to any form of political regime. Others, such as Cardinal Chiaramonti, the future Pope Pius VII, highlighted the evangelical character of the principles of equality and fraternity (Leflon 1958: 414–51).

However, these positions were considered deviations from the Vatican's official stance. The church naturally sided with "tradition," attacking the Revolution for its atheism and considering the modern project as a work of the Devil. From a Catholic perspective, Joseph De Maistre—a counterrevolutionary thinker par excellence—was right. The Revolution was not only the final manifestation, indeed the culmination, of errors profoundly rooted in modernity; it was also the divine punishment that served to atone for the errors and purify the evils that the impenetrable plan of God's Providence had allowed.

In 1799, the Revolution was coming to an end and the Napoleonic era was about to begin. Rome turned into a republic that declared revolutionary France a revolutionary "sister republic." 1799 was also the year in which the Camaldolese Monk Bartolomeo Cappellari (1745–1846), the future Pope Gregory XVI (1831–46), wrote a book titled *Il Trionfo della Santa e della Chiesa contro gli assalti de' novatori respinti e combattuti colle stesse loro armi* (*The Triumph of the Holy See and the Church against the Assault of Innovators, Repelled and Combated with Their Own Weapons*). The text was directed against the Jansenists and dealt primarily with theological matters (Congar 1960: 96–7; Alberigo 1964: 359–67; Korten 2016).[1] At the same time, the text also had a broader appeal, touching upon the crucial question of the church's role after the French Revolution. Cappellari rejected revolutionary ideas and categorically refused that the state had the right to oversee religious matters. In line with tradition, he staunchly proclaimed the church's independence from civil society and secular politics. He also insisted that its earthly guide remained infallible in matters of faith. Cappellari set the tone not only for the evolution of ecclesiological thought but also for the substantial attitude of the church toward political modernity and against liberal regimes during the entire nineteenth century. This position would establish as a so-called "intransigent" attitude in decades to follow. Thus, the church retreated into its grandiose solitude and locked itself up in a missionary attempt to reconquer the world. This struggle with liberal democracy would last an entire century (Clark and Kaiser 2003).

---

[1] Several scholars, most notably Dale K. Van Kley (1996), have argued that the intellectual origins of the French Revolution are to be found in Jansenism more than in the Enlightenment.

1.1 Pope Gregory XVI and Lamennais

The French Revolution eventually ended in Napoleonic dictatorship, followed by a long and bloody period of European warfare, the Napoleonic wars. In a way, the historical events seemed to prove the church right. The Napoleonic wars can indeed be seen as the first instance of "total warfare" (Bell 2007). However, much to the Vatican's regret, the prolonged warfare and the ensuing peace agreements did not put an end to the idea of the modern nation-state: quite the contrary. In fact, in the short period that followed the Congress of Vienna, the church briefly sought to engage in European politics and society more constructively (Chadwick 1981: 535–608). However, the election of Cappellari as Pope Gregory XVI and ruler of the Papal States in 1831 signaled the beginning of a new phase of retrenchment and hostility vis-à-vis the politics of the new time (Korten 2016).

In 1832 (on August 15), Gregory XVI's encyclical letter *Mirari vos*, subtitled *On Liberalism and Religious Indifferentism* condemned the proposal of Félicité Lamennais (1782–1854) to welcome the new society and its civil liberties as an opportunity for Catholicism to "baptize," in Lamennais's words, the Revolution. The text reads as follows: "At the present moment a brutal malevolence and imprudent science, an unrestrained arbitrariness prevails" ("Alacris exultat improbitas, scientia impudens, dissolute licentia"). The problem of the church was not only the ideas and consequences of the French Revolution, but also the attitudes of certain sectors within Catholicism that argued for a *ralliement* with those ideas and its stalwarts. The most important and staunch representatives of the idea that democracy and revolution were not necessarily incompatible— in fact, they were perfectly congenial to Catholicism and the Christian spirit— were Lamennais and his friends (see Lamennais's writing in Milback and Lebrun 2018).

From the pages of the daily *L'Avenir*, whose motto was "God and Liberty," Lamennais and his group struggled on a double front in 1830 and 1831. On one side, to the liberals, Lamennais declared that he unreservedly embraced the modern liberties that descended from the French Revolution; he included in such liberties the freedom of teaching, which many liberals were reluctant to concede fearing a clerical invasion of the field. On the other side, he tried to convince Catholics that it was time to get rid, once and for all, of the past and the *ancien régime*, and to look confidently to the future (as indicated by the journal's title). In other words, *L'Avenir* was open to national Romanticism. It invited people and states to embrace peace, disarmament, and the unification of Europe. At the same time, the journal backed the "national" insurrection of the Irish and the Poles in the name of the rights of people and nations to decide their destiny. Lamennais and the writers of *L'Avenir* declared being in favor of universal franchise and the republican order, and they deemed the revolutions that were sweeping away a large part of Europe providential. They also reflected on the social and economic aspects of democracy, on the need for a "Christian" political economy, and on the redistribution of goods—an issue that, at the time, was obscured by the more pressing problem of the production of goods in industrializing societies.[2] The writers of L'Avenir wanted to translate their ideas and intellectual activity into a political and pragmatic plan. Therefore, they created a General Agency for Religious Freedom (Agence générale pour la Défense de la liberté religieuse). On the suggestion of the Dutch journalist Le Sage ten Broeck, it extended its scope to Europe to fight for political and religious freedom and build a "Holy Alliance of People" in contrast to the monarchist "Holy Alliance." From this perspective, the papacy should reject the monarchy for being an oppressive force of the church and the masses and ally itself with the people.

The political and cultural project of L'Avenir essentially distinguished a bad Revolution (1789) from a good Revolution (1793). It thus accepted the Declaration of the Rights of Man and of the Citizen while at the same time strongly rejecting the centralized Jacobin state that oppressed religious freedom and local autonomies and diversities. In other words, when Lamennais proposed to "baptize democracy" he meant not so much the democracy of 1789 and its theory of national sovereignty, but the democracy of 1793 that located the source of power in a more abstract and mythical "people."

However, this was not an easy position to uphold at the time. The preaching of L'Avenir fell on deaf ears and encountered firm opposition from almost every sector of Catholicism and almost everywhere in Europe, except in Belgium.[3] The Holy See firmly held on to the old regime's political ideals. The French hierarchy banned the liberal Catholic paper in a number of dioceses and its program was labeled as revolutionary and contradictory. This happened even before Gregory XVI's reaction, expressed in the Mirari vos.

The pope's problem was not so much cultural modernity (or the attempt to overturn the traditional culture and metaphysics at the core of the Western and European project) or the challenges of a socioeconomic project (i.e. the rise of new forms of community and economic life), but political modernity: the attempt to overthrow the traditional political order that conferred on the pope the status of European sovereign and ruler of the Papal States (a third of Italy). The challenge of political modernity was the most immediate and urgent question for Gregory XVI, as it would be for his successor, Pius IX. Indeed, political modernity struck

---

[2] This section draws on Le Guillou 1966; Verucci 1967: 13–64; Prelot 1969: 102–9.

[3] It was in Belgium that "liberal Catholicism" first emerged in Europe. The reason for this is that, after the Congress had united Belgium and Holland under the name of the Kingdom of the Netherlands in the hope that they would form a barrier against France, Belgian Catholics and liberals collaborated to obtain the independence of their country between 1828 and 1839. It is still unclear whether Lamennais had a direct or even an indirect influence in Belgium. Either way, Belgian Catholics shared some of the liberal principles of Lamennais, thought that the church could still flourish in conditions of general freedom and toleration, and joined forces with liberals in the name of the principle of respect for human freedom. On this issue see Viaene 2000.

the papacy and its holy authority within the Papal States at the core. Likewise, it challenged the very existence of the Papal States themselves, and thus of the Catholic Church as a temporal power, well beyond the mere question of its place in Italy. This was the reason why Gregory XVI ignored social and economic issues—the consequences of the Industrial Revolution—and was particularly concerned with the more political and institutional issues that the French Revolution and its ideas had raised. The point was that, in France, the modern state was formed *against* the church, and the same was happening elsewhere. National and nationalist movements struggled against the church's role as a bulwark of the old regime. In Italy, the first *moti* of the *Risorgimento* (literally resurgence, i.e. the process of national unification that culminated in the establishment of the Kingdom of Italy in 1861) had strong anticlerical and anti-church connotations. In addition to this, the pope was skeptical about a doctrine that "linked the thrust of Christianity to the collective judgment of humanity" rather than to tradition and about the "adoration of the masses" that pervaded Lamennais's thoughts and words, which presented a remarkable similarity with those of the Italian revolutionary Giuseppe Mazzini (Coppa 2013: 71).

For this very reason, Gregory XVI went on to attack the program of Mazzini's Young Italy, the political movement for the Italian youth (under the age of 40) that the latter had formed in 1831 while in exile in France, and which was to become one of the most important and influential movements of the Italian *Risorgimento*. The movement's cultural and political project was to make Italy a united, independent, and republican nation, where citizens were equals. The direct derivation from the ideals of the French Revolution was evident. Not unlike Lamennais, and inspired by the civic and pre-Romantic religion of Jean Jacques Rousseau, Mazzini believed in a new faith in progress based on a humanity united toward the achievement of the common good. As Mazzini wrote: "[T]he time has come to convince ourselves that we can only rise to God through the souls of our fellow man." He continued by saying that "we can neither improve without the improvement of Humanity, nor can one hope that one's own moral and material condition will improve without the improvement of the whole" (Mazzini 1936: 47). For Gregory, the theology, ideology, and politics of Mazzini were no better than those of Lamennais; consequently, he did not hesitate to denounce and condemn them.

1.2 The Revolutionary Years of 1848 and 1849

Gregory XVI's condemnation of *L'Avenir* and its attempt to bridge Catholicism and liberalism was scathing and set the tone for what would happen next. The encyclical *Quanta cura* and the attachment written by his successor Pius IX (Giovanni Maria Mastai Ferretti, 1792–1878), the aforementioned *Syllabus errorum*, opened a deep conflict between the church and modern civilization and politics that lasted at least until World War II but also beyond, until the Second Vatican Council.

Yet, the hopes and expectations of liberals and reformers within and outside the church could not have been higher at the moment of Pius IX's election in 1846. He was considered a "liberal," to use a secular term that does not quite apply to the church, and a champion of modernization and reform. For many, Pope Pius IX would undoubtedly find a new way to confront modernity in its multifaceted aspects—certainly in a better way than his predecessor, who had even defined the newly invented railroads as a machination and a tool of the Devil. The action of the new pope initially met with these high hopes and expectations, and it convinced both patriots and reformers that they had found a leader. In July 1846, acting as head of the Vatican state, he granted amnesty for political crimes. Encouraged by public opinion, in 1847 he granted (limited) freedom of the press and appointed a *consulta di stato* (which could be seen as similar to a parliament), a civic guard, and a council of ministries. Alarmed by and worried about such reforms, Austria (a bastion of conservative Europe) occupied Ferrara (part of the Papal States) in July 1847, but in doing so pushed the pope to raise his voice against the occupation, thus stirring up national opinion.

The revolutionary events that swept across Europe and Italy in 1848 and 1849 changed everything. At first, following the example of other sovereigns, the pope was forced to grant a constitution and concede a lay government led by the cardinals Gaetano Recchi and Giacomo Antonelli, which included a few liberals and members of the Holy See. With the first war of Independence of the *Risorgimento*, the pope initially decided to support the nationalist and unification movement led by the Piedmontese dynasty of Savoy, but then changed his mind and abandoned the national camp (April 29, 1848). After a few "moderate" attempts failed, public disorder and riots spread. Cardinal Pellegrino Rossi was assassinated and Pius IX fled Rome. Disguised as a common priest, the pope took refuge in Mola di Gaeta (today's Formia) under the protection of Ferdinand II of Bourbon, King of the Two Sicilies. Rome thus became a republic (February 1849), led by Mazzini and the patriots Carlo Armellini and Aurelio Saffi. Its founding decree, publicly proclaimed to a Roman crowd from the Campidoglio, read as follows:

Art. 1. The papacy is removed from temporal power *de facto* and *de jure*.

Art. 2. The Roman Pontiff will have all the necessary guarantees for the independence of his spiritual powers.

Art. 3. The Roman state's form of government will be pure democracy and will take the glorious name of the Roman Republic.

Art. 4. The Roman Republic will have relations with the rest of Italy as required by ordinary nationality.

It was clear that some of the more radical principles of the French Revolution nurtured the republican movement. From Mola di Gaeta, the pope urged the Catholic powers (France, Austria, Spain, and Naples) to intervene and take action against the usurpers, which they did. In July 1849, the French General Oudinot overthrew the Roman Republic; the pope's authority was restored. Pius IX returned to Rome in April 1850, with the firm intention of defending his temporal power by any means, even if France invited him to act with moderation.

This was a pivotal period. The events of 1848 and 1849 brought back to life—with even greater intensity—the almost insurmountable issue that the Catholic Church had tried to cope with for half a century: how to tackle the modernizing world that remained imbued with the political, intellectual, and cultural ideas and spirit of the Revolution from the end of the eighteenth century onward? In particular, what was to be done about the civil and religious freedoms stated in the Declaration of the Rights of Man and of the Citizen? How could the consequences of the principles and ideas of 1789 be controlled? For many Catholics and the Vatican, the violence caused by the liberal and national insurrections of 1848 and 1849 was the ultimate confirmation that there was a direct link between 1789 and the destruction of religious and moral values and the threat to social order.

The case of the Jesuit Taparelli D'Azeglio (1793–1862), the brother of the Catholic liberal Massimo D'Azeglio and one of the founders of the influential Jesuit journal *La Civiltà Cattolica* (1850), is crucial in this regard (De Rosa 1993). In his youth, Taparelli D'Azeglio was close to the neo-Guelph views of Gioberti and Cesare Balbo, trying to bridge the gap between Catholics and moderate liberals. Neo-Guelphism represented a position that sought to unify the nation and the church: the neo-Guelphs believed that the process of national unification and the establishment of a unified Italy were impossible without religion and the pope. They insisted that the elimination of the papacy would not make Italy politically modern. Taparelli D'Azeglio solicited the Society of Jesus to avoid closure to anything that was new—reaffirming and confirming its reputation as champion and advocate of the absolutist order—and to support, instead, the participation of Catholics in secular politics in the new representative order that had developed in Europe shortly after the French Revolution and throughout the first half of the nineteenth century. Such participation, he thought, was all the more necessary as it would defend the interests of the church in what was a difficult and complicated situation. In the first instance, Taparelli D'Azeglio had positively judged the uprising of 1848, which resorted to violence and revolution for the accomplishment of the national cause. However, his devotion to the pope and the ecclesiastical institution did not falter. After 1848, anticlericalism became much more radical and pervasive. In 1850, the government of Piedmont—led by Taparelli's brother Massimo—promulgated the Siccardi law, which restricted the powers of the Catholic Church and abolished the ecclesiastical tribunals and the right of asylum. Taparelli D'Azeglio, then, embraced a negative stance on liberalism, the representative system, and democracy. He therefore considered 1848 a key turning point because it was the end of any possible relationship between Catholics and liberals. Such a stance found its more radical expression in his *Esame critico degli ordini rappresentativi nella società moderna* (1854, "A critical examination of the representative orders in modern society"), which deeply influenced the "intransigent" Catholic culture (Traniello 1998: 55–61).

Ironically, Taparelli D'Azeglio—adopting a Thomist perspective and starting from Aquinas's natural law philosophy, seen as the basis for a theoretical model for the church's engagement with the modern world—was also the man who forged and invented, in the 1840s, the term *giustizia sociale* ("social justice"). He used it in his work in five volumes titled *Saggio teoretico di diritto naturale appoggiato sul fatto* ("A theoretical essay on natural law based on facts"), printed in 1843 (Behr 2019). In Taparelli D'Azeglio's understanding, "social justice" was a formal and not a substantial or material concept. It had nothing to do with the way the concept is used today, or how it was used after World War II; it was also unrelated to the idea of social justice as developed by John Rawls in his 1971 *A Theory of Social Justice*. For Taparelli D'Azeglio, social justice was a branch of the concept of justice—analogous to "commutative" or other types of justice—and did not convey a specific worldview. It could be liberal, conservative, or even Socialist. In short, "social justice" suggested that the concept of justice as traditionally understood spilled over into a different field: that of social life. Thus, what was needed for such a translation was not the elaboration of a new philosophy, but the creation of new conditions that would serve to make its application possible.

In the following decade, social justice became a ubiquitous term, and not only for Taparelli D'Azeglio. It was picked up by the Jesuits, by John Stuart Mill in *Utilitarianism* (1863), by Antonio Rosmini, by the English Christian Socialists, and—as we will see in the next chapter—by Leo XIII in his encyclical *Rerum novarum*, which was to become the most authoritative text and source for twentieth-century Catholic social teaching. In several writings, Taparelli D'Azeglio discussed at length and elaborated another crucial concept, which would later prove enormously important for Christian democrats across the globe: subsidiarity. Subsidiarity, which Taparelli D'Azeglio also defined as a "hypotactical right," means that "every consortium must conserve its unity in such a way that does not damage the unity of the whole; and every larger society must provide for the unity of whole without destroying the unity of the consortia." Since a large society is inevitably composed of smaller associations or communities, "the duty of the *consortium*" is to seek the unity of the *Whole*; at the same time, "the duty of the *Whole* is to not destroy the being of the consortia" (Taparelli D'Azeglio quoted in Behr 2019: 206, italics in the original). In short, subsidiarity permanently became a pillar of modern Catholic social teaching. Leo XIII would confirm this principle in *Rerum novarum*, as would Pius XI in his encyclical *Quadragesimo anno* (1931). Thanks to Christian Democratic influence, the principle of subsidiarity would eventually be encoded in post-World War II constitutional systems, including the EU's Treaty of Maastricht (1993). The crucial point here is that these Catholics, who thought hard about the place of the church vis-à-vis the modern world, came from Turin and other areas of the peninsula that were directly experiencing the challenge of *modernity*—in terms of industrialization, the market, and socioeconomic matters. From their privileged point of view, they could see and grasp socioeconomic, political, and cultural aspects and issues that the Holy See, located in a city that was far from yet still rooted in a quasi-feudal world, hardly even noticed.

1.3 Wishing for Reform: Gioberti and Rosmini

After 1848 and 1849, the space for those Catholics who believed that a return to the concept of restoration was detrimental and counterproductive shrank dramatically. The possibility of maneuvering had become increasingly limited for the neo-Guelph Catholics. In fact, neo-Guelphism was politically defeated in 1848, but it would not disappear. Quite the opposite: it would later resurface in what would become known as a Catholic modernity. This line of thought and action, which had at first seen the election of Pope Pius IX positively, found its major expression in the work of the priest and philosopher Vincenzo Gioberti (see Forlenza and Thomassen 2016: 60–2, on which the following is based). Gioberti came from the northern city of Turin and knew very well the political, social, and economic situation of France and other European countries. He lived in Paris as well as in Brussels, places that were much more modern than a city like Rome, still locked in an aristocratic and medieval world. These experiences heavily influenced his thoughts about Italy, the Holy See, and role of Catholicism writ large.

During the 1830s and the 1840s, Gioberti argued for a federal union under the pope, concisely contrasting his ideas with the French model. These ideas found their clearest expression in *Del primato morale e civile degli Italiani* ("On the moral and civil primacy of the Italians"), which became a fundamental text for various generations of nationalists. Gioberti was very clear on this point: Italy should *not* simply imitate the other European powers as it had a moral and civil *primacy*, its own foundational values, and its own starting points. For Gioberti, this primacy was inescapably linked to the Catholic religion. Gioberti summarized his entire intellectual engagement with these words:

> I propose to prove that Italy contains within itself, above all through religion, all the conditions required for its national and political resurrection [*Risorgimento*], and to bring this about it has no need for a revolution within, and still less for foreign invasions or foreign examples. (Gioberti 1846: 104)

In Gioberti's reading, Italy had become *impoverished* because it had become imitative. The country had to find its roots, and those roots belonged to its history. Gioberti praised Vittorio Alfieri (1749–1803)—the poet, dramatist, and fervent patriot and prophet of the unity of Italy—for embodying the true fire of Italian genius and arguing that Italy's salvation lies "in political and literary independence from France." Gioberti was adamant that the pope should remain a unifying figure for the new Italian confederation. He therefore went against those forces that saw the pope as a political obstacle, "a foreign idea born in the confused brain of a French priest," referring to Lamennais, "whose recent condemnation [in the 1832 papal encyclical *Mirari vos*] proved that Gallic whims do not prevail over the common sense of Rome" (Gioberti 1846: 112). For Gioberti, the French model for political and spiritual modernization remained a rather primitive one. Italy should set its own standards; it could do so by remaining spiritually anchored in the church and recognizing the pope's authority.

In other words, Gioberti was convinced that there could be a different model for Italian political modernity and the modern nation, one alternative to the French model, in which the roles of religion and the pope would be central. Gioberti's position on the church, seen as a founding value of modern nationhood, would never completely disappear from the intellectual horizon. Gioberti's stance would never become hegemonic within the *Risorgimento*, and at the practical-political level, the union with the church never worked out the way he had wanted. Yet, his ideas left an important legacy which would be picked up by later generations, including twentieth-century Catholic thinkers and politicians.

The priest and philosopher Antonio Rosmini was another important representative of the neo-Guelph perspective. The latter was embraced by those Catholics defined "conciliatorist," who were committed to a non-traumatic but positive solution to the issue of the relationship between the church's temporal power and the nascent Italian nation (Traniello 1966: 140–9; De Giorgi 1999: 305–13, 2003; Malusa 2011). Rosmini favored a democracy that promoted social justice and was based on the centrality of the person, guaranteeing freedom and rights. He believed that the church must not refuse the modern world but be open to and confront modernity. He insisted that faith and reason, on one hand, and faith and science, on the other hand, needed to enter into dialogue. In such a context, the relationship between the state and the church was of paramount importance. Rosmini wished for the promotion and enhancement of the right of religion and freedom of consciousness, but in a situation in which the state and the church remained free to act in their own spheres. As he wrote in 1848, "the Catholic religion does not need dynastic protection but instead liberty...religious Italy has the mission to liberate Catholicism from infamous servitude" (Rosmini 1848: 14; Rosmini 1985).

Thus, Rosmini imagined a non-confessional constitutional system that explicitly recognized the church's freedom. Without a state religion, it would become much simpler to exercise the freedom of consciousness. For Rosmini, this also meant that, while the state did not have the right to intervene in matters of the church, the alliance between the throne and the altar could not be a feasible form of social and political engineering in modern times. Although this had been the situation in the Middle Ages, it was no longer a viable model.

Rosmini was held in high esteem by secular thinkers and politicians committed to the process of national unification, and he gained explicit and public recognition for his modern political thought. However, he was particularly intent on pushing for an internal reform of the church. His proposal took a more comprehensive form in his *Delle cinque piaghe della Chiesa* ("Of the Five Wounds of the Church"). In this prophetic and passionate text, Rosmini denounced the sins and the errors of the church, at the same time pointing out that only a return to the sources—the gospel, the tradition of the Fathers of the Church, and the praxis of the first centuries of its life—could ensure its renovation and resurgence, again making the church a credible and reliable carrier of the evangelical message. Rosmini closely analyzed the entire history of the church, pointing out the errors it had made over the centuries: from the subordination of secular power to the church's conflation and compromise with it; from the longing for wealth and power to ritual practices that were detached from common people, who should be seen as the real core of the church. To correct such errors, Rosmini proposed to relaunch the high and deep spiritual values of communion and the unity of the church—the values that had permeated the first centuries of the church's history and whose abandonment had contributed to creating divisions within Christianity, and hence to the Reformation.

Between August and October 1848, just when Pius IX had become the hope of the reformers, Rosmini went to Rome (see Della Missione 1998). He had accepted to act as a messenger and a diplomat for the Savoy House of Piedmont, which many reformers, nationalists, and patriots considered the force that could make Italy a united nation. The importance of and respect for Rosmini within the pontifical court rose rapidly; yet, it dissolved equally rapidly. Pius IX moved to the anti-constitutional and intransigent side. Some of Rosmini's writings were included in the 1849 Index, the list of publications that were forbidden by the church. After a brief opening to the conciliatorist line, the intransigent paradigm—supported especially by the Jesuits who, in 1850, founded the combative journal *La Civiltà Cattolica*—evidently regained its hegemony (see Menozzi 2007). In 1882 (thirty-two years after Rosmini's death), the Vatican promulgated the *Post Obitum* ("after death") decree, in which forty propositions taken from the writings of Rosmini were judged heretical. Only in 2001 was Rosmini eventually rehabilitated.

The events of 1848 were a turning point that generated a profound change of perspective on the path toward national unification. To begin with, in the crucible of the events of 1848, the permanent connections between the national movement and constitutional principles came to the fore and, with them, the crumbling of the principle of legitimacy on which the institutional order of the Italian states was founded. 1848 opened a new period in the history of Italy, with as yet uncertain outcomes. Such a change of perspective strongly and variably affected the role of the church. Ample sectors of Catholicism felt that the times were changing and something had to happen. Writing to the influential Cardinal Castracane on May 17, 1848, Rosmini argued that the movement that was under way could not be halted "before Italy becomes a nation" (Rosmini 1892: 327).

According to Rosmini, it was time to accept the idea that the move toward the national state was unstoppable because it dovetailed with "unanimous consent," and that such a move would inevitably follow the road to a constitutional and representative system. The only uncertain aspect was the exact way in which this move would be accomplished. For Rosmini, the translation of the nation into a modern state system should occur in harmony and not in conflict with the church. From an institutional point of view, Rosmini endorsed and promoted a type of constitutionalism inspired by a representative system, but one that could simultaneously yield principles and institutions that were different from those prevailing in the French-inspired constitution.

Rosmini and his attempt to bridge the gap between the church and modernity sowed important seeds. His ideas inspired the conciliarism of the so-called liberal Catholics. These included Alessandro Manzoni, Massimo D'Azeglio, Luigi Tosti, Antonio Fogazzaro, Monsignor Geremia Bonomelli, and other Catholics who supported a political alliance between the new Italian state and the Holy See, and a cultural agreement between religious Catholic tradition and modern thought (Traniello 1970; Passerin D'Entrèves 1981). Rosmini's ideas also influenced other twentieth-century Catholic thinkers who worked to find a positive encounter between Catholicism and modernity, such as Augusto Del Noce (1983).

In the context of the 1848–9 period, there was no space for the ideas of Lamennais, Gioberti, Rosmini, and other Catholics who wanted the church to come to terms with modern politics. As the Italian *Risorgimento* and the process of national unification progressed and accelerated, challenging the temporal power of the church, the Vatican's reaction and response to political modernity and its generative factor—to be found in the principles of 1789—became harsher and more insistent. Precisely in the name of modern liberty, based on the ideals of 1789, the popes' temporal power was put under strain. In 1854, with the *bolla papale* ("papal bull") *Ineffabilis Deus*, Pius IX re-affirmed the importance of tradition as well as the harmony and the continuity between the church of the past and that of the present. Among other things, the *bolla* reinforced papal authority, thus opening the way to the dogma of his infallibility, encouraged Marian devotion, and highlighted the religious truth that was rejected or neglected in modern thought, such as the supernatural order, original sin, redemption, and the elevation of man as the son of God. It was in this charged atmosphere of restoration and reaffirmation of tradition that, in December 1864 (three years after Italy's unification), Pius IX published the encyclical *Quanta cura* and *Syllabus errorum*.

1.4 Pope Pius IX and the Errors of Modernity

Quanta cura referred to modern thought, secularism, and other "current errors" provoked by the "nefarious enterprises of wicked men" ("nefariis iniquorum hominum molitionibus"). The encyclical was accompanied by the *Syllabus errorum*, a list of propositions condemned as erroneous in past papal statements. The most famous "error" was the belief that "the Roman pontiff can, and ought to, reconcile himself, and come to terms with progress, liberalism and modern civilization" ("Romanus Pontifex potest ac debet cum progressu, cum liberalismo et cum recenti civilitate sese reconciliari et componere"). The *Syllabus* crystallized a holistic critique of modernity advanced by an intransigent school of thought. The period that followed became the heyday of Catholic positions fighting against modernity.

In the encyclical, Pius IX also stressed that the errors of modernity could open the way to "fearful calamities" in both "the spiritual life of the church and its faithful" and "civil society." The calamities that the pope had in mind were the regime of Terror, which he traced back directly to the French Revolution and the political disorder that it generated, nationalism, and the political processes of national unification that happened in Europe during and after the 1848 revolt. In other words, the pope drew a direct line of connection between theological, ideological, and intellectual errors and a specific political outcome. Modernism and its consequences, namely secularization and rationalization, were considered the result of a movement (or better, a series of subsequent and consequential movements) that placed the individual at the center of human development: the Renaissance, the Reformation, the Enlightenment, and the French Revolution.

On September 20, 1870, Rome was captured by the Italian army commanded by General Raffaele Cadorna: the event would become known as the *presa di Roma* ("the capture of Rome"). In 1860, the nascent Kingdom of Italy had invaded and occupied Romagna, the eastern section of the Papal States, leaving only Latium under the pope's temporal authority. Latium and Rome itself were annexed to the Kingdom of Italy through the *presa*. It was the culmination of the dreams and hopes of the patriots of the *Risorgimento*; for them, and all Italians, as Bettino Ricasoli said (the successor to the first Italian Prime Minister Camillo Benso, Count of Cavour), to go to Rome was "not simply a right" but "an inexorable necessity."

For the pope, the church, the Jesuits, and conservative defenders of Catholicism, the event was a nightmare—the nefarious enterprises of wicked men, to use the words of *Quanta cura*—that had finally been accomplished. The crucial institutional question that emerged was the pope's liberty and independence, and it soon became known as the *questione romana* ("Roman question"). "To protest and to wait" was the general motto—coined by Cardinal Giacomo Antonelli—of the intransigent line after the end of the temporal power of the popes. This intransigent line centered around two points: first, its supporters considered the pope a prisoner of the usurping liberal state; second, they rejected modern politics and ruled out positive participation in the political life of the new Italy, against the views of those transigent and conciliatorist Catholics who, instead, believed that participation in national political life was useful and could open the way to other, future developments.

Already in 1868, Pius IX had uttered his now famous *non expedit*, Latin for "it is not expedient," which until 1904 remained the church's official position and the expression that best captured the attitude of intransigent Catholics vis-à-vis the political life of the new state. With the *non expedit*, the Holy See prohibited Italian Catholics from actively and passively participating in the political life of the nation. To them, the church ordered, it was "not expedient" to exercise their active as well as passive right to vote. In fact, the formula *ne eletti né elettori* ("neither elected nor electors") represented a common political practice for all Catholics since the national unification of 1861. Father Giacomo Margotti had launched it on January 7, 1861, in the daily *L'Armonia*, inviting Catholics to abstain from voting in the first election of the Kingdom of Italy. Rather ironically, such a practice—as Stathis Kalyvas has argued—had the unintentional consequence of "creating the basis for the emergence of Catholic political identity" (Kalyvas 1996: 180). Indeed, electoral abstention did not mean that Catholics refused to engage in the political realm of the new Italy and were excluded from public life. Thus, in the following years, the very *preparazione nell'astensione* ("preparation through abstention") became the means to turn the refusal to vote into the organization of the political struggle of the future (Ambrosoli 1958: 13–14; Kalivas 1996: 180). In reality, as the Jesuit Father Gaetano Zocchi wrote in 1879, abstentionism from the poll and the intransigent line were in themselves a political move and a political stance. To believe that political life begins and ends with participation in the poll was "a miserable and ridiculous mistake" (quoted in Traniello 1998: 72). The decisive struggle, the Jesuit added, did not concern elections but the founding principles of a society.

Additionally, while at the national level virtually every Italian followed the *non expedit*—even though participation in the elections remained an individual choice—and the few Catholic members of the parliament resigned after 1870, things worked very differently at the local level.[4] Catholic lists were presented,

---

[4] According to Gabriele De Rosa, after 1870, abstentionism became a "qualifying aspect of militant Catholicism" (De Rosa 1966: 98). However, the real impact of abstentionism is difficult to assess. Statistical and historical analysis seems to indicate that, in the first decade of unified Italy, Catholics continued to go to the poll *en masse*, thus satisfying their national-patriotic feeling (see also Mellano 1982).

obtaining good results, at the local elections in Bergamo, Florence, and even Rome. Here, in 1871, the *Unione romana per le elezioni amministrative* ("The Roman union for local elections") was established, which aimed at introducing a "Christian element" (Mazzonis 1970) into the heart of secular power, the Campidoglio. After all, Pius IX himself—while talking to the parish priests of Rome in July 1872—said that participation in local elections could be one of the means to prevent "the advancement of impiety and the depravity of youth."[5]

The need to engage in the social and political life of the new state, through participation in the local elections, was explicitly reaffirmed again at the second congress of the Italian Catholics, which was held in Florence in September 1875 (Secondo congresso 1875: 116). Some Catholics thought that participation in the local elections was not enough and could certainly not ensure appropriate and adequate Catholic participation in political life. Debates emerged around the idea of creating a "Catholic party" as opposed to a "conservative party" (Traniello 1998: 67–77). Hence, already in the mid-1870s, sectors of Catholicism supported the idea of overcoming the *non expedit*. The pope, however, reaffirmed the validity of the formula proposed by Margotti in 1861 in a letter to the president of *Società della Gioventù Cattolica Italiana* ("Society of the Italian Catholic Youth"), Giovanni Acquaderni.

1.5 The Emergence of Social Catholicism

After the unification and despite the *non expedit*, Catholics were relatively active in the social and political life of the new state. Indeed, it was precisely in this novel context that they started to define and defend their interests and those of the church, embryonically formulating a platform for some kind of social thought and social action. The vast majority of Catholic intellectuals and thinkers rejected the idea that structural reform was needed to improve the life and working conditions of the proletarian workers and peasants. Therefore, during and after the unification and in the third quarter of the century at the more general (European) level, groups of lay Catholics, priests, and bishops started to realize that the poverty and misery of workers were a problem of both Christian charity and justice.

Interestingly, such a penchant for social problems did not emerge in the circle of the liberal, conciliatorist, and transigent Catholics—that is, those sectors of Catholicism that, influenced by Rosmini, Gioberti, and Lamennais, were more open to modern political democracy. It emerged instead precisely from the more conservative sector of Catholicism, including those who firmly opposed democracy and were, therefore, searching for a solution to the social question in a non-democratic perspective. This might appear paradoxical, but it is nonetheless true: the trailblazers of social Catholicism came from the social class of landowners

---

[5] The pope's speech is reported in *La Civilta Cattolica*, s. VIII, 4, 1872, 233.

and landed aristocracy. Compared to liberal Catholics, they were much less committed to and engaged in the world of business, trade, and market; they were therefore less sensitive to the imperative and the iron law of competition and competitiveness. Moreover, they saw in social action a way to convince the popular masses of their—and the church's—cause, setting them against the anticlerical and oligarchic bourgeoisie, which they profoundly detested for two reasons: because it was anticlerical, and because it pretended to replace the traditional social authority with the power of money and materialism. Consequently, conservative Catholics willing to cope with and solve the social question were inspired by the highly idealized desire to go back to a patriarchal and corporative (read medieval) past, rather than by the realistic need to adapt Catholicism and themselves to the new and irreversible situation generated by the Industrial Revolution.

In fact, the connection between anti-liberalism and opposition to modern politics, on one side, and social concerns, on the other side, had already emerged from the pages of *La Civiltà Cattolica*. In *Quanta cura*, Pius IX himself had denounced not only Socialism and its pretension to replace Divine Providence with the secular state, but also the pagan nature of economic liberalism that pretended to keep morality out of the relationship between capital and labor. These ideas inspired the activists of the *Movimento Cattolico Italiano* ("The Italian Catholic Movement"), such as Giulio Cesare Fangarezzi and Giovambattista Casoni (the founders of a short-lived association that aimed to "defend the liberty of the Church in Italy", 1865–6), Giovanni Acquaderni, Mario Fani and his brother Alfonso, and Francesco Malvezzi, who in 1867 founded the aforementioned *Società della Gioventù Cattolica* (see Bedeschi 1959; La Gioventù cattolica 1972). In 1875, Pius IX favored the establishment of the *Opera dei Congressi e dei Comitati Cattolici*, a federation of the more intransigent lay Catholic associations whose aim was to lay the foundations for the building of a more just, Christian state (on the *Opera*, see the old but still detailed and informative text by De Rosa 1966; cf. Gambasin 1958). Under the protection and the auspices of the *Opera dei Congressi*, whose activists and members were openly hostile to the secular and liberal state and to the idea that political democracy was the necessary condition for effective social reforms, a series of charities and associations with a strong social and economic character arose, especially in northern Italy, where Socialist actions and campaigns were growing fast. The aims of these attempts to work and act in society were to meet the demands and the needs of popular classes. As we will see in the next chapter, these attempts were accompanied by the development of proper theoretical reflection, which emerged from the *Opera dei Congressi*. This theoretical reflection was to be a "sociology" that primarily stressed the requirements of morality and religion in relation to material interests. The most important representative of this "Christian sociology" was Giuseppe Toniolo, who was very influential in the future development of social and political Catholicism (see Chapter 2).

1.6 Liberal Catholicism and Catholic Liberals in Unified Italy

Under the influence of Gioberti, Rosmini, Manzoni, D'Azeglio, and Balbo, many Catholics in post-unification Italy endorsed Cavour's formula *libera Chiesa in libero Stato*: a free Church in a free state. They found their ideal and ideological justification in Gioberti's last work, where he abandoned neo-Guelphism (i.e. the idea that Italy must be a federation of states under the pope's guidance) or, better still, repositioned it in the framework of a secular and national state characterized by the absolute separation of two different jurisdictions: the church and the state. The title of this provocative work was *Del rinnovamento civile d'Italia* (*On the Civil Renewal of Italy*). It was published in 1851 in Paris, although it became known only after Gioberti's death in 1852. In it, Gioberti made references to Dante and Machiavelli (above all others), but also to other intellectuals of the more recent past, such as the poets Vittorio Alfieri and Giacomo Leopardi, who did not really belong to the canon of the church. Gioberti also returned to arguments and discussions from his previous works.

However, after the post-1848 disillusionment, he deepened his analysis of the place of religion in Italy. This time, though, he was much more pessimistic about the strength, role, and weight of religion in society. Catholicism, Gioberti wrote, was losing "its power over souls and minds" and becoming unable to halt the spread of atheistic rationalism. A more important reason for the decline of Catholicism was the "combination of the temporal and the spiritual." Rome, he argued, had not only allied with "despotic and absolute lordships"; it had also appropriated a form of power and regime that was alien to the evangelical spirit and translated this power into the government of the church, choosing the weapons of coercion and subjugation instead of the much more effective and evangelical tools of persuasion and preaching (quoted in Gioberti 1969: 1.26–7, 2.372–3; see also Traniello 1998: 52–5). In his work, Gioberti also maintained that, within the wider frame of a European renovation, Italy had a new primacy: to bring about a scientific and Catholic reform of religious doctrine through a deal between the state and the church. For Gioberti, the fate of religious European civilization had to be linked to the establishment, in Italy, of a new national state, accompanied by the emergence of a new, future Rome: the *Roma dell'avvenire*. In this new Rome, thanks to the abolition of the temporal power of the pope, to whom many—not territorial—guarantees and privileges were to be granted, the spiritual and the temporal "will bloom . . . mixed but not confused, in harmony and not in opposition" (Gioberti 1969: 2.113).

Del rinnovamento civile d'Italia was quite open and favorable to the line followed by Cavour, who at the moment of its publication was not yet the head of government of Piedmont. Ten years later, while discussing the Roman question in one of his first speeches as prime minister to the parliament of the Kingdom of Italy,

Cavour included Gioberti, Manzoni, and Rosmini among those "great thinkers" who had worked "to reconcile the spirit of liberty with the religious sentiment," the two "principles on which modern society must rest" (Cavour 1872: 359–60; on Cavour see Salvadori 2011: 3–41).

The speech reflected Cavour's attempts to bridge the gap with sectors of liberal Catholicism precisely at a moment when the church–state conflict had become even more problematic, with unification accomplished and the Roman question knocking at the door. However, Cavour was not really thinking of Gioberti, whose democratic line was too radical for him as well. Nor did Cavour have the limited sectors of Catholic high culture in mind; instead, he was thinking of a vast area of Catholic public opinion, including the clergy, which he considered indispensable for the consolidation of the new state. The events of 1859–60 created a deep rift between the nascent state and the church. Yet, it was precisely for the support that many liberal Catholics had given to the state that the fracture within the Italian body politic was not so deep and serious as the hierarchy had predicted. Cavour cautiously confronted the critical moment of the emergence of the new state, proposing—without success—a direct negotiation with the Vatican, and choosing among his collaborators a few representatives of the Catholic-liberal milieu. These included, for example, the former Jesuit Carlo Passaglia (who embraced Cavour's cause after having collaborated with Pius IX) and the *rosminiano* Father Jacopo Molinari.

After Cavour's death, the liberal Catholics relaunched the theme of conciliation between the church and the state. By then, large sectors of Catholicism had moved to the position of anti-temporalism, thus emphasizing the pope's main role as a spiritual authority. In 1862, they promoted the *Indirizzo del clero Italiano a Pio IX*, inviting the pope to reconcile the state and the church and allow Rome to become the capital of the new state. The *Indirizzo* gathered nine thousand signatures, 90 percent of which were by the secular clergy (i.e. deacons and priests who were not monks or members of a religious institute). The year before, at the time of national unification, Bishop Giuseppe Maria Mucedola—in a speech to the pope and the congregations of Rome—exhorted to "not convert a political contest into a religious war." Other influential bishops, such as Giovanni Battista Scalabrini and Bonomelli, agreed on this point and expressed their aversion to the *non expedit*. In one of his writings, Bonomelli proposed what was effectively done: the creation of an autonomous state of the church with a symbolic territory. From Milan to Naples, from Rome to Turin, many *società ecclesiastiche* ("ecclesiastical societies") were created that gathered, outside the church's institutions, a clergy not aligned with Rome and that adopted liberal and national positions. Journals expressing such positions proliferated (Confessore 1999), like *La Rivista Universale*, which promoted the formula "Catholics with the Pope, liberals with the *Statuto*" (the constitution of the Kingdom of Italy). From the pages of *La*

Rassegna Nazionale, other Catholics—including a woman, Sabina Parracino Revel—supported the thesis of "Americanism," that is, the separation between churches and the state in the United States. Other intellectuals, writers, and politicians who adhered to the liberal Catholic front included Francesco Paolo Tosti, Ruggero Bonghi, and Antonio Fogazzato.

The Holy See opposed these positions by condemning liberalism (even before *Quanta cura* and the *Syllabus*, in Pius IX's previous encyclical *Maxima quidem* of 1862), adopting disciplinary measures against those who had signed Passaglia's *Indirizzo* (many were forced to withdraw) and condemning the *società ecclesiastiche*. However, the atmosphere was not favorable to the conciliatorists. The *presa di Roma* and the need to defend the pope dramatically limited the grounds for a positive confrontation. Moreover, the end of the government of the Destra Storica (the "moderate" wing of the patriots who contributed to the *Risorgimento*) and its replacement with the traditionally anticlerical Sinistra inflamed the political atmosphere.

In short, while the unification did not destabilize Italy from a religious point of view, it was neither the beginning of the great religious renaissance that many liberal Catholics had hoped for after the Holy See was deprived of its temporal power. Many of them gave the birth of the nation a palingenetic meaning that was implicit in the term *Risorgimento*, which referred to the process of national unification and had a religious etymology: Resurrection (Forlenza and Thomassen 2016: 7–10, 2017: 292–4). In fact, the term conjured up the central belief of Catholicism: Jesus resurrecting from death. The creation/resurrection of the nation, therefore, conveyed a religious and hence universal meaning. Other liberal Catholics had moved toward the national movement in the name of liberty. They mainly came from the more advanced areas of the peninsula, where the effects of industrialization and the modern organization of society made the sheer restoration and re-affirmation of traditional religious principles impossible. They thought that this could be a historical opportunity for the church, and obviously also for Catholicism, to positively confront the needs and demands of a changing society. For liberal Catholics, the birth of the modern nation reflected an occasion to retrieve a religion that was followed and practiced in liberty and, therefore, more authentically lived as a source and a collective moral law that was more appropriate for the modern citizen.

The whole liberal Catholic front thought that what had happened in Italy—because of its history and tradition, and because the peninsula hosted the Vatican, the universal center of Catholicism—reverberated on a broader horizon, answering wider religious questions that, in fact, concerned the entire European civilization. Liberal Catholics—that is, men (and, less likely, women) who belonged to Italy's social, economic, and intellectual elite—time and again missed crucial aspects of popular religious life and underestimated the widespread presence of the church in the texture of Italian society. These aspects did not necessarily invalidate the Catholic liberal project, but for its ideas to be successful, the road would prove to be long and difficult. The advent of the modern nation-state radically changed the frame of Italian religious life, but not necessarily in the sense that liberal Catholics had wanted and wished for.

2

Democratizing from Below

This chapter deals with the relationship between church, state, and society in the period from unification to the early 1900s. In many ways, the period was marked by a constant culture war between ecclesiastical and anti-ecclesiastical attitudes and positions. At the same time, the period saw an opening from within the church allowing for new types of social and political engagements. In this context, the chapter zooms in on the consequences of Pope Leo XIII's encyclical *Rerum novarum* (1891) on social, cultural, and political matters.

As we have seen in the previous chapter, the church's official response to the advancement of the national secular project, which was institutionalized by the establishment of the Kingdom of Italy, was to pronounce anathemas and excommunications against the "subalpine usurpers," as Pope Pius IX called the Savoy royal family, and all others who had assisted and participated in the despoliation of the church and the conquest of Rome (Papenheim 2003). This position would become the model to follow in all other liberal countries, resulting in a continuous cold war between the Vatican and the state. Clericalism and anticlericalism would split European countries not only at the political and institutional level but also at the level of ordinary social life—a schism that would develop into separate and opposed ways of life.

The Catholic engagement in society and politics was, as we have also seen, not an absolute novelty. Despite the *non expedit*, Catholics had not abstained from engaging in political, social, and cultural fields. By contrast, Catholics were active in a variety of ways and had started to associate, from the middle of the nineteenth century, to advance the design of God on earth and defend the church and the pope from the attack of the secular modern world. Yet, when Pius IX died in 1878, the church found itself at odds with modern civilization. It was in conflict not only with the Kingdom of Italy, but also with Russia (which had severed diplomatic relations with the Holy See), the United States (which had closed its legation in Rome), and a few Latin American states that had taken anticlerical stances and measures (Coppa 2013: 117). The most problematic situation regarded the German Empire. Starting in 1782, the Prussian chancellor of the recently united nation, Otto von Bismarck, launched a political and cultural struggle against the indigenous (Catholic) Center Party and the Church of Rome, a veritable *Kulturkampf* against the church. While the struggle initially had to do with questions of education and ecclesiastical appointments, it concerned the very shape of

Italy's Christian Democracy: The Catholic Encounter with Political Modernity. Rosario Forlenza and Bjørn Thomassen,
Oxford University Press. © Rosario Forlenza and Bjørn Thomassen 2024. DOI: 10.1093/oso/9780198859864.003.0003

the modern German state and Bismarck's declared wish to reduce the public role of Catholicism to a minimum (Anderson 1981, 1986; Gross 2005; Borutta 2003; Bennette 2012).

Sectors within the Catholic Church—especially the Catholic liberals—were openly hoping that Pius IX's successor would put aside his resentment against the modern world, overcome the ultramontane stances of his predecessors, and adopt a flexible policy with the secular states. The election after a surprisingly brief conclave of Vincenzo Gioacchino Raffaele Luigi Pecci (1810–1903), the cardinal bishop of Perugia, as Leo XIII was seen in a positive light by Catholic liberals. Yet, the new pope was not a liberal. It soon became evident that he flatly rejected the idea of the increasing secularization of political and social institutions, and of the world as such. Instead, he aimed at re-Christianizing such institutions, putting the church back in the place it had occupied for centuries: that of a spiritual guide of humankind. At the same time, Leo XIII wanted the church to re-establish a more positive dialogue with the world, showing to be less hostile to modern ideas and politics. He therefore invited Catholics to make use of constitutional liberties for their own advantage and that of the church. Further still, in several of his speeches and writings, he made a theoretical and theological effort to integrate liberal and secular institutions into a Catholic conception of state and society.

In this context, it is worth describing Leo XIII's background, as his papacy would become a decisive turning point in the church's engagement with the modern world. In 1843, he had been appointed Apostolic Nuncio to Belgium, where he was forced to deal with the question of education that was hotly being debated by the country's Catholic majority and liberal minority. He had also spent time in England, carefully reflecting—during and after the visit—on the condition of the church in a country where it clearly occupied a minority position. During his papacy, and also as a consequence of these experiences and interests in countries where industrialization had already taken off, Leo XIII made more than an effort to formulate a positive, updated, and modern Catholic doctrine of the state, open to the aspirations and demands of a modern democracy (Hellemans 2001: 118; Burleigh 2005: 344–411; Kraynak 2007).

To formulate such a doctrine, Leo XIII wrote over seventy documents, including four encyclicals: *Diuturnum illud* (1881), *Immortale Dei* (1885), *Liberta, praestantissimum* (1888), in which he defined *libertá* ("freedom") as "God's most prestigious gift," and *Sapientiae Christianae* (1890). Strong Catholic opposition to democracy and liberalism, as well as to the separation between the state and the church, did not disappear overnight. Nevertheless, Leo XIII started to move away from ultramontanism and the traditional teaching of the church toward a process that he made possible even though he could not fully pursue it himself. This was also because, as Murray already argued in the 1950s, the constraints of the historical context in which he operated as well as the weight and inheritance of centuries of tradition and authoritarianism were not easy to overcome (Murray 1953).

However, Leo XIII drafted a rough sketch of an alternative Catholic perspective on government and law that was adapted to a society where the *ancien régime* had waned. In many ways, Leo XIII indeed set in motion a transformation toward more modern forms and concepts. For example, he did not simply claim the rights of the church; at the same time, he strove to define and pinpoint the rights of secular power and its legitimate independence from the pope's hierarchy and power, guaranteeing the autonomy of the secular state within its own spheres of action and interest.

Pope Leo XIII did not limit himself to an intellectual elaboration; his ideas were translated into practical and political action in a variety of ways. For example, he recognized the end of monarchy in France and encouraged French Catholics to vote and participate in the political life of the Third Republic, much to the consternation of Catholic monarchists in France who opposed the church's *ralliement* to the Republic. He did the same with Spanish Catholics, inviting them to adhere to the new regime, or at least not to reject the modern outright. He therefore invited Catholics to renounce a form of legitimism that was very common within Catholic circles, whose members did not want to accept or even recognize the dramatic transformation that society was undergoing. He also allowed Russia to open an embassy in Rome and instituted diplomatic relations with Japan.

Leo XIII also dealt with Otto von Bismarck in a prudent, and perhaps even calculating, fashion. While the Iron Chancellor pursued his anti-Catholic stance to the point where it became counterproductive, the pope encouraged a softening of the culture war by dealing directly with him in matters of diplomacy and church appointments. This policy meant recognizing Germany's conservative monarchy and eventually led to three visits by Kaiser Wilhelm II to the Vatican. Leo XIII's arbitration of the contest between Germany and Spain regarding the Caroline Islands in the Pacific showed that the relationship with Bismarck had certainly improved and yielded positive consequences: the *Kulturkampf* ended. Without a doubt, imperial Germany maintained control over religious education as well as the right to object to ecclesiastical appointments. Yet, as Chadwick noted, the Holy See came out stronger from the conflict with Germany: "Bismarck failed in his main objective—to crush the Center Party and make the Roman Catholic in Germany what he regarded as 'truly German.' On the contrary, the Kulturkampf did for German Catholicism what Napoleon did for French Catholicism—it made them more Roman" (Chadwick 1998: 228).

Such a prudent approach was bound to be more complicated and ultimately less successful in Italy. Too much was at stake and substantial territories were directly under dispute. While recognizing that Pius IX's demand for a return of the Papal States from the Kingdom of Italy was the only guaranteed support for the freedom of the church in the age of the nation-state, Leo XIII never realistically expected to get them back. Yet, in the hope of securing a deal for a sovereign Vatican State in a territory that would protect the freedom of the church from political interference by the Italian government, Leo XIII maintained the ban on voting and participating in politics within the Kingdom of Italy. Political prudence is not always successful in balancing the demands of the spiritual and temporal realms.

Naturally, Leo XIII's opening to liberalism was nothing akin to a Christian Democracy as it would emerge later. In fact, in the last quarter of the nineteenth century, Catholic liberals had nothing in common with Lamennais: they were typically representative of a "constitutional" Right, devoted and loyal to individual liberties even if rather conservative from a social point of view; they defended the classic liberal principle of *laissez faire, laissez passer*; and they were often quite reluctant to embrace the principle of a genuinely universal franchise.

In sum, by reappropriating and re-signifying what was reasonable and sensible in the view, theory, and insights of the Catholic liberals of the previous generation, using wisdom and prudence to bring liberal ideas into harmony with official doctrine, Leo XIII decisively expanded the sphere of influence of liberal Catholicism. In addition to this, his doctrinal clarification led Catholic political forces to reposition along new lines of division. As we shall below, in Italy as in other countries, such as France and Belgium, late nineteenth-century Christian Democrats, whose political program was partially inspired by some of the principles of 1789, would descend from the circles of intransigentism that had passionately argued against Catholic liberals and their plea to embrace modern society and politics for at least two decades.

2.1 On *Rerum Novarum*

With his doctrinal fine-tuning, Leo XIII unlocked the Catholic prejudices against and aversion to the political regimes and institutions that belonged to the genealogy of 1789. At the same time, he forced Catholics to come to terms with their social responsibilities, seen not only as a demand for the evangelical call to individual charity but also as a wider and comprehensive rearrangement of the social and economic structure in the name of (social) justice. In this way, the two most fundamental aspects of Christian Democracy as it would unfold in the first half of the twentieth century, political democracy and social justice, were recognized and given new meanings, functions, and nuances.

Leo XIII's decisive intervention in the social sphere came with the encyclical *Rerum novarum* (1891). The document is widely recognized as the beginning of a modern Catholic social teaching that since then has been developing to contribute toward a Catholic action-oriented interpretation of the modern. The circumstance that convinced the pope to conceive and release the encyclical was a controversy among Catholics on the state's right to intervene in social matters. However, well before the last decade of the nineteenth century, as we have seen in the previous chapter, various sectors of Catholicism had started to tackle the question. In 1884, for example, a "Catholic Union of Social Studies" was established in Freiburg, whose aim was to formulate a corporatist doctrine of society in line with Catholicism appropriate for modern times. The reports of the Union were sent to the pope and, on top of other initiatives (including those of a lay group of Catholics), became the preparatory work for *Rerum novarum*. Several hands drafted the encyclical. In fact, Leo XIII only wrote very few, if any, of the sections of the document. However, he meticulously and thoroughly revised the final version and certainly imposed his thought, leaving an unmistakable mark.

The encyclical was a refutation of Socialism as a theory suited to society and the world, as well as the outline of an alternative solution based on class solidarity and corporatism, rooted in Catholic tradition and particularly in Thomism. The principal themes and arguments of *Rerum novarum* were the following: the rejection of the Socialist response to the social question, and the demonstration that private property was founded on natural law; the justification of the church's intervention in social affairs to ease the "boundless poverty of workers"; the state's right to intervene in economic life to guarantee a fair salary and a more just and better distribution of properties; the usefulness and importance of professional and worker's unions as well as of associations founded by Catholics in favor of workers. Much of the inspiration of the encyclical came from the fear of seeing ample sectors of Catholic workers join Socialism, and hence from a reactive and defensive approach; it was full of moralistic and abstract generalization. Yet, it also had important positive aspects. Social Catholicism previously reacted to modernization and the advancement of bourgeois society by proposing an impossible return to the past and a rural and pre-capitalistic world still anchored in the corporatism of the *ancien régime*. Leo XIII, instead, left behind such romantic utopias, engaging in the complexities of the real world and descending to the same ground as reformist Socialists, thus seeking to improve the conditions of workers in real history. Additionally, it was crucial that the pope—the highest spiritual authority—proclaimed and defended the rights of workers and denounced the injustice of liberalism and capitalism. This denunciation contributed to legitimizing the worker's movement, distancing workers' rights from the revolutionary character that had frightened the bourgeois world. One passage of the encyclical reads as follows:

> Among the most important duties of employers, the principal one is to give every worker what is justly due to him. Assuredly, to establish a rule of pay in accordance with justice, many factors must be taken into account. But, in general, the rich and the employers should remember that no laws, either human or divine, permit them for their own profit to oppress the needy and the wretched or to seek gain from another's want. To defraud anyone of the wage due to him is a great crime that calls down avenging wrath from heaven.

Rerum novarum is, beyond doubt, one of the most important papal documents in the history of the Church. As said, it is rightly considered the first encyclical with an explicitly "social" and political agenda. Furthermore, it can and should be read as a reflection on modernity and its challenges; it provided some explicit guidelines for Catholics and how they should navigate, faithfully, this modern world. In sum, it inspired Catholics to engage with the world around them and to no longer sit back passively and watch it change.

Catholics, in Italy as elsewhere, were now urged to actively unite in all kinds of social domains and respond to the threat of liberal and anticlerical governments as well as to the challenge of Socialism.[1] By this time, it had become clear that modern society was more than revolutionary chaos, soon to collapse. Leo XIII's encyclical inspired a whole range of Catholic associational initiatives across the Italian peninsula: youth organizations, literary and recreational circles, organizations of Catholic workers, and Catholic unions. This period was also marked by the development of the so-called "mutual societies," the Catholic response to corporatist models based on Socialist ideas. Important outcomes of this wider process included the emergence of institutions like the *casse rurali*, that is, banks functioning as cooperative companies that lend money to peasants. The banks were based on a Catholic philosophy of personhood and morality: they were to be centered on people and not on money. One of the church-affiliated credit unions that appeared in this period was the Banco Ambrosiano, founded in 1896, five years after the release of the *Rerum novarum* (Taccolini and Cafaro 1996; Istituti di credito 1998; Forlenza and Thomassen 2016: 65, on which the following is based).

A young Sicilian priest, Luigi Sturzo, founded a *cassa rurale* in his hometown Caltagirone in the same year. Important figures in the wider Catholic movement, like Giuseppe Toniolo, to whom we shall return below, were active in the so-called "white credit" sector, a term used in contrast to the "red credit" of Socialist orientation. Another important figure in this context was Luigi Cerutti, the priest who in 1896 founded the Società Cattolica di Assicurazione (Catholic Insurance Society) in Verona (Tramontin 1968). In short, a full-fledged and well-organized Catholic subculture—a Catholic "pillar" or compartment within society—was established in anticipation of Catholic modernity proper. In many ways, the movement resembled the Socialist labor movement that was active around the same time in Europe and beyond. The *Rerum novarum* thus endorsed the already existing networks and spurred the emergence of Catholic associational initiatives in Europe and Latin America: credit unions or *casse rurali* in Italy and Germany; trade unions representing the Catholic Polish workers of Poznania and Upper Silesia and those of Mexico; literary circles and cultural and charitable associations in Belgium, Switzerland, and Chile; transnational youth movements active across

---

[1] On the *Rerum novarum* and the birth and development of Catholic "social thought," see Misner 1991; Williams and Houck 1993; Furlong and Curtis 1994.

the globe that put the social doctrine into practice in everyday life. Additionally, Catholics founded newspapers and bulletins, amplified papal statements and documents, wrote articles and essays, organized conferences on social issues or the problem of indigenous integration (in Latin America), mounted public campaigns, and created study groups. It is important to note that there was already a tendency toward Catholic associational and organizational life even *before* the *Rerum novarum* was published, both in Europe and Latin America. Therefore, the encyclical gave systematic and ideological coherence to hitherto loose and disparate initiatives, and further spurred Catholic activism (see Misner 1991 and, more specifically on Latin America, Linch 1986: 584–90).

2.2 From the Social to the Political: Christian Democracy

The Catholics' activism in the social sphere *naturally* invaded the political sphere. Social Catholicism stimulated its political manifestation and Catholics came to identify as Christian Democrats. In other words, despite resistance and hesitations, Catholics in Italy and elsewhere were forced to admit that something had to change and that the solution to the problem of the modern could not be a return to corporatism. It had to be something else: Christian Democracy.

The Vatican remained skeptical of national political movements and independent Catholic parties not controlled by the hierarchy. Rather, it attempted to detach itself from the failures, or fortunes, of political groups. After all, any idea of a Catholic independent national party was not easily acceptable by Rome: electoral outcomes could not be controlled, nor could party platforms and programs be decided and imposed by the Vatican. Yet, the call for Catholic social action launched through the *Rerum novarum* generated a bustling profusion of enterprises and activities that the Vatican could in no way manage to control. The direct consequence of this "figuration" was the emergence of a proper Catholic political milieu, which in Italy and elsewhere turned Catholicism into a political identity (Kalyvas 1996: 171–2).

In the years that followed the publication of the *Rerum novarum*, a profusion of groups officially embraced the ideal of Christian Democracy across the globe. Yet, this embrace was all but unproblematic. First, many representatives of Social Catholicism thought that the institutional changes destined to improve the conditions of workers could only be made following the age-old formula "everything for the people, nothing by the people." Second, the very notion of Christian Democracy was, to say the least, ambiguous, contested, and subjected to different interpretations. It suggested a democracy that was different from "false," radical, and individualistic democracy. Yet, how was the strong reference to Christianity to be interpreted? For some, it meant the construction of a confessional political party, whose aim had to be the building of a Christian state with a popular basis.

For others, the reference to Christianity simply implied a Christian inspiration, which had to be combined with selected elements of the liberal inheritance to create a secular state in which believers and non-believers, Catholics and non-Catholics, would collaborate in the name of social justice. The controversy and the debates were intense and crossed national borders, especially in Belgium, France, and Italy.

In Belgium, the Ligue démocratique belge was founded in 1891, a year before the *Rerum novarum* was released. In a few years' time, it became an essential force within the Catholic party, pushing it to embrace reformist politics in favor of workers and within the country's professional, economic, cultural, and religious life. In France, alongside the traditional and paternalist sectors of Catholicism, the "second Christian democracy" (defined as such to distinguish it from the failed attempt of 1848; see Montuclard 1965) emerged in the last decade of the century. The members of the group were priests and lay Catholics committed to social action, and labor activists coming from Catholic associations. They were united by a common ideal: to re-establish a connection between the church and the *peuple*, the popular masses that had abandoned the church because of the hierarchy's endorsement of, or frank support for, conservative or reactionary regimes in the past. The most active among the French Christian Democrats were the members of a combative group of young priests, the so-called "democratic abbots," including Hyppolite Gayraud, the author of a fundamental work titled *Les Démocrates Chrétiens: Doctrine et Programme* ("The Christian Democrats: Doctrine and Programme," 1898). The young abbots' stances generated hot debates within the Catholic world. They had controversial ideas on sensitive issues, such as the position of Catholics in a secular society and the call for a new social and political order, opposed to the hierarchical conception of society that the church had traditionally embraced. For many conservative and integralist Catholics, the young priests conflated and confused love for the lower class with hate for the higher classes.

The movement of the abbots lost strength and disappeared after a few years, but their democratic efforts and attempts did not. Marc Sagnier's movement Sillon, for example, galvanized the energy of young Catholics, leaving a profound mark on the next generations of French Catholics. However, the democratic line was abruptly halted in 1910 when, as we will see below on pp. 54–6, Pope Pius X condemned all "modernist" tendencies. At the same time, at the beginning of the twentieth century, a new moderate line within French Catholicism slowly emerged and structured itself around associations and organisms, like the first Christian unions, the Jesuit Action Populaire, the "social weeks" of France, and the Sécretariat Social founded by Marius Gonin.

This line of action remained limited and temporarily without the support of the episcopate and the hierarchy. In Italy, by contrast, the social question occupied an increasingly important place within the debates and the concerns of the

Opera dei Congressi. As we have seen in the previous chapter, the Opera was a stronghold of intransigentism. Yet, this does not mean that it was conservative in social matters, or that it embraced the social conservatism of the bourgeoisie. Quite the opposite, for the world of Italian social Catholicism, the bourgeois ideology of liberalism was the prime cause of social maladies and the emergence of Socialism. The Opera's lively second section was supported by the vast majority of the clergy and by the Catholic press. This included, in particular, the *Osservatore Cattolico* directed by Don Davide Albertario. While intransigent and hostile to liberal Catholicism, Albertario made a strong effort to inform the Italian Catholics about the social question. He also proposed to replace the formula *né eletti né elettori* with *preparazione nell'astensione*, roughly "to start getting ready, while still abstaining from participation in liberal politics" (see Canavero 1988: 167–8). He was followed by a vast sector of Catholic intransigentism, which had hitherto rejected any possible collaboration with the liberal and secular state. These sectors reconsidered the opportunity to re-enter public life; contrary to the "transigent" and "conciliarist" Catholics, they did not do this on the basis of a passive acceptance of the current political order and renouncement of Catholic principles, but with the aim of advancing social demands and claims opposed to the politics and policies of liberal governments. In 1896, even *La Civiltà Cattolica* endorsed Albertario's proposal. In two articles, titled "I cattolici e l'ora presente" ("Catholics and the Needs of the Moment") and "I cattolici e il Regno parlamentare" ("Catholics and the Parliamentary Kingdom") Father Raffaele Ballerini suggested that "preparamento nell'aspettazione," that is, "getting prepared while waiting" (Traniello 1998: 79–80), was a duty for all Catholics who were loyal to the pope. Ballerini added an important clarification: Catholics could be called to contribute to the defense of the social order against Socialism and to comply with a de facto authority requiring actions and behaviors that were not in opposition to Christian consciousness. However, they could not be forced to support and defend a political constitution embedded in and structured around erroneous principles from both a religious and an ethical point of view. Catholics were therefore forbidden from "entrare nell'edificio del sabaudismo" ("entering the framework of the Savoy ideology").

Socialist thinkers understood that something was happening in the Catholic world. For example, Gaetano Salvemini talked explicitly of a Catholic party in an 1898 article published in *Critica Sociale*. He called it "a large army," composed of aristocrats and poor peasants, "the active and combative young man," the "peaceful grocer," and many other people with different "ideas, interests, education," cemented together by the clergy, with "its wealth" and "the secular organization of the church." To approach such a complex organization—Salvemini continued—with "four more or less trivial insults" or the "the eternal aphorism: priests are allies of the bourgeois" was convenient and easy, but it was also "contrary to the truth and ineffective" (quoted in Traniello 1998: 78).

There was, however, an unresolved issue in the composite world of Catholic intransigentism. On one hand, it was clear that the movement possessed a great ability for social and political mobilization: it had a doctrine, structure, and political culture alternative to both Socialism and liberalism, and was therefore ready for real political action. On the other hand, one of the crucial doctrinal elements of this movement was the complete obedience to an authority that continued to officially hamper access to the modern right of citizenship expressed through the political vote.

Inspired and encouraged by the example of French and Belgian Christian Democrats as well as by the social achievement of the German Catholics, whose unification in a powerful political party had—paradoxically—been reinforced by the struggle against Bismarck, the young Catholics of the Opera, starting from the 1897 congress in Milan, made a decisive move toward the creation of an efficient popular liberation force, progress, and positive engagement with the world. Thus, the need for a party emerged from the formula *preparazione nell'astensione*. The young generation of Catholics started to realize that only a political democracy could ensure the fulfillment of social democracy, and a political democracy required the constitution of a political actor: a party. It is in this context that, in 1901, the young priest Romolo Murri (1870–1944)—a member of the Opera, promoter in 1894 of the birth of the Federation of the Italian Catholic University Students (Federazione Universitaria dei Cattolici Italiani, FUCI), and the initiator and director of journals that were very active in the public debate—founded the *Democrazia Cristiana* movement, famously defined by the Italian historian Francesco Traniello as "the party that was never born" (Traniello 1998: 77–100; on Murri see also Saresella 1994 and Biaglioli et al. 2004).

2.3 Murri and the First Christian Democracy

In founding the movement, Murri was—like so many others—inspired by the *Rerum novarum*, but also by the writings of the jurist, sociologist, and economist Giuseppe Toniolo (1845–1918). Toniolo was one of several central figures who laid the groundwork for a full-blown Catholic, modern outlook (this section is again based on Forlenza and Thomassen 2016: 66–70). Toniolo was the founder, in 1889, of the *Unione Cattolica per gli Studi Sociali in Italia* ("Catholic Union for Social Studies in Italy"). He consciously worked to develop a Catholic social and economic platform that stood in contrast to Socialism. He stressed the duty of labor and defended the social function of property, while also inspiring the formation of Catholic unions. He worked behind the scenes of the weekly *Democrazia Cristiana*, which was first issued in Turin in 1896. His most famous and important publication is *Trattato di Economia Sociale* ("Treatise on Social Economy"), which sought to lay the scientific and ethical foundations for a

Catholic-inspired political economy, a corporate model based on solidarity and social justice. In a social science article published in 1897, titled "The Christian Concept of Democracy," Toniolo was the first to define "Christian democracy," describing it as:

> that civil order in which social, legal, and economic forces, in the fullness of their hierarchical development, harmoniously work together toward the common good, and in such a manner that the greatest benefit of all is reaped by the lower classes. (Toniolo 1897: 325; see also Toniolo 1949)

Already in 1894, Toniolo warmly invited—not without encountering resistance— the direction of the Opera to accept his *Programma dei cattolici di fronte al socialismo* ("Program of Catholics vis-à-vis Socialism"). The young members of the Opera enthusiastically embraced Toniolo's ideas. He championed the reorganization of society based on professional trade unions. He also highlighted the importance of other reforms: from municipal autonomy to administrative decentralization, from the calculation of the maximum working hours and minimum salary to a more just and equitable allocation of taxes and resources, from the freedom of teaching to the defense and promotion of small private properties as collective property. Naturally, a similar program required political action, but Leo XIII could not allow Catholics to participate in the political life of the liberal state, at least not until the Roman question was solved.

Yet, Toniolo's ideas sowed the seeds of change and, time and again, resurfaced in the subsequent history of political Catholicism. As we will see in the following chapters, Alcide De Gasperi, an important figure in the history of Italian political Catholicism in later times, remained immensely influenced by Toniolo's early writings. In 1949, De Gasperi announced the re-publication of a series of Toniolo's most important works, including the abovementioned essay of 1897, in which the notion of Christian democracy was pinned down with precision for the first time (see Toniolo 1949). In a sense, De Gasperi considered Toniolo his political "patron" and the inspiration behind his political activity, in much the same way as Palmiro Togliatti liked to see himself as an interpreter and active codifier of Antonio Gramsci.

Directly inspired by these ideas, Murri made considerable efforts to disseminate a Christian social movement in and alongside the Opera. Murri elaborated a quite detailed project for economic, social, and political reforms aimed at a radical transformation of the liberal state. He wanted to bring to life the idea of Christian democracy in all aspects of human affairs. In May 1899, he wrote the following in the *Osservatore Cattolico*:

> In Italy, we have called our young movement of ideas and souls Christian democracy. It is a complex of clear and firm principles and criteria for action

that must reform our entire public life.... It was not meant simply to be a critique of revolution, the reaction of religious thought: it was, instead, meant to be an act of reconstruction, of reconquest. (quoted in Tornielli 2011: 70)

Catholic thinkers were consciously moving away from a defensive position, actively seeking to reform and mold the—ideational as well as institutional—contours of modern life. In fact, Murri considered what the official church hierarchy failed to realize a *fait accompli*: that the church would necessarily have to accept political democracy. Furthermore, the church would have to *identify* with political democracy as understood and interpreted by Murri and his followers, that is, as a "direct participation of the people... with special reference to the most humble and numerous classes, in economic and political institutions." It is important to note how Catholic thinkers of the time had become ardently aware of the issue of class. They were not going to give the "class struggle" away to the Socialists; rather, they wanted to take up the class issue, but absorb it in the folds of their own playground.

While other young Catholics—such as Filippo Meda, who came from the school of Don Albertario—criticized liberalism from an ideological point of view, Murri pushed forward and motivated his critique in the name of a social and historical analysis imbued with quasi-classist content (Murri 1898; see also Traniello 1998: 86–8). For Murri, organized Catholics represented every social sector that was oppressed and subjugated by the dominance of a bourgeois oligarchy except for those sections of the proletariat already conquered by Socialism. In other words, Murri tentatively defined the contours of a social basis for the Catholic party. This was a radical innovation in Catholic thought and action; such radicalism pervaded not only Murri's idea of a party but also his conception of political democracy, which was completely opposed to the liberal, political democracy of the Italian state.

This radicalism was also the result of Murri's attentive reading of Marx. In 1893 and 1894, he attended classes on historical materialism held by the Marxist philosopher Antonio Labriola at the University of Rome, La Sapienza. Encouraged by Labriola's ideas and also by the thought of the prime philosopher of liberalism in Italy, Benedetto Croce, Murri "suggested a distinction between historical materialism, and dialectic materialism, believing it possible to accept the analysis of contemporary society provided by the former and thus opening up the way to an exchange between Marxist philosophy and the Catholic world which would be useful to many believers in the years to come" (Saresella 2019: 14). Murri felt that the cultural and political beliefs of Catholicism vis-à-vis the modern world and Socialism were problematic. He considered "the social contradictions introduced by capitalism to be far more serious than the unresolved bickering between the two states," the Holy See and the Kingdom of Italy (Saresella 2019: 13). For many

Catholics, even those of the young generation close to Murri, a Catholic political action in Italy remained subordinated to the resolution of the Roman question. For Murri, the latter was the manifestation of the Catholic movement's non-involvement in and unrelatedness to the bourgeois arrangement of the state and society (Traniello 1998: 87). In 1905, Murri even proposed an alliance with the Partito Socialista Italiano (PSI, Italian Socialist Party) and its leader, Filippo Turati. Murri thought that there could be a *political* convergence between Christian Democrats and reformist Socialists who had abandoned the revolutionary dream that was not necessarily less important than the Catholics' *religious* convergence with other forces (Murri 1905). This way, Murri "challenged the idea that Christ's message could or should [be] interpreted in one way only from a social and political point of view" (Saresella 2019: 13).

Murri essentially claimed that modern democracy, originating from the French Revolution, represented "the very life of Christianity in human history."[2] By inserting modern democracy into Christian history, Murri was urging his movement to elaborate and implement a Christian society *here* and *now*, in the given historical context of the time. For Murri, modern political democracy had no meaning and function in itself; it could only be imagined as an appropriate political modality to establish a social democracy, which to him (as for Toniolo) could not be but a *Christian* democracy.

In Murri's view, Christian democracy was political and social democracy at the same time. It was, therefore, an authentic alternative to a liberal democracy that, founded on individual political representation and pursuit of wealth, would never be able to generate a "social" democracy. Likewise, it was a real alternative to Socialist democracy, whose collectivistic objectives would inevitably pave the way for the tyranny of the state over individuals and society. Even in terms of its social content, Christian democracy as described by Murri—namely as an "organic" democracy founded on corporatist professional associationism and the autonomy of the intermediate bodies—would never become a finished product or a fully designed social model. Because it should be rooted in social reality and shifting historical circumstances, Christian democracy would have to be constantly in becoming. This is precisely why it substantially distinguished itself from Socialism. Murri wrote the following:

> For us, Christian Democrats, the highest program is not a social state possessing certain characteristics, conceived as the outcome of a series of upheavals and reforms leading to it. We are more positivists than the Socialists. (quoted in Are 1963: 459)

[2] See the "maximum and minimum program of Christian democracy" and the "program of Christian Democracy" in *Cultura Sociale* of August 1, September 1, and November 1, 1901, quoted in Are 1963: 459–70; see also Traniello 1998: 91–3.

The idea that modern democracy could not be separated from the method of liberty, that liberty had a Christian origin, and that it was inherent in Christianity was the great novelty, and true discovery, of Murri and the wider movement around him. Here he followed Lord Acton's reflection on the history of liberty as coinciding with the history of Christianity and Judaism alike. This interpretation, which might be said to be the embryonic of a distinctive "political spirituality," to adopt Foucault's concept, was in open contrast to the Enlightenment-based version of liberty, namely as a condition that states and individuals had obtained from the church—and *against* the church. However, this interpretation also diverged from the authoritarian attitude of Christian medieval society, still dominant within the official church hierarchy at the beginning of the twentieth century.

2.4 Murri and the Cultural Struggle

One of the most important and qualifying points of Murri's Christian democracy was not only the pessimistic view on the state of Catholicism in Italy, which obviously implied a negative assessment of the nineteenth-century Catholic movement, but also the conviction that the religious crisis was eventually a cultural crisis. Murri and his followers placed two crucial and interrelated aspects at the center of their analysis: first, they acknowledged the intrinsic and hegemonic power of modern culture, pervaded by the inductive, critical-historical, and scientific-comparative method; second, they recognized that Catholic popular consciousness was weaker and had no modern answers—or no appropriate answers to modern times—vis-à-vis the insidious forces of Socialist and liberal culture.

From this point of view, Murri's Christian democracy was an attempt to redefine a new relationship between culture and religion, starting from the core of Catholic culture, which was in direct competition with other cultures while at the same time appropriating their methods and motivations. Thus, Murri abandoned a—from a religious point of view—merely defensive position and initiated a profound and critical examination of the real conditions of Italian Catholicism, especially at the popular level. Catholics must go to the *popolo* to organize and educate them, as Gennaro Avolio wrote in *Il Popolo Italiano* in 1897 (quoted in Traniello 2007a: 213). In a similar vein, in 1898, Murri wrote the following in the same journal:

> [I]f [the Catholic movement] wants to avoid the weakness and dissipation of the past, it must try to educate non only the religious but also the political consciousness of Italians, thus establishing itself more widely and efficiently in the field of popular organization. (quoted in Rossi 1977: 44)

In short, Murri proposed a cultural revolution, considered as the trailblazer of a religious and political revolution (on this see Traniello 2007a: 211–19). The manifesto of such a revolution was a series of articles that Murri (under the name of Paolo Arcari) published in 1900 in his journal, *Cultura sociale*, in the column *Vita cristiana oggi* ("Christian Life Today"), subsequently collected in the volume *La vita cristiana sulla fine del secolo XIX* ("Christian Life at the End of the Nineteenth Century"). Murri noted that while "the church's external and visible activity before civilization, at this time, is summed up in the defense of the Catholic self, the dogma, and Catholic disciplines," the (still popular Catholic) masses and the lower classes "offer inert and passive resistance to the invasion of modern life and civilization, marked by the expansion of capitalism." The consequence, Murri argued, was the erosion of Christian life and conscience that had made the lower classes the prey of Socialism. Another consequence was growing religious indifference, generated by a religion reduced to mere habits, and a superficial form unable to engage and compete with modern culture and society. The Catholic response in the nineteenth century had been a total failure, Murri continued. The "reactionary politics" of Catholic legitimism, the paternalism of "clerical religious" movements, and the separation between Catholic high culture and Catholic actions on the ground had caused the detachment of the bourgeoisie from Catholicism and the church, and subsequently produced the same result with "the fourth state and the new current of civil and social action that led it to dominate the public cause."

For Murri and his companions, modernity was a profound and pervasive sociopolitical, cultural, and existential revolution, which was paving the way for the liberation and intervention of the lower classes. As such, it could not be tackled with the traditional Catholic paternalistic approach. Rather, old principles and values needed to be critically re-examined, and the new Catholic movement should go beyond rural classes, artisans, the *petit bourgeoisie*, and the marginal sectors of the new urban and capitalistic society—often unable to initiate a modern social action (Murri quoted in Are 1963: 559)—and bridge the gap with the newest social classes generated by the Industrial Revolution. This new Catholic movement should, then, initiate a careful examination of the socioeconomic structure, thus going well beyond religious and ethical considerations. Sturzo, a close collaborator of Murri, said the following in 1902: "[W]ork classifies and unites men…it created class" (Sturzo 1961a: 47). For Sturzo, Murri, and the other Christian Democrats, the success of Socialism among the lower classes forced the new Catholic social culture to make a distinction between ideology and the "social movement" of the proletariat. Thus, Christian Democrats formulated a class theory that was very different from Socialist ideology and that was specifically characterized by the role and function of professions and categories. As Sturzo suggested:

work, which is a fundamental and vital basis for cooperation and common interests, synthesizes the whole problem of life for the worker; he cannot, from his point of view, look at other problems, which offer him a clearer perspective and vision on life. (Sturzo 1961a: 87)

From the perspective of Murri, Sturzo, and other progressive sectors of Christian democracy, it was necessary to establish an element of discontinuity with the Catholic tradition and recognize the principle of the autonomy and self-organization of social classes.

2.5 Christian Democracy and the Challenge of Modernism

The Vatican was not ready to embrace the ideas of the most radical thinkers of Christian democracy. Not surprisingly, it remained skeptical about modern political institutions and the involvement of Catholics in national politics. In his 1901 encyclical *Graves de communi re*, Pope Leo XIII insisted that the label "Christian democracy" must be employed "without any political significance." The pope certainly preferred the label Christian democracy over social democracy. Yet, he condemned the Catholic efforts in active politics to protect their rights and those of the church. Leo XIII thus consciously downplayed the political ambitions of Christian democracy, which should be understood—he wrote—as no more than a "beneficent Christian action on behalf of the people." In other words, he emphasized the moral role of Christian democracy, playing down its political role. In this reading, the "democratic" element had nothing to do with institutional politics; it simply meant to act and do good among the "people." From such a viewpoint, the pope positively referred to Toniolo's ethical and social viewpoints, and wholly rejected what the French democratic abbots had said: *tutto per il popolo e dal popolo* ("everything for the people, and from the people"). However, Leo XIII did not obstruct the continuation of moderate reformist action, although this was not what Murri and his radical friends had in mind. Murri's project was indeed political, openly geared toward deep social reforms within the framework of state and society, to the point of challenging the liberal order.

Murri and his circle of friends were soon accused of modernism. Indeed, at the time of the emergence of Christian democracy, the Vatican had to face a new movement from *within* its own ranks, which went still further; this movement was incidentally called "modernism." It was an intellectual, amorphous movement that developed among Catholics in the late nineteenth century and early twentieth century, first in France and England, with the proclaimed aim of creating harmony between the church and modernity as well as the post-Enlightenment world (Schultenover 1993; O'Connell 1994; Jodock 2000). In the insightful reflections of Antonio Gramsci and other sectors of secular culture, modernism was the Catholic intellectual circle's reaction to the challenge of the modern world, with its rationalistic and scientific criticism (on this issue see Saresella 2019: 48–51).

Church authorities were the first to employ the term "modernist" condemningly. The official condemnation of modernism in 1907, in Pope Pius X's encyclical *Pascendi dominici gregis*, marked a victory for Catholic anti-modernists and the emergence of an anti-modern position within the church that would spread across Europe throughout the first half of the century. Anti-modernists such as Joseph Lemius, the man who drafted the majority of the papal document that condemned modernist roots and branches, described themselves as "integralists," a title that clearly revealed how they saw the church and its ideology (Poulat 1969 and 1996 [1962]; Daly 1980: 184).

Murri maintained contact with modernists, aiming for a common front of scholars and social activists who were exasperated by hierarchical control. This affirmed the integralists' suspicion that the essence of modernism consisted in excessive claims for autonomy and an inbuilt intolerance of authority: in short, that the modernists were troublesome reformers who had to be controlled or, if necessary, expelled. Murri was a Thomist in the classical sense and remained skeptical about various aspects of the wider modernist movement. Yet, the church would eventually classify him as a modernist (Scoppola 1961: 158; Guasco 1995: 140–1). The confrontation with the official church hierarchy seemed inevitable, especially after the death of Leo XIII in 1903. His successor Pius X saw modernism as nothing but an enemy to combat. In his 1906 encyclical, *Pieni l'animo*, Pius X explicitly addressed the situation among the Italian clergy. In this letter, which in many ways directly addressed Murri and his followers, the pope put his fingers on what he defined as a "spirit of insubordination and independence displayed here and there among the clergy." He continued:

> This unfortunate spirit is doing damage especially among young priests, spreading new and reprehensible theories concerning the very nature of obedience among them. In order to recruit new members for this growing troop of rebels, what is even more serious is the fact that such maxims are being more or less secretly propagated among youths preparing for priesthood within the enclosure of the seminaries.

In the same encyclical, seminarians were forbidden to take part in "external" activities, which meant any activity not under the direct control of the church. In its final clauses, the encyclical explicitly prohibited seminarians and members of the clergy from becoming members of the National Democratic League, the association founded by Murri and Giuseppe Fuschini in 1905 as a non-denominational party of Catholic inspiration (Giovannini 1981). The conflict became a public affair.

Pius X summed up his position on the modernists very explicitly in the encyclical of 1907, the aforementioned *Pascendi dominici gregis* on the doctrines of modernists, which was nothing other than a long attack on "the errors of modernism." In 1910, Pius X issued the equally famous *Oath against Modernism* that he promulgated in the *motu proprio* ("on his own impulse," a document issued at the pope's initiative and signed directly by him), *Sacrorum antistitum*. Swearing this oath was compulsory for all Catholic bishops, priests, and teachers, up until its abolition by Pope Paul VI in 1967.

In the years of Pius X, the church simply considered it one of its most fundamental tasks to protect the world against modernism. It was a genuine culture war, fought not only against secular threats but also within the ranks of the church, hence the condemnation of Antonio Fogazzaro's best-selling novel *Il Santo* (1905), which fictionally combined the social, scholarly, and church reform movement. Murri himself was *sospeso a divinis* in 1907, and then excommunicated in 1909.[3] He was eventually extremely disappointed about the possibility of reforming the church from within. Thus, while the church emerged victorious against modernist tendencies, the seeds for a modern Catholic social and political movement had long since been sown. Murri lost his battle, also because the people in Rome at the time were strongly opposed to democratic ideas and practices, but others were soon to pick it up. He was followed by the more active of his young collaborators, those who preferred to stay in the church. This was particularly the case of one of his earliest collaborators, the Sicilian priest Luigi Sturzo. Already in 1905, in his speech *Per un partito nazionale di cattolici in Italia* ("For a national party of Catholics in Italy"), Sturzo opened the way for the most typical manifestation of Christian democracy in the first half of the nineteenth century, namely the Italian Popular Party. First, though, as we shall see in chapter 3, the Christian democratic idea had to overcome a demanding trial: the Great War.

2.6 Christian Feminism

One salient theme concerning the meaning of the word "modern" was the role of women (the following is based on Dau Novelli 1996: 23–36; Gaiotti De Biase 2002; Dawes 2011). In a series of documents, Leo XIII discussed the family, stressing how Christian doctrine had effectively raised the issue of women's inferiority, giving them the same dignity as men, as well as the same rights and duties. From the pope's perspective, however, a woman fulfilled herself exclusively as a wife and mother, and therefore exclusively within the family. She was the angel of the house. Work, activities, and any other occupation outside the family and

---

[3] The suspension *a divinis* is not a deprivation of the clerical state, commonly known as "defrocking," but a penalty barring the exercise of the power of office (e.g. celebrating the Mass). Murri's excommunication was revoked in 1943, shortly before his death. Ironically, and perhaps somewhat tragically, Murri died only months before the new Democrazia Cristiana party started to take shape, initiating a rise to power that would make it more triumphant than Murri could ever have imagined.

within society would have meant a deviation from women's proper role, which would not bring them any gratification.

Yet, in the final years of Leo XIII's papacy, within the Catholic movement and strongly related to the experiences of the *Opera dei Congressi* and Murri's Christian democracy, a so-called "Christian feminism" emerged—a term that became popular in the Christian Democratic press around 1900. It was the *Rerum novarum* and its call to tackle the consequences of the social and economic transformation that convinced groups of Catholic women to become involved in activities outside the home and the family. Unlike secular feminism, whose primary aim was women's emancipation, the main objective of Christian feminism was to promote Catholic values in Italian society, while at the same time engaging with the social issues of a society in rapid transformation. The historian Paola Gaiotti De Biase well explained the difference between secular feminism and Christian feminism:

> Secular feminism has its historical point of departure in the declaration of rights and the new structure of production, and its logical basis in the assertion of equality with men. Christian feminism, instead, originates from a whole new set of apostolic problems posed to the church by modern society, and it is logically founded on the equality of the spiritual vocation of man and woman. (Gaiotti De Biase 2002: 22)

Unsurprisingly, the center of emerging Christian feminism was Milan, the most modern place in Italy, even though the Catholic women's movement was by no means limited to this city. Thanks to periodicals such as *L'azione muliebre* ("Women's Action") and *Pensiero e azione* ("Thought and Action") and groups like the *Fascio democratico cristiano femminile* ("Women's Christian Democratic Association"), Catholic women (typically from the middle and upper classes) established a network that generated exchanges and ideas, as well as activities at a high cultural level. Their aim was to expose the errors and flaws of liberalism (because it supported capitalism) and Socialism (because of its willingness to overturn the social order). They tackled issues such as women's right to vote, divorce, the conditions of working-class women and—more in general—female laborers, public schools, and the condition of children. At the same time, they continued to address more traditional questions, such as charity, popular (religious) education, and services for the disabled.

Pensiero e azione, the organ of the Fascio that was directed by Adelaide Cori, launched the initiative for the foundation of a Milanese women's federation ("Federazione femminile") that could coordinate all Catholic women's associations. It began its publication of the periodical *Cultura sociale*, which was founded by Murri. The periodical promoted a wide debate on the woman question from a social and cultural perspective, respectful of Christian and Catholic principles, but outside the guidelines of Catholic organizations proper. In 1907, the Federazione promoted a congress that was held in Milan and open to secular and Socialist feminists. The aim was to elaborate a common strategy to directly tackle social, civil, and political issues. Pope Pius X disapproved of any relationship between Catholic women and secular feminists, and Christian feminism was increasingly associated with modernism. Simultaneously, large sectors of the Catholic press—especially on its more conservative side—started to campaign against the openly feminist agenda of the Federazione and *Pensiero e azione*, given their demands for full civil and political rights. *Pensiero e azione* was suppressed in 1908; one reason for this was the fact that the periodical had recommended a book by the Socialist Augusto Bebel as holiday reading for a schoolteacher. Its suppression marked the momentary end of Christian feminism.

In 1909, a new and more conservative organization quickly emerged from the ashes of previous experiences: the *Unione fra le donne cattoliche d'Italia* ("Union of Catholic Women of Italy"). Founded in Rome by a group of women close to the clergy and the hierarchy, the Unione received an official papal endorsement on April 21, 1909, when Pius X received its representative. The Unione was born not to defend and improve the condition of women but to protect religion. The quintessential themes of feminism thus disappeared from the agenda of the Unione. Its objective was rather to connect Catholic women and prepare them for the fulfillment of their individual, domestic, and social duties. The latter primarily included charitable activities and assistance to the poor, ill, and needy. In line with the will of Pius X and against earlier attempts at creating alliances with the secular feminists, the Unione aimed at countering the secularization process and fighting the anti-religious and anti-Christian spirit, as well as anything neutral or indifferent to Catholicism and the church. Members of the organization were educated through publications, conferences, and vocational schools. Yet, despite the call for an exclusive religious commitment, the Unione made its entry into other fields, such as the defense of Catholic women workers, and promoted the birth of many Catholic professional organizations for women. In short, the programmatic assumptions were progressively circumvented, and the initial apolitical attitude turned into dynamic and spirited activism in battles such as those against divorce, questions related to civil and religious marriage, and the teaching of religion in schools. Although the Unione did not advance explicitly feminist demands, it can certainly be compared to secular women's emancipatory associations.

This development was in line with a broader trend that become more and more visible from the end of the nineteenth century. Growing sectors of the Catholic world would leave behind defensive attitudes and engage with the rapidly shifting political and economic contexts in which they were living. This was much in line with the activist spirit found in *Rerum novarum*. At the same time, many of the political actions taken in the name of Catholicism were eventually critiqued and, in some case, rejected by the very same church. This was a tension that would be continued throughout much of the twentieth century.

3

Popular Democracy

This chapter focuses on how the experience of World War I was decisive for Catholic politics, opening the way for the emergence of a Catholic political party and therefore for what can be called the "first generation" of Christian Democrats. Until the war, and despite the changes of the later decades of the nineteenth century, Catholic approaches to political democracy and national politics were still rife with obstacles. The Great War changed everything. In 1919, Pope Benedict XV lifted the ban on Catholics participating in national political life. Luigi Sturzo founded the Italian Popular Party, Italian Catholics' first sustained experiment in mass politics. The word "popular" indeed encapsulates what happened during the first two decades of the twentieth century: a significant rethinking of the roots of democracy. The experiment came to an end in 1926, when the PPI was outlawed by the Fascist regime.

For Catholics, the nineteenth century ended in 1904. The new Pope Pius X (Giuseppe Melchiorre Sarto, 1835–1914), elected in August 1903, decided to dissolve the *Opera dei Congressi*, the main association that promoted Catholic intransigentism. While it was not the only Catholic association operating in post-unification Italy, it certainly had the most significant imprint on wider sectors of Italian Catholicism. The end of the Opera had immediate consequences at the organizational level but also signaled deeper changes in terms of Catholic thought and actions from a wider perspective. Three associations replaced the Opera: the *Unione Popolare* (the "Popular Union"), the *Unione Elettorale* (the "Electoral Union"), and the *Unione Economica e Sociale* (the "Economic and Social Union), which were supposed to constitute the new pillars of Catholic organization and action in Italy. The new associations followed lines of thought and orientations that diverged from traditional intransigentism. This did not mean that intransigent culture and mentality disappeared overnight; rather, they remained operative in the background and texture of the Catholic world, while adapting themselves to the changing times and conditions.

The first crucial transformation involved the political sphere. Indeed, this is when the process of inserting Catholic organizations into the fabric of the national liberal-political institutions began, slowly at first, then more rapidly. The *non expedit* was suspended in various dioceses. Many Catholics went to the polls in electoral colleges and tended to vote for Catholic candidates, who then became their representatives in the national parliament. These politicians would be called

Italy's Christian Democracy: The Catholic Encounter with Political Modernity. Rosario Forlenza and Bjørn Thomassen,
Oxford University Press. © Rosario Forlenza and Bjørn Thomassen 2024. DOI: 10.1093/oso/9780198859864.003.0004

cattolici deputati ("deputies who were Catholics"), and not *deputati cattolici* ("Catholic deputies"), because Pius X did not want them to be seen as representatives of Catholicism at large.

This was only the tip of the iceberg. There were many dimensions to the Catholic entrance into political matters. For example, at the local level, many Catholics built alliances with the liberal moderate groups, opposing the so-called "popular blocs" of Socialists and radicals. After all, already in 1904, the pope himself informally had permitted going to the polls to halt the success of the Socialists. Catholics were now starting to become not only an important part—even if still indirectly and partially—of the political contest from which they had hitherto been excluded but an influential part, one which could decide the outcome of the elections. This was even more the case in 1913, when new political elections were held.Thanks to the reform introduced by Prime Minister Giovanni Giolitti in 1912, these were the first elections with universal male suffrage extended to all citizens aged 30 and above, and with no further restrictions. Crucially, on this occasion, Giolitti and the President of the *Unione Elettorale Cattolica*, Ottorino Gentiloni, made an agreement known as the "Gentiloni Pact," pushing Catholic voters to support Giolitti's liberal-moderate coalition. In exchange, Giolitti promised that his new government would support Catholic policies and measures, such as funds for private (Catholic) schools and opposition to divorce. Around two hundred deputies were elected through the Gentiloni Pact, allowing Giolitti to win the majority of the seats. The Pact marked the alliance between Catholic and liberal-moderate forces, or the "clerical-moderates" as their opponents—including Murri's former collaborator Luigi Sturzo—contemptuously called them.

The Catholics' entry into the political arena manifested and, at the same time, signaled the attenuation of a conflict between the church and the liberal state. Giolitti understood that the relationship between the two forces resembled two parallels, two lines that never intersect. This metaphor expresses the idea of an increasing distance between church and state, and hence of a reduction of reasons for controversies and debates. Compared to the previous period, Giolitti's legislation was undoubtedly less anticlerical, if at all. This was, in fact, the main driving force of Giolitti's politics and approach to the life of the nation: to avoid, or solve, conflicts within the Italian body politic—between classes, geographical areas, stakeholders, and secular institutions, on one hand, and the church and Catholicism writ large, on the other hand.

Such an engagement in the political life of the nation had a crucial consequence: Catholics became increasingly aware of this issue and tended to reclaim their role in the defense and support of the interests of the nation, even—and above all—in an international dimension. This was not simply a matter of political alliances. It was, rather, a question of identification. Catholics were more and more inclined to identify as such within the nation, claiming to be truly Italian and affirming that Catholic opposition was opposition not to Italy but to liberal

Italy, hence opposition not to the nation but to the prevailing liberal political-institutional order. From this point of view, Catholics wished to be recognized as the best among the Italians. In other words, the Catholic stance changed from the nineteenth-century rejection of the liberal nation to a position that, without involving the entirety of Italian Catholicism, could be defined as Catholic patriotism. Catholics thus started to reconquer and resignify the value of the *Patria*, that is, the homeland, which they indeed considered purified thanks precisely to the Catholics' contribution.

One of the reasons for the Catholic embrace of the nation was the conflict that opposed Catholicism to Socialism—or large sectors of Socialism—and its internationalism, which tended to undermine the importance of the nation. Whereas Socialism proposed to overcome the idea of nation and *Patria* in the name of internationalism and universal brotherhood among workers, Catholics rediscovered and relaunched national identity, coming close to the positions of nationalists. This happened in 1912, in particular, during the war in Libya. The vast majority of the Catholic world endorsed the war for a series of reasons, including the fact that Libya was controlled by the Turkish Empire and the massive amounts of money that the Banca di Roma (a stronghold of the Catholic financial system) had invested in Libya.[1]

At the same time, the Catholic engagement with the issue of the nation was not an easy task, as the church was pitted against the state and the national identity it claimed to represent. Yet, Catholics openly tried to balance "solid patriotism" and "true nationalism" with Christian and Catholic doctrine (Traniello 2007b; Gentile 2009: 115–21; Formigoni 2010: 13–59). The church had by then toned down, if not set aside, its disapproval of the myth of the nation born out of the French Revolution. This "myth" considered the nation the expression of a new principle of people's sovereignty against the monarchic sovereign of Divine origin. The church, the Jesuits of the influential journal *La Civiltà Cattolica*, and—increasingly—large groups of Catholics were now committed to building a competing Catholic myth of the nation that stressed the religious factor in the formation of national identity. In doing this, they sought to reject the accusation of being unpatriotic and, in fact, accepted the existence of a unitary state.

This Catholic encounter with the idea of nation is crucial. Ever since the Reformation, the church had come to see nationalist tendencies as a threat to its integrity. With modern nationhood, as conceived and enacted through the French

---

[1] The Italo-Turkish or Turco-Italian War, also known in Italy as *guerra di Libia* (Libyan War), was fought between the Kingdom of Italy and the Ottoman Empire from September to October 1912. As a result of the war, Italy captured several territories that became the colonies of Italian Tripolitania and Cyrenaica, which would later merge into Italian Libya. Although a minor event, the war was a significant precursor of the Great War. It sparked nationalism in the Balkans; seeing how easily the Italians had defeated the weakened Ottomans, the members of the Balkan League attacked the Ottoman Empire before the war with Italy had even ended.

Revolution, nationalism had come to represent a menace to Christian civilization at large. At the same time, it was clear that, by the turn of the century, the church could not simply fight against the existence of nation-states and the national identification process as such.

According to the Jesuit Agostino Gemelli (the founder, in 1921, of the Università Cattolica), nations are neither the product of individual desire nor a fact of nature. Nations are, he said, "wished for by the God Providence"; consequently, "the source of love for the *Patria* is God himself, as one country is the instrument of power, goodness, and Divine providence, [and therefore] love of the *Patria* is included, like the least in the most and the detail in the general, in the cult that is God's right" (Gemelli 1918: 52, 60–1). However, Gemelli was writing in 1918, when Italy and the world had already been devastated by a cataclysmic event: World War I.

3.1 Catholicism and World War I

On the eve of the war, Catholics had started to participate in the modern democratic life of the nation and developed their thoughts on the question of the nation. At the practical level, however, Catholic approaches to national politics were still prone with obstacles. As with so many other things, the Great War and its aftermath proved a watershed, injecting slow but substantial changes. Although the papacy and some sections of the Catholic movement opposed Italy's intervention in the war, Catholics played their part loyally in the war efforts; their patriotism removed the last major hindrance to full participation in national politics.[2]

For the church and all Catholics, the Great War was a profound and wrenching rupture with the past. Despite the Gentiloni Pact, the contrast between the secular and the religious—that is, the liberal state and the church—had not disappeared. As long as the Roman question had not found a solution, a genuine and lasting reconciliation could not be foreseen. Moreover, the dilemma of peace and war, in a profoundly Catholic country, came to the fore with great strength and evidence. The traumatic experience of the war, which opposed armed Catholic nations against each other, highlighted critical paradoxes and tensions. The war was the period of Italian history in which the Catholic world put the historical opposition to the *Risorgimento* behind itself. Catholics entered the national community as a visible and self-conscious political force.

Elected quite unexpectedly and just before the beginning of the war, on September 3, 1914, the new Pope Benedict XV (Giacomo Della Chiesa,

---

[2] This section is based on Malgeri 1995; Rocca 1980, 1995, 2005; Gibelli and Stiaccini 2006; Menozzi 2008a: 15–46, 2008b, 2010, 2015; Malpensa 2010; on World War I in Italy, in general, see Gibelli 2007, 2001; Isnenghi and Rochat 2014.

1854–1922) saw the war as a divine punishment and urged Catholics to implore that "you lay down the curse of your wrath, with which you do justice to the sins of the nations." In an allocution to the consistory of cardinals held on January 22, 1915, the pope reaffirmed the neutrality of the church, which rejected "with all its forces every violation of the law regardless of where it is committed." At the same time, he also rejected the attempt to "involve the papal authority in the warmongers' disputes." The Holy See as well as a large and significant sector of Catholicism saw the experience of the war, its traumatic incivility, and the daily confrontation with death, suffering, and endless pain as a condition that could eventually reawaken a religious renaissance among soldiers and their families, thus activating a process of re-Christianization of the world. This was the moment to oppose the process of de-Christianization generated by modernity and its sociopolitical manifestations. The war certainly provoked a return to a religious spirit, at least in its more evident manifestation of cults, rituals, and symbolism. For example, the church took initiative to print almost 2 million images of the Madonna, as well as three thousand small portraits and 1.5 million medallions.

On the internal front, local councils led by Catholics as well as the vast networks of Catholic associations and organizations made significant efforts to assist families of combatants and fallen soldiers. While the Holy See remained neutral, large sectors of the clergy and the entire population—in Italy as elsewhere—instantly turned in favor of the war, leaving behind neutralism and embracing interventionism. Bishops were generally patriotic and invited Italians to be loyal to secular authority and to understand the defense of the *Patria*, on the frontline as on the internal front, as a proper duty. Very few bishops were neutralists, just as few were ardent nationalists. The traditional Catholic distinction between just and unjust war—in this context, interventionism was considered just—found more than an echo among Italian bishops, but the prevailing orientation was to adapt to the contingent situation and patriotically obey, postponing deeper and more careful reflections to the post-war period.

This was not only the case in Italy. In fact, a divergence emerged between the Church of Rome and the different national churches in several parts of Europe. The Great War was not a war of religion, but Catholics took sides with their own countries, justifying the conflict as a just war fought to defend themselves, their families, and their country against an enemy identified as the anti-Christ. Catholicism and nationalism merged and started living side by side, not without contradictions and tensions. These tensions were heightened by the fact that Italy's main enemy, Austria, was predominantly Catholic (albeit within a multi-confessional empire). In fact, Austria had been the Catholic political power *par excellence*, defending the church and traditional Catholic values from the menace of revolutionary ideology and uncontrolled secularization throughout the nineteenth century.

The patriotism of the Italian church was much more prudent and cautious compared, for example, to the Belgian and, especially, the French church.

Indeed, in France, despite its proclaimed political and institutional *laicité*, the clergy's patriotic mobilization and the propaganda of religious authorities, aimed at soldiers and the faithful, resorted to tones and modes of expression that were deeply nationalistic and aggressive.

For Italian Catholics, and eventually for the church itself, a real turning point that led Catholicism to embrace the cause of the war without reservation came when General Luigi Cadorna, a diehard Catholic, decided to assign military chaplains to the Italian armed forces, which amounted to 2,500 individuals by the end of the war. Lured by the idea of providing soldiers at the front with spiritual assistance and support, Catholics and the church were permanently convinced of the importance of the war. Many Catholics, priests or not, decided to support the cause of Italian soldiers as chaplains or doctors. These included Angelo Maria Roncalli (the future Pope John XXIII), Padre Pio (now the most famous saint of Catholicism), and Don Giovanni Minzoni, holder of a silver medal for his merit in the war, killed by a Fascist squad in 1923. The popular writer Giosuè Borsi converted to Catholicism during the war and soon became the epitome of conciliation between faith and the *Patria* in the name of nationalism. His figure was then appropriated and politicized by Fascism, which transformed him into a martyr who had sacrificed himself for the cause of a better and bigger Italy.

The Catholic press, at the higher and the grassroots levels, enthusiastically endorsed the war effort and supported the morale of soldiers and their families. Public speeches of bishops and priests did the same. And yet, there was a divergence between the public and the private, the propaganda effort, and the real perception on the ground. Letters, diaries, and other personal accounts and narratives of Catholic soldiers, as well as chaplains and bishops, clearly showed that the choice of the war and the endorsement of the national cause were not easy, and that it was difficult to find compatibility between faith and the violence of the war. For many, faith became not an irrational refuge but, rather, an anchorage: a place for one's own social, spiritual, and existential self-grounding that the chaplains and the family helped to keep open and free from the war and its traumatic incivility—in the end, a very hidden, personal, internal, and almost exclusive space.[3]

In this process, the traditional conceptual equipment of Catholicism, inherited from the ancient Christian reflection on peace and war, crumbled. In Italy, as elsewhere, Catholics tended not only to legitimize the wartime violence but also to justify it from a religious point of view, even sacralizing the violence and the war. In short, for Catholics, the war became not only "just" but also "holy." Popular prayers and worshipping practices that emerged spontaneously from Catholics at the grassroots level were profoundly imbued with the idea that the

---

[3] For an excellent transnational comparative history of Catholic everyday religion in Germany and Austria during the Great War, see Houlihan 2015.

war was sacred, something that needed to be fought like a proper crusade. In the traditional *santini* (literally "little saints," that is, icons printed on small pieces of paper that were very popular among Italians), the words of the pope—even those that rejected the war and its violence—were inserted to justify the war and the Catholic engagement with it. Papal statements were, therefore, being decontextualized and resemanticized via the recombination of iconographical content devoted to an aggressive and violent culture of war.

The world of Catholicism was composite; different tendencies coexisted. For example, men such as Francesco Crispolti, an important representative of the Catholic movement, rejected any possible sacralization and divinization of the national cause, in the name of obedience to the pope. At the same time, he was aware that the participation of Catholics in the war was a sort of test for their incorporation into Italian body politics. Given their sacrifice in the war, Catholics could not be denied their Italianness and their whole and legitimate membership in the nation. There were differences between the popular rural (especially southern) area, more inclined to peace and the rejection of the war, and the urban and bourgeois Catholics, more sensible to the need for international law and justice and the nationalistic appeal, and therefore more open to the war. The sectors of Catholicism that were more open to civil and religious renewal, such as the Democratic League and other groups close to modernism, participated in the conflict with more awareness and in the name of democratic interventionism; the popular sectors—evidently more conservative from a religious point of view— were, instead, closer to the position of neutralism.

Either way, the generally disciplined and patriotic behavior of Catholic combatants and the Catholics' commitment to the support of the internal front did not diminish after Benedict's uncompromising condemnation of the war as an *inutile strage* ("a useless slaughter") in 1917, which also provoked the harsh reaction of Italy's allies. The Italian Foreign Minister Sidney Sonnino intervened, asking the Allies not to respond to the pope's Note. Italy also opposed the participation of representatives of the Holy See at the Peace Conference of Paris. This was yet another sign that the relationship between liberal Italy and the Vatican was still problematic and controversial.

3.2 After the War

Immediately after the war, in 1919, Pope Benedict XV lifted the ban on Catholic participation in national political life. The Sicilian priest Luigi Sturzo was quick to take action. He had collaborated with Murri and was still quite active in the political life of his region. He considered local politics and the promotion of local autonomy, which expressed one of the crucial principles of Catholic social teaching, namely subsidiarity, an ideal school and formative experience for political activity. He had been the "pro-sindaco" (sort of deputy mayor) of Caltagirone since 1905 and maintained this role until 1920. The time was ripe—he thought after the war—for the founding of a party of Christian, democratic inspiration. He came to these ideas not simply through a theoretical orientation but precisely because of his experience in local politics. He obtained the authorization of Benedict XV for such an endeavor.

In January 1919, appealing to "all strong and free men," he founded the Partito Popolare Italiano (PPI, Italian Popular Party).[4] For Antonio Gramsci, this was "the most important historical event after the Risorgimento," an assertion that anticipated what historian Federico Chabod said decades later, defining the PPI's birth as "the most remarkable event of twentieth-century Italian history" (on Sturzo and his project see Formigoni 2008a: 95–105, 2010: 83–103; De Rosa 1977; Traniello 1998: 141–83; Crivellin 2010). The party was an immediate success, gaining 20.5 percent of the national vote and one hundred seats in the Chamber of Deputies in the 1919 elections. The result was largely confirmed in the 1921 elections. The party was particularly strong and gained almost half of the votes in a region like Veneto, where Catholic associational life was extremely present and active. It thus captured what since then has been called, and rightfully so, Italy's "Catholic vote."

Sturzo very consciously, and closely following Murri, posited the party in opposition to both Socialism and liberalism. His sense that Italy had something genuine to offer to modern politics, and that this "something" must be grounded in its religious history, was expressed quite explicitly in the second to last clause of the "appeal" with which he had presented the party in early 1919: "We present ourselves to political life with our moral and social banner, inspired by the firm principles of Christianity that consecrated the grand civilizing mission of Italy." In Sturzo's words, this "civilizing mission" had to show its real worth in the concrete historical situation that presented itself after World War I, with the collapse of empires and the simultaneous emergence of new forms of imperialism, be they Socialist or liberal. In this context, Christian principles had not lost their importance. Quite the contrary, they had become all the more necessary in modernity: the only reservoir of wisdom and ethical guidelines from where a true alternative to liberalism and Socialism could be established. It was in this precise sense that Gioberti's old notion of Italy's "primacy" and its "civilizing mission" came to life again.

The model proposed by Sturzo guaranteed the overcoming of the historical fracture that emerged, in the nineteenth century, between the liberal "conciliatorism" of the "transigent Catholic" (who sought an accommodation with the less anticlerical elements in the ruling liberal establishment) and the social

---

[4] The text is published in Sturzo 1951: 1–7. Sturzo made his appeal on January 18, 1919, the day when the Paris Peace Conference opened.

commitment of the intransigent Catholics (who, true to the spirit of Pius IX, abstained from any contaminating involvement in national politics). This fracture had come to appear insourmountable in Italy and much of Europe. Sturzo's "invention" had a huge effect on the subsequent history of Catholic involvement in politics and on Italian political history as such.

3.3 The Moral and the Political

The first two clauses of the PPI's program formulated the general principles of a party that, without being confessional, found its inspiration in Catholic doctrine: integrity and defense of the family, concern for public morality, protection of infancy, freedom of teaching. Point 8 of the program claimed:

> [f]reedom and teaching of the church in the full explication of its spiritual teachings. Freedom and respect for the Christian conscience considered as the foundation and bastion of the nation and of popular liberties, and for the growing achievements of civilization.

The other nine clauses of the program had technical content and could easily be embraced by any democratic party attentive to the public good, regardless of the philosophical and religious beliefs of its members. These clauses included social legislation devoted to ensuring and protecting the rights of workers and small private property; the power of consultation and orientation accorded to professional associations and unions in case of governmental decisions regarding workers; the redistribution of land (especially large estates abandoned by land owners) to poor and landless peasants in exchange of compensation to the legitimate owners; struggle against unemployment and emigration in the general context of a valorization of the natural resources of the nation, especially of the *Mezzogiorno*. The PPI's program furthermore included a fiscal reform based on progressive taxation; administrative *decentramento* and autonomy for local councils (*comuni, province*, and *regioni*); a proportional electoral system; enfranchisement of women; international cooperation; and struggle against the rearmament of the nation.

Yet, the PPI was not merely to be an expression of pragmatism, deprived of any moral and religious consideration. Quite the opposite, a rightful approach to political commitment for the common good required—in the understanding of Sturzo—the harmonization of politics and morality, overcoming any possible contrast between science and belief. Only such a harmonization could ensure an ordered society and an authentic democracy, based on the moral principle "that is historicized in the diversity of social realities and the pluralities of social units and forms," as Sturzo wrote in 1935 (Sturzo 1960: 236). The priority of the moral order was crucial for him; it was the basis for true democracy, as he wrote in *Politica e Morale*, first published in 1938:

> We include the authority of morality in the political system, the values of the conscience of private life in public life, and respect for others in the domain of political and economic relations. This is true democracy. (Sturzo 1972: 72; see also Sturzo 1957: 195–6, 1972: 262)

3.4 From Christian Democracy to a Popular Party of Christian Inspiration

Sturzo and other leaders were former Christian Democrats and close collaborators of Murri. Nevertheless, they decided to renounce the *democrazia cristiana* label for two reasons: first, to avoid a past that had positive as well as negative connotations and that had been the object of too much discussion; and second, because the PPI's leadership wanted the party to be more than a confessional group, open to all Italians who saw the need for an alternative to both Marxism and liberalism.

In the intention of Sturzo and his followers, the new party should refer to and be informed by Christian principles but, different from Murri's Christian democracy, it should be "a-confessional." Sturzo thus distinguished its scope of social, political, and cultural actions from those of the clergy and Catholic Action, a loose network of Catholic lay associations advocating and acting for greater Catholic influence in society. This "a-confessionality" was not meant to put aside or bracket off the party's religious element, but to trigger the fermentation *from below* of fundamental Christian values already existing in popular life. All this should be combined with the assumption of the direct responsibility of Catholics in politics, in terms of being autonomous from the Vatican and the church hierarchy, while nevertheless recognizing the mission of illuminating personal and collective conscience in the name of the gospel (see, for example, Sturzo 1996: 21).

As Sturzo wrote in 1902, Christian democracy was—and had to be—a historical movement that, founded on the message of "social redemption" of Christianity, complied with "a real and urgent need of the society" (1961a: 3). The profound link between Christianity and democracy cannot mean a modernist kind of secularization of the church's mission in the this-worldly realm; nor can it be an integralist and reactionary sacralization of a movement that, inspired by Catholic social teaching, wants to operate in the political and social sphere. A few decades later, in a 1937 article, Sturzo defined "our democracy" in the following terms:

> We want it to be Christian not because we want the Christian religion to express itself in political terms, but to exclude the entire anti-Christian democratic

tradition, from Rousseau to the present.... The adjective "Christian" is therefore
not characteristic...of the name of democracy and hence does not define it.
(Sturzo 1972: 263)

Sturzo, in reality, had already prefigured and anticipated the idea of a party of
Christian inspiration with a strong democratic and reformist imprint at the
famous Caltagirone speech (December 24, 1905) devoted to the "problems of the
nation." This is a document that the historian of the Catholic movement Gabriele
De Rosa defined as the "magna charta of popularism," a "lucid and brilliant
analysis of the past experience of intransigent Catholicism and a conscious and
courageous anticipation of what would have become the future national party
of Catholics" (De Rosa 1973: 57). Here the use of the word "Catholic" as an
adjective, in the sense of "popular," meant the abandoning of the traditional
intransigent stance that remained outside history—a Catholic one, tout court
(Sturzo 1906).

3.5 The People and the Popular

For Sturzo, the notion of *popolo* referred not to a confused and indefinite mass of
individuals, but to an organic whole of social groups defined and characterized by
their position within the relations of production. This was a consciously different
philosophical starting point from both liberal individualism and socialist collectivism, and would remain a defining feature of any Christian democratic position
up until today. Essentially, Sturzo wanted to position Catholics as a *social group*
and not as an ecclesial community within national political life. He wanted the
party to work from the basis of a political platform that was not dependent on
cultural universes opposed to Catholicism. In this way, he thought, the degree of
secularization that followed the process of political participation would not have
devastating and disruptive consequences for the traditional Catholic doctrinal
context.

Sturzo's idea of a people's party marked a huge and daring step forward in the
process of modernizing the Catholic world. It sought to develop a Catholic platform from which to respond to the challenges posed by two crucial passages of
modern democracy: the process of secularization and the process of political participation (on this see also Bobbio 1995: 113–14). In his inaugural speech for the
first congress of the PPI, held in 1919, Sturzo gave the most straightforward formulation of how politics and religion merged, and culminated, in the PPI, in a
new distinctive form of political spirituality:

From the beginning, we have excluded that our label should be religion and
have consciously chosen to situate ourselves on the specific terrain of politics,

which has as its specific object the interest of the nation.... However, it would be illogical to deduce from this that we have fallen into the error of liberalism, which treats religion simply as a matter of individual conscience. On the contrary, this is precisely what we stand against when we posit religion as the *vivifying spirit* for the entirety of individual and collective life.... While keeping that firmly in mind, we cannot allow ourselves to be transformed into an organism of the Catholic Church, nor would we even have the right to speak in the name of that authority, either in parliament or outside it. It is only in our name, albeit as Christians, that we can fight on the same terrain as other parties. (Sturzo 1961b: 82; quoted in and translated by Invernizzi Accetti 2019: 177)

As we have already stressed, the decisive point that qualified Sturzo's idea of democracy was that democracy must necessarily be a "social" democracy, and not (only) a political democracy. Democracy, of course, should not be indifferent or unrelated to political forms. However, Sturzo saw that the establishment of a political system must correspond to, reflect, and represent a "democratic" ideal social order. The crucial question here is, in fact, the difference between "formal" and "substantial" democracy. Already in 1900, in his discussion of Murri's ideas, Sturzo had argued that any notion of "Christian democracy" had to work from the premise that democratic political participation could not be reduced to formal electoral rights, but had to be grounded in concrete forms of social engagement through which individuals could find their worth and dignity within their encompassing political communities. In other words, a truly Christian democracy involved an ordering of society in all its aspects, based on the "popular will" and without succumbing to the logic of majoritarian rule—it was to be a political, social, and economic democracy. As Sturzo wrote in 1900:

[t]he democracy we want as Catholics is not simply a political form of society in which the people play a role in deciding who rules them. After all, even today the people already participate in the political lives of their nations.... Such acts of power are only popular in name but not in fact, because the action of those we call the representative of the people, just because the latter have put a piece of paper in a ballot box, most often develops in an anti-popular sense, both in its laws, in its economic purposes and in its concrete social effects.... In contrast, Christian Democracy means a popular organization of the whole structure of society whether that concern politics, law, economics, finance or concrete social practice. (Sturzo 1958: 58; quoted in and translated by Invernizzi Accetti 2019: 92)

Consequently, as Invernizzi Accetti insightfully writes, a popular form of government must involve "some kind of *objective* counterpart to the practice of collective self-government" and, more specifically, a "concrete measure to improve the people's lot and well-being" (Invernizzi Accetti 2019: 92, italics in the original).

In fact, Sturzo—Invernizzi Accetti continues—played on the ambiguity between the people and the popular, "the people as a social whole," and "the people as the lowest and the most disadvantaged class within the social whole." A popular government, therefore, means to undertake concrete measures in favor of the poorest sectors of society.

Invernizzi Accetti furthermore notes that Sturzo made this very clear by unraveling the "substantive" aspect of democracy and conjuring up what Toniolo, too, had written in 1897, in the *Appeal to the Free and the Strong*: "The necessary and urgent reforms in the field of social security and assistance, the regulation of labor and the formation and protection of small property…must all tend towards the elevation of the working and popular class" (Invernizzi Accetti 2019: 93).[5] Yet, for Sturzo, social democracy did not mean indifference to political forms; it meant, instead, that the political system must correspond to a democratic social order, representing and reflecting it—an awareness of the distance between a formal and a substantial democracy. This is the decisive aspect of Sturzo's idea of Christian democracy as formulated in a speech of 1902, titled "The social struggle as a law of progress": "[T]he democratic or popular principle is the main means and objective of social implementation or reform; hence the now common motto 'all for the people and all by means of the people"' (Sturzo 1961a: 24–55, here 52). This speech clearly expressed, already in the title, the modernity of Sturzo's culture, which descends from his conception of history, which is quite a deviation from the dominant Catholic approach to the question. In this speech, Sturzo affirmed that the "social struggle exists" and is "a massive dynamic force that comprehends the problems of life." Hence, to him, Socialism and liberalism received their strength from their willingness to accept and deal with "the principle of struggle" from different theoretical perspectives. Both conceptions possessed a kernel of truth, which Sturzo wanted to explain following the principle that the soul of truth is to be found in the error. The intimate and ineliminable movement of social life was for him the product of the immanent contrast between a static and a dynamic element, "one tending to limit social life to a few, the other to enlarge it to many; one holding power and seeking to impersonate, [to] intensify the principle of authority, the other to extend it, [to] diminish it." In the current situation, he added, the force moving the social flux (*divenire*) was the "disintegrated people, reduced to a state of permanent social suffering; that is the necessity of the democratic character." In other words, the democratic was the popular.

---

[5] As noted by Invernizzi Accetti, in his 1897 article "The Christian Concept of Democracy," Toniolo stated that since "a truly democratic order" is "oriented toward" reciprocal aid in the pursuit of the temporal common good, it implies that "those who can do more also ought to do more, whereas those who can do less ought to receive more." Therefore, the Christian concept of temporal common good eventually "flows back to the ultimate advantage of the lower class," and it is precisely here that the "deepest essence" of the democracy system emerged (see Toniolo 1897: quotes respectively at pages 332 and 330). On this discussion see Invernizzi Accetti 2019: 93.

3.6 The Modernization of Catholic Culture and the Catholic *Popolo* through Education

Sturzo's *popolarismo*, based on the good sense of the people who actively participate in politics through parties, can therefore not be equated to the replacement of representative democracy with a direct relationship between masses and leader, which—with an anachronistic and perhaps imprecise word—could be defined as "populism." As he wrote in 1936, "*popolo* means not only the working class, but the entire citizenry, because everyone must enjoy liberty and participate in the government" (see Sturzo 1971: 108, and also 1945a). Thus, *popolarismo*, at a doctrinal and a political level, also implied the "moral education to public life" (Sturzo 1972: 98).

To sustain the renovation of Catholic action in politics and society, Sturzo considered the renovation of Catholic culture and the valorization of the cultural dimension of social and political problems crucial. This is important to understand. In a preparatory text for a 1904 conference, Sturzo wrote that "if we lose the field of ideas, if we stay away from it in the daily scientific debate, the influence of religion will diminish, it will be lost; the impact on families, on the people, in society will be enormous" (Sturzo 1974a: 253). In an article from 1902 (which he signed *il crociato*, "the crusader"), aware that new political participation would be impossible without an original and pervasive cultural elaboration, he insisted on the need for Catholics to forge and at the same time appropriate a "large and vast modern culture" (Sturzo 1902: 1). It is for this very reason that, since the beginning of his political action, Sturzo committed himself to the cultural education of seminarians and the laity. In 1898, he reflected on the "social culture" that had to characterize and motivate both clerics and nonclerical Catholics, inviting them in particular to engage with the study of sociology, which he considered the mother of all sciences that relates to the welfare of society, including the religious sciences (Sturzo 1898: 3).

He insisted that the clergy should possess a culture solidly grounded in Christian principles and yet open to the problems and the demands of modern society—a Christian and Catholic new culture open to the challenge of modernity yet without appearing modernist and willing to adapt even only slightly to the modern, losing its specificity. In a text from 1902, Sturzo reflected on the mission of the clergy in modern society, inserting theological, historical, sociological, and psychological perspectives in a project of great reach and depth. He started his reflection on the negative consequences of preventing future priests from entering into contact with contemporary reality.

> [T]he priest who is thrown into the vortex of modern life without criteria...will end up bringing into the environment of Catholic associations a small and ancient world, which we could call the antechamber to the seminary, the sacristy, and the curia. (Sturzo 1974b)

While the clergy must be prepared—culturally and spiritually—to understand the complexity of modern society, the Catholic laity had the fundamental task, through their commitment to live the social teaching of the church, to elaborate a creative bridge between faith and history, the political and the secular, the state and the church. This bridge has its core and axis in natural love, enlivened by and pervaded with Divine Grace.

3.7 The End of *Popolarismo*

The PPI conserved its strength in subsequent elections, both at the local and the national level, in which the Socialists also obtained remarkable success. The advance of mass parties in post-World War I Italy was an important indicator of the crisis of the liberal system, incapable of dealing with the social and economic consequences of the Great War and failing to understand the new dynamics of mass politics. In many respects, the PPI was the axis of any possible parliamentary majority. Given the Catholics' unsurmountable repulsion for an alliance with the Marxist Left, the PPI—unless it wanted to render the functioning of the parliamentary system impossible—had only one viable strategy: an alliance with the liberal and conservative forces. However, the political conceptions and social orientations of liberals and conservatives diverged greatly from those of the PPI's militants, for example on matters of decentralization, agrarian reforms, and social legislation, to cite only a few. These were not easy situations to deal with for the new party, its members, and its leadership, which very often consisted of young men lacerated between the secular and the sacred, the political and the religious, the spiritual and the terrestrial. As a consequence, a gap started to open while tensions and controversies emerged between two wings of the party: a "progressive" wing, disappointed by the party's immobility, and a conservative wing, whose opposition to social reform was only reinforced as a result of the mobilization of the extreme Left and the revolutionary wave that, fueled by the example of the Bolshevik Revolution in Russia, swept across Italy during the so-called *biennio rosso* (the two red years, 1919–20). The *popolari* rapidly had to take a position on another novel political creature: Fascism. Thus, some politicians of the PPI joined the first Mussolini government alongside liberals (1922).

Weakened by the defection of PPI members from the party's right-wing and left-wing factions, merely tolerated by the liberal elites and the old members of parliament who considered it an intruder, and frowned upon by the king and the court, the industrials, and the big landowners, the PPI lost the Vatican's protection. Pius XI considered the rapprochement with Mussolini and the ascent of Fascism as a minor evil vis-à-vis the persistence of the revolutionary peril and the liberal regime's anticlericalism. After all, pluralism as such was bound to remain a problem for an institution with universalistic aspirations. The secretary of state, Cardinal Pietro Gasparri, had called it the "least bad" of all Italian parties (quoted by Molony 1977: 47–8). The Holy See eventually turned against Sturzo and supported factions that were unquestioningly prepared to collaborate with Mussolini (Kertzer 2014).

The party's decline, which began in 1922, was exacerbated during the fourth national congress held in Turin in 1923. It culminated in 1926, when the last group of hardcore *popolari*—gathered around the new secretary Alcide De Gasperi and the daily *Il Popolo*, founded and directed by Giuseppe Donati—was wiped out by Fascism with the introduction of the *legge fascistissime*, which outlawed all political parties and opposition to the regime. Sturzo went into exile in London, and later in New York City. From abroad, he tried to keep in touch with the representatives of other European Christian democratic parties. De Gasperi was first imprisoned and then found shelter in the Vatican library, where he retired to study and contemplation while also writing for journals of the Holy See, mainly—if not exclusively—on matters of international politics.

Catholic politics, as any other non-Fascist politics had been eliminated by decree. The only space that was left for some kind of Catholic social and cultural engagement, apart from exile, was Catholic Action which, as we will see in the next chapter, preserved at least a partial autonomy from the Fascist regime, to which we will now turn.

4

Death and Resurrection

The Challenge of Fascism

The relationship between the Fascist regime and the Catholic Church has been one of the most important subjects of Italian historiography during the last five decades. Yet, time and again, this crucial aspect of twentieth-century Italian history has been approached through simplistic categories of analysis, such as clerical Fascism, philo-Fascism, a-Fascism, hidden anti-Fascism. Such oversimplifying dichotomies have reduced the complexity of such a relationship to the instrumental use of Fascism by the church, or to the regime's appropriation of the church for its own ends. Such simplifications run the risk of obscuring what was indeed a complex relationship, changing over time. Mussolini's position regarding the church was in constant evolution, and much the same can be said of how the popes and clergy regarded Mussolini and Fascism. Moreover, there were huge internal difference within Fascism and within Catholicism in their attitudes toward each other. There was a functional convergence of interests between the Holy See and the regime, ideological similarities as well as profound contrasts and tensions. The aim of this chapter is twofold: to reconstruct this complexity and to show how the 1930s were a crucial, formative moment for Catholic thought and politics, in which something new started to emerge, including what would be later dubbed the "second generation" of Christian Democrats.

4.1 *Instaurare omnia in Cristo*

Fascism came into power in 1922. Within the Fascist movement, profoundly anti-clerical views flourished. Mussolini himself, before coming to power, had time and again launched fierce critics against the church and its very right to exist. However, once in power for the Fascist regime Catholicism became an *instrument regni* and a means to reach large sectors of the Italian population on the fringe of modern mass politics, peasants especially. Indeed, the church played a fundamental role in the stabilization of the regime and gained Catholic consensus for Mussolini. At the same time, the Holy See tried to take advantage of the regime in order to re-Christianize society. In this sense a mutual interest moved the actions of both parts (Ceci 2014).

Italy's Christian Democracy: The Catholic Encounter with Political Modernity. Rosario Forlenza and Bjørn Thomassen, Oxford University Press. © Rosario Forlenza and Bjørn Thomassen 2024. DOI: 10.1093/oso/9780198859864.003.0005

Following in the footsteps of Pope Benedict XV, Pius XI (1922–39) embarked on a project of Catholic restoration and re-Christianization of the world, a Christian restoration of society in a Catholic sense, which had been shattered by the war that was seen as the consequence of materialism and secularism; the latter were, in turn, the consequence of liberalism and modern society. His motto was *Instaurare omnia in Cristo*, that is, "restore all things in the image of Christ." Pius XI set forth a program of Christian reconquest of a society dominated by the evils of secularism and anticlericalism already in his first encyclical of December 1922, just weeks after Mussolini had come into power, *Ubi arcano Dei*. In the encyclical *Quas primas* of 1925, he went a step further. *Quas primas* was indeed a true programmatic manifesto. The pope once again exposed the opposition to modernity as previously formulated by Pius IX and, in a different form, Leo XIII. With this encyclical, Pius XI announced the institution of the feast of Christ the King and celebrated the regality of Christ, seen as an affirmation of his role as an alternative guide to modern society:

> When once men recognize, both in private and in public life, that Christ is King, society will at last receive the great blessing of real liberty, well-ordered discipline, peace and harmony. Our Lord's regal office invests the human authority of princes and rulers with a religious significance; it ennobles the citizen's duty of obedience.

Referring to the duty of obedience was also an indirect support for the legitimacy of the secular state, and therefore for the regime. Yet, there was still an unresolved question concerning the political power and diplomatic standing of the Catholic Church that had been lost when Italy seized Rome in 1870. On February 11, 1929, a historic treaty was signed between the Fascist government and the Vatican. The so-called Lateran Pacts (also known as the "Concordat") established the Vatican City as an independent state, restored the civil sovereignty of the pope as a monarch, and regulated the position of the church and the Catholic religion within the Italian state. Furthermore, a financial convention compensated the Holy See for the loss of the Papal States (Pollard 2008: 85–7, 2005; Pertici 2009: 143–52).

From 1929, the Holy See attempted to take advantage of the privilege granted to the church by the regime through the Lateran Pact to bring Italian society back to the church. In other words, the Holy See came to embrace the idea that, through an alliance between the secular and the religious order (the pope and il Duce, the altar and the throne), a "superior interest" could come to fruition (Ceci 2014).

The dream of the church was to use secular power, namely the regime, to align secular laws and customs with Catholic precepts—especially on matters such as family and education, where a convergence between the Catholic and the Fascist morale was indeed strong. In short, the church saw this as an opportune historical moment to win back society to Catholicism. Catholic Action played a crucial role in this attempt.

4.2 Catholic Action during Fascism

A few months after the Concordat, the pope invited the national president of Catholic Action, Luigi Colombo, to adopt a positive approach to Fascism and proposed a collaboration: "[T]he pope is convinced that, if God assists us, and if we work, Catholic Italy will have a bright future" (quoted in Formigoni 2010: 109). After such an authoritative endorsement, Catholic Action started to think about a possible collaboration with Fascism.

The Lateran Pacts had institutionalized the model of Catholic action in politics, a model that developed in the Italian context and was then promoted globally. Until October 1923, when Pius XI approved the new structure of Catholic Action, the latter had been a loose and disparate network of initiatives, its name serving only as a generic brand for the activities of Catholics in society. Through this new structure, Catholic Action became the umbrella organization under which the religious, social, and cultural activism of lay Catholics was to be organized and developed under strict ecclesiastical control, instead of being led by lay autonomous initiatives exposed to the nefarious influence of the ideologies of the modern world.

The different branches of Catholic Action (composed of men, women, workers, students, and youth) existed at the level of parishes and dioceses, and then on a national scale. Each level had an ecclesiastical assistant monitoring and channeling the lay organizational efforts and initiatives, as well as providing "spiritual" and theological support. Statutes written by the bishops, under the directive of Rome, guided the entire machine.

After the experiences of the early 1920s, when the distinction between the activities of Catholic Action and those of the party led by Sturzo had blurred, Catholic Action was ordered—through the Concordat—to remain strictly apolitical. This model was exported in every other context. While severing ties with Catholic party politics and groups in Europe and Latin America throughout the 1930s, the Vatican allowed and encouraged Catholics (as individuals and private citizens outside the institutional church) to participate in the political process, joining political parties and seeking the common good based on Christian principles, at the same time forcing Catholic Action to abstain from direct political activity. Thus, the realm of politics became contested not only between the church and the secular state, but also within the church itself: the distinction between the political action and activities of Catholics as individuals, on one hand, and associations run by the clergy such as Catholic Action, on the other hand, was dramatically thin. Members of Catholic Action had to follow the principles of social action dictated by the organization and could act in the public sphere according to those principles but separated from clerical control. Catholic Action was prohibited from participating as a group in party politics. There was, then, a sharp line of separation between lay groups led by the clergy and political parties. Again, the crucial point here is that the Vatican wanted to deal directly with secular governments to secure the church's rights. Recourse to a Catholic party, the Vatican thought, would fundamentally undermine its negotiating position.

After 1931, the (Italian) non-party political model of Catholic Action was promoted globally (Pollard 2013; Faggioli 2014: 48–52). It worked as a Vatican-directed means of social, political, and cultural control, also defined by Vaillancourt as a "normative and manipulative means (e.g. through socialization and co-optation)" (Vaillancourt 1980: 2). As has also been written about Latin America (but this holds at a wider level), "in essence, the Vatican desired to monopolize political power within ecclesiastical ranks and sought to do so by redefining Catholic activism" (Andes 2014: 4).

In Fascist Italy as well as in other authoritarian regimes in Europe and Latin America, Catholic Action was never completely put under the regime's control. The Concordat did not mean the complete fascistization of social and political Catholicism. Catholic Action essentially continued to function as the only non-Fascist organization in Mussolini's totalitarian state—despite il Duce's repeated efforts to restrict its activities. Somewhat ironically, considering its *raison d'etre* and the Vatican's weariness over sociocultural action crossing over into the political—and even party political—sphere, in the interwar years Catholic Action became perhaps the most important way to prepare Catholics for constructive political engagement in post-World War II Italy, as well as in Europe and the world, especially South America.

4.3   Can Fascism Be Catholicized?

The mutual benefits of the collaboration and functional convergence between the regime and the church were obvious and went beyond the merely instrumental aspect. Catholic rhetoric could turn il Duce into a man sent by Providence for the fulfillment of the church's plan. Conversely, Fascist rhetoric could exalt religion as an element instrumentally subjected to the construction of national identity. The two narratives could merge and contaminate each other, but not always without conflict or contradictoriness. This was, for example, the case with the Fascist stress on the "crusade" of the colonial war in Ethiopia, which the pope did not like very much as it involved a superimposition of missionary and imperial themes (Riccardi 1979: 23–32; Gentile 2007a: 131–57; Ceci 2010). Another example is the war against the Spanish Republic, which led the Holy See and the regime to go hand in hand in supporting Franco. On October 28, 1935, at the beginning of the Fascist colonial adventure in Ethiopia, and the day of the anniversary of the March of Rome, the Cardinal of Milan Ildefonso Schuster solemnly proclaimed that the Christian mission had found its ultimate expression in the will of il Duce and in the Fascist civilizing mission. This very "mission" was no longer perceived as national or Catholic: it had become one and the same thing (De Felice 1974: 624–5).

Hence, in addition to functional convergences, a deeper ideological nexus existed that could bridge the gap between the two camps. In the same period, Catholics and the Holy See sought a moral and spiritual rebirth of Italian and, more generally, European society (Pollard 2007: 435). As John Pollard has argued, the Holy See and many Catholics were attracted to Fascism because both the church and the regime engaged in a palingenetic project. In the understanding of Roger Griffin (1991, 2015), Fascism was a political ideology whose mythic core was a palingenetic form of populist ultra-nationalism. Fascism, in other words, was a revolutionary attempt based on a quest for rebirth. It was the attempt to institute a different civilization, a new historical and political order, and a new—but historically rooted—culture. It was the search for a new beginning and for the resurrection of a nation that, from the perspective of Fascism, was in imminent danger.

Not only did both sides wish for a rebirth of society, but they also shared the same enemies: above all else, Bolshevism and capitalism, both considered as a product of materialism. Catholicism and Fascism shared other beliefs such as ruralism: the idea that a rural and agrarian society, threatened by evil capitalism and its entailing products, industrialization, and urbanism, was a bearer of "healthy" moral values. This is also why bishops and clergymen supported the Battle for the Grain that Mussolini started in 1925, that is, the attempt to make Italy self-sufficient in the production of cereals. Another ground of convergence was corporatism, or the idea of a "third way" between godless Communism and heartless capitalism, which was both a crucial aspect of Catholic social teaching as well as a central social and economic policy of the regime. Finally, we must not forget the not-so-hidden and unclear connection between modern Fascist anti-Semitism and old-fashioned Catholic anti-Judaism.

The deeper objective of the Vatican and of large sectors of Catholicism was to Catholicize the regime. This related to Pius XI's specific theological conception of history, outlined in *Quas primas*. The vision of Pius XI might be seen as a sort of modern temporalism or modern theocracy, imbued with a total distrust of the social and political manifestation of modernity, such as party politics and the clamor of political passion. The church's role was to remind states of the spiritual and moral principles that they must follow, urging them to promote the Kingdom of God.[1] This line of interpretation was imbued with a theocratic vision, which Pius XI

---

[1] See, for example, the pope's speech to the French federation of Christian unions (September 18, 1938; in Discorsi 1961: 810–16).

himself defined as *totalitarismo cattolico* ("Catholic totalitarianism"). Through this line, the pope claimed the right of intervention for the church in all matters that involved the eternal fate of human beings. The tools to implement such a vision were the Concordats—which in Italy, as in other countries where such an agreement had been made, granted the church ample space for autonomous activities—and, as already discussed, the strengthening of Catholic Action (defined by the pope as the *pupilla dei miei occhi*, "apple of my eye"). The aim was to develop Catholic values and instances through activities in culture and society, under the clergy's direction.

Such a vision offered little room for Sturzo's *popolarismo* and liberal Catholicism, opening the way to other lines that were at the opposite end of the political and cultural spectrum. Already in 1922, before the March of Rome and the PPI's participation in the first government led by Mussolini, a few Catholics had embraced Fascism. Sturzo defined them as "clerical Fascists." In June 1923, a group of Catholics distanced themselves from Sturzo and anti-Fascist politics, drafting a *Manifesto dei cattolici nazionali* that stated the following: "[We] proclaim openly and without understated reservation, our attitude toward the Fascist government. Our agreement must be shown to be complete now." The Manifesto went on to highlight that Fascist politics and policies respected the moral, social, and ideal demands and needs of true Catholics (Ricciardi 1981; Pollard 1990; see also Arpaia 2015; Baragli 2015: 278; Nelis 2015).[2]

During the first years of Fascism, the sectors within Catholic political culture that had been skeptical of Sturzo—accusing him of having put *Cristo in soffitta* (literally "to store Christ in the garrett," i.e. "to get rid of Christ")—and the a-confessional stance of the PPI became more and more popular. Such accusations came especially, and unsurprisingly, from the Jesuits, and more specifically from Father Agostino Gemelli and Father Francesco Olgiati (1919a, 1919b).[3]

The Università Cattolica in Milan was, in addition to Catholic Action, at the heart of Pius XI's plan for the redemption of Italy; it was intended to be the "intellectual powerhouse of a new, Catholic Italy, providing the intellectual cadres for

[2] The *Manifesto* also reads as follows: '[Our consensus] stems from the fact that Fascism, in the form of the National Government of which this movement is the only authoritative expression, recognizes openly and honors those religious and social values that constitute the basis of every healthy political regime, profession, against antiquated democratic and sectarian ideologies, principles of hierarchical discipline and order in the state, in harmony with the religious and social doctrine always affirmed by the Church.' The *Manifesto* is published in Misciattelli 1924: 139–41, also quoted in Baragli 2015: 278 (no. 7).

[3] Sturzo's response, formulated in the speech at the PPI's first congress, was as follows: "[T]oday…an act has ripened, which, without constituting a rebellion, was instead the affirmation in the political [sphere] of the conquest of one's personality and [which] could rally [those who could agree] on a program and a political thought not of simple defense but construction, not only negative but positive, not religious but social" (Sturzo 1956: 77).

its 'reconquest' by the Church" (Pollard 2008: 94). Gemelli wanted to render the Cattolica the center of cultural elaboration for the global restoration of society. The renovation had to be pursued with new tools, forming and transforming the new leadership destined to Christianize the world. Gemelli saw precisely in the political reality of those years—with Fascism in full swing—a more favorable ground and more opportune occasion to proceed with the Christianization not only of Italian society but also of the regime and the state's institutions. At the moment of the Conciliation, Gemelli wrote: "I believe we are on the threshold of a renewal of Catholic Christian civilization." He added:

> There is a great number of men who, tired of wandering under the deceptive guidance of erroneous systems, turn to Catholicism to regain the inner useful-ness that guarantees the fruitfulness of life. (Gemelli 1929: 17)

The Cattolica, in Gemelli's mind, should be at the forefront of the cultural battle to "give God back to Italy, and give Italy back to God," which—according to the pope—had been opened by the Lateran Pacts, exploiting the opportunities that the authoritarian regime had made possible. Along with the colonial adventure in Ethiopia and the economic sanctions decided by the League of the Nations against Italy, Gemelli's nationalism unfolded entirely through the rhetorical and con-vinced support of a regime that, Gemelli explained, had "taken on the task of guiding Italy toward the diligent completion of its civilizing mission in the world" (quoted in Formigoni 2010: 123).

Other Catholics likewise thought that there was a need for Italian spiritual imperialism, resulting from the marriage between Fascism and Catholicism, and between *Patria* and religion, to save European Christian civilization from Bolshevism and Western "plutocracy." For example, the writer and intellectual Giovanni Papini—one of the most representative voices of interwar Catholic culture—wrote the following in 1941:

> The salvation of civilization—which to no small degree is our fathers' and our own merit—is primarily up to us.... Today, Italy is like a besieged fortress, an entrenched camp, the last citadel of what made and will remake the unity of Europe: the Pax Romana and the Church of Christ. We, our children, [and] our grandchildren have been assigned the immense task of saving those two sacred institutes, and not only saving them but imposing them again on Europe, so as to perpetuate that superior, human and divine civilization that they promote, protect, and embody. (quoted in Formigoni 2010: 124)

Gemelli, Papini, and other Catholic thinkers thought that a positive change for Catholicism was about to occur, as many initiatives and ideas of the regime seemed to demonstrate: from anti-Bolshevism to corporativism, from the respect of order to the hierarchical system. Such a confident expectation, however, was eventually disappointed as the Fascist regime would develop worldviews (such as the racial laws) that clashed with the spirit of the gospel.

Ultimately, from the church's perspective the dream of a perfect marriage turned out to be illusionary and misleading. To be sure, large sectors of Catholicism long believed that it was indeed possible to Catholicize Fascism. The Lateran Pacts had fed the conviction—or rather the illusion—of a return to a Catholic state based on the binomial throne and altar in the name of *Italianità* and Catholicism. However, such a hope definitively came to an end by the late 1930s, when the rapprochement with Nazi Germany made it clear to Catholics that Fascism associated with and embraced its neo-paganism, which was frontally opposed to those moral and Christian values that should have been at the basis of the alliance between Catholics and Fascists. It became clear that Fascist respect for Catholic values was mostly of a formal nature. Emblematic in this sense was the existential and cultural path of Egilberto Martire, perhaps a more convinced supporter of the potential to Catholicize Fascism. He ended up being confined, at the end of the 1930s, as he had harshly criticized Mussolini for his alliance with Nazi and Lutheran Germany, an act that—according to him—wrecked any possible symbiosis between Catholicism and Fascism.

Already in 1935, when the war in Ethiopia was ongoing and the adhesion of Catholics and the clergy to Fascist politics seemed at its height, Domenico Tardini, undersecretary for the Congregation of Extraordinary Ecclesiastical Affairs, denounced the dangers posed by Fascism to Italy and the church in a series of notes devoted to "thirteen years of Fascism," written on behalf of Pius XI. It was not a personal denunciation but, rather, a consideration echoing reflections that circulated within the church and in Vatican circles on the dangers posed by Fascism, which was considered a problematic form of political religion. Among the more problematic aspects, Tardini listed a number of themes, including the totalitarian tendency toward a consensual culture, the cult of personality, Fascism as a political religion, and the rivalry between Catholicism and Fascism for the control and the formation of the minds and the education of the new generations. More than a year before, Pius XI had ordered the Jesuits to gather documentation and materials on themes such as nationalism, racism, and totalitarianism—preparatory work that the pope would then use for his anti-Nazi encyclical *Mit brennender Sorge* (1937).[4] The Fascist drift toward Nazi paganism was unacceptable to the church.

---

[4] The document, which can now be consulted in the Vatican Secret Archives, is reproduced in Ceci 2008; on Tardini, see Casula 1988. On the Catholic interpretation of Fascism and Nazism as a political religion, see Gentile 1990, 1996, 2010; R. Moro 2005; Nelis 2011. See also Voegelin 1999.

4.4 The Church and the Jewish Question

One of the most sensitive issues of the relationship between the church and the regime relates to the Jewish question. The racial laws promulgated by Fascism in 1938 were a ground of contrast between the Holy See and the regime (for a thorough treatment of this contrast see Foa 2011). The church considered it the manifestation of a pagan and national-Socialist drift that it could no longer tolerate. Once again, things were complex and the various sectors of Catholicism expressed different views on the matter. It was sometimes difficult to distinguish between old, traditional Catholic anti-Judaism and the modern form of racial anti-Semitism.

For example, *La Civiltà Cattolica* waged a harsh anti-Semitic campaign that, time and again, reiterated the usual accusations (i.e. ritual murder, economic exploitation) and recalled the Protocols of the Elders of Zion (Kertzer 2001). It is true that violent Catholic anti-Semitism was isolated, and anti-Semitism was not even on the Fascist agenda until the mid-1930s. More importantly, as John Pollard has argued, "the kind of synthesis, or dare one to say it miscegenation, of Christian theology and fascist racial ideology was not possible in the Catholic context" (Pollard 2007: 439). After all, being Catholic meant being universal, and "whatever forms of racial discrimination and segregation might actually have been *practiced* by Catholics," in the end, the "theological essence of Catholicism remained universalistic." The command of the gospel to "go forth and preach to all nations, baptizing in the name of the Father, the Son, and the Holy Ghost" remained "the mission statement" for the church even in the twentieth century (Pollard 2007: 437). Time and again, Pius XI spoke out against racialism, paganism, and exaggerated nationalism, most notably in the 1937 encyclical against Nazism, *Mit brennender Sorge*. In 1938, a decree of the Sacred Congregation for Seminaries and Universities condemned the proposition that the "human race, by their natural and immutable character are so different that the humblest among them is furthest the most elevated than from the highest animal species" (Passelecq and Sucheky 1997: 114; Pollard 2007: 437).

The pope initiated an encyclical against racist ideology entitled *Humani generis unitas*, which, however, remained in draft form because of his death. Without a doubt, the content of the draft was still cautious and feeble, and unable to clarify the nexus between old and traditional Catholic anti-Judaism and modern, aggressive, and totalitarian anti-Semitism. However, its publication would certainly have shocked people for its neat and clear distancing from nationalism, defined as "a true perversion of the spirit" (Formigoni 2010: 117). Not surprisingly, the pope condemned the introduction of racial laws in September 1938 (Gilette 2002: 76).

The only serious attempt, from a Catholic perspective, to embrace the regime's racism was made by Gemelli,[5] but even this attempt was short-lived and disavowed

---

[5] See the words on Gemelli in a 1939 conference, in Gemelli 1939: 11; see also Bocci 2003: 539.

by the church. At the same time, as the historian and Jesuit Giovanni Sale has argued, the Vatican certainly maintained a "prudent" political approach to the racial laws and the anti-Jewish turn of the regime, to the point that "it is embarrassing for the Catholic historian" to justify such a politics with "moral or religious categories" (Sale 2009: 89–90; on the Jews in Fascist Italy see also Sarfatti 2000). Despite stances such as that of the influential Cardinal of Milan Schuster, who protested against the "anti-Roman heresy" the approach to the discrimination of the Jewish was arguably mild and too compromising. In fact, racial thinking was sometimes smuggled in through the back door, as when the economist Amintore Fanfani explained, in 1939, that "for the power and the future of the nation, Italians [must be] racially pure." In other words, the Catholic nation had to be defended and protected in its religious and racial homogeneity (Fanfani 1939: 256; Formigoni 2010: 128–9).

Several Italian historians have thoroughly analyzed Catholic anti-Judaism and anti-Semitism between 1870 and 1938, and its complex and ambiguous relationship with racial anti-Semitism (R. Moro 1992; Miccoli 1997). Most have followed the lessons of George Mosse, who introduced the term "infected Christianity" (Mosse 1978). For Mosse, both Protestants and Catholics had the instruments to resist and react to racism thanks to the values and beliefs of Christian thought. Yet, they had not been able to do so and ended up being "infected by racism." One crucial aspect of such contamination is the following: the naturalistic and physical conception of "the Jew" as emphasized by racial doctrine clashed with the possibility of conversion, that is, the idea that baptism can transform a Jewish person (or any human being) into a Christian. This was a limit that the church could not cross, the stumbling block that hindered any possibility of conciliation between Fascist racism and Catholic anti-Judaism. The overturning of the emancipation gained with the *Risorgimento* that was introduced with the 1938 laws potentially had a positive impact on the church, confirming the traditional anti-Judaic ideology. However, the rejection of conversion was—for a church that had put conversion and proselytism at the center of its politics toward the Jewish people—an unacceptable rift with its constitutive principles.

Either way, the Holy See's objections to the racial laws were limited to what was defined the *vulnus*, the breach of the Concordat of 1929 as a result of the rejection of mixed marriage and the introduction of biological racism. This was not simply the manifestation of the willingness to not take care of the converted Jewish men and women and to abandon those who had not converted to the Catholic faith. It was, instead, the manifestation of a profound concern for the question of conversion. Facing norms that considered a Jewish person an individual simply on the basis of blood, independently from the religion that such an individual professed, the church realized that it should now renounce the possibility of receiving converted Jews into its fold. This would challenge the universalism of the church, that is, the principle that baptism in the name of Christ made everyone equal, like brothers and sisters. Hence, having renounced a protest in spiritual and prophetic terms, the only objection that the church advanced against the racial laws unfolded on the only ground that was granted to the church itself: the politics of the Concordat. It was also the only ground that allowed the church to keep together its rejection of racism and the teaching of disdain for "the Jews." This disdain had never, in the entire history of the church, aimed to expulse the Jewish population. However, the church's suspicion towards the role of the Jewish minority population had become even more intense after the *Risorgimento* and the unification of Italy.

This is important to understand. In order to grasp the church's reaction to the racial laws of 1938, it is necessary to go back to 1870; by then, in a Rome deprived of its role as the center of Christianity, the Jews were indeed considered equal to other citizens. Thus, they could freely exercise directive functions in politics, society, and culture. The foundational principle on which the uneven balance between Jews and Christians had been based was subjection: the subjection of Jews to Christians and Catholics, of errors to the truth, of the incredulous to the believer. The emancipation of the Jews that unified liberal Italy had made possible was the highest and most consequential assertion of what the intransigent Catholics would define as "religious relativism," that is, the principle of tolerance, the idea that every religion could have equal value, juridical status, and recognition by the secular power. However, 1870 marked the end of a history of inequality.

A sense of betrayal emerged from Pius IX's public pronouncements after 1870. Welcomed and loved paternally by the church, the Jews had beaten the hand that had fed them by stabbing the church in its back. The emancipation of the Jewish peope, the act that made them equal to Catholics and to any other citizen, was difficult to accept. In those years, Pius IX—talking to pilgrims who visited him in the Vatican—spoke out violently against the Jews, calling them the "sons" who had turned into "dogs," which "we hear barking everywhere, disturbing us" (quoted in Miccoli 1997: 1407; on the metaphor of Jews as dogs see Stow 2006). More than anything else, this reaction from the church shows how reluctant it was to endorse pluralism and religious freedom, the necessary pillars of any democratic regime.

4.5 Contrasts between the Church and the State: Catholic Action Regains Agency

As we have already shown, the relationship between the regime and the Holy See was not always one of agreement or understanding. Other than the church's fear of Fascism turning into neo-pagan Nazism, especially after the racial laws, the church and the regime competed in the field of social services in state and civil society. The church hoped to transform society through Fascism that, in the church's view, should emanate laws in line with the moral precepts of the church, especially on matters of school and education. The church welcomed the school reform introduced by the prime philosopher of Fascism, Giovanni Gentile (1923), which made the teaching of religion mandatory—and "religion" meant Catholicism. Yet, it was precisely in the world of education that a major contrast between the church and the regime started to emerge.

The battle over the education of youth and, more specifically, Catholic Action and its role in Fascist society was perhaps the most evident manifestation of the tensions running between the two sides of the Tiber. The agreement with Fascism was more the result of a marriage of interest than an intimate alliance. As discussed above, Catholic Action was the instrument for the Christian restoration of society that Pius XI had wanted. Catholic Action also worked as a pressure group within the regime, in terms of public morality and censorship (Pollard 2008: 94). The main contrast, though, regarded the autonomy and independence of youth organizations and Catholic mass associations. The church and the regime competed for the cultural and social, hence not only religious, education of large sectors of Italian society.

The regime was aware of the danger of giving free reins to the church in the field of the ideological education of youth—evidently a foundational element of the process of building "consensus" for the regime. The latter feared that the culture of Catholic Action made young people impermeable to the ideological pressure of Fascism. The crisis was always latently there but erupted in 1931 (Giuntella 1975; Chiesa 1983; Koon 1985: 130–6; Malgeri 1994: 56–9).

On May 26, after a few weeks of press campaigns against Catholic Action and violence and assault against members and headquarters of its youth branches, the prefects in the provinces received instructions from the minister of the Interior (Mussolini himself) that imposed the dismemberment of all youth organizations not directly subject to the Fascist party and the Fascist youth association Opera Nazionale Balilla.

The headquarters of Catholic Action were sealed, and goods and documents—particularly the list of members—confiscated. On June 3, an announcement of the Partito Nazionale Fascista (PNF, National Fascist Party) proclaimed that it would "not tolerate that under any flag, old and new, the residual anti-Fascism that has so far been spared finds refuge and protection" (quoted in Scoppola 1967: 257). The measures against Catholic Action were politically motivated, denouncing the fact that former *popolari* were now acting under false names within the organization, germinating anti-Fascist stances to be eradicated. Pius XI reacted immediately and strongly. Already on May 30–1, the pope told the Salesians and Scolopians on the occasion of his birthday:

> One may ask for our life but not for our silence in case of an attack on that which forms the most vivid predilection of our hearts. . . . Attack, we say, because it was

prepared first by a press campaign based on inventions, disrespect, [and] slander, then by a campaign out in the streets and squares, made up of subjugation and— not infrequently—bloody violence, quite often perpetrated by many against our few, always defenseless, sons and even daughters.

On June 1, the pope convened the cardinals who were in Rome, suspended the Eucharistic Congress, and prohibited the processions for the feast of Corpus Domini (the Body of Christ) in all parishes. The leaders of Catholic Action were hosted, for their own safety, in the Vatican. At the end of June, the pope wrote the encyclical *Non abbiamo bisogno* ("We Do Not Need"), published at the beginning of July. Two years after the Conciliation, the climate of agreement between the Holy See and the regime was on the verge of crumbling. The Concordat safeguarded the autonomy of Catholic organizations provided that they remained in the sacristy and did not invade the public space. Yet, when it came to the educational question, the church could not accept being managed and directed by a regime whose ideology "clearly revolves itself into a true... 'statolatry' which is no less in contrast with the natural rights of the family than it is in contradiction with the supernatural rights of the church," as the pope wrote in the encyclical.

Contesting the unjust accusations against Catholic youth, the encyclical neither disputed the agreement reached in 1929 nor condemned the party and the regime as such. It instead dwelled on what, in Fascism, was incompatible with the doctrine of the church. Thus, the pope denounced the educational moment of Fascism, which instigates people to "hate, violence, irreverence." More specifically, the pope criticized the oath requested to obtain the party's membership card, which at the time was an almost necessary condition to get a job and build a career. The pope wondered:

> what is to be thought about the formula of the oath, which even little boys and girls are obliged to take, that they will execute orders without discussion from an authority which, as we have seen and experienced, can give orders against all truth and justice and in disregard of the rights of the church and its souls.

With *Non abbiamo bisogno*, the pope condemned aspects of what he perceived to be the false religious elements in Fascist ideology. The encyclical denounced the regime's intention to monopolize the education of the young, an effort that Pius XI qualified as a clear example of pagan "statolatry" and a "new religiosity... that becomes persecution." The denunciation was tempered by the statement that the encyclical did not want to condemn Fascism as such, but only those practices of Fascism that went against Catholic teaching.

In the following negotiation, entrusted to the Jesuit Pietro Tacchi Venturi, the aim was to avoid a traumatic rupture. A compromise was reached: the circles of Catholic youth could reopen, but their activities had to be restricted and brought under the full control of the ecclesiastical authority. Catholic Action was forbidden to engage in politics, as well as in sports and athletics. It was essentially reduced to discussion groups. On its part, the regime lifted the ban on simultaneous membership in the party and Catholic Action groups (Koon 1985: 136–7).

The compromise that marked the end of the conflict demonstrated that neither the Vatican nor the regime was interested in continuing the battle. Exiled Catholic anti-Fascists such as Sturzo hoped that the crisis would mark the beginning of a political turning point for the entire country, with the church acting as a driving force. In the end, though, the Vatican aimed to safeguard the space of autonomy—however limited—that the regime had granted to Catholics. This space of autonomy, or room for maneuver, included the autonomy of Vatican politics on the national and international plane, the regime's nonintervention in Catholic associations, and respect for the norms of the Concordat more in general. At the same time, the church and the regime were far from able to always control their bases. At the local level, Fascists and Catholics entered into verbal fights that could even become physical. However, the leadership of both organizations wanted to pacify a controversy that could have unpredictable consequences. For the Vatican hierarchy and for the leadership of Catholic Action, the idea of becoming the head of an anti-Fascist movement was out of question and far removed from their mentality. Rather, Catholic Action—especially its intellectual groups, FUCI and the *Movimento Laureati*, to which we will return below—looked for an autonomous ground, clear of the regime's ideological and political conditioning and of the nationalistic and bellicose myths that the regime tried to inculcate in the minds and habits of the younger generations.

After a few years of peaceful existence, which peaked at the time of the Spanish war and the adventure in Ethiopia, the tension between Catholic Acton and the regime reached a new breaking point in 1937–8. The regime did not want Catholic Action to become too attractive and distract young Italians from Fascist discipline. The regime remained concerned that Catholic Action could spur the growth of an alternative culture, a potential incubator of anti-Fascist politics. The PNF's secretary, Achille Starace, declared that the leaders of Catholic Action could not become leaders of the *Gioventù Italiana del Littorio* (the Fascist youth organization) and vice versa. Roberto Farinacci, an "intransigent" Fascist, declared the incompatibility of double membership in his city, Cremona: one could not simultaneously be a member of the PNF and a member of Catholic Action. Violence against members, leaders, and structures of Catholic Action resumed. On July 28, the pope reacted with a speech at the Collegio di Propaganda Fide:

> Who strikes Catholic Action strikes the church, because he strikes Catholic life…. You would do better not to strike Catholic Action…. Please, for your own good, because who strikes Catholic Action strikes the pope, and who strikes the pope dies.

In the same speech, the pope denied that there was an anti-Semitic tradition in Italy and blamed il Duce for following Hitler and his racist and pagan policies. The pope once again presented himself, the church, and Catholic culture as a bastion against the totalitarian pretenses of the regime. On August 20, 1938, another agreement was reached, which renewed the measures of 1931. Starace retreated from the policy of incompatibility and returned party membership cards to members of Catholic Action. The latter, in turn, had to participate in or send their children to the parades and activities of the *Gioventù Italiana del Littorio*, and the association was forbidden from engaging in activities other than religious ones. Despite the agreement, tensions continued to grow with the so-called "battle of the badge" launched by the Fascists, who wanted to dissuade members of Catholic Action from wearing their badges in public. This culminated with the prohibition to wear the Catholic Action badge in public in May 1940, while assaults against members and clubs continued (Ponzio 2015: 162–4; see also Moro 1980; Casella 1992: 238–42).

It is precisely within Catholic Action and its intellectual branches that we can trace the most significant development of the 1930s—a turning point that had immense consequences for the subsequent history of Catholic politics in Italy, and more generally for the history of democracy in Italy after World War II. Among the younger generations, a Catholic subculture started to develop that would eventually open up to democratic thought. However, it first had to free itself from the Fascist temptation.

4.6 Catholic Action and the Fascist Temptation

At the beginning of the 1930s, the notion of democracy and political modernity was still alien to Catholic culture in Italy and beyond (the following is based on Forlenza and Thomassen 2016: 73–85). Catholic assertions of moral absolutes and the belief in an objective order of truth did not leave space for the dialectic and dynamics of democracy, based on the recognition of subjective rights, free competition between ideas and worldviews (pluralism), and the majority principle.

At the same time, Catholic Action continued to function as essentially the only non-Fascist organization in Mussolini's totalitarian state despite il Duce's repeated efforts to restrict its activities. The two intellectual branches of Catholic Action, the FUCI (Federation of Catholic University Students) and the *Movimento Laureati* (Association of Catholic Graduates and Professionals), functioned as active cultural and formative spaces aimed at the re-Christianization of Italian society, spaces that eventually would create openings for a political imagination beyond Fascism.

In the 1930s, the young intellectuals of Catholic Action (also known as *fucini*) endorsed and upheld almost all of the policies enacted by the Fascist regime, from the demographic battle to the invasion of Ethiopia and the proclamation of the Italian Empire (1936), which for many of them seemed to herald a time in which "Catholic Italy" would play a leading role in the new world order (Dagnino 2007, 2012, 2017). Many of them were also members of the Gruppi Universitari Fascisti (GUF, Fascist University Youth).[6] The *fucini* had a mostly positive view of the regime's anti-capitalist and corporativist economic policies and other aspects of Fascist modern politics that resonated with the tradition of Catholic social thought. Some of the *fucini* worked for the regime's economic agencies. For example, the former *fucino* Sergio Paronetto became an important manager of the *Istituto per la Ricostruzione Industriale* (Institute for Industrial Reconstruction, IRI), the public holding company established in 1933 by the Fascist regime to rescue, restructure, and finance the banks and private companies that went bankrupt during and after the Great Depression.

Other Catholics, such as the young academics of the Cattolica, shared these views. The Cattolica represented an assertive, intransigent, and anti-modern Catholic cultural institute that was engaged in Fascism without any inferiority complex, trying to Catholicize the regime. The economist Fanfani, a professor at the Cattolica, joined the PNF in 1933, endorsing the regime's socioeconomic policies. Corporativism was seen as a "third way" between liberal capitalism and Communism, which—he thought—suited Catholics and Fascists alike. For Fanfani, corporativism had a Christian underlying meaning, which he identified in social peace and class collaboration (or fraternity) as the moral basis for the reconstruction of the nation. The Fascist doctrine was, in his view, "not contrary to faith and morale," and Catholics must therefore "elaborate and apply it" (quoted in Galli 1977: 17; see also Fanfani 1937; Ornaghi 2011). Fanfani shared with the *fucini* not only a deep concern for social justice but also sincere nationalist feelings. He celebrated Italian imperialism for bringing "Roman virtues combined with Christian consecration" to Ethiopia. He also praised Mussolini as "the conqueror of all in the struggle for civilization," who was instilling a new form of patriotism in Italian youth and raising Italy's stature abroad (quoted in Fanfani 1936).

For Fanfani, the *fucini*, and large constituencies of Italian Catholicism, Fascism was the normal and natural regime for modern Italy, the best possible sociopolitical model for the preservation of Christian values and the promotion of the anti-Communist struggle (Formigoni 2010: 105–44). Socialism and Soviet Bolshevism represented the main threat. Giuseppe Dossetti, another young professor of the Cattolica and an expert in Ecclesiastical Law, explained this in a series of speeches given at the Fascist Institute of Culture between 1933 and 1935 on "the originality

---

[6] Already by 1929, over 50 percent of the FUCI members were concomitantly members of the GUF; throughout the 1930s, many *fucini* participated in the *Littoriali*, the cultural activities sponsored by the regime (Moro 1979a: 81).

of Fascism," "Bolshevik experiment and Fascist renewal," and "Bolshevism and Roman Civilization" (Galavotti 2006: 85–92).[7]

From a Catholic perspective, the historical experience of liberal democracy before and after World War I represented a total failure. Catholics saw democracy as a regime pervaded by "disorder," as it prevented the disciplined and organic harmonization of order, truth, and justice. The *fucini* were quick to criticize the "degeneration" of democracy: anticlericalism, liberalism, and parliamentarism, that is, the "false principles of 1789" (R. Moro 1979a: 465–8). "Laicism," if not the openly anticlerical politics of the Third Republic in France and the Spanish Republic, was considered the main reason for the endless subversion of social order so intrinsically tied to democracy. In this sense, the rebellion against God and the church was almost automatically conducive to the rebellion against the state, family, army, and nation.

The violence of the "reds" in Spain and the religious persecutions in Mexico and the Soviet Union were anathema to these intellectuals, much in line with Pius XI's encyclical *Divini Redemptoris* (March 1937), and they soon took sides with the "whites." They saw in Franco, Primo de Rivera, and Salazar a healthy alternative to anti-religion, anticlericalism, and anarchism: in other words, a Latin and southern Mediterranean spiritual response to the paganism of Nazism and the materialism of Bolshevism (R. Moro 1975: 757–73; other testimonies and memories can be found in Crivellin 2000). The older generation of the *popolari* (the activists and politicians who had militated in the PPI) were substantially on the same line. In 1934, De Gasperi—under the pseudonym of Spectator—rejoiced in the defeat of the Austrian social democrats who "were de-Christianizing and fanaticizing the young people of their country, and using political power to destroy the Family and suffocate the Faith" (De Gasperi 1934). In 1937, he wrote that the German church was correct in preferring Nazism to Bolshevism (De Gasperi 1937).

4.7 Winds of Democracy from Across the Alps

This line of intransigence, however, did not deprive the young Catholic intellectuals of independent mentality, ideas, and culture. The real challenge for them was to reinvent and recreate a "vital" and autonomous Catholic culture that could engage with the modern world and Catholicize Fascism. The overall objective was more to correct Fascism than to build democracy, which was either an unfamiliar

[7] Dossetti's certificate of membership of the Fascist party (card number no. 264094, from 1935 onward) is held in the Archivio Centrale dello Stato, Ministero della Pubblica Istruzione, Direzione Generale Istruzione Superiore, Divisione I, Liberi Docenti, III serie, 1930–50, b. 190. The document was first retrieved by historian Paolo Acanfora.

or an undesirable objective for them and, in any case, unattainable in the 1930s. At the same time, the new generation of Catholics thirsted for new cultural inspiration. In this search, they dealt with an eclectic and rich combination of cultural references, awakening Italian Catholicism from its provincialism. European Catholic thought had not come to a standstill in the interwar period. Quite the opposite, it had developed as a meditation on the failures and setbacks of the interwar period. Catholic thinkers started to embrace crucial aspects of modernity and human rights, considered indispensable to a proper Catholic view of the world. Jacques Maritain (1882–1973) and Emmanuel Mounier (1905–50) became the moral and intellectual compass in this search for a Catholic ground in the midst of a civilizational crisis that was t ever more acutely felt.

It would be wrong to limit this development to the French context. What slowly took shape among Catholic thinkers and activists during the 1930s happened in a transnational context. As Samuel Moyn has explained, also in reference to James Chappel's work, the idea of the human person as the bearer of "constitutional dignity" can be traced back to the Irish constitution of 1937. A hugely influential document in this regard was Pius XI's 1937 papal encyclical, *Divini Redemptoris*, which declared the fundamental dignity of the human person. The encyclical was a rebuttal of the secular narrative of "rights" and dignity bestowed upon the "depersonalized individual" from the French Revolution onward and taken to extremes by the Communist regimes. *Divini Redemptoris* is, in fact, primarily a scathing attack on Communism (Chappel 2011; Moyn 2014, 2015: 25–64).

However, there is no doubt that French intellectual developments were of primary importance in the Italian context. Maritain's ideas had the most direct influence. Maritain had been close to the quasi-Fascist Action Française in the 1920s but abandoned the movement when the Vatican condemned it in 1926.[8] Working within a neo-Thomist philosophical framework, in the 1930s, he started to embrace human rights and modern democracy. In particular, his 1936 study *Humanisme Intégrale* and his 1942 pamphlet *Christianisme et démocratie*, which Allied planes had dropped over Europe in 1943, had constituted a decisive endorsement of the ultimately Christian nature of democracy (Thomassen and Forlenza 2016a).

Central to Maritain's theory and definition of democracy was the concept of the "person" and its opposition to the "individual." The "person" has a spiritual and transcendent nature, is irreducible to biology, and is concerned for the good of all. The person flourishes only within the community and in relation to God—and, through God, for the good of all.

---

[8] This section is largely based on Doering 1983; Barré 1995; Di Joseph 1996; Müller 2011: 134–8, 2008; Doering 1983.

Maritain's writing influenced the emerging philosophy of "communitarian personalism." For a while, Maritain even acted as a mentor to its leading proponent, Emmanuel Mounier (Rauch, Jr 1972; Hellman 1981; Delbreil 2001: 60–2). During the 1930s, Mounier and the group around the journal *Esprit* condemned both Communism and liberal individualism as forms of materialism. Liberal individualism, in particular, was held responsible for what Mounier disdained as *le desordre établi*, his designation for the corrupt parliamentary politics of the French Third Republic and a political culture associated with the heritage of the French Revolution; as he put it, "on the altar of this sad world, there is but one god, smiling and hideous: the Bourgeois" (quoted in Moyn 2011: 89). As an alternative to the materialist twins of liberalism and Communism, Mounier insisted that the "person"—as opposed to the isolated "individual"—always realized themselves in a community, while retaining a spiritual dimension that could never be absorbed into the politics of this world. At the practical level, Mounier and the personalists endorsed a society with a vigorous group life (not unlike Harold Laski and the English pluralists, with their emphasis on local voluntary communities). This society was characterized by the decentralization of the decision-making process, brought down to the grassroots level or to communities with a human dimension—in essence, a subsidiarity principle at work throughout society. Mounier's concrete proposals could perhaps appear harmless. However, his rhetoric and expectations were revolutionary and highly anti-liberal. Therefore, because of their anti-liberal ideology, the personalists could embrace the Vichy regime during the war, and Communism and Soviet Marxism after the war (Judt 1992: 86–90; Hellman 1997; for a balanced and "engaged" assessment of personalism written in the period, see Ricoeur 1950).

Maritain's philosophy had effects outside intellectual circles. Maritain played a key role in drafting the United Nations Declaration of Human Rights. Charles de Gaulle made him French ambassador to the Vatican after the war, from 1945 to 1948—a timeframe that coincided with the birth of Italian democracy and the emergence of Catholics as the country's new ruling class (see Chapter 6). He likewise played a crucial role in the Second Vatican Council (see Chapter 9).

Both Maritain and Mounier were, in fact, not necessarily in favor of founding explicitly Christian parties; rather, in Maritain's understanding, Christianity should be something like the "yeast" of political life, making the liberation from pagan Fascism the first step to a new political culture based on morality and, to some degree, religion (Belardinelli 1990: 251). "The question," he wrote, "does not deal…with Christianity as a religious creed and road to eternal life, but rather with Christianity as a leaven in the social and political life of nations and as the bearer of the temporal hope of mankind…as historical energy at work in the world" (Maritain 1943: 37). In 1934, intervening in a fracas between Mounier and Catholic philosopher Paul Archambault, Maritain insisted that the new Christianity could not be equated with a party program, being "of a freer and more elevated order, which on the contrary seeks to renew the very manner of posing the problem." Integral humanism "could not be reduced to any of the operative ideologies in the political formation and still extant" (Maritain 1934; see also Rauch, Jr 1972: 113–25).

Mounier was even more explicit on this point (the following is based on Rauch, Jr 1972). He had next to nothing to do with the drafting of the United Nations Declaration of Human Rights, and he could not accept Christian Democracy. In fact, he opposed himself to Christian Democracy as a party project both in France, in the 1930s, and in the post-World War II era. Elections, party politics, and coalition governments—he thought—meant compromise and, consequently, corruption. His "democratic" credential should not be overstated; in reality, his anti-liberalism sometimes bordered on anti-democratism.[9] In this regard, as with a whole range of other issues, he characteristically adopted ambivalent positions. Transcendent truth existed, he believed, but its human manifestation was invalid and unjustifiable. Like his mentor Peguy, his main concern was to "incarnate the temporal to the spiritual" but he exposed the "temptation to political action," writing the following in one of his essays from the early years of *Esprit*: "Is not any action condemned to inefficacy to the extent that it will be pure, impure to the extent that it will be efficacious?" (Mounier quoted in Rauch, Jr 1972: 77–8). Throughout his political career as editor of *Esprit*, he was firmly caught on the horns of this dilemma. His conviction that Christians must be *in* but not *of* the world forced him to walk his theological-philosophical tightrope publicly. He was strongly anti-bourgeois but found himself cooperating with bourgeois politicians during every major crisis of the thirties, from the Spanish Civil War to the Munich crisis and beyond. He consistently criticized the Christian Democrats for being too clerical and confessional, yet his faith kept him from an outright commitment to the Popular Front. His antagonist Archambault accused him of imprecision, the negation of capitalism tout court, and doctrinal incoherence. For Mounier, then and later, the Christian Democrats were compromised by the liberal established disorder of the Third and Fourth Republics. He was consistently severe with regard to "Christian Democratism," its inadequacies, and its dishonest compromises. The question that plagued him was one that Italian Catholic intellectuals could more than identify with: can one make a temporal commitment, especially one to radical anti-capitalism, without being involved in the established disorder?

4.8 The Opening of the Democratic Horizon

The writings of Maritain and Mounier were translated and published by *Azione Fucina* (the organization's journal) and widely read by the *fucini*. Perhaps the

---

[9] The historian Zeev Sternhell defined Mounier as a representative of those anti-democratic, "neither Right nor Left" ideologies of the 1930s that eventually led to a form of Fascism (Sternhell 1983).

most enthusiastic interpreter of French neo-Thomism was Guido Gonella, who would become secretary of Christian Democracy in the post-World War II years and the main editor of its newspaper *Il Popolo*. In 1934–5, he insisted on the concept of "person," which for him was the only way to solve the otherwise puzzling and unsolvable relationship between citizen and state. The "person," as opposed to the "individual," was the watershed that separated Catholicism from collectivism (Fascism and Bolshevism) and individualism (Gonella 1935a, 1935b). Giovanni Battista Montini, the future Pope Paul VI, translated Maritain's *Trois réformateurs* into Italian in 1928, and wrote an introduction to the Italian version of *Humanisme Intégral*, whereas Giampietro Dore translated Maritain's *Primauté du spirituel* into Italian, again in 1928. The distinction between the "spiritual" and the "temporal," on the eve of the Lateran Pacts, ignited an important reflection among the *fucini* on laity and the relationship between religion, philosophical/cultural convictions, and politics. Many young Catholics, not necessarily members of Catholic Action, read Maritain in the 1930s. There is no doubt that for them, the French Thomist was a genuine "reading experience" in the sense given to that term by Arpad Szakolczai: a formative and transformative "encounter with a certain work that struck a chord with personal experiences" (Szakolczai 1998: 2, 12), generating an intellectual drive.

For example, the Catholic philosopher Augusto Del Noce read *Humanisme Intégral* in full and in French already in 1936, the year of its publication. In the post-World War II period, Del Noce would elaborate and conceptualize a Catholic modernity, bridging a positive encounter between Catholicism, democracy, and freedom. The year 1936 was the year of the Italian war against Ethiopia, the event that marked the period of maximum consensus on the regime (De Felice 1974). Del Noce, instead, felt a sense of utter disgust at and moral opposition to Mussolini and Fascism, which he regarded as the mere reign of violence, a brute force with no foundation in justice.

Maritain was widely and avidly read and carefully commented upon by other Catholic intellectuals and politicians, such as the abovementioned Del Noce, the intellectual and Dominican lay brother Giorgio La Pira, the former *fucino* and young manager of the IRI Sergio Paronetto, and a group of young academics formed in the intellectual climate of the Cattolica in Milan, whose prominent figures were Dossetti and Fanfani. Like other Catholics, Dossetti and Fanfani had seen Fascism in a positive way, namely as the best available option at the time for the preservation of Catholic values and as a harbinger of corporativist and anti-capitalist economic policies. Yet, with the increasing association of Fascism with Nazism and its racial policies, followed by the existential uncertainty engendered by the war, they drifted away from traditional Catholic intransigence—still advocated in 1940 by Agostino Gemelli (Galavotti 2013: 11)—and began searching for a Catholic response to the challenge of modern mass politics and for the basis of an alliance between the church and the modern world. However, De Gasperi also closely followed and reflected upon Maritain's search for a renewed Christianity from his exile in the Vatican. In his review of Maritain's essay "Idéal historique d'une nouvelle chrétienté," published in *Vie Intellectuelle* on January 25, 1935, De Gasperi wrote that Maritain's new Christendom could positively become a "myth" and provide Catholic political action with a weapon that was indispensable to oppose totalitarianism.

> The attempt to draw the architectural lines of an ideal Christian state...corresponds with a need for the Spirit.... The "myth" in a Sorelian sense runs ahead of all modern political movements; and thus, why should the vision of an "ideal" Christendom, yet compatible with reality, not run ahead of Catholic youth, as the column of fire led Israel through the desert? (De Gasperi 1935)

On an even more emphatic note, De Gasperi claimed, a "myth" or a "mystique" is "a necessity in our time, an epoch more inclined to accept simple formulae, sentimental and at times irrational"; it is "a yeast needed for every popular movement and every political system." Without mystique, "one does not win over the masses, and the working class is not swept along." After all, he concluded, "Fascism, Socialism, and Nazism, all of them have their own mystique" (De Gasperi 1936). With regard to the experience of totalitarianism and modern mass politics, De Gasperi and the old generation of *popolari*—those who had entered politics before World War I, approaching it with the modes and thoughts inherited from the nineteenth century—began to abandon the traditional Catholic hostility to mythical thought and accept its historical functionality and importance for the elaboration of a modern political language.

Thus, only in Jan-Werner Müller's very superficial reading could the interwar years be seen as "disastrous" for political Catholicism (Müller 2011: 134); on the contrary, Catholic thought and positions transformed into a reflection on the fatalities of the interwar period (for similar developments in Austria, Germany, and France see Chappel 2018). In the 1930s, the most important developments undoubtedly did not occur in the area of institutional assets and party politics. And yet, the search for the foundations of a new social and political culture that marked the experience of the young—and less young—Catholic intellectuals and politicians in the 1930s proved highly relevant and influential in post-war and post-Fascist Italy, not only on an intellectual-cultural level but also in terms of the political-institutional outcomes. Their encounter with Maritain and their readings happened at a crucial moment. In the mid- to late 1930s, with the increasing association of Fascism with Nazism and its racial politics as well as the acceleration of totalitarian dynamics, the Catholic infatuation, if not fascination, with the regime showed signs of crisis. The *fucino* Paolo Emilio Taviani dated his detachment from Fascism and the beginning of his search for an alternative back to the 1938 racial laws. The same holds for other *fucini* and Catholics (Taviani 2002: 23–6), but for many, the real change came with World War II and the political and existential crisis that it ushered.

5

Democratic Conversion

This chapter deals with the Catholic experience of World War II. The war shattered the fragile balance between Catholic and Fascist identity and the idea that there could be a convergence between the two. It became clear to Catholics that Fascism could not be the carrier of Catholic values and principles. For the young generation of intellectuals who had grown up in the 1930s this amounted to a deeper existential crisis. They had to confront the foolishness of Fascism and the foolishness of Catholics, including themselves, who had believed in Fascism. This political and existential crisis, however, triggered the emergence of new state of consciousness and the conviction that Catholics must act as a Catholics not only in the cultural sphere but especially in the political realm. Thus, between 1942 and 1945 the Catholic milieu (the young second generation formed in the 1930s, the old first generation of *popolari*, and others) became an incubator of proposals for the political and social order of post-Fascist Italy. Catholics elaborated, in a series of documents (such as the *Camaldoli Code* and *The Reconstructive Ideas of Christian Democracy*), a rich Catholic democratic political project in clear discontinuity with their own tradition, a project that can be termed as a "political spirituality," using the concept of Michel Foucault. Furthermore, under the leadership of De Gasperi, they rejoined in a new party: the Democrazia Cristiana (DC), soon to become the most successful political party in modern European history.

5.1 War Experiences and Learning How to Think Politically

If the 1930s were crucial for the development of a Catholic-inspired political way of thinking that was open to democracy, the years that spanned World War II can be considered decisive. The racial laws and the pact between Rome and Berlin had shattered but not entirely broken the alliance between Catholicism and Fascism. The idea that it was possible to Catholicize the regime was still alive. The racialism and paganism professed by the Nazi regime were unacceptable, as the pope himself wrote in the encyclical *Mit brennender Sorge*. The first seeds of doubts and uncertainty had been sown in the minds of Catholics. Yet, at the end of the 1930s, many Catholics still believed in the marriage between Catholicism and the regime (Galavotti 2013: 11). Fanfani, for example, signed the 1938 *Manifesto of Race* and actively wrote for the infamous official Fascist magazine

Italy's Christian Democracy: The Catholic Encounter with Political Modernity. Rosario Forlenza and Bjørn Thomassen, Oxford University Press. © Rosario Forlenza and Bjørn Thomassen 2024. DOI: 10.1093/oso/9780198859864.003.0006

La Difesa della Razza ("The Defense of the Race"). In the already quoted article from 1939 (see Chapter 4), he endorsed the "segregation of the Semites from the national demographic body" introduced after the racial laws (Fanfani 1939: 256). With the war, everything changed.

With the onset of the war, patriotism still offered a ground on which Catholicism and Fascism could find a point of convergence. Patriotic sentiments and the dream of a Catholic world civilization initially encouraged many *fucini* to support the Fascist war efforts. In 1941, their president, Aldo Moro—certainly not one of the most radical and radicalized among patriots—wrote that "we can truly say that [to] serve the *Patria* in arms is a great moment of life" (Moro 1941; see also Dagnino 2009). This was in line both with the fervid patriotic appeal to the association's members formulated in June 1940 by Catholic Action's general director, Evasio Colli, and with the "love of *Patria*" of which Pius XII spoke to the diocesan leaders of Catholic Action in September 1940.[1]

With the war on the Eastern Front happening alongside the *Wehrmacht*, the regime brandished Bolshevik Russia as the merciless destroyer of Italian (and European) Catholic values. In this regard, the regime relied not only on Fascist principles but, rather, resorted to cultural-religious categories to explain "why we fight," adopting a Catholic semantics of ultimate ends (Stone 2008: 334, 2012). While it is true that the Vatican, urged by Washington, moderated its heated anti-Communism and Pius XII tempered his condemnation of Bolshevism, as Nazism now appeared a more dangerous threat, the military chaplains and the Catholic press pronounced the Russian war a "holy crusade" to bring "faith to barbarians," to the "blasphemous and heinous enemies of God," "destroyers of churches," and "murderers of Christ's followers" (quoted in Pertici 2003: 281–4; see also Forlenza 2017b: 229–30). The *fucini*, including De Gasperi, embraced the war in Russia as a patriotic effort, a sacred mission to bring Christian civilization back to an entire people, liberating them from atheism and materialism (on De Gasperi see Vecchio 2009: 670–1).

However, as the war proceeded, a "crisis of meaning" hit Italian Catholicism hard (R. Moro 1998; Traniello 2007c). In fact, Italy as a whole and the Italian body politic entered a liminal time of deep uncertainty. On July 25, 1943, the Fascist regime collapsed because of heavy casualties, an economic crisis, food shortages, and other setbacks caused by the war. Forty-five days later, on September 8, Marshal Pietro Badoglio announced over the radio that an armistice with the Allies had been signed five days earlier. Accordingly, he ordered the Italian armed forces to stop fighting the Allies, though without giving the Italians

---

[1] The appeal, with the title "L'Italia in armi. L'appello dell'A.C.," can be found in *Gioventù Nova*, June 22, 1940; see also the police report of July 14, 1942, in Archivio Centrale dello Stato, Ministero dell'Interno [hereafter: ACS, MI], Direzione Generale di Pubblica Sicurezza, Affari Generali e Riservati, G1 Associazioni, b. 10, f. 127 (Azione Cattolica); see also De Felice 1981: 819.

any precise instructions. The announcement was followed by King Victor Emmanuel III's ignominious flight from Rome. A void in the leadership of the nation was thus created, and soldiers and civilians were left without any clear military and political direction. As the Anglo-American armies advanced from southern Italy into the German-occupied North, civil war broke out between the forces of resistance and the forces of Fascism. This led to a situation of unprecedented uncertainty. The spread of warfare into society, pitting neighbor against neighbor and bringing material devastation, massacres, retaliations, and bombings, ruined the structures of everyday life. The legal framework of the nation evaporated. Civilian life became a front-line experience, destroying patterns of trust and social consensus, and undermining beliefs in elites and authority. In short, as we have discussed in details elsewhere, the final two years of the war constituted a liminal moment of deep uncertainty, confusion, and disorientation (see, in particular, Thomassen 2014a; Forlenza and Thomassen 2016: 149–55; Forlenza 2019b: 19–21).

For Catholics and especially the young generation of Catholics born on the eve of Mussolini's ascent to power, the war shattered the fragile balance between Catholic and Fascist identity. Such a balance hinged on the perception that there was a convergence and a commonality between the objectives and mission of the nation in the overall framework of a Catholic civilization, of a Catholic Italy. It was becoming increasingly clear to Catholics that Fascism could not be the carrier of Catholic values and principles. In fact, to an increasing number of Catholics, the war revealed that Fascism was their main enemy.

For the young generation of intellectuals, the war turned into an existential crisis. Acquired universes of symbolic and cultural worldviews collapsed. The *fucini* had believed in the regime, its patriotic/civilizational wars, and the alliance between Catholicism and Fascism. The political failure of Mussolini, the superficial preparation of the Italian soldiers, and the "gruffly slapdash attitude" (Taviani 1988) with which Italy fought the war became dramatically evident to them. The foolishness of Fascism and the foolishness of those Catholics, including themselves, who had believed in Fascism became painfully visible. How could they face this new situation? The past did not offer them any reference points; they knew little, if anything, of the pre-Fascist democratic politics of Christian inspiration and some of them rediscovered Sturzo and Francesco Luigi Ferrari only after World War II (Vecchio 1997: 272–3). Few of them had an anti-Fascist democratic background. They had been taught that the church was indifferent to and equidistant from every political regime and had not been educated to "understand" Fascism, as Dossetti and others—including the *fucino* and scholar of Classics at the Cattolica, Giuseppe Lazzatti—later put it when they reproached those who, in the interwar years, had acted as their spiritual leaders. Thus, in the immediate post-war years, Dossetti gently rebuked his spiritual guide Dino Torreggiani by saying that he "did not help us to understand Fascism" (Dossetti quoted in

Spreafico 1989: 729). Their "anti-Fascist education," Taviani admitted, had been "insufficient, almost non-existent" (Taviani 1988). Lazzatti made his criticism of teachers and spiritual guides who taught them to be indifferent to political regimes shine through (Dossetti quoted in Lazzati 1989: 163–5). In a similar vein, Giorgio Battistacci from Perugia wrote:

> Catholics who turned 20 at the beginning of the 1940s and 1950s found themselves—like most of their peers—lacking any political training and the ability to make political choices. Even if they were in contact with priests and lay people who had experienced political life before Fascism...such priests and lay people made few references to their past. (Battistacci 1978: 466–7)

Lino Monchieri, a young Catholic partisan and member of Catholic Action at the moment of Mussolini's declaration of war (June 10, 1940), exposed the failures of Catholic Action, which prevented him from understanding what Fascism had really been. Discussions within the organization regarded the war, its uncertain outcome, and the concerns about the future; and yet, there was "no open condemnation, no reasonable criticism" (L'Azione Cattolica Bresciana 1987: 23). Monchieri also explained that the young members of Catholic Action in 1942 advanced the request to engage with social, political, and cultural issues, but after their guides refused, many resigned and abandoned the organization (L'Azione Cattolica Bresciana 1987: 24).

However, in the middle of this political and existential crisis, something new started to emerge. The crucial point here is that religion and faith provided Catholics not only with psychological refuge, consolation, and a meta-ideological meaning to understand incomprehensible events, but also with a path to the future and an inspiration to take action. Stories from the Bible became a reference point. For example, a priest from Parma who joined the Resistance referred to the Book of Maccabees:

> Our revolt could not have more valid and enlightening precedents.... [T]he battle of those who defend the borders of the spirit, freedom, [and] human and divine rights will always be just and holy. (quoted in Vecchio 1997: 270–1)

At the same time, in his famous 1942 Christmas address, Pope Pius XII urged Catholics to act: "the call of the moment is not lamentation but action; not lamentation over what has been, but reconstruction of what is to arise and must arise for the good of society." This was an exhortation to action but also the acknowledgment that the new historical conditions were paving the way for and, in fact, *required* a qualitative transformation in the Catholic attitude to politics.

In many ways, and as had often happened before, the papal message was only a reflection on what was happening on the ground. In a moment of great crisis, faith and religion were becoming a mobilizing force for Catholic activists and thinkers, an incentive to act personally on the public stage. Starting in 1941–2, that is, *before* the pope's authoritative intervention, the Catholic intellectual and political milieu showed important signs of political vitality. This implied not only a return to the *popolari* and De Gasperi, back in the field of active politics but also renewed and almost febrile activities, like conferences and working groups on sociopolitical themes at the Cattolica (Bocci 1995). The young generation (i.e. the *fucini*, the academics of the Cattolica, and other individuals) took a leap from the cultural to the political sphere.

The collapse of the old markers of certainty triggered the emergence of new states of consciousness and the search for a meaningful interpretation. In this period of prolonged crisis, young Catholics started to question their own (Fascist) past and their present, asking themselves *what was to be done*. The awareness that Catholics must act as Catholics not only in the cultural sphere but, especially, in the political realm started to emerge, introducing into politics the novelty, richness, and spiritual resources of Catholicism—the only way to heal the evils of the world.

Examples and personal testimonies abound. It was the tragic experience of war and imprisonment in a German camp, a time of desperation and crisis, "hope" and "grace," and "expiation,"[2] that urged Giuseppe Lazzati to commit, in Maritain's words, to the "spiritual animation of the temporal." His decision to enter politics was the consequence, he wrote, "of the cultural concerns which moved us" in the years of the war, "allowing us to pin down precise programmatic points." The war pushed him to understand: the rejection of Fascism became a rejection of any authoritarian and repressive regime. Furthermore, the war taught Lazzatti that Catholics had been unable to think politically. Thus, Lazzati decided to "establish a cultural commitment destined to prepare Catholics to think politically."[3] It was the time spent in concentration camps that triggered a new state of consciousness among many Catholics. In his diary, Enrico Zampetti wrote the following on March 2, 1944: "If it was God's wish that these three years passed in this way, they did not do so in vain. The formation, or better, the transformation of my character and conscience is a fact that the naive, 19-year-old 'I' could not even have imagined at the time" (Zampetti 1992, 176; on the experience of the concentration camp for Catholics more in general, see Vecchio 1997: 283–94). Decades later, another Catholic former internee remembered the German camps in this way: "[T]he years spent in the camps, for us officers, gave us the rare opportunity to reflect like hermits in a desert; I grew from a careless boy into a conscious man" (quoted in Vecchio 1997: 287).

---

[2] As in the memory of another Catholic internee; V. Giuntella 1979: 259–64.
[3] See the diary written by Lazzati during his imprisonment, Dossier Lazzati 1993; see also Lazzatti 1989. The quotes are taken from an interview with Lazzati (Magri 1984).

The year was 1943 and a dramatic transformation convinced Emi Rinaldini, a teacher from Brescia who would be tortured and killed by the Fascists and the SS in 1945, to change his perspective. "Until today," he wrote in his diary, "we worked in the school, locked between four walls, and we struggled to believe that we had men before us, to be trained to a stronger life by will, moral discipline, [and] conscience; the men of tomorrow, continuers of an ideal" (Rinaldini 1957: 105). The war and the existential uncertainty that it entailed convinced Dossetti and many other young Catholics to abandon Catholic intransigence in favor of direct involvement. This meant joining the anti-Fascist Resistance, even at the cost of collaborating with Communists and Socialists (V. Giuntella 1981; Pavone 1991: 169–89; De Rosa 1997a; Vecchio 1997, 2011).

5.2 Rebels for Love

It was the events of the war that convinced Telesio Olivelli, one of the most radical young Catholic-Fascists until 1942-3, to become "a rebel for love": to live the struggle against Fascism as a "moral revolt," as liberation from Fascism understood not only as an external force but also as an internal attitude that had contaminated Catholicism, and as a purification that required a personal sacrifice. This change of attitude should not be reduced to mere opportunism. Calling young Catholics to battle in 1944, a few months before his death in a German camp, he wrote:

> We are rebels: ours is first of all a moral revolt. Against the decay in which a weakened Italy, subdued, ungoverned, turned into prey, torn apart, turned into a prostitute in her values and in her men…. Our revolt is not contingent on this or that moment, it is not against this or that person, it does not aim toward this or that specific political objective: it is a revolt against a system and an epoch, against a way to think and a way of life, against a worldview. We never felt as free as when we found, in the depth of our consciousness, the capacity to rebel against the passive acceptance of the brutal fact, to rebel against the bovine yoke of the alien, to rise again to a life of intense and adventurous morality. (quoted in Caracciolo 1975: 211–15)

The *fucino* Ermanno Gorrieri, a loyal Fascist soldier and subsequently an anti-Fascist partisan, explained his transformation and the beginning of his taking the initiative using similar words: "[It was] the desire to react to the national humiliation of September 8, and it was a subterranean, perhaps unconscious aversion to Fascism" that he had absorbed through Catholic Action (Gorrieri 1966: 68). Likewise, the Catholic partisan from Reggio Emilia Gianni Morselli admitted the confusion within Catholic Action and the process of transformation that he and his fellow activists underwent between 1942 and 1943. In this timeframe, the awareness emerged "that the time in which we, as Catholics, had lived with our heads in the sand was coming to an end"; the transformation was "slow and confused" and "for almost all young Catholics the choice of the Resistance came after an anguished process" (quoted in Spreafico 1989: 760).

Letters, diaries, and memories of young Catholics living the war contain many traces of its transformative dimension. Changed life perspectives and disrupted trajectories of bourgeois life opened up new "horizons of expectations" (Koselleck 1985) toward a democratic order. This is what Gorrieri wrote to his mother on November 1, 1942, a few months before joining the Resistance:

> My thoughts about the future have slowly transformed; if I once thought about a career to pursue…now it seems to me that something much more important can be done in life, that there is something higher to be achieved in the world, which is not a personal aim or an egoistic career goal. I do not feel I am called simply to be a pharmacist all my life: I feel I am called for something higher, there are so many truths to study and delve into, so many ideas to diffuse, so much work to do toward the *Christianization of the world*, so many ideas to fight for.[4]

As Benigno Zaccagnini wrote decades later, the commitment to the anti-Fascist struggle and the Resistance aimed at "demonstrating that the Catholics did not side with Fascism and that they also endeavored with dignity and resoluteness to make amends for past errors…. it was we, lay Catholics and many parish priests, who discovered this autonomous dimension, who wanted to experience our being Christians day after day" (Zaccagnini 1975: 47).

In the maelstrom of World War II, Catholics—like many other Italians— rejected Fascism and chose the anti-Fascist Resistance not in the name of a clear political and ideological vision but for moral, cultural, and even existential reasons (what follows is based on Forlenza and Thomassen 2017; 2020). This choice was based on confessional motivations (i.e. against what was seen and perceived as anti-Christian) more than political ones (i.e. against what was perceived as antidemocratic); it was a search for social rather than political foundations (Parisella 2001: 144–5), even if it culminated in a clear political decision.

For many, the idea of an independent *Patria*, the cultural memory of the *Risorgimento*, and the long history of hostility to the Germans were also important factors. Within large sectors of Catholicism, the themes of patriotism and the "second *Risorgimento*" became more and more common. The "first *Risorgimento*" was the process of national unification and liberation from foreign oppression

---

[4] The letter is held in the Archivio del Centro Francesco Luigi Ferrari, Modena, Carte Gorrieri (italics added); for other testimonies and memories, see Lanzardo 1989: 201–58; Crivellin 2001.

that had culminated in the establishment of the Kingdom of Italy—a process that had pitted Italians *against* the Catholic Church and its followers. The "second *Risorgimento*" was the new national and patriotic war of liberation, supported by the entire population, rallying around partisans and soldiers. Catholics appropriated this narrative, which would become the dominant narrative of post-Fascist Italy, shared by virtually all anti-Fascist forces, while at the same time resignifying it; the second, new *Risorgimento* was the "real" *Risorgimento*, as this time it did not exclude the moral nation that is the Catholic nation.

Catholic partisan bands—especially in the Veneto region, where there was a strong "white" (i.e. Catholic) subculture—took names inspired by the *Risorgimento*, such as the "Osoppo" band, from the name of the Osoppo fortress in Friuli, which was defended for seven months against the Austrian troops in 1848 (Giuntella 1981: 119). Decades later, Lazzati recalled "the sense of *Risorgimento*" he had inherited from his family at the time of World War I, "the war of my adolescence" (Lazzati 2009: 247). Taviani, another Catholic partisan, had been conquered as a child by his grandfather's "*Risorgimento* stories," to such an extent that, at the age of 9, he had become a "republican and enthusiast of Mazzini" (Taviani 2002: 9–16). Dossetti's grandfather was a devout follower of Garibaldi (Dossetti 1988: 41). Evidently, the "national-patriotic" pedagogy implemented by liberal-monarchic Italy since 1870—via the army and public school, rituals and artistic representations, public commemorations, and the erection of museums and monuments—and continued by Fascism had percolated into Italian society, including into Catholic families, and resurfaced in a time of deep collective and individual crisis. In this sense, the Resistance was the arrival point of the nationalization of Catholic masses (Mosse 1975). The tortuous path that had started with the Catholics' opposition to the nation born from the *Risorgimento* culminated in the embrace of those *Risorgimento* ideals, which now had a religious meaning: as a moral, cultural, and religious rebirth and resurrection of the nation.

5.3 The Spiritual Reconstruction of Italy: Building Christian Democracy, 1942–5

Between 1942 and 1945, the Catholic intellectual and political milieu became an incredible incubator of ideas about and proposals for the political and social order of post-war and post-Fascist Italy—and for the role of Catholics in this new order. It is exactly in this timeframe that Catholic intellectuals and politicians abandoned their constitutional agnosticism or their authoritarianism and embraced democracy without reserve. They thus elaborated, in a series of important collective and individual documents (Idee e programmi 1984), a rich and articulated Catholic democratic political project in clear discontinuity with the premises of their political and cultural tradition. More importantly, such a movement toward democracy proved to be irreversible. In the following decades, anti-democratic temptations and nostalgia for authoritarian regimes persisted in certain sectors of Catholicism. However, differently from the previous formative periods in whichdemocratic Catholicism emerged from the end of the nineteenth century until 1922 (i.e. at the time of Rosmini, Murri, and Sturzo), the path to democracy was now a one-way road (Campanini 1997; Casella 1984; Scoppola 1997: 26–31).

The crucial factor in this transformation from authoritarianism to democracy was the awareness that any reflection on and consideration of forms of government must begin with the rights and freedom of the person, as Augusto Del Noce wrote time and again in those years (Thomassen and Forlenza 2016b: 186–9). From the French Revolution to 1922, when Fascism took power, the central question for Catholics vis-à-vis the secular state was how to defend the rights of the church. In this respect, the 1929 Lateran Pacts between the Vatican and the regime provided Catholics with enough guarantees. Between 1942 and 1945, the Catholics' priority became that of defending the rights and freedom of the person. Thus, any consideration of the forms of government necessarily had to take into account the fact that the fundamental aspect in the passage from totalitarianism to democracy was not simply the church but the human being. Decades after the Resistance, one of the representatives of the Catholic Resistance, Ezio Franceschini, who would later become rector of the Cattolica (1965–8), explained the transformation and the Catholic rejection of Fascism with great clarity. Catholics understood that "dictatorship and democracy were utterly incompatible" and that "liberty is the most important value for human beings" (Franceschini 1983).

In this transformation, Maritain's lesson remained important. However, the historical experience of totalitarianism, the regime's totalitarian drift, and the devastation of the war that had tarnished the integrity and the liberty of the person were even more important. Catholics had not only been external spectators of this process: they had lived and experienced it.

Violence against and disdain for the person were not the infantile illnesses of Fascism, as Catholics had believed, hoping to heal it through the regime's Catholicization. The illness was the most profound essence of the regime—and it was incurable. Thus, Catholics slowly but surely came to understand not only the historical but also the conceptual incompatibility between Catholicism and Fascism.

The premises of Catholic traditional social and political thought, namely the idea that the church and Catholics were equidistant from and irrelevant to political regimes and various forms of governments, were rendered untenable by the outcomes of Fascism. This view presupposed that any regime was acceptable for Catholics provided that such a regime or political order recognized the rights of the church and respected the fundamental natural rights of the person. The former and the latter were radically questioned and threatened by the totalitarian nature of Fascism. The revelation of the totalitarian face of Fascism and its final threat to the person convinced many Catholics to convert to democracy, not only in Italy but also in France and Germany. What had until then been considered *one* of several possible forms of government became, for Catholics, the only choice that could effectively guarantee the fundamental rights and freedoms of the person and, eventually, the freedom of the church and the freedom of religion.

The option of democracy involved not merely the old generation of "Catholic-democratic" *popolari* but, crucially, the second generation: the young intellectuals of the 1930s who were entering the political stage for the first time during the war. Even Pius XII, in his radio message of Christmas 1944 on "the problem of democracy," expressed a favorable predisposition and an opening toward the values of democracy and the dignity of the person against every form of totalitarianism, from the Right and the Left of the political spectrum: "[T]he democratic form of government appears to many as a postulate of nature imposed by reason itself." As the Concordats with Fascist Italy and Nazi Germany were signed, the church thought that it could establish a protected area for Catholics and Catholic Action within authoritarian and totalitarian regimes. The underlying idea was that the liberty of the believers could, in the end, coexist with the lack of liberty for citizens. History had demonstrated that it was impossible to maintain a distinction between the space of the church and the space of secular power. There was only one space, that of the human being, and in such a space it was necessary to recognize and respect the liberty of all human beings, not only that of the believers. Seen with the benefit of hindsight, the pope's words were cautious and much less advanced than the elaborations of Catholic intellectuals and politicians (Ruffilli 1980: 29–42; Campanini 1997: 496–500; Traniello 2007a: 223–39; Chamedes 2019: 237–41). Yet, his words resonated with what was happening on the ground, as Catholic politicians and intellectuals found in Pius XII an authoritative endorsement and confirmation of their democratic and anti-Fascist choice. In 1945, a Catholic activist thus wrote that "democracy in this radio message is elevated to human dignity," and saw in it a legitimation of "Christian democracy in a universal sense" (Giordani 1948: 567).

This embrace of democracy did not imply giving up Catholic ideas. Quite the opposite: from a Catholic point of view, democracy must be infused with a spiritual, transcendental meaning. This meta-political dimension was seen as necessary to prevent democracy from reverting to a mere liberal order, which had proven itself defenseless against the totalitarian threat. Catholics, with their spiritual resources, had to step forward in the process of rebuilding the nation to avoid "new slavery and new debris."[5] Christianity and religion would infuse

---

[5] Aldo Moro, "Prospettive," *La Rassegna* (August 10, 1944), in Moro 1982a: 50–1.

democracy with the "spirituality" that could deflect Fascism's venomous legacy, its "moral decadence," "exhaustion of the spirit," and "loss of the sense of life."[6] The same call for spirituality pervaded Catholic reflections on democracy and the post-war order, such as Olivelli's "Christian-inspired" socioeconomic "reconstructive program" based on a "revolution of the spirit"; similarly, Fanfani wrote thoughtful pages on "person, goods, and society" in a "renewed Christian civilization" (Fanfani 1945; Giuntella 1981: 124). For Laura Bianchini, a real democracy and the political and social reconstruction of Italy would require the spiritual reform of the consciousness of citizens and the rediscovery of the centrality of the person (Bianchini 1944a, 1944b).

Democracy and spirituality: the former was meaningless without the latter. Democracy without spirituality could not last as it would be overwhelmed by the evil of the world. In fact, between 1942 and 1945, the political, institutional, constitutional, and structural aspects of democracy were barely at the center of the Catholic elaboration of what post-war Italy should look like. The main concern was the spiritual, ethical reconstruction of the democratic order; indeed, a political spirituality.

The crucial point is that the reflection on and elaboration of a "Christian," "spiritual" democracy happened precisely when Catholic thinkers and politicians were living through dramatic experiences of war, civil war, and devastation—when their existences were pushed to the limit. The vision of democracy that emerged from the documents written by Catholics was shaped by their existential path as well as by their experiences of crisis and the consequent search for a Catholic alternative in a time of mass politics, totalitarianism, and total war. They experienced the structural incompatibility between Catholicism and authoritarianism in a German camp, on the battlefield, or in a Fascist prison. Adopting Voegelin's approach (Voegelin 1987), their political ideas crystallized not as second-order reflections of reality, but rather as symbolizations of real human experiences: how Catholics lived through a transitional period of Fascism and war and reacted to it. In this limit situation, in this critical juncture of politico-existential creativity, the immediate connection between thought and experience came to the fore with great strength.

5.4 From the *Reconstructive Ideas* to the *Camaldoli Code*

In this pivotal moment for Catholic politics, a milestone of Catholic thought on democracy appeared: *The Reconstructive Ideas of Christian Democracy*. Elaborated by De Gasperi in collaboration with other *popolari* and men of the second generation such as Paronetto, this document circulated secretly

[6] Aldo Moro, "Crisi spirituale," *La Rassegna* (February 10, 1944), in Moro 1982a: 14–16.

since the spring of 1943 and publicly after the fall of Fascism. The *Ideas* echoed central aspects of Maritain's thought: the value and dignity of the "person," the principle of "political liberty," and the appeal to "fraternity" and other Christian values that, alone, could open the way to Italy's democratic reconstruction and reconcile people and nations (the *Ideas* are Atti e Documenti 1968: 1–8).

The same can be said for the most original, comprehensive, and programmatic of these Catholic documents: the so-called *Camaldoli Code*, which was produced by the *Movimento Laureati* and the FUCI with the contribution of the intellectuals of the Cattolica. In the very same days that Fascism collapsed, these young intellectuals met in the Tuscan monastery of Camaldoli to discuss the principles of a social, political, and economic order from which a new Italy could be built. Meetings and workshops in Rome were regularly held in the following months, until 1945, when the *Code* was finalized and published (Per la comunità 1945; see Parisella 2001: 145–6; Campanini 2006: 402–4; Civitas 2013). The *Code* supported the idea of state intervention in the economy and pleaded for the promotion of the "intermediate collectivities" (*collettività intermedie*): the regional, provincial, and municipal units; the professional categories; and the family. It also reaffirmed the dignity of the person and its primacy over the state—a categorical refusal of a totalitarian view of politics that chimed with the explicit encouragement to disobey unjust laws. At the same time, and significantly, the *Code* abandoned the conception of a confessional state and located the primary values of the political community in solidarity, social justice, and defense of freedom. Finally, the *Code* claimed the need to reject war and violence and promote peace and collaboration between nations through new international institutions (see Parisella 2001: 145–6; Campanini 2006: 402–4; Civitas 2013).

It is no coincidence that the sections devoted to economic and social questions are the most significant of the entire *Code*; after all, it was drafted in a time of political uncertainty and suspension, when Catholics were increasingly detaching from Fascism but not yet sure what the best political regime to follow was. Written by Paronetto in collaboration with his colleague at the IRI, Pasquale Saraceno, and Ezio Vanoni, these sections represented a rethinking of the quintessential themes of Catholic social thinking. This is not surprising: in addition to parts on a just salary, cooperation, urbanism, social justice, and the social function of private property, there was an entire chapter on "public economic activity." The "specific private economic activities" had to be coordinated and attuned to the common interest of preventing the possibility that "they remain in a potential state or are hampered in their development." In this way, economic planning was introduced, which would prove crucial in post-Fascist Italy.

Saraceno and Paronetto's experience in the IRI was central; it moved them away from the vague and indistinct elaboration of Catholic social teaching on themes such as corporativism, leading them to embrace, instead, a vision that was much more modern, efficient, and pragmatic, founded on the priority of industrialization. Both men were sensible to the moral instances that descended from their Catholic inspiration and, particularly, to the demand for social justice linked to such a moral instance. Furthermore, their experience in the IRI had allowed them to insert the problem of the Italian economy into a global dimension in a more comprehensive, proactive, and forward-looking way than the private sector had been able to do. Saraceno and Paronetto, along with the other men of the IRI, were criticized as conventional and orthodox supporters of liberalism and a laissez-faire economic doctrine, little attentive to the problems and the imbalance of the Italian economic system. The *Camaldoli Code*, in fact, shows that Saraceno, Paronetto, and their fellows had already concentrated on important aspects in the early 1940s, such as the aim of full employment through industrialization, sustained also by public actions. This vision was much more effective and less ideological than the vision and ideals of many economists and intellectuals in those years who evoked and invoked Keynes.

From 1945 onward, when Catholics became the dominant political force of post-Fascist Italy under the banner of the DC, these visions and ideas would be institutionalized in a variety of ways.

5.5 Institutionalizing Spiritual Democracy: Politics and Spirituality from the War to the Post-War Period

The layers of meaning that emerged in the Catholic elaboration of a spiritual democracy in the period 1942–5 had a direct impact on post-Fascist Italian democracy (Forlenza 2019b).

Many of the Camaldoli's supporters entered the rank of the DC. The *Code*, together with De Gasperi's *Reconstructive Ideas*, inspired some of the socioeconomic reforms launched by Christian Democracy in the late 1940s and early 1950s, such as the housing development scheme (a law written by Fanfani), the introduction of "progressive" taxation by the Minister of Finance Ezio Vanoni (one of the Camaldoli's advocates), the agrarian reform, and the public investments in the South called Cassa per il Mezzogiorno (Forlenza 2010). The Camaldoli's supporters were men of the second generation, that is, former *fucini* and academics of the Cattolica—those Catholics who had endured the political and existential crisis of the last years of Fascism and the war and who had converted to democracy, actively searching for a bridge between Catholic faith and political responsibility. It was this new elite that rendered Christian Democracy a new "political animal" (Judt 2005: 80) and something very different from the pre-Fascist PPI.

One of the first and most tangible embodiments of the call for spirituality and transcendence that informed Catholic political discussions and debates during the war was the Italian Constitution. Catholics started to debate the theme of the constitution with effervescence in the months following the end of the war, generating a profusion of ideas that confronted Italian Catholicism with political modernity. Catholic-inspired thinkers and politicians played a pivotal role in the writing of the Constitution. They managed to inscribe a "personalist" worldview into the wording and spirit of the first section, thus contributing to the building of a post-liberal democracy with distinct spiritual foundations (see Chapter 7 for a full discussion of the constitutional process).

The emergence of ideas rooted in spirituality did not stop with the Constitution. In the first years of democratic Italy, Catholic politics remained strongly motivated by "spiritual" concerns. As discussed in the Introduction, spirituality here does not refer simply to an inner experience but rather an experience and view of the world that concretely came to shape life-conduct (in the Weberian sense) and political choices. This resonates with Foucault's notion of "political spirituality," as we read it. Political spirituality for Christian Democratic thinkers and politicians was not simply an insistence of a predefined set of beliefs. It involved instead *new* techniques of self-transformation, *new* capacities, *new* possibilities for an alternative regime of truth to emerge—a movement of creation and re- creation.

For the Catholic politicians engaged in the tremendous task of Italy's reconstruction, spirituality meant translating their internal life into a political one, "an apostolic, missionary, and compassionate commitment" (Giovagnoli 1991: 94). For Christian Democrats, it meant that democracy necessarily had to be rebuilt on Christian foundations and that the only alternative to Christian Democracy was totalitarianism, which in the Cold War context was no longer Nazism or Fascism but Soviet Communism. Only Christianity applied through a Catholic-inspired party could ensure Italy's political, spiritual, and moral renewal (Acanfora 2007). This was, indeed, a kind of "religious democracy" that many Christian Democrats derived from the writings of Maritain but that ultimately rested on their personal experiences of crisis in the last years of Fascism and the war.

From De Gasperi's viewpoint, spirituality meant operating within politics with the conviction that democracy has its origin in the values of the gospel (De Gasperi 1948; see also Craveri 2006). While De Gasperi's days as prime minister were obviously burdened with pragmatic tasks, he always gave importance to prayer, contact with God, and daily participation in Mass. Likewise, although he always employed a sober and "rational" political vocabulary in his speeches, writings, and personal notes (diaries), at the same time, one can find endless references to the Bible (both the Old Covenant and the gospel) and to the *Imitatio Christi*, which served as a means to explain and analyze sociopolitical and mundane questions (see De Gasperi 1974: 1.93). It is well documented that he was particularly attentive to the Book of Job. This section of the Old Covenant is perhaps most pervaded by a sense of the transcendence of God's plans that man can never fully comprehend (Scoppola 1981; Durand 1984; Acanfora 2015). "In the democratic system," De Gasperi said in 1950, "a politico-administrative mandate is conferred with a specific responsibility." He continued: "[A]t the same time, there is a moral responsibility vis-à-vis one's consciousness, and the consciousness to make decisions must always be illuminated by the doctrine and teaching of the church" (quoted in De Gasperi 1990: 243).

For Dossetti and other politicians and intellectuals of the second generation, spirituality meant injecting Maritain's and Mounier's ideas into the new democratic culture of post-war Italy, striving for the realization of Christian values in the state, economy, and society at large (as we shall see in Chapter 7). For Paronetto, spirituality meant measuring socioeconomic issues in their own right, albeit firmly rooted in a Christian conscience and in what he defined once and again as the "ascetic of the man of action" (the title of a posthumous collection of his writings). For the southerner Aldo Moro, spirituality meant the need to create a "party for the Mezzogiorno" that, through the agrarian reform, could respond to the call of the gospel in favor of the impoverished peasants of southern Italy, liberating them from centuries of subjugation (Moro 1955; see Chapter 6 for a full discussion of these aspects). For Moro it also meant fighting for—as he wrote in 1947, echoing Maritain—an "integral" democracy based on the "demands" and "resources" of human beings and inspired by Christianity, the only force that could enrich the "cold...myth of a *political* democracy" with "humanity and justice" and a superior vision of liberty (Moro 1947; see also Chapter 6). For Fanfani, finally, spirituality meant that the economy had to be guided by politics which, in turn, must be inspired by Christian ethics; spirituality involved placing the economic dimension in a broader horizon in which the struggle against poverty, unemployment, and the lack of housing was ascribable to a Christian vision of the duty to assist the poor (Fanfani e la casa 2002).

Giorgio La Pira was a prominent member of the Constituent Assembly and mayor of Florence, from 1951 to 1957 and then again from 1961 to 1965. Deeply committed to the struggle for peace in the world, he was the first Western non-Communist politician to visit the Soviet Union (1959). For him, spirituality meant meeting the "expectations of poor people" and acting in "defense of poor people," as the titles of his two most famous articles recite (La Pira 1950a, 1950b). The purpose of spirituality was to build houses for poor people in need of shelter, to defend those who had been evicted, and to take sides with workers in their struggle against owners. Having been accused, not least by conservative Catholics and the Vatican, of being a "white Communist" and a "statist," he made the following remark before Florence's town council, on September 24, 1954:

You do not have a right to tell me: Mr. Mayor, you should not care about human beings without a job (fired or unemployed), without a home (evicted), without assistance (the elderly, ill, children, etc.). This is my fundamental duty: a duty that does not leave space for discrimination and that before my position as mayor of the city...derives from my consciousness as a Christian: what is at stake here is the very substance of grace and the gospels. (La Pira Sindaco 1988: 445–6)

Seen from the present, anachronistic perspective, Christian Democracy in the post-war period may indeed seem like a "bargain of ideas" (Müller 2011: 138): an empty signifier with no real ideological core, or a container into which one could throw almost anything. Together with leading Christian Democrats, De Gasperi insisted on democracy, human rights, and a sort of controlled capitalism, recognizing the need to increase production and encourage the growth of a private sector to become the motor of economic development. They insisted, at the same time, on housing policies in the cities and loan systems and agrarian reforms in the countryside: in other words, a hodgepodge of liberalism and Socialism or, to say the least, ideological confusion.

However, such a reading fails to recognize the spiritual sources that lurked beneath the—only apparently—pragmatic-relativistic political measures taken by Christian Democrats in Italy as in many other parts of Europe. For them, such measures were not contradictory, nor were they pragmatic reconciliations of liberal and Socialist ideologies. They were rooted in Christianity and in a proper *Christian* democracy. The adjective was no mere decoration. It was the animating source of inspiration, the glue that gave coherence to their political action. Christian Democrats sincerely believed that through these measures, Italy's socioeconomic conditions and the lives of the poorest would substantially improve (Giovagnoli 1982; Scoppola 1997: 115–18). They believed that these measures would allow citizens to act and create value outside the strict control of the state. Their embrace of democracy and a reconfigured political modernity stemmed from Christian principles and religious motivations—in fact, from the evangelical call to charity (Giovagnoli 1991: 95–6).

In short, at the end of the war and following the politico-existential crisis engendered by the war itself, the ambiguous infatuation with—if not embrace of—Fascism that, despite the antagonism beneath and sometimes on the surface of the church–state relationship, had captured significant sectors of interwar Italian Catholicism was shattered and eventually destroyed. Catholic political culture had moved toward a political and social model that reincorporated transcendence as a legitimate perspective of truth and reason and re-anchored democracy, justice, and freedom in a religiously argued ethos. In 1945, these attempts were still no more than ideas but they were soon to be institutionalized in a series of ways, influencing constitutional formulations and party politics.

5.6 Rediscovering the Church

The crucial development towards a spiritual, Christian Democracy happened outside the church. However, the church itself gained a new role linked the very same process of political transformation characterizing the end of the war and the immediate postwar years. At the end of World War II, Catholicism and the church had emerged as an important reference point for Italian society and its members (Forlenza 2019b: 207–9). Aside from Fascist leadership, the most important war-time elite was, of course, the church hierarchy. The structural reorganization overseen by Pius XI and the rapid expansion of Catholic Action in the interwar period ensured that the church was particularly well placed to seize the new opportunities created by the war (Conway 1997: 40–4). Uncertainty, the crisis of meaning, and the material suffering caused by the war contributed to a rapid rise in religious observance and a dramatically increased demand for welfare assistance. After the regime collapsed, and in the absence of any other legitimate governments, the bishops, local clergy, and leading Catholic laity constituted the social and political force best endowed with the moral legitimacy and financial resources to lead local communities (Giovagnoli 1985; Felice 1993: 355–75; Mazzonis 1997; for a similar development in Germany, see Blessing 1988). Moreover, there was a return to religious practices, especially the "ancient religion of pain and tears," imbued—especially in the South—with Marian piety and devotion, and with a sense of mercy and consolation, and expressed through public prayers, pilgrimages, and other forms of ancient ritual devotion (Malgeri 1980; Violi 1997: 114–15). Catholic tropes and images deeply ingrained in popular culture and the Italians' cultural memory—such as sacrifice, victimhood, and resurrection after suffering—were common in large sectors of the population, composed of humble people tormented by the events. Letters, diaries, and memoirs of these years are typically filled with religious images (e.g. the deposition of Christ, the Via Crucis, the martyrdom of the Saint, and the sorrowful Mary) that helped Catholics, but not only, to symbolize the otherwise incomprehensible events of the war and reconstruct a meaningful existence. German massacres and violence, after all, were only one side of the picture (on this see Forlenza 2012, 2019b: 163–8).

The political vacuum and the existential crisis of meanings were mitigated by the spiritual resource of religious belief and by the figure of the *Pastor Angelicus*, Pope Pius XII.[7] In July 1943, only a few days before the king dismissed Mussolini and the latter met Hitler in Feltre, in the Veneto region, the pope upstaged him after the American bombing of Rome's working-class San Lorenzo district. Pius was quick to bring spiritual and material comfort to the victims, appearing in person among the ruins (Riccardi 1979: 270–1).

Over the following months, the desire for solace and understanding led many Italians to rediscover the certainties of religion and the pastoral role of the church. For a young mother in the northern town of Varese, for example, the disaster that

---

[7] *Pastor Angelicus* was the title of a 1942 film about Pius XII on the twenty-fifth anniversary of his ordination as a bishop. This fascinating portrayal of papal charisma later played a crucial role in mobilizing the Catholic vote in the 1948 elections, when it was shown across the peninsula, using cars donated by the Vatican and adapted for film projection (see Chapter 8).

had befallen Italy was a punishment for the sins people had committed. She believed that everyone should entrust their fate to "the guardian angel of Italy, the pope, in whom alone all our hope resides."[8]

There is no doubt that the church's wartime action, and the people's response to it, prepared the ground for the emergence of Catholicism as a major political force in post-war Italy. It was significant for the history of post-war democracy that the generations of lay elites that had gathered, in the 1930s, in the ranks of Catholic Action, the only organization not to have been taken over by the Fascists in interwar Italy, were able to move smoothly into the organization and structure of the Christian Democratic party (Pollard 2008: 93–5). As we will discuss in the next chapter, Pius XII, the Vatican, and the church hierarchy were initially mistrustful of the secular regime that emerged from the war, fearing the revival of anticlericalism. These anxieties, however, were soon dissipated when the DC gained political power at the national level, offering the Catholic world and the church's interests more consistent opportunities than those promised by the unpredictable Fascist regime in the 1930s (on the church's strategy in Italy, France, and Germany, see Warner 2000).

---

[8] Diary entry for July 26, 1943, by Maricilla Piovanelli, *Dio*, Archivio Diaristico Nazionale, Pieve Santo Stefano, DP/95.

6

Integral Democracy

This chapter deals with the crucial years 1945–8, the most intense and critical years of Italy's political and economic reconstruction; it examines how Catholics, in collaboration and in contrast with the other parties, became the dominant party of Italian politics, the party that, at the first parliamentary elections of 1948, received almost half of the popular vote. Our focus is on Christian Democracy's effort to face the social and economic emergence of the immediate post-war years; on its commitment for the institutional and political reconstruction of the country and the transition from monarchy to republic and from Fascism to democracy. The chapter also follows closely De Gasperi's efforts to keep together the party, to resist the pressure of the Vatican and to bring Italy back into the international system of democracy system in a context marked by the dramatic emergence of the Cold War.

Shortly after the war ended, Christian Democracy not only established itself as a formal political party; it also, and in almost no time, became the biggest and most popular political party in Italy. With the benefit of hindsight, this seems "obvious" and almost a foregone conclusion. The final sequence of Roberto Rossellini's *Rome Open City* (1945) shows a group of boys sadly trooping away after the execution of the priest, Don Pietro, who had collaborated with the Communist Manfredi for the liberation of Italy. They are shown in the foreground of a panoramic shot of the city (the only one of its kind in the entire film), in which the skyline is dominated by St. Peter's, the pre-eminent symbol of Catholicism. What other destiny was possible? Could Italy take a different direction?

Yet, at the time, this outcome was anything but a given. Indeed, the development can even be considered paradoxical. After the end of the war, the DC established itself as the main actor in the nation's political scene and *the* decisive force in the reconstruction of Italian democracy. Heir of a specific political culture, it had originated in opposition to political modernity and the idea of Italy as a unified nation—a country that had largely been "made" in the nineteenth century, in contrast to such a culture. This development can be seen as a genuine "rite of passage." As we have seen in the previous chapter, the preceding years of war were lived through as a highly liminal period, with no certainty of outcomes. The years 1945-8 can, in continuation, be seen as the final stage of a rite of passage, e.g. the phase of re-aggregation, when the transition from one state to another is ritually

Italy's Christian Democracy: The Catholic Encounter with Political Modernity. Rosario Forlenza and Bjørn Thomassen, Oxford University Press. © Rosario Forlenza and Bjørn Thomassen 2024. DOI: 10.1093/oso/9780198859864.003.0007

completed, and a new sense of normality becomes institutionalized. In this sense, Christian Democracy represented an answer to a highly liminal period as well as the historical agent that brought this period to successful completion. If the democratization of Italy after World War II can be seen as a rite of passage, or as a threefold sequence of separation, liminality, and re-aggregation (Van Gennep 1960; V. Turner 1967; Thomassen 2012a, 2014a; Forlenza 2019b), then Catholic politics in the form of Christian Democracy must be approached as a performative act that both sustained and guided the closure of liminality and the emergence of a new, different order.

It is again important to stress that the DC established itself as a hegemonic force in a period marked by deep crisis. After the end of World War II and until the end of the 1940s, Italy lived through an intense time of social, political, and economic reconstruction. Italy was an extremely poor country in 1945. Fears and hopes blended with extreme uncertainty about the future. The immediate postwar years saw the end of the Savoy monarchy and the birth of the Italian Republic after the institutional referendum of June 1946. On January 1, 1948, the new, republican constitution came into force. The first parliamentary elections were held in the same year, while the first elections at the local and administrative level had already been held in the spring of 1946. New international alliances took shape as the Cold War began. Fascism, and a global war that had also developed into a civil war, had made Italy a deeply fractured society. Italians and the political community had to confront almost unsurmountable socioeconomic, institutional, and cultural challenges. Christian Democracy, under the strong and decisive guidance of Alcide De Gasperi (Malgeri 1988; Formigoni 2008b), played a central role in this critical juncture of Italian history, rapidly establishing itself as the dominant party of Italian politics.

De Gasperi himself was appointed prime minister in December 1945 and remained in office until 1953. The launch of the republican constitution, the agrarian reform, and other social policies, the ratification of the Peace Treaty, the adoption of the Marshall Plan, Italy's membership of the Atlantic Alliance, and the country's commitment to the incipient process of European integration were among the main acts of his governments. The entire historical process was anything but smooth. The DC had to deal with a series of important national and international actors: from the leftist parties to the productive classes, from peasants to urban sectors, from Washington to the church, from the trade unions to the other European countries. In these formative years of Italian history, Christian Democracy elaborated a specific response to the challenge of a post-Fascist, modern mass democracy. It furthermore articulated and developed—in competition or cooperation with non-Catholic forces—political and institutional, cultural, and socioeconomic platforms and a modern welfare state that led Italy into a more stable democratic age.

6.1 Democracy and the Gospel: Arising from the Ashes of War and Fascism

How, then, was it possible that after the war, a political culture that—until the late 1930s—had been at least lukewarm about democracy and political modernity became the main actor in the process of reconstructing democratic Italy? The same happened in other European countries, most notably in Germany. Christian Democracy became the new "political animal" of post-World War II Europe (Judt 2005: 80; see also Conway 2003; 2020), the central forum for institutionalizing Catholic modernity and a distinctively Christian approach to democracy. This was a decisive turn in Italian and European politics. Indeed, the Christian Democratic conversion to democracy through the historical juncture of the 1930s and the 1940s was perhaps the most important political phenomenon of European history since the French Revolution; and yet, this passage remains to be explained. While there is a thriving literature on Christian Democracy in Europe and in Latin America, scholars typically neglect the personal background experiences that nurtured the politics and ideology of Christian Democrats in the passage to democracy. Following the dramatic events of the 1930s and the 1940s, religiously inspired political principles emerged as new markers of certainty and conviction. Following Eric Voegelin (1987), the constellation of political concepts that Christian Democrats embraced and formulated represented the crystallization of their existential responses to their direct lived experience.

But what did "Christian democracy" really mean? Was "democratic" the same as "popular" in the meaning Sturzo gave it after World War I? Or was it something different? In other words, what "democracy" did Christian Democrats have in mind? In what sense and to what extent was it "Christian," and what exactly was the political project of De Gasperi, the party's founder and indisputable leader?

Once again, at the level of ideas, Maritain remained an important reference point for Italian Christian Democrats committed to the rebuilding of democracy. This also meant that such a project could not simply revert to pre-Fascist liberal foundations, which had proven themselves unstable vis-à-vis Fascism. Since Charles de Gaulle persuaded Maritain to serve as French ambassador to the Vatican from 1945 to 1948, Maritain actually lived in Rome during the time frame that coincided with the most intense phase of reconstructing Italian democracy and the emergence of Catholics as the new ruling class. Sturzo was acutely aware of the important occasion this offered Christian Democrats in Italy.[1] Writing in

---

[1] On February 11, 1945, while still in the United States, Sturzo wrote a letter to Igino Giordani, editor of the Catholic newspaper *Il Quotidiano*, inviting him and Italian Christian Democrats to welcome Maritain: "Jacques Maritain will give my greetings to you.... I am sure Roman Catholics know

1945, while still in exile in New York City, Sturzo advocated "personalism," "pluralism," and "institutionalism" as the philosophical pillars of Catholic involvement in the politics of the new nation (Sturzo 1947: 12). He also insisted that in the past, liberty had been "badly understood by clericals" and now had to be "relinked to the Christian tradition of popular sovereignty and to the democratic regime" (Sturzo 1945b: 309; see also Müller 2011: 135). In 1947, echoing Maritain, Aldo Moro—one of those young Catholics who had grown up and was formed in Fascist Italy (see Chapter 4)—explicitly called for an "integral" democracy to be built in post-Fascist Italy.

The term "integral" had, and still has, a deep meaning that is crucial to understand if we want to grasp the particularity of Christian Democracy—then as now. It is indeed an important word that needs qualification. It was taken from Maritain and his seminal *Humanisme Intégrale* of 1936. With "integral democracy," Maritain essentially indicated a communitarian, personalist, and pluralist democracy—a political order that could implement Christian and Thomist beliefs in the worldly sphere and that was an alternative to liberal democracy. Time and again, in their writings and speeches, the leaders of Christian Democracy mentioned the "integral democracy" that they claimed they were building and that was to be the antidote to materialism and totalitarianism. Following Maritain, Moro and the other Christian Democrats believed that democracy could and must become alive, meaningful, and effective—a "social" and not simply a "political" democracy—through Christianity and via the commitment of Catholics in the political, socioeconomic, and cultural spheres. Moro, for instance, wrote the following in this regard:

> We, Christians, more than others should feel the need to give democracy complete and concrete content of working solidarity.... It would be a grave mistake for Christians to create the myth of political democracy, which is the indispensable premise, the basis of the system, but it is not the whole of democracy, which is made up not only of freedom, but of humanity and justice. (Moro 1982a: 126–7)

De Gasperi did not dare to affirm that democracy had its origin in the value of the gospel and in Christianity itself. Yet, De Gasperi closely followed the lessons of Maritain and the philosophy of Maritain's mentor, Henri-Louis Bergson. In a conference held in Brussels on November 20, 1948, titled "The moral basis of democracy," De Gasperi said: "[I]t is our duty to offer democracy the

how to approach the French philosopher who comes to them as a French ambassador to the Holy See. His mission is the mission of any Christian: to offer a testimony of truth. But he knows very well how to offer the truth so purely and clearly by addressing the mind's thirst for truth, and it would thus be a pity not to benefit from his presence." See Giordani-Sturzo 1987: 106–7. Sturzo first met Maritain in 1939, in London, and then many times in the United States during the war.

contribution of our philosophy, our morality, our tradition." Christianity, De Gasperi added, gave decisive impulses ("impulsi") to democracy. The most important and strongest of these impulses was love. Quoting Bergson, De Gasperi also stated that "democracy is in its essence evangelical: its driving force is love" (De Gasperi 1948; on the importance of "love" see also Moro 1944).

De Gasperi and other DC leaders affirmed that democracy necessarily had to rest on Christian foundations, arguing that the alternatives to Christian Democracy were either a return to the pagan totalitarianism of the past or the atheistic totalitarianism of the present, and that only applied Christianity could ensure Italy's political, spiritual, and moral renewal. This was a kind of "religious democracy" that many Christian Democrats derived from Maritain and Bergson but with implicit references to *Risorgimento* ideas, as expressed in Giuseppe Mazzini's political thought (see for example Sala 1945). In the context of post-World War II, the notion of a spiritual form of democracy proved attractive for many reasons. To begin with, there was the motivating idea of an Italian—but also European and Western—revival, the vision of a better future, and the "spiritual" reconstruction (or Renaissance) of a world shattered by the atheistic, pagan materialism of Nazism. In other words, a Christianized democracy offered both a diagnosis of and an appropriate treatment for the decline of the West and its spiritual vacuum. Materialism and the fall of God had plunged Europe into fanaticism, nihilist totalitarian dictatorship, and war—a thorough crisis of meaning. Salvation lay in the re-rediscovery of Europe's religious roots and the teaching of the Catholic faith, which only Christian Democracy could guarantee. This narrative asserted that interwar Fascism had actually been a form of materialism; the political spirituality of Christian Democracy—a party endowed not only with a political program but also a religious view of human life and a "missionary" mentality—was, then, the antidote to a return to the past (Conway 2003: 51).

Ideas and inspirations, however, were not enough. Christian Democrats were well aware that the force of Christianity and its impulses, in the historical condition of post-Fascist Italy, needed to be channeled into politics and society through a party. On this point, De Gasperi, Sturzo, and the other Christian Democrats held a view that strongly diverged from Maritain's thought. The French philosopher was, in fact, not in favor of founding explicitly Christian parties. Rather, as he often repeated, Christianity and the gospel should be "the yeast" of political, social, and civic life, a formulation that the *Reconstructive Ideas* and several writings of Christian Democrats also evoked.[2] For Christian Democrats, instead,

---

[2] "The question," Maritain wrote, "does not deal...with Christianity as a religious creed and road to eternal life, but rather with Christianity as a leaven in the social and political life of nations and as the bearer of the temporal hope of mankind...as historical energy at work in the world" (Maritain 1943: 37). On his opposition to the reduction of the "new Christianity" to a party program, see Maritain 1934. The *Reconstructive Ideas* affirmed that "it is thus in democracy's specific interest that this Christian yeast ferments throughout the entire social life." See also Belardinelli 1990: 251.

actions in the temporal sphere—in society and politics—required the creation of a Christian, albeit not confessional, party. In other words, Catholics must act in politics through a party, the historical agent and political tool called to transform Christian moral values and Catholic social doctrine into political reality and effective policies. "Christian theories will bear no weight, even as theories," Sturzo wrote in 1945, "if there are no politico-social currents that give them actualization and experimentation" (Sturzo 1945b: 15). "To operate in the social and political sphere," De Gasperi said at the 1954 party congress, rethinking the experience of Catholics in power, "neither faith nor virtue is enough: it is required to create and nurture an instrument suited to the times: the party, a political organization with its own program, method, autonomous responsibility, and democratic life. It is not possible to operate in a twentieth-century democracy with the paternalism of Bossuet" (De Gasperi 1954: 69).[3]

From De Gasperi's point of view, Maritain and French Catholic thinkers were too concerned with religious aspects and less so with the concrete historical conditions of mass politics in the post-Fascist era. Their writings thus had to be translated to be able to cope with the reality of Italian contemporary society. This was in many ways inevitable. After all, De Gasperi's approach to politics and democracy—as that of Sturzo and other Christian Democrats—had a historical, sociological, and profoundly political character. Maritain, instead, was a political philosopher and a theologian, and his approach was quite different. For his entire life, De Gasperi had been an active politician, living through several formative experiences: a native of the Trentino region (which at the time was part of the Austro-Hungarian Empire), he had acted as the Catholic representative of a national minority in the parliament of Vienna before entering Italian politics (when Trentino became part of Italy after World War I), then participated in the foundation of the PPI and then experienced Fascism and war. By contrast, Maritain was primarily a thinker and had lived a life of rigorous, Thomist philosophical reflection. For De Gasperi, the historical conditions of post-Fascist Italy and the need to relate to the masses—overcoming the limits of pre-Fascist liberal politics and the Fascist totalitarian organization of society—required the construction of a religiously inspired, not simply Catholic, political party. In De Gasperi's mind, the DC was to become a genuine *partito nazionale*, a national, cross-class people's party or "party of the nation," as he claimed time and again, for example at the November 1947 party congress in Naples:

> It is necessary, dear friends, that we make an effort to project our party on a national plane, becoming a true party of the nation ....I say this because there is

---

[3] Jacques Bénigne Bossuet (1627–1704) was a French theologian and bishop, renowned for his sermons. A court preacher of Louis XIV of France, Bossuet was a strong advocate of political absolutism, the divine rights of kings, and paternalistic monarchy.

no alternative if we wish to stay on a democratic path: a party does not win on the basis of the number of its members, or at least not just on that basis, but rather on the basis of its capacity to interpret the popular will as a whole, mediating and overcoming the conflicts that exist within it. (De Gasperi 1947: 33, quoted by Invernizzi Accetti 2019: 200; see also Scoppola 1977; Malgeri 1997: 95; Masala 2004: 89; Müller 2013a: 85–6)

6.2 The Party of the Nation and the *Risorgimento*

The *partito della nazione* formula did not imply the Christian Democratic party's transformation into what political scientists would coin a catch-all party. Rather, with this formula, De Gasperi brought the DC to fully accept and embrace the national responsibility that derived from the historical circumstances. In De Gasperi's mind, the DC had to identify the destiny of the nation with its own destiny, assuming the duty to defend Italian civilization and identity, democracy, as well as the liberty and independence of the nation against an anti-national, anti-Christian, and foreign party (the Italian Communist Party) that "because of its doctrine... broke the umbilical bond between us, the generation of 1945–1946, and the previous generations of the Christian Italian civilization" (De Gasperi 1956: 1.118, quoted by Gentile 2009: 324).

De Gasperi's strategy to turn Christian Democracy into a "party of the nation," with deep roots in national history, was underpinned by the rereading and reinterpretation of nineteenth-century Italian history and the recovery of the *Risorgimento* tradition. This was not exactly an easy task. The *Risorgimento*, after all, had been a struggle for national liberation and independence that culminated in the establishment of the Kingdom of Italy in 1861, much against the will of the church. The *Risorgimento* was reappropriated at different levels. The overall strategy was to marginalize the historical conflicts between Catholics and the state but also to valorize the first revolutions—or *moti*—of the *Risorgimento*, in which Catholics had been quite active. Opposing both liberal and Fascist readings of the *Risorgimento*, the party had to interpret the major political cultures of the *Risorgimento* (liberalism, Mazzini's republicanism, and democratic Socialism) as derivations of Christianity. Within this historical narrative, De Gasperi and the leading Christian Democrats referred to the insistence on continuity between the first, historical *Risorgimento* and the second *Risorgimento*. The latter was the Resistance, the new struggle for liberation against Fascism and Nazism in the 1943–5 period in which Catholics claimed to have played a fundamental role, although it was also the country's material and moral reconstruction that Catholics wanted to actively pursue in the immediate post-war years. From a Catholic standpoint, in the new Cold War situation, the "second *Risorgimento*" was the rediscovery of liberty and democracy vis-à-vis Soviet Communism.

On June 1, 1948, De Gasperi told the Chamber of Deputies that in post-World War II Italy, thanks to the engagement and commitment also of Catholics, Italy had seen a rebirth of "spiritual energies of faith, liberty, and civilization," which had "made the nation great in its first *Risorgimento*."[4]

Through this narrative, the Catholic party waged its own battle for legitimacy as the leading force in the democratic Republic, at the same time delegitimizing its adversaries, above all the Communists who were characterized as alien to Italian national history and culture. In this sense, the DC's victory on April 18, 1948—the first parliamentary elections of the Republic, when Communists united in a popular front with Socialist and other leftist forces suffered their most decisive defeat—became a symbolic date for national reconstruction as it confirmed and strengthened Italy's "civil and Christian conscience" (Domenidò 1948). April 18 became the symbol of the triumph of Italian civilization as the Italian people had regained contact with the roots of its most genuine idealism and spirituality, thus achieving—as one commentator put it—"the greatest peaceful revolution of modern times" (Francia 1948). Subsequent commentators would go even further. The mythification of April 18 was given universal significance: Europe and the West had found new possibilities for rebirth. The Italian rebirth (or the quasi-revolutionary Catholic-national-religious battle of Italy) was self-consciously turned into a model for the broader battle against Communism that Europe and the free world were waging (Spataro 1949; Taviani 1949; Arata 1951).

6.3 Italy as a Catholic Nation

Interrelated with the rereading of recent national history, the central aspect that characterized De Gasperi's "party of the nation" project was the recovery of the neo-Guelph paradigm of Italy as a "Catholic nation" and the idea that a perennial "Catholic Italy" was eventually re-emerging. This Guelph perspective merged with the representation of Christian Democracy as the manifestation of the soul of such a Catholic nation (Acanfora 2007; Formigoni 2010: 145–64, 2008a: 26–33; Gentile 2009: 37–8).

Guelphism was a broadly defined culture, a perspective, and an attitude that many Christian Democrats shared. Within the several Catholic groups that De Gasperi was able to unite in the Christian Democratic movement in 1942–3, there were also the small Milanese circles of Piero Malvestivi and Gioacchino Malavasi, among the very few Catholics who were explicitly anti-Fascist during the years of the regime. They defined themselves as the Guelph movement,

---

[4] De Gasperi 1985: 373. See also his speech to the Chamber on June 16, 1948, in De Gasperi 1985: 412; see also Gonella 1946a; Sturzo 1946; for further details on these aspects, see Forlenza and Thomassen 2011, 2017, 2020.

whose members wanted to translate the age-old identification between the church and the (Italian) nation into democracy and anti-Fascism. However, in a certain sense, De Gasperi was himself the champion of a distinctive Guelph proposal.

Born and educated in Habsburg Trentino and, therefore, not really implicated in the Roman question, De Gasperi repeatedly talked and wrote about the greatness of the *civiltà italica* (Italic civilization), which had deep roots in the traditional soil of the pre-modern mixture of religion and civilization, Christianity, and the myth of ancient Rome (Monticone 1984; Giovagnoli 1991: 119–23). It was a strong and pervasive, albeit mythical and ideal, cultural vision of nationality. On February 15, 1948, shortly before the first parliamentary elections of April 1948, De Gasperi lambasted—using typically Fascist expressions and clichés and quoting Dante Alighieri, *the Sommo Poeta*, and *Padre della Patria*—the Communists, saying that "we serve and defend the Italic civilization in which Christ is Roman; we defend the Italian people: workers, sailors, discoverers, colonizers, the light of the Universe" (De Gasperi 2008: 1161). Echoing Gioberti, a very central aspect of Christian Democratic political culture was the insistence that Italy could only regain its moral force from *within* and should not simply adopt external models. As De Gasperi put it at the 1947 party congress, where he talked about the "party of the nation":

> We defend the humanist ideal of Greco-Latin civilization that was spiritualized on these shores, [and] renewed and fertilized by Christianity; we defend not foreign interest but our own history, our own vitality, our own culture. (De Gasperi 1947: 47; see also Gonella 1946b)

At the beginning of the twentieth century, in the liberal years under Giolitti, the invocation of a Catholic Italy was—from a Catholic point of view—the right way to oppose the *paese reale* ("real Italy," i.e. the supposedly Catholic masses) to the *paese legale* ("legal Italy," i.e. the liberal law-making class). With Catholic participation in the politics of liberal Italy, World War I, and the Resistance, Catholic national awareness was by now sedimented and taken for granted as a fact of history, as various intellectual bourgeois sectors also admitted. In other words, De Gasperi's appeal for a Catholic Italy was not simply a defensive reaction against the old anti-Catholic accusation of not being part of the nation—or being its enemy. It reflected, instead, the need to find a new ground on which a new national identity, different from the aggressive proposal of Fascism but also pre-Fascist nationalism and the more radical proposals of anti-Fascism, could be founded.

Crucially, as the Italian historians Paolo Acanfora (2013) and Guido Formigoni (1996, 2010: 160–4) have insightfully highlighted, the rediscovery of the myth of a (Catholic) nation did not clash with De Gasperi's choices in international Cold War politics. Quite the opposite: in De Gasperi's mind, by siding with the West, the Atlantic Alliance, and the process of European integration, in which the

Italian Christian Democracy and De Gasperi himself—together with other European Christian Democrats—played a foundational role (Kaiser 2007; Forlenza 2017a see also Preda 2004), the Catholicity of Italy would not lose its originality and function. For De Gasperi, the Roman and Christian foundations of Catholic Italy were indeed the foundational, fundamental, and primigenial characters of Western (Occidental) civilization; Italian (Catholic) identity thus inserted itself in the wider concept of the West (Occident). In fact, because of this wider context, De Gasperi constantly thought and said that Italy must enter into the new Western bloc not in a marginal position but, instead, as a central actor, fully legitimized in this role. Italy should have ample autonomy and room for maneuvering in its traditional role as a mediator (between East and West, North and South, Europe and the Mediterranean) and a creative agent of civilization. Italy could significantly contribute to the creation of a supranational community drawing on its Christian, Roman, and hence profoundly Italian civilization. De Gasperi already made such an ideological argument in public in 1946, in the context of the discussion of the Peace Treaty, when Italy was in a difficult situation; he thus asked the Allied forces to change the course they had taken in the first draft of the treaty and soften the attitude toward Italy, which seemed punitive. Inaugurating the Congress of the Catholic Graduates and University Students in Rome, De Gasperi said that during the war, the great powers had appealed to "Christianity against the politics of force." He added:

> Do not judge a people by fifteen minutes of madness, but by the centuries of fruitful and glorious history. Italy is not simply a political organization: Italy is a civilization, indeed, a current of civilizations that merged with Christianity and has spread across the world.[5]

On May 15, 1949, a few weeks after Italy signed out of the NATO Treaty (April 4, 1949), De Gasperi gave a speech in which he commemorated the *Rerum novarum* and specifically evoked a Catholic and altogether Italian path toward Atlanticism: "If we have joined a security pact, this was not out of servility, foreign ideals, or interests, but to introduce what comes from our civilization, what radiates from our civilization, into this peace alliance" (De Gasperi 1956: 1.235). The same approach sustained De Gasperi's commitment to the ambitious project of the European Community of Defense, which should have been a super-national organism with specific political functions and the expression of a cultural and identitarian value of Europe, culminating in the Treaty of Rome (1957).

Many Christian Democrats did not entirely endorse the participation in the Atlantic pact and other international choices that De Gasperi made. Within the

---

[5] As reported by the article "I congressi dei laureati e degli studenti universitari di azione cattolica inaugurati dalla fervida parola di Alcide de Gasperi" in "L'Osservatore romano," January 5, 1946; see also Formigoni 2008a: 27–8.

DC, there were certainly diverging and contrasting views (Vezzosi 1986; Capperucci 2003, 2004). For example, leftist sectors (*correnti*) within the party advanced different perspectives and alternative ways to act in international politics. For some Christian Democrats, Italy had to work toward détente and pacification between blocs to be achieved not through military means but in the name of neutrality, based on people's collaboration and willingness to build peace. Some attitudes and tendencies were based on different motivations: religious, humanitarian, pacifist, and anti-American motivations based on a supposedly anti-Christian nature of the socioeconomic model of American capitalism. For example, men like Giovanni Gronchi remained anchored in Italy's Mediterranean and Latin identity, and then in a European "third way" freed from any military pacts. Others, such as Dossetti (see also Chapter 7), held supranational and identitarian views not too dissimilar from De Gasperi's but certainly based on different diplomatic and political methods and ideological approaches. Within his party's majority, De Gasperi had to deal with the less convinced stance of Mario Scelba and Giuseppe Pella, tied to a strong anti-Communist position and a more traditional way of interpreting nationalism. De Gasperi was, instead, a realist and quite a pragmatic politician. He knew that the Atlantic choice and Italy's anchorage in the Western European world would be a deterrent to the Soviet and Communist threat—which for Italy was an internal as well as an external threat (Forlenza 2017b)—but also a real necessity for Italy to avoid being trapped, without protection, between the opposing blocs.

Notwithstanding the resistance and opposition within his own party and the difficult situations faced at the level of international politics, De Gasperi was an important figure in the creation of a "new political identity" (Acanfora 2013: 245) for large sectors of Italian society. Despite the opposition of the Partito Comunista Italiano (PCI, Italian Communist Party), De Gasperi and the party leadership around him managed to convey an image of the DC as the only political subject able to embody the original and fundamental character of the Italian nation, hence as the only party able to defend and protect its identity.

Christian Democrats, through the "party of the nation" project, presented themselves as Catholics, Italians, and democrats. This threefold identification made the indissoluble link between Italianness and Catholicity manifest, anchoring democracy within it.

6.4 The Catholic Nation Seen from the Vatican's Perspective

In the context of post-Fascist Italy, there were different visions of what a Catholic Italy should be or look like, visions that did not comply with De Gasperi's approach and at times frontally opposed it. The church of Pius XII had reinforced its role in Italian politics and society through its wartime actions and the spiritual resource of religious beliefs in times of crisis (see Chapter 5). However, the church expressed a different and more conservative approach to the idea of Italy as a Catholic nation, placing much less emphasis on the democratic dimension. An important background of the teaching of Pius XII was the vision of a Catholic *Reconquista* of society. Such a *Reconquista* was based fundamentally on an "ideology of Christianity" (Menozzi 1993: 165–7; Riccardi 1998; Formigoni 2010: 153–6) that was distant from the kind of political modernity that Christian Democrats were articulating in the post-war years. In other words, a large sector of the Vatican still cherished the idea of an "integralist" kind of democracy, diametrically opposed to the integral democracy that Christian Democrats, inspired by Maritain, were conceptualizing and building. After all, at the end of World War II, the church continued to condemn modernity. Integralism, the form that Catholic fundamentalism adopted to fend off the challenge of nationalism, secularization, and political modernity as defined by the modernizing nation-states ever since Pius IX's *Syllabus*, was still in evidence during the pontificate of Pius XII. While the defeat of Fascism, the post-war triumph of democracy, and the threat of Soviet Communism made the church's confrontation with the modern world less and less plausible, the official doctrines of the church still seemed to distance themselves from social and political developments. While it is true that, as we have seen in Chapter 5, Pius XII—in two famous Christmas addresses (1942 and 1944)—had expressed a favorable predisposition and an opening toward the values of democracy and modernity during the war, the pope warned of possible abuses even when he praised democracy. In 1950, making an implicit reference to heated theological and political debates in France, the pope published the encyclical letter *Humani generis* in which he reprimanded the fact that "some [Catholic teachers]...desirous of novelty, and fearing to be considered ignorant of recent scientific findings, tend to withdraw from the sacred Teaching Authority," with the risk of "departing from revealed truth" and "drawing others along with them into error" (see Daly 1985: 774).

In the Italian context, the Vatican's version of a "Catholic Italy" reinforced the inclination toward what has been defined as "clerical and Catholic exclusivism" (Miccoli 1994: 580). Such Catholic and clerical "exclusivism" was hardly compatible with the democratic climate of the post-war era. The Constitution was the first battleground on which different visions of "Catholic Italy" came to confront each other: one of the Vatican and the other of Christian Democracy. The Vatican, the hierarchy, and many conservative sectors of the Catholic world thought that the time was ripe for the implementation of a Christian Constitution, which should have as its crucial components the Lateran Pact, and a stringent Christian vision of the school and the family (Casella 1987; Sale 2008). A few days before the opening of the Constituent Assembly, De Gasperi met the Apostolic Nuncio Borgongini Duca. Their discussion is revelatory of what they thought of a "religion of the state" and the more general relationship between politics and religion in a modern democracy. Giving proof of a sense of political realism necessary to act politically in the context of a pluralist democracy, De Gasperi said that "it is impossible to fully obtain what the Church demands; one cannot but admit freedom of thought, freedom of conscience, freedom of religion." Borgongini replied: "[W]e cannot forget that true religion must reject... freedom of error, freedom to deny absolute truths" (quoted in Sale 2005: 41; Formigoni 2010: 152).

The Vatican's battle for the implementation of a Christian Constitution was attuned and incorporated thanks to the clever mediation and cautious political moves of Dossetti and his friends, the group of the so-called *professorini* who, as we will see in the following chapter, played a crucial role in the writing of the Constitution. The *professorini* managed to present the ideological and cultural agreement on the personalist and communitarian platform of the Constitution's first section as "substantially" Christian. Giorgio La Pira, one of the Dossettian *professorini*, could thus write in the party's organ *Il Popolo* that the Italian Constitution was based on the "organic conception inherent to Catholic sociology" (quoted in Pombeni 1995: 93). The Lateran Pact was included in the new Constitution thanks also to the Communists' agreement. Even if the Constitution did not include direct confessional arrangements and measures, it could be seen as accommodating the hopes and expectations of conservative sectors of the Catholic world.

In the following years, the Vatican continued its battle for a Catholic Italy with even more emphasis. For the Jesuits of *La Civiltà Cattolica*, a resurrected Catholic Italy must make itself manifest in the historical context of the post-World War II era (Sani 2004). As the Jesuit Riccardo Lombardi wrote in 1947, now was the time to implement a "grandiose Christian social experiment," an attractive example for all nations to follow. This was conceived as an "eternal Italian mission" that, Lombardi claimed, must inspire a strong and autonomous Italian action, offering a genuine alternative to the bloc politics in the emerging Cold War crisis "in the name of Christ." This Catholic alternative was conceived as a religious, international "third way" that should give Italy a new role, rooted in its history and essentially Christian nature. The confessional aspect and religious exclusivism were strong elements in this vision. Indirectly quoting Gioberti, Lombardi highlighted that in the current historical moment, "to be a good Italian means to be a Catholic; to be anti-Catholic means to betray the *Patria*" (quoted in Formigoni 2008a: 30–1).

The anti-modern sectors of the church relaunched Guelphism and the vision of a Catholic Italy in a very "integralist" way, especially before and after the elections of April 1948. In a leaflet for the activists of the *Comitati Civici* (Civic Committees), a Catholic grassroots movement created to bring as many Catholics as possible to vote for the Christian party and against anti-Christian parties (i.e. the PCI), it was claimed that the "dawn of a new civilization" linked to the " vitality of Christianity" was soon to come and that this would ensure Italy's recovery from the political, socioeconomic, and military "great depression" into which the country had plunged. After all, Italy possessed a "unique" role and location in the world, which was its "spiritual primacy" over the entire world.[6]

Many Catholics—that is, ample sectors of Catholic Action, the *Comitati Civici*, and its leader Luigi Gedda, the Jesuits of *La Civiltà Cattolica*, the Vatican, and most of the hierarchy—thought that the result of the elections was the manifestation of an "officially Christian" Italy (see Formigoni 2010: 153). This was, in many ways, a self-deception. For these sectors, though, 1948 appeared as the end of a historical cycle that had begun with the earlier experience of the intransigent Catholic movement and now culminated with the healing of the fracture between different ideas of the nation through the definitive triumph of "Catholic Italy." In his argument against Communism, Gedda time and again sustained that "there is no *Patria* without faith, there is no Italy without a Catholic religion." The very same motto of the *Comitati Civici* pro aris and foci might better be translated as "for the altar and for the *Patria*" (Gedda 1951: 15–16; see also Formigoni 2010: 155–6).

This inward-looking and reductive vision cultivated a reassuring image of Italy as naturally Catholic, in a problematic and self-referential manner. It prevented the Vatican from understanding how Italian society was changing, and it was precisely such an approach that kept Italian Catholicism from rethinking the religious condition of a country whose society was undergoing a process of secularization. Cherishing the myth of a Catholic Italy, Catholicism failed to take seriously the reduction of the Catholic world to a sociologically circumscribed— although still solid—reality. While the Catholic hierarchy and the laity were inclined to a form of pastoralism based on the conservation of faith and directed against the enemy of faith and the nation (i.e. the Communists), Italians were progressively abandoning traditional religious behavior and principles (on these aspects see Formigoni 2008a: 32–3).

6.5 The Church and Christian Democracy: Under the Sign of the Cross?

The enthusiastic and triumphalist Guelph proposal was much more extreme than that of De Gasperi, which remained firmly rooted in democratic grounds. Yet, time and again, it tried to influence Christian Democracy and restrict the space of constitutional democracy. The Vatican and the more conservative and reactionary circles of Italian Catholicism continued to seek unofficial influence within the DC. For example, it put pressure on Christian Democracy to limit the freedom

---

[6] See *Tutti alle urne! Corso propagandisti C.[omitati] C.[ivici] D.[iocesani]* (1948), ed. Comitato Civico Nazionale (Rome), p. 31.

of the press, clearly aiming to target the anticlerical press and the supposed manifestation of "errors" against the only possible truth: the Catholic truth.

In fact, in the immediate post-war years, Christian Democracy was not the Vatican's first choice (what follows is based on Forlenza 2017b: 223–5, 233–5). Some sectors of Catholicism supported the idea of a Catholic state or a clerical regime based on the model of Franco's Spain. These sectors openly opposed collaboration with parties of different political and ideological backgrounds within the frame of a secular and pluralist state. Although the church guided by Pius XII had accepted democracy, it had not fully changed its attitude toward it and remained hesitant about its implementation. Moreover, at the end of the war, only a small section of the hierarchy favored the commitment of Catholics to the nascent Christian Democracy. Unsurprisingly, the Vatican Catholics were uncertain about, if not frankly opposed to, the insertion of Catholicism into a state that was perceived as still hostile to the church, despite the Concordat of 1929 and Catholic participation in society after the unification.

Until 1946–7, the Vatican primarily encouraged Catholics to vote against Communists. Additionally, it encouraged Italians to vote for candidates and parties respectful of the Divine Law, religion, and the rights of the church. There was no clear directive to vote in favor of Christian Democracy.[7] Pius XII and the church hierarchy wished for a clerical, conservative, authoritarian regime like that of Franco or Salazar, with or without the support of a Catholic party. Despite the claim of the church's neutrality in institutional matters, bishops as well as the majority of Catholics from the South were in favor of the monarchy when the institutional referendum was held. The leadership of the DC, however, was in favor of the Republic. In the end, the DC gave its electorate freedom of vote, at the same time underscoring that the party had the right to express its republican leaning (on this see Traniello 1998: 304–31). The Vatican abhorred the DC's governmental collaboration with the Communists and Socialists, a continuation of the politics of national solidarity that had started in the context of the anti-Fascist struggle during the war, which lasted until May 1947. Other sectors of Italian public opinion were equally critical of De Gasperi's continuation of the politics of national collaboration. This became evident during local elections, when the electorate of the southern provinces and regions voted for right-wing parties or the Fronte dell'Uomo Qualunque, or when they boycotted the poll, punishing the DC's governmental collaboration with the PCI (Setta 1995; Forlenza 2008: 50–66). The Undersecretary of State Giovambattista Montini (the future Paul VI) made many efforts to persuade the pope to accept the DC as "the" Catholic party, but Pius XII mistrusted Christian party politics. What mattered was Christian action.

---

[7] However, provincial police reports highlighted the fact that Catholics leaned toward the DC especially when the party's local representatives assumed firm anti-communist positions; see ACS, MI, Atti di Gabinetto, 1944–6, b. 164, f. 15377 (report from Puglia, August 1, 1945).

In the end, pluralism was still a problem for an institution with universalist aspirations. The fear was that the Catholic faith would be reduced to one political faction among others and ceased to be the moral glue that kept society together (see also Scoppola 1997: 102–18, 239–63; Pollard 2008: 111–13).

After the elections of 1948, hardcore Catholics still believed that a neo-Guelph solution was a real possibility: the transformation of the secular state guided by a Catholic party within the wider democratic and pluralist frame ensured by the Constitution, in a confessional Catholic state. In the following years, the church did not abandon such a "Spanish" plan for Italy. It promoted a "sacred union" between the DC, the monarchists, and the neo-Fascists to form a common anti-Communist front for the 1952 local election in Rome, where the possibility of a Communist victory was anything but remote. Furthermore, Sturzo, who a few years earlier had said that he could only obey the Vatican (Sturzo 1959), was involved in the creation of a large anti-Communist front in Rome. The project was intended as the first step in the transformation of the entire national political landscape, tilting the DC's politics to the right and creating a Francoist Italy (Riccardi 1983, 2003; Gedda 1998: 154–5; D'Angelo 2002; Forlenza 2002: 520–1, 2008: 106–7). Between the end of the 1940s and the beginning of the 1950s, De Gasperi also received Catholic pressures to outlaw the Communists. In this regard, conservative Catholics formed a common front with Washington; time and again, the Americans asked De Gasperi to outlaw the PCI, especially after the arrest of the French Communist leader Jacques Duclos.[8]

Nonetheless, the DC never became the secular arm of the church and De Gasperi resisted the Vatican's plan, for example by rejecting the creation of an anti-Communist front that included the DC, the monarchists, and neo-Fascists at the election in Rome in 1952. It is certainly true that the party took advantage of one of the church's organizational resources, namely its reputation, enhanced by its role during the war, which proved crucial for the DC's electoral triumphs. Also, it was sometimes difficult to distinguish the anti-Communism of the church from that of the DC and, likewise, the church's vision of Catholic Italy from that of the DC. This was especially the case on the occasion of the election of 1948, when the entire Catholic front presented the challenge in strictly binary terms, as a holy crusade: religion or atheism, church or anti-church, good or evil, civilization or barbarism. As the pope repeated in St. Peter's Square two weeks before the vote, on Easter Day, "either with or against Christ" (see Forlenza 2020).

---

[8] Harry S. Truman Presidential Library, Independence, Mo., Staff Member and Office File, Psychological Strategy Board File, b. 11, fo. 091.4: "French and Italian Elections," July 6, 1951; National Archives, Washington, DC, General Record, 59, 62D333, b. 1, PSB D-15: "Remarks by the Department of State Member of the Psychological Strategy Board on the Psychological Strategy Plan for Reduction of Communist Power in Italy," February 2, 1952; "Analysis of the Power of the Communist Parties of France and Italy and of Measures to Counter Them," CIA report, September 15, 1951, available at: https://www.cia.gov/readingroom/document/cia-rdp80r01731r003200020013-5 (last accessed October 18, 2023).

Yet, the DC was able to distinguish itself from the church. This was one of the most important achievements of De Gasperi's political action. As Sturzo's PPI, the DC was not simply a Catholic party but a party of Catholics. Sturzo never sought the political unity of Catholics, which was a paramount objective of De Gasperi. In his idea of the relationship between faith and politics, reference to Christianity always remained a moral and individual fact, while politics was the field in which the autonomy of the believer could and should be expressed and defined: a lay vision of politics. A much easier reconciliation between faith and politics was possible in post-World War II Italy because the Roman question had finally been resolved. This was perhaps the most important discontinuity between the PPI and the DC, and between Sturzo and De Gasperi. Sturzo had to openly declare the PPI's non-confessional nature. De Gasperi did not need to make any such declaration. He could simply refer to Christianity and Catholicism from an ideological standpoint, choosing the Vatican as the party's interlocutor without putting its political allegiance to the secular state under strain. The PPI had been a *partito fra cattolici* ("a party among Catholics"); the DC overcame this by building a *partito dei cattolici* ("a party for Catholics"; on this see Formigoni 2008a: 47–9; Capperucci 2009: 447–9), with the declared aim of representing the political unity of Catholics. Of course, not all Catholics voted for the DC. Most voters to both the left (including the PCI) and the right of the political spectrum were also Catholic, at least in a nominal sense. However, the DC did manage to represent itself as the party that served as a platform to collect, elaborate, and formulate the demands and policies of Catholics. In such a party, the political program was a flexible tool, adaptable to the external situation. The party could build its identity with reference to Christianity and base its unity on "Catholic discipline" but without any confessionalization project or claims toward a general Christianization of society. Christian inspiration and secular political action could seem a contradiction in terms, but all this was framed in a general conception of the state and the relationship between party and state, which was perhaps the most distinctive aspect of De Gasperi's politics.

6.6 Catholic Anti-Communism and Christian Democratic Anti-Communism

There was a profound difference between Catholic anti-Communism and Christian Democratic anti-Communism. The former was rooted in the church's struggle against modernity; the latter was, instead, amalgamated with liberal and democratic values. De Gasperi and other Christian Democrats wanted liberty, in the first instance, and were thus against totalitarianism, be it from the Left or the Right. For De Gasperi and other Catholic politicians, anti-totalitarianism was much more than an abstract principle; it emerged as a marker of certainty that could direct the democratic experience without simply reverting to a liberal order, which had proven itself defenseless against totalitarian regimes. After their infatuation with Fascism in the 1930s, and as a result of their experience of the war and the political and existential uncertainty it had entailed, De Gasperi and his collaborators began a search for a Catholic response to the problem of modern mass politics. This search ended with the recognition that, to resist pagan totalitarianism, democracy had to rest on Christian and spiritual foundations.

Hence, more than a mere political or electoral tactic (see Barbanti 1988), De Gasperi's anti-Communism was a real belief and a personal commitment, shaped by cultural and existential concerns. Atheist Communism and Nazi or Fascist paganism did not belong to a *Weltanschauung* that situated Christianity at the origins of European civilization.[9] Collaboration with Communists had thus been a "necessity of public safety," as De Gasperi put it in October 1944 (De Gasperi 1956: 1.24), or "a forced cohabitation" (quoted in Forlenza 2017b: 225) as one of his collaborators said in November 1946. After 1947, and prior to the first parliamentary elections of April 1948, the tension between Communists and Catholics became less radical. The DC fully embodied the political unity of Catholics, including their anti-Communism; it would end up giving political shape and substance to the instinctive anti-Communism of large and barely politicized sectors of Italian society, channeling potentially anti-democratic views into fragile but effective democratic politics.

De Gasperi's opposition to any harsh measure against the PCI was also the consequence of a simple consideration: How could one go about presenting Communists as alien to Italy? The Communists were a constituent part of Italy's body politic. They had collaborated with Catholics in the anti-Fascist struggle, the transition to democracy, and the writing of the Constitution. At the bottom of the Italian Constitution, still in force today, there is the signature of a Communist and president of the Constituent Assembly, Umberto Terracini. Communists were, in short, a legitimate component of the republican democratic space. Eight million Italians cast their votes in favor of the Popular Front in 1948. By the end of the 1940s, one out of three Italians was a Communist—one out of two in the regions of central Italy. Italy in the post-war period has often been described as a divided nation, with Catholics and Communists pitted against each other from the political propaganda at the national level to village life at the local level. While there is certainly a kernel of truth in this view, in reality, and especially at the local level, the situation was more complex and often more a case of interweaving realities than separate identities. Catholic-Communist families (usually divided along generational and gender lines) were the norm rather than the exception in post-war Italy. People often reconciled Catholic religious practices and values with communist militancy. A specific "Communist" lifestyle, as opposed to a specific

---

[9] On De Gasperi's anti-Communism as a "philosophy" and "ideology" rather than a mere tactic, see Del Noce 1957; Scoppola 1977; Pertici 2003: 304–13.

"Catholic" lifestyle, did not exist; instead, Communists and Catholics shared "Italian" forms of everyday conduct, traditions, morals, prejudices, and even worldviews rooted in the same set of religious values. In contrast to the United States, where domestic Communism could be cast as alien and un-American, in the Italian situation, a thorough demonization was unsustainable.

For this reason, De Gasperi and the DC, while emphasizing anti-Communism to maintain the unity of Catholics and attract non-Catholic voters concerned about the Communist threat, resisted the Vatican's authoritarian plan. This is also why De Gasperi refused the American project to outlaw the PCI, which would have labeled the Communists as unpatriotic Italians. With the Korean War marking the peak of the Cold War, the DC government engaged in repressive anti-Communist measures in line with De Gasperi's idea of "a strong state" and a "protected democracy." Yet, the international Cold War and the Vatican's reactionary plot had a limited impact on the DC. De Gasperi never renounced the anti-Fascist principles enshrined in the Constitution, not even in the name of anti-Communism. As he explained to the Americans, democracy was a young and delicate flower in Italy. To "go outside the Constitution [and] suppress the Communists" could lead to "the destruction of democracy" (quoted in Brogi 2011: 153–4; see also Del Pero 2001: 207–95). Communism could not be a reason for depriving citizens of their civil rights; rather, the upholding of democratic rights was a litmus test for Italian democracy. For De Gasperi, Communists had to be challenged in the parliament, and in local politics, with ideas and reformist policies. Catholic Italy had to be a democratic and pluralist Italy.

De Gasperi frontally and skillfully rejected the pressure of large sectors of Catholicism but also other conservative forces that wished for a Catholic repositioning in a vast moderate front, cemented by and imbued with pervasive anti-Communism. De Gasperi, instead, forced the DC to further its collaboration with other "centrist" parties (*partiti laici di centro*): the Social Democrats, the republicans (members of the Italian Republican Party), and the liberals. He resisted the doubts of Dossetti and his followers, among others, who saw in the alliance with the centrist parties a serious hindrance to the development of proper Christian and evangelical politics—a politics that had as its first objective what La Pira famously defined the "expectations of poor people." A clever reader of the real historical contingencies, De Gasperi knew that Italy was a fragile sociopolitical and economic system and that it was crucial to mediate the interests and expectations of many powerful stakeholders, while reconciling a country that had been devastated by a traumatic civil war.

6.7 The Party of the Nation: Interclassism and Centrism

De Gasperi's politics of moderation and mediation implied the duty and mission to bring together Italian citizens from all social classes (*interclassismo*) in the name of the material and spiritual reconstruction of the nation after the disaster of war and Fascism. For De Gasperi and other Christian Democrats, "interclassism" was not simply an electoral tactic: as Moro wrote in 1946, it was the result of a "deep spiritual intuition" (Moro 1982a: 266–7).

For De Gasperi, as a "party of the nation," the DC should not govern alone; it constantly had to seek the collaboration of other forces, thus taking "interclassism" to the political and institutional level and ensuring real pluralism. In De Gasperi's understanding, "interclassism" and pluralism involved not only the socioeconomic dimension but also the politico-institutional level. His "party of the nation," based on the model of pluri-confessionalism of the German CDU, was meant to ensure political and cultural pluralism, enabling a democratic cohabitation between Italians. A few days before his death, he wrote to his successor Amintore Fanfani that, at the time, the DC "became…an Italian party," managing to heal the conflicts that had historically ridden Italy (De Gasperi 1974: 1.334). At the fourth congress of the DC in 1952, he said:

> Ours is the party of the nation and we must therefore adopt an all-encompassing action, trying to subordinate all interests to that of the community and, especially, directing them to a social justice intervention. This means…interclassism. (De Gasperi 2009: 1757)

De Gasperi's political project was based on the idea of consensual democracy. De Gasperi was not afraid of making clear-cut choices, formulating precise objectives, or taking drastic decisions. While his priority was to collaborate with other parties, he was also convinced that the most important party—the "party of the nation"—must take responsibility for the construction of a parliamentary majority, and thus for the precise targeting of the policies to be implemented.

The case of 1947, which is rightly considered the beginning of *centrismo* (the overcoming of the historical division with non-Catholic forces and the political line that derived from such an alliance), is most significant in this respect. Since 1944, the DC had governed with the PCI and the PSI in the so-called *tripartito* ("three-party alliance"), which had guaranteed a quite smooth recovery of the country, all things considered and given the dramatic historical events that occurred in the transition from Fascism to democracy and from the monarchy to the Republic: the institutional referendum of June 1946, the first local elections (March–April 1946), the return to democratic life, and the country's first material reconstructions. However, in May 1947, the Communists and Socialists were expelled from the government. There were many reasons for this political move. A few weeks before this decision, De Gasperi decided to include the liberal economist and thinker Luigi Einaudi—the first president of the Italian Republic—in his cabinet. Einaudi's line of political economy was based on the containment of public expenses, monetary stability, control over credit, and measures against inflation. This was an opening to the so-called *quarto partito* ("fourth party"), the expression De Gasperi used to indicate the productive classes and the economic and financial stakeholders. It was impossible to govern while ignoring such an important sector of society. De Gasperi was put under strain. On one hand, important sectors wanted to replace him with a representative of the old, pre-Fascist liberal classes; others within the party, such as the leader of the "social" wing, Gronchi, considered his decision a deviation from the politics that the DC had to pursue in post-war Italy and wanted him to abandon office and go into opposition. De Gasperi resisted; he did not want to leave the nation to the old elites. He wanted its political direction to remain in the hands of a mass party, and this had to be the DC. However, it was necessary to reassure the productive forces and form an alliance with them for the reconstruction of the country.

The Einaudi policy was inevitably a problem for the Socialists and Communists. Their popular bases would undoubtedly oppose privatization and the sacrifices imposed by his line of action. In light of this, the breaking up of the three mass parties was probably inevitable. For decades, scholars, commentators, and political opponents of the DC have considered the disbandment of the "three-party" government a direct consequence of De Gasperi's visit to Washington at the beginning of 1947, and therefore as a top-down consequence of the Cold War. Building on new archival documents, more recent scholarship has argued—without undermining the actions of international powers—that the crisis was more a product of the combination of international and national factors. While the international Cold War was creating new conditions for the transformation of the domestic political struggle, the crisis was nevertheless the consequence of internal socioeconomic and financial issues that convinced De Gasperi to change direction (Formigoni 2003; see also Giovagnoli 1996: 42–3; Mistry 2014: 76–94). Still, at the time, the crisis was not perceived as a definitive and irreconcilable rupture; that would only become the case with the full onset of the Cold War in the summer of 1947, with the implementation of the Marshall Plan and the Truman doctrine. In May 1947, the Communists and Socialists still thought that their collaboration with the DC could resume or at least remain on the horizon.

This was indeed De Gasperi's political masterpiece: he made the DC central in the Italian political system through "centrist" politics. Thus, on one hand, the DC increased its presence and participation in the institutions of the new post-Fascist and democratic state; on the other hand, it sought to share the responsibility with the other parties even when the DC reached its main triumph. For example, after the first parliamentary election of April 1948, De Gasperi imposed his choice of a non-Catholic president of the Republic. After the candidacy of the republican Carlo Sforza was withdrawn, the parliament elected Einaudi, who then became the arbiter of Italian political life while his policies were continued by his successor Giuseppe Pella.

Centrismo continued to inspire De Gasperi's governmental action from 1947 to 1953. *Centrismo* was not simply anti-Communism, nor—as Togliatti once famously said—a "capitalistic restauration" that united the Vatican, the US, and Christian Democracy. In reality, with the beginning of an alliance between popular classes and the productive sectors, guided by Catholics, the crisis of 1947 became—for the DC—the premise of a politics of "interclassist" mediation, which opened the way for the possibility to intervene in the redistribution of wealth and the promotion of social reforms (as we will see in Chapter 8). Obviously, after the summer of 1947 and even more so after April 1948, *centrismo* did not lose its initial objectives but increasingly linked such objectives, in the Cold War context, to anti-Communism.

The first republican legislature of 1948–53 was not only a period of hard-line approaches to the intense social conflicts that swept across the country. The Minister of the Interior Mario Scelba formed rapid-response police units (*celere*) to crush, often with violence, protests and unrest by peasants, workers, Communist oppositions, and unions. Workers' demonstrations in the towns and cities of the North and land occupations by peasants in the South were often met with uncompromising toughness by the police. On January 9, 1950, the police famously opened fire during a workers' demonstration, killing six workers, whereas two hundred people were wounded. Yet, this was only a part of the story. Between 1948 and 1953, the governments guided by De Gasperi reconciled the Einaudi (and then Pella) policy—a quasi-liberal approach based on the containment of expenses and monetary stability—with crucial social reforms that were being introduced. To this end, De Gasperi followed different political directions, which depended on the objective he wanted to achieve, while always remaining firmly anchored to *centrismo*. For example, in order to implement the agrarian reform and the Cassa per il Mezzogiorno, in 1951, De Gasperi kept the liberals out of office, collaborating with the republicans and Social Democrats; for other policies, he would seek collaboration elsewhere, including with the liberals.

With the development of *centrismo*, De Gasperi and the DC laid the foundations and the premises for the rapid development of the entire country. The economic reconstruction was relatively fast, even though it also created deep social tensions and did not solve the historical dysfunctions of Italian society and economy. The "southern question," the socioeconomic and cultural rift between the northern productive areas and the southern much poorer regions where the economy struggled to take off, anything but disappeared. Yet, the foundations for the economic miracle of the 1950s and 1960s were laid. The "party of the nation" became "the Italian party," as the historian Agostino Giovagnoli wrote: a party able to express the demands and the needs of many and different social and geographical areas, achieving the most comprehensive and effective mediation in a country marked by political, social, and cultural differences and divisions (Giovagnoli 1996; see also Pombeni, Formigoni, and Vecchio 2023). The politics launched by De Gasperi also inspired his successors Fanfani and Moro, who tried to advance the potentialities implicit in the centrist line, seeking collaborations with other forces and eventually including them in the governmental area: the Socialists in the 1960s and the Communists in the 1970s. In fact, post-war Italy was held together by a collaborative effort across the political divide, rooted in anti-Fascism and in the Constitution that took effect on January 1, 1948. The contribution of Catholics to this fundamental document, as we will see in the next chapter, was immense.

7

Instituting Catholic Modernity

The Writing of the Italian Constitution

The writing of the Constitution in the immediate aftermath of World War II compromised the viewpoints of republican Italy's founding fathers, that is, politicians and intellectuals with different ideological and cultural backgrounds: from Catholicism to Socialism, from liberalism to Communism. It thus fostered a compromise between the composite segments of the Italian population that had voted the members of the Constituent Assembly on June 2, 1946, the very same day the Republic was born. This chapter discusses the momentous turn in Italian politics that the writing of the Constitution signaled. Approaching the Italian constitution as a "rite of passage" and as a "performative utterance," we wish to foreground one aspect of the Constitution: the specific way in which the Italian citizen became symbolically "coded" as a "person" and not as an "individual," inspired by Catholic principles. Our focus then is not so much the legal dimension of citizenship, or the social consequences of the formulations that were eventually adopted; what we primarily wish to understand is the underlying semantics and the wider symbolic universe that came to underpin those legal dimensions, trying to give Italy not only an institutional skeleton but also a heart and spirit. The Constitution was indeed also linked to a certain kind of "political spirituality," as we have argued throughout.

Our argument rests on the assumption that what is at stake in the writing of a constitution is indeed the grounding of political legitimacy in philosophical anthropology. As Eric Voegelin famously argued in his dispute with Hans Kelsen, probably the world's most famous constitutionalist ever, the political language adopted in constitutional writing must be understood as symbols of ideological self-interpretation. In *The Authoritarian State* (1936), Voegelin fundamentally accused Kelsen of ignoring the content of human life in his approach to politics, thus disregarding the necessary sociological and anthropological foundations of any political theory (Voegelin 1999; on the Voegelin–Kelsen dispute see Thomassen 2014b; see also Thomassen 2012b).

It must be remembered that the Italian Constitution was written in a truly "empty place of power," with no foregone conclusions, in a historical figuration of

Italy's Christian Democracy: The Catholic Encounter with Political Modernity. Rosario Forlenza and Bjørn Thomassen, Oxford University Press. © Rosario Forlenza and Bjørn Thomassen 2024. DOI: 10.1093/oso/9780198859864.003.0008

radical contingency.[1] Liberal, pre-Fascist constitutional traditions were potentially available but could not meet the challenges faced. The Constituent Assembly elaborated the final document under a cloud of uncertainty. As such, its members were forced to focus on the (imagined) future more than on present aims and objectives, opening the ground for a virtuous and vital compromise across political, ideological, and philosophical divides.[2] Unlike Japan and—albeit to a lesser extent—West Germany, the Anglo-American allies did not join the constitutional process. The future was up for grabs.

The Italian Constitution must be seen as a significant example of the wider phenomenon of the Catholic "appropriation of modernity" and multiple paths toward modernity (Eisenstadt 2000; see also Roundtable 2011). At the end of World War II, a reliable ideological and cultural body, or theoretical essence, had to be formulated against the background of Fascism to mark the break and discontinuity with the past. From a Catholic perspective, this body had to appear authentically universal, without succumbing to the church's dogma, yet present itself as particularly Italian. In this way, Christian Democrats formulated a profusion of ideas that were conducive to the adaptation of Italian Catholicism to the standards of a modern democracy and a fairly advanced welfare state. We will focus on a group of Catholic politicians and intellectuals guided by Giuseppe Dossetti, who sat as a Christian Democratic representative on the so-called *commissione dei 75* ("commission of the 75") and was selected among the members of the Constituent Assembly, elected on June 2, 1946, which was assigned the task of drafting the constitutional texts. We will also describe the contrasts between Dossetti and his followers (the *dossettiani*), on one hand, and De Gasperi and the party's leadership, on the other hand.

7.1 Post-War Deliberations and the Role of the *Dossettiani*

Catholic debates on the new constitutional architecture of post-Fascist Italy started while World War II was still on, and even before Mussolini's fall from power on July 24–5, 1943. From 18 to 24 July 1943, members of the *Movimento Laureati* (see Chapter 4) and exponents of the *Istituto Cattolico di Attività Sociali* ("Catholic Institute of Social Activities") met at Camaldoli, on the Apennines, to articulate and formulate a Catholic proposal to build a new social, political, and institutional order at the end of the war; this was then outlined in the

---

[1] On the concept of the "empty place of power" as constitutive of modern democracy, see Lefort 1986: 28; Forlenza 2019b.

[2] Time and again, scholars and observers have defined the 1948 charter as the result of a "constitutional compromise"; see Pombeni 1995: 103–43.

Camaldoli Code (see Chapter 5). Catholic debates on the new Constitution continued with even more energy in the months following the end of the war (R. Moro 1979b; Casella 1987; Pombeni 2006; 2010). For example, the nineteenth "social week of Italian Catholics," held in Florence in October 1945, dealt directly with the "Constitution and Constituent Assembly" (Costituzione e Costituente 1946).

A group of left-leaning Christian Democratic thinkers and politicians became involved in the drafting of the Constitution by sitting on the board that was appointed to draw up the new charter. Dossetti, La Pira, Fanfani, Lazzati, Moro, and Angela Gotelli were the most prominent figures in this group of intellectuals, often called—not without sarcasm—the *professorini* ("fledgling professors"), or also the *dossettiani*. The movement Civitas Humana (founded in 1946) and the journal *Cronache Sociali* (1947–51) served as a platform to articulate the group's ideals and plans for the institutional, social, and economic design of post-war Italy (Pombeni 1976, 1979a; Galavotti 2011a). The *professorini* and others Catholic intellectuals and politicians, including the passionate *dossettiana* Laura Bianchini, met regularly to discuss on political and constitutional matters, in what became known as "la comunità del porcellino" (Portoghesi Tuzi and Tuzi 2010).

In 1945, Dossetti became vice-secretary of the Christian Democratic party and tried to open the party to pacifist and even Socialist ideas (for a biography see Pombeni 2013). He had been deeply impressed by the British Labour party's election victory in 1945. In an article titled "Triple Victory," published by the newspaper *Reggio Democratica* on July 31, 1945, he praised the outcome of the elections as the triumph of "substantial" democracy, opening the way to "solidarity and equality" (Dossetti 1982: 193). He and his circle of friends and collaborators became enthusiastic admirers of Stafford Cripp's "Christian Socialism" and engaged with John Maynard Keynes and William Henry Beveridge, mistaking them for Labour politicians.[3] La Pira, in particular, drew extensively from Keynes, Lord Beveridge, *The Economist*, and Jesus Christ—all seen as the ultimate economic and spiritual points of reference for Catholics in politics. In 1950, he published two controversial articles in which he explained the relevance and the revolutionary potential of Keynes's theoretical postulations for post-war Italy, which he saw as the embodiment of "the economic and financial policy of the gospel" (La Pira 1950a: 3–4, 1950b).

The *professorini* were formed in the 1930s, in the intellectual climate of the Cattolica, which at the time was engaged in a sharp controversy with the idealist conception of the ethical state as developed by the Fascist prime philosopher Giovanni Gentile. In the intention of the university's founder and rector,

---

[3] In 1947, Achille Ardigò, in an analysis of the "Labour experiment," praised "the British evolutionary drive which, in contrast to what often happens in continental Europe and elsewhere, hardly ever stops for long" (Ardigò 1947: 9). The *dossettiani* sponsored the translation of Cripp's *Feet on the Ground* in 1950. On Keynes's influence on the *dossettiani*, see Pombeni 1979a: 378, 380–1; Biagini 2007: 238–9.

Agostino Gemelli, the Cattolica had to forge the leadership of a Catholic-inspired Fascist state to react to the liberal anticlericalism that had permeated the entire political process of post-unification Italy, as well as to prepare a coherent and holistic reaction to the threat of Socialist and Communist forces (Bocci 1999). Dossetti and his friends were also fascinated by French legal-social currents of thinking, including authors such as Léon Duguit, Maurice Hauriou, and Georges Gurvitch, not to mention the "institutional" ideas of the Italian constitutionalist Santi Romano, who had always expressed concern about the social reality on which legislation should be based.[4] They were all members and activists of Azione Cattolica and, like many young—and not so young—Catholics, they had flirted with Fascism, then considered to be the best social model for the preservation of Catholic values. Yet, confronted with the growing association of Fascism with Nazism and its racial policies, the experience of the war, and the existential uncertainty it entailed, Dossetti and the others drifted away from traditional Catholic intransigence and "romanità" (the cult of ancient Rome), still advocated in 1940 by Gemelli (Galavotti 2013: 11). They began a search for a Catholic response to the problem of modern mass politics and for the reconciliation of the church with the modern world.

Dossetti and his friends began to meet regularly in Milan in the house of the Cattolica professor Umberto Padovani. During these clandestine meetings, which can be seen as the genesis of *dossettismo*, a series of ideas emerged that were outlined in a "programmatic document"—which has been lost—on post-Fascist Italy (Lazzati 1989: 179; Parola 2007; Galavotti 2011a: 1368–9). The bottom line of the project was that after the disappearance of Fascism, a new state was needed that was different from the liberal tradition, which the *dossettiani* accused of being the main culprit for the advent of Mussolini. In other words, the new state had to give life to a true democracy that, putting aside the elitist perspective pursued by the liberal state until 1922, had to include the popular masses in the decision-making process: a democracy and a state that placed the self-realization of the person at the top of everything else. Initially, Dossetti and his circle of friends were hostile to the idea of a Catholic or Christian-inspired party, and they hesitated to commit directly to such a party. To them, what was needed was an essential "cultural" effort intended for Italian Catholics, with the aim of educating them and teaching them the basic principles of democracy. This effort was all the more needed after their forced exclusion from political life and embrace of Fascism, before they eventually founded the Civitas Humana. Dossetti and the other participants in

---

[4] Dossetti, Fanfani, and Lazzati studied at the Cattolica and were then appointed as professors (Dossetti in Canon and Ecclesiastical Law, Fanfani in Economic History, and Lazzati in Ancient Christian Literature). La Pira became a professor of Roman Law at the University of Florence in 1933 but soon started to engage in academic discussions with the *milieu* of the Cattolica. The younger Aldo Moro, who studied at the University of Bari where he was also appointed professor of Penal Law, had a different cultural background and was unrelated to the Cattolica. On Dossetti's youth see Galavotti 2006.

the meeting at Padovani's house shared the idea that Italian Catholics were not yet sufficiently mature and able to formulate their own political proposals, and it was therefore important to help them take this step through a patient educational, edifying, and illuminating activity.

The idea survived after the collapse of Fascism and the beginning of the civil war, which rendered the meetings at Padovani's house impossible. Dossetti, like others of his generation, chose direct involvement in the Resistance, fighting alongside Communists and Socialists. This was an existential and political choice, driven by the desire to embrace the new that was about to come. Yet, in this period, Dossetti continued to study the Catholic movement's history, deducing that the church had a serious responsibility in the advent of Fascism and its rooting (A colloquio 2003: 28–9, 107). Furthermore, his collaboration with the Communists led him to reconsider and examine in depth the essence of Marxist ideology. Writing to the priests of the Apennines in March 1945, he insisted that Catholic criticism of Communist ideology must be "objective... scientific" and based on perfect knowledge (the letter, titled *Il Movimento Cristiano Democratico*, "The Christian Democratic Movement," is in Dossetti 1995a: 18–25, quoted at p. 23). In the same letter, Dossetti confirmed his choice of direct involvement in history and politics, accepting the idea of a Catholic party. The singularity and exceptionality of the historical juncture strongly required the hard work of political commitment as a way to face and contrast the ongoing dramatic crisis—a crisis that was primarily a cultural crisis of Catholicism vis-à-vis modernity, which seemed more and more determined to get rid of it. As he wrote in the letter of March 1945, the crisis could be tackled and overcome by abandoning the "indifference to any political activities and responsibility, which has become a centuries-old tradition of Italian life" (Dossetti 1995a: 22).

When Dossetti was appointed vice-secretary of the Christian Democratic party, in August 1945, he quickly tried to re-establish his relationship with the circle of friends who had shared the discussions at Padovani's house. The new task was to expand the new democratic culture of post-war Italy with the thoughts of thinkers such as Maritain and Mounier, who had led the way in embracing crucial aspects of modernity and human rights by considering them indispensable to a proper Catholic view of the world, and whose works the young Catholics of Azione Cattolica had avidly read and carefully reflected upon in the 1930s (Chapter 4). They became the major source of inspiration for Dossetti and the *professorini*, in their commitment to the social, political, and institutional reconstruction of post-Fascist Italy.

7.2 The Person and the Moral Community

Without losing all its open-ended questions and unresolved tensions, the thought of Maritain and Mounier came to constitute an important reference point for

Christian Democrats in Europe and Italy, including for De Gasperi and the *professorini* (Ardigò 1978; Durand 1996; Müller 2013a: 85–7). The language of personalism was one that they would make their own as they became involved in the constitutional process.

For the *dossettiani*, the Constitution was not simply the cold manifestation of constitutional engineering, merely destined to regulate the "traffic" of the state; rather, it was the juridical expression of a deeper feeling that, by distancing itself from the disruption of the liberal era and the individualism of capitalism, must be able to define the underpinning structures that favored the promotion of the person (Pombeni 1996). On the eve of June 2, 1946, the day of the institutional referendum and the elections for the Constituent Assembly, Dossetti wrote a stringent working plan for the constitutional project. It focused on pursuing a "democratic republic" that must aim at the transformation of the industrial structure, financial reform, the abolition of the latifundium, and the nationalization of monopolistic industries. Dossetti pointed out that this was not the program of the Left but an update and a reconsideration of the "old social program of Catholics." Dossetti and his friends thought that a "political," "economic," and "moral" democracy must be put together to form an "integral" democracy. In terms of "political" democracy, contrary to the Left's demand for one chamber, Dossetti advocated a second elective chamber, which was the expression of intermediate bodies. With regard to "economic" democracy, Fanfani insisted on the idea of defending property that descended from "honest work" against the "abuses of the state," at the same time highlighting the need to "destroy big properties." Finally, Dossetti explained that moral democracy should be understood as the complex of rules that ensure freedom of religion, press, and teaching, which had to be protected at the level of the individuals and at the level of associations and communities (quoted in Pombeni 1979a: 221–2; see also Melloni 1994: 31).

In the mind of Dossetti and his friends, the new Constitution should be the result of a common effort, a convergence of different and even contrasting ideologies, experiences, and inspirations (Catholic, Socialist, Communist, liberal, social-democratic) that nevertheless found its unifying elements in anti-Fascism. The *dossettiani* were simply hostile to the idea of a Constitution *against* someone or something. For this reason, in the preliminary debates, Dossetti and his friends—unmovable in their defense of the proportional electoral system—seriously evaluated the idea of transforming Italy into a presidential republic. De Gasperi, however, soon put aside such an option. The fear was that the Socialists and Communists could outpace the DC at the elections, imposing their men at the top of Italy's institutional system (Melloni 1994: 43–4; A colloquio 2003: 63–4). The dedication and efforts of the *dossettiani* in the constituent workshop went in multiple directions. Their work aimed at producing an original text, specifically tailored to Italy and resulting from the country's reality and the specificities of its history and politics, and not simply the variation and translation of other constitutional documents. This was also because the *dossettiani* were perfectly aware of the fact that Italy was a peculiar country in the European context, with the biggest Communist party west of the Balkans. Moreover, as Dossetti recalled fifty years later, the millions of casualties of World War II forced all political forces to make an agreement and forge a foundational pact, far beyond the logic of consociationalism, in which all the contractors felt intimately bound (I valori 1995: 17–20; Scoppola 1997: 211–12). On this point, there was a clear difference between De Gasperi and the young intellectuals from Dossetti's circle. For the prime minister as well as the men of his generation, the turning point, the catastrophic event that marked a watershed in European and world history, was World War I. Such a different perspective also explains why De Gasperi refrained from any deep involvement in the process of writing and elaborating the new Constitution, in which he evidently put much fewer expectations than the *dossettiani*, directing all his efforts to governmental action.

In the Constituent Assembly's discussions, occasionally unsurmountable contrasts and misunderstandings emerged between the *dossettiani* and the other political forces, especially the Communists, who obviously pursued a different constitutional design (L. Giorgi 2002). However, resistance against and skepticism toward the *dossettiani* was perhaps stronger within the DC, particularly among those sectors of the party that did not share its anti-liberal thrust and, instead, considered liberalism the most efficient deterrent to the aggressiveness of Communists and Socialists. Hence, the strongest opposition to the line that the *dossettiani* followed in the process of writing the Constitution came from within the party and, additionally, the old and still combative Luigi Sturzo. This went so far that, during a conference of Civitas Humana in November 1946, Dossetti made the following accusation:

> [S]ince some of us manage to give the constitution new formulas and a new approach based precisely on the concept of the person, he who is supposed to be the most genuine interpreter of the Christian democratic spirit—Don Sturzo— complains that the constitution becomes too ideological, and with him a rabble of conservatives in our party protest that too insistent and abstract applications of the concept of the protection of the human personality are made in it. (Pombeni 1980: quoted on p. 259)

The "person" was indeed the polar star of the *dossettiani*. Closely following their French inspirers, the *professorini* criticized individualistic liberalism and saw the person as deeply embedded in a moral community. They saw their role and their analytical-moral effort within the larger picture of political modernity and what had gone wrong within this historical experience. They were driven by the idea of "transcending the principles of 1789," as La Pira once put it (quoted in Pombeni 2008: 35) or, as La Pira said, commenting on the Constitution a few weeks after it took effect, "the human personality unfolds through the organic belonging to the successive social communities in which it is contained and via which it steadily develops and perfects itself" (La Pira 1948). Harking back to Hippolyte Taine, he explicitly stated that Rousseau's "individualistic" principles must be revised in the return to an "organic" universe. La Pira quoted Mounier and his *Déclarations des droits des personnes et des communautés*, which was written in 1941 and debated at the height of the Resistance in the pages of *Esprit*, in an article with the questioning title "Should We Rewrite the Bill of Human Rights?"[5]

The *professorini* were aiming at an Italian version of a labor-based, "substantial" democracy founded on a holistic vision of the human person, which could generate Christian solidarity throughout Italian society and its institutions. The central belief that post-war Italy needed socioeconomic reordering was rendered by their credo, "First the person, then the market." Throughout the post-war period, this idea would not be easy to implement within a wider socioeconomic context of advancing capitalism and slowly unfolding consumerism based on the American way of life, exploding with the economic miracle from the mid-1950s onward (Masala 2004: 90, 92–4; Müller 2013a: 86).

7.3 Dossetti and De Gasperi

There were profound disagreements between Dossetti (and his group) and De Gasperi (Baget Bozzo 1974; Scoppola 1997: 114–18). The *dossettiani* wanted a sharper distinction between "Catholic" and "political" action, or—as Maritain would have said—between the "temporal" and the "spiritual." Building on Maritain, Lazzati expressed strong criticism of the invasiveness of Catholic Action in Italian politics. Following the French theologian, Lazzati explained that the "natural" order and the "supernatural" order were two "distinct but not separate realities," or "two levels of reality that coexist and intersect with one another within man." A Christian must always act as a Christian, even on the political plan, moving away from the mistakes of Machiavellism. On the supernatural level (i.e. that of the church), Lazzati said that "[we] act as members of the mystical body of Christ"; by contrast, on the natural plan, or the plan of the world, "[we] act as members of the earthly city." Consequently, Catholic action and political action belonged to two different, separate, and distinct plans of action: "[T]he direct goal of Catholic Action is the goal of the hierarchy. Such a goal is entirely supernatural." He continued: "[I]n itself, the action of the hierarchy, and the action of the Catholics who collaborate with the hierarchy within Catholic Action, entirely belong to the first plan. It binds Catholics as Catholics [*in quanto cattolici*]; it binds the church." Political action, instead, "does not belong to Catholic

---

[5] See *Déclaration des droits des personnes et des communautés* (1941) and *Faut-il refaire la déclaration des droits?* (1944), in Mounier 1963: 96–104.

Action. On this frontier, Catholic Action must stop" (Lazzati 1948; see also Fanfani 1946; Trotta 1996: 276–80; Giorgi 2007: 204; Melloni 2013).[6] Lazzati and the *dossettiani* thought that the De Gasperi and the party's leadership were too weak and submissive to the pretensions and the invasiveness of Gedda's Catholic Action.

They also believed that the party must operate not only as an anti-Communist force and a general public opinion movement gathering consensus, but also as the center of cultural elaboration and an advocate of reformist political action. Ultimately, the *dossettiani* thought, the limits of De Gasperi and his governmental actions were ascribable to the DC's structural flaws and deficiencies. For them, the DC was unable to express leadership, a comprehensive plan for Italy that was not simply a governmental program, and a method. All these elements could be found in the PCI, a party that—despite its limits, which Dossetti denounced and exposed, namely conformism, Machiavellism, anticlericalism, anti-DC preju-dices, and intellectual deficiencies—was at least concerned with the crucial task of educating the popular masses and trying to establish a positive relationship with them. Thus, in the view of Dossetti and his friends, a DC that was con-demned to govern indefinitely, because of its electoral strength and the interna-tional conjuncture, but lacking a real and effective reformist project was a real danger for Italy. A country with a limited perspective—due to the DC's inability to give it a project and a future—seriously ran the risk of becoming a "Levantine country" marked by the decadence of public customs, a place where everything was easy to purchase and the state would become a "huge feeding trough," as Dossetti said in a conference of November 1946.

More importantly, Dossetti and his friends shared another conviction, which was difficult to espouse in public but which became a significant aspect of their political vision and action. This was the idea that Italy's main problems did not descend from historical and political contingencies (i.e. the economic crisis, the PCI's action, and the international context) but from a *longue durée* factor: and this involved the weight and role of the church. In the aforementioned conference organized by Civitas Humana on November 1, 1946, Dossetti specifically lamented the cultural deficit of the clergy, unable to formulate an analysis and prevision of social and political phenomena: a clergy that was also subjected to hierarchical conformism and ecclesiastical functionarism and whose morality had been shrinking dramatically (Dossetti's report can be found in Pombeni 1980).

The radicalization of the contrast between the *dossettiani*, on one hand, and De Gasperi and his closest collaborators who led the party, on the other hand, emerged clearly and vividly with the *mozione di sfiducia* ("motion of no confidence") that

[6] In those same weeks, Lazzati noted that the *dossettiani* were following, and would continue to follow, the line of the hierarchy: "[I]f AC as such wants to be in politics, we only ask for a statement from the hierarchy that will correct what has thus far been declared and open a new path. We bow down to the hierarchy" (quoted in Parola and Malpensa 2005: 559).

Dossetti and Lazzati proposed at the party's national council of December 1946. The reason for this move was the need to develop a "new method in the action of the party" that could positively transform the action of the government. Lazzati and Dossetti urged the party and De Gasperi to:

> replace the method of delayed and forced adherence to the initiatives of others with the method of making decisive and convinced party decisions, one that the present leadership has not only failed to apply but which it likewise indicates that it does not intend to adopt. (quoted in Lazzati 1988: 32)

The criticism here was directed to the very idea of the party, what it should be, how it had to work, and what role it had in a democracy. De Gasperi and the party's leadership remained anchored to a classic liberal nineteenth-century approach: the party's function and role were electoral mobilization and parliamentary support to the action of the executive.

Dossetti and his collaborators—but eventually also the entire young generation of intellectuals and politicians, Catholics, and non-Catholics who entered the public stage in the immediate post-war years, in Italy and elsewhere—saw things differently. For them, the party was the place in which the cultural basis of the political action had to be elaborated. Therefore, the lines and directives of the political action had to be set, defined, and detailed within the party and not within the parliament, and even less so by the government (Pombeni 1976: 19). In a letter to De Gasperi of 1946, Dossetti explained that it was crucial to prefer the "method of an organic action of the party" that could inspire and generate a "vital and renewed Catholic elan," abandoning the "method of government" and bargains between ministries (De Gasperi 1974: 290). Unsurprisingly, thanks to the joint effort of the *dossettiani* and the leftist forces, the crucial role of parties as the privileged and main instrument for the actualization of real political participation would be encoded in the Constitution.

It is on the pages of *Cronache Sociali* that the *dossettiani* conducted their internal struggle and pressed the party's leadership with a series of articles, which were proper manifestos, through which they made their political and cultural proposal more and more explicit. In 1947, with the ousting of the Socialists and Communists from the government and the beginning of *centrismo*, Dossetti himself addressed a firm and concerned invitation to De Gasperi so that the new government would hold on to its programmatic line, rejecting deviations and pressures that might come from the Left but also independent, financial, or frankly neo-Fascist sectors responsible for a rampant distrust of the DC and more and more intolerant of any plan for real reform in the country. To this end, Dossetti continued, economic decisions and initiatives had to be taken by Christian democratic ministers and not by independent experts or *tecnici* (Dossetti 1947). In a similar way, in the circle of the *dossettiani*, the result of the

April 1948 elections was evaluated not so much in terms of the defeat of the leftist Popular Front and the triumph of Christian Democracy, but through careful consideration of the responsibility that the vote put on the party. While David Maria Turoldo offered a lucid and comprehensive interpretation of those crucial elections (Turoldo 1948), Amintore Fanfani commented—in the rush of the moment—that the 12 million votes for the DC were undoubtedly a lot, but that it was sensible to think about the 8 million Italians who voted against the DC. The 12 million had the task of "recovering" the 8 million, and the 8 million could be found not "in the churches" but in "fields and factories." "If we have failed," Fanfani concluded, "we have failed as politicians . . . as prophets . . . as Christians" (Fanfani 1948: 8).

The political and cultural proposal of the *dossettiani* encountered growing resistance and opposition, within and outside the party. For this reason, Dossetti soon considered the idea of abandoning direct political action. His commitment to the constitutional project pushed him to postpone such an idea. After the Constitution took effect, in January 1948, he reconsidered his earlier intentions, as he thought that he had completed his assignment. With the elections of April 1948 behind the corner, and the need for the Catholic front to keep the level of mobilization high and intense, and employ all possible resources against the Communist threat, the Holy See rejected Dossetti's request for retirement from active politics. Lazzati too wanted to retire and dedicate his life to research and academia. However, Cardinal Schuster (the archbishop of Milan) rejected his request, forcing him to remain active in politics. Although the church and the *dossettiani* debated hotly and had strong disagreements about several issues relating to Catholic politics, apparently the Holy See and the hierarchy esteemed the *dossettiani* and considered them vital and significant resources for Christian Democracy. It is also for this authoritative relegitimization of the Vatican that Dossetti became even more determined to pursue his political and cultural line.

The *dossettiani* deeply committed themselves to the electoral battle. Yet, they were increasingly uneasy about the decline of Christian Democracy's identity and anti-Communist program. They feared that, because of the struggle against Marxist-inspired forces, the governmental action could fall into an impasse, which would benefit the very Communists and those conservative sectors of society that aimed at the stabilization and preservation of the social and economic status quo. On February 23, 1948, Dossetti wrote to the party's secretary, Attilio Piccioni, that the electoral contingency must not become a permanent character of the party. His choice, he continued, had been made: he wanted to retire and commit to "Christianity and its historical task in our time" (Dossetti 1995b: 195–6).

Yet, Dossetti decided to again postpone his decision, trying to see if the DC would change its political line. In the end, Dossetti despaired of any possibility of Christian Democratic reformism and was deeply dissatisfied with De Gasperi's government line with regard to politics and economy, which he criticized for lacking a serious social program. He was appalled by Italy's accession to NATO and the government's aggressive attitude toward the East.[7]

For Dossetti and his friends, Italy's accession to NATO as it was being designed ran the risk of being a complete subjugation to the United States (for the different positions in international politics within the DC, see Vezzosi 1986; Capperucci 2004; Formigoni 1996). This way, Italy would lose its centrality in the Mediterranean, a centrality that would allow Italy to overcome the bipolar logic of the Cold War and freely dialogue with non-aligned countries. Italy would lose, precisely at the moment of the rebirth of the democratic state, a qualifying factor for the solidity of the state, that is, its autonomy and independence in foreign policy decisions.

For Dossetti, such a situation would recreate the same kind of relationship that Italy had nurtured with the Third Reich during Fascism, with all the entailing bleak consequences. Dossetti and the *dossettiani* did not question the international collocation of Italy in the Western camp, nor did they underestimate the Soviet threat; rather, they objected to the passivity of Italy in the negotiation phase and insisted that it was crucial to work toward unity in Europe, excluding only those who "deliberately obstruct" such a "constructive and peaceful" unity (Dossetti 1994: 372). In the end, the *dossettiani* were essentially distrustful of the ability of the United States to understand the continental dynamics beyond the mere interest in using Europe as a tool to counter Soviet hegemony in Eastern Europe (see Dossetti's 1946 speech, quoted in Pombeni 1980: 272–3).

The *dossettiani* aligned with the party's official position and voted for Italy's accession to NATO. Their final choice was influenced by the willingness to respect the principle of the majority, the Vatican's pressure, and a bitter and lucid consideration of Lazzati, who—decades later—remembered that he had literally dragged Dossetti to the vote: "[B]e careful," Lazzati warned Dossetti, "[for] we have not yet been understood and a refusal to vote would mean a loss of consent for us" (Lazzati 1988: 166).

7.4 Success and Decline

Despite the obstacles that Dossetti and the *dossettiani* encountered, between the end of the 1940s and the beginning of the 1950s, they managed to push through a series of crucial legislative measures to promote structural reforms, such as the

---

[7] In 1948–9, Dossetti advocated a position of neutrality between the two Cold War blocs and repeatedly criticized the ratification of the Atlantic Treaty before voting it in the parliament, following party discipline; see "*L'o.d.g. Dossetti al gruppo Dc sulla politica estera (1.12.1948)*" in Dossetti 1948; cf. Dichiarazioni 1949; Dossetti 1994: 372. In a 1946 speech, Dossetti defined the USSR as a "more vital" society than the United States. Americans, he said, "do not understand" European "problems"; the Russians were, instead, capable of "admirable and sensitive participation" in the European debate. The text is in Fondazione per le Scienze Religiose Giovanni XXIII, Fondo Cronache Sociali, E, 1, 2.

Fanfani law on public housing, the agrarian reform, the Cassa per il Mezzogiorno, and the fiscal reform based on progressive taxation promoted by the Minister of Finance Ezio Vanoni, one of the participants in the Camaldoli meeting and a *dossettiano* (Forlenza 2010).

These were, in fact, projects that had already been formulated in the *Camaldoli Code* and other programmatic documents elaborated by Christian Democrats in the final years of the war, and which had become a rallying cry for the *dossettiani*. In their final formulation, such projects fully complied with their expectations and wishes. However, they had managed to remove the projects from the dead-end track in which they had been put because they feared that their approval would undermine entrenched economic interest and the balance of local powers. It was a clear triumph for Dossetti and his friends, indeed, a double triumph: in terms of the projects' content but also because the projects had been introduced after the party had taken the lead and insisted on the government to act in this way, and for the *dossettiani*, the party must always have the initiative. Dossetti thought that this was a turning point, the beginning of a different story in which many within the party started to lean toward acceptance of the idea that "some requests" could eventually obtain "practical acceptance."[8]

Christian Democracy was becoming—Dossetti hoped and thought—not only a party that could win the election thanks to its anti-Communism, but also a body able to make projects and pursue a series of interventions in social and economic structures, which prepared or integrated the activities of the state and the public offices. And yet, what appeared to Dossetti the "apex" of his work—and that of his friends—within Christian Democracy was also the beginning of the end, that is, the beginning of the rapid decline of the *dossettiani* (Tassani 1988: 243). The reasons for and causes of this swift decline were multiple: the beginning of the Korean War and the stiffening of international relations, which complicated the implementation of reforms in a country with a powerful Communist party; the resistance of Italian land owners, businessmen, and capitalists to the reformist action of the government; and the Vatican's pressure to overcome the struggles and quarrels between the various sectors of the DC.[9] Two further reasons were Dossetti's opposition to the party's decision to ally—on a case-by-case basis—with monarchists and *missini* (members of the MSI, Movimento Sociale Italiano) at the local elections of 1951 in Sicily and, not least, the difficulty for Dossetti to talk and make himself heard without generating prejudicial hostility among most of the party's members.

[8] Archivio Storico dell'Istituto Luigi Sturzo [hereafter: ASILS], Fondo Guido Gonnella, Personalità DC, b. 38, f. 28; see also Dossetti 2008: 189.
[9] On May 13, 1951, Fanfani wrote in his diary that Pius XII had asked him and La Pira to put aside their contrasts and quarrels with other leaders and sectors in the name of party cohesion; Archivio Storico del Senato della Repubblica, Fondo Amintore Fanfani, Diari, May 13, 1951.

The most evident manifestation of the crisis is a long and unsigned article published in *Cronache Sociali*, in which Dossetti, starting from an analysis of the 1951 local elections, contested the entire political line followed by De Gasperi after 1948. This line, Dossetti explained, had systematically privileged the logic of coalition and made too much room for authorities and forces that were external to the party, weakening the DC's capacities and exposing the party to the threat of clericalism and moderatism. Dossetti deplored the opportunities that the DC had missed after 1948 and the party's rejection of what should have been its task. There is no doubt that the challenges of such a crucial historical juncture had been formidable, as it had been necessary to thwart "social disintegration, economic deterioration, [and] administrative decomposition," which had reached a level of "national decadence" after Fascism. To respond to such challenges, there was a need not for "a plurality of heterogeneous forces," as had been attempted through *centrismo* (see Chapter 6), but something diametrically different: "[A] homogeneous force, equipped with a spiritual backbone, a complete program, a strong organization, and a massive membership." Since Christian Democracy—Dossetti continued—possessed all these characteristics, it could truly be different from the PPI, not "a party in an *already given* state," but "the sole instrument for the construction of a new state—no longer semi-democratic and semi-oligarchic but purely democratic—to be given to the Italians" (Dossetti 1951, italics in the original).

To continue weakening the action of the DC—as had hitherto been done—by focusing on what Dossetti called the *polipartito* ("multi-party"), implied a worsening of the crisis of society and the crisis of the state. Dossetti's bitter feeling was that reformism was no longer within the horizon of Christian Democracy. Thus, in 1951, Dossetti chose to dissolve his faction in the party and retired to monastic life, only to briefly return in 1956 to unsuccessfully run for mayor in the Communist stronghold of Bologna.[10] In the end, Dossetti believed that it was impossible to reform Italian politics: or rather, he remained convinced that Italian politics could be reformed only on the condition that the church be reformed and regain its leading role in history. This conviction led him to assume an important role in the Second Vatican Council (Alberigo 1998; see Chapter 8). However, to assess the political legacy of Dossetti, we have to go into some more detail with his role in the writing of the Constitution.

7.5 The *Professorini* and the Constitution: Catholicism at Work

Through their work at the Constituent Assembly, which started in June 1946, the *dossettiani* acquired visibility, credibility, and prestige far beyond the limits of the

---

[10] Having retired from public life nearly forty years earlier, Dossetti shortly reappeared in public in 1994, when he publicly expressed his concerns about the proposed changes to the Constitution underway with the new Berlusconi government. Dossetti died in 1996 (see Chapter 11).

party and the Catholic milieu. Their strength lay in the ability to insert themselves into the crucial foundational moment of the Republic, formulating—differently from other sectors of the DC—a comprehensive, organic, and fascinating plan for the future of Italian democracy. Dossetti was very young and had virtually no parliamentary experience. Yet, he gave proof of an extraordinary capacity to master the mechanism and procedure that enabled the functioning of the Assembly, the commission of the 75, and the three subcommittees in which the constitutional work was organized.[11] It was Dossetti who defined the working procedure for the subcommittees and their related matters, and it was again Dossetti who decided the *ordine del giorno* ("agenda") for the subcommittee in which he took part. La Pira and Moro (in the first subcommittee) as well as Fanfani (in the third), even if with their own cultural and personal sensitivity, also added to the constitutional process instances that had emerged and had been elaborated and refined in their discussions (Pombeni 1979b; Scoppola 1980; Novacco 2000: 99–101).

Implementing Catholic philosophy in real life was never going to be an easy task. Yet, as far as the preparation and writing of the Constitution are concerned, the enterprise was largely successful. Let us briefly explain at what level and to what extent.

In the first place, the *professorini* managed to have their version of the first article of the Constitution passed: the "personalist" wording "Italy is a democratic Republic founded upon work," elaborated and proposed by Amintore Fanfani (one of the young *professorini*), prevailed over "Italy is a democratic republic of workers" proposed by the Communist leader Togliatti and a number of Socialists (see also Pombeni 1995; Canfora 2008: 182–4). The difference may seem minimal at a first glance, but Fanfani's proposal instantly steered the wording of the entire document away from a Socialist worldview.

An expression in Article 2, which makes a strong allusion to the rights of man, can be traced to a Catholic viewpoint and social philosophy:

> The Republic recognizes and guarantees the inviolable rights of man, both as an individual and in the social groups where human personality is expressed. The Republic expects that the fundamental duties of political, economic and social solidarity be fulfilled.[12]

---

[11] The first subcommittee dealt with the Rights and Duties of Citizens; the second with the Constitutional Order of the State (in turn divided into two "sections": executive power and judiciary power); and the third with Socioeconomic Rights and Duties. Being among the more important representatives of *dossettismo*, Dossetti himself, La Pira, and Moro were members of the first subcommittee; Fanfani of the third. Lazzati was elected in the Constituent Assembly but did not take part in the commission of the 75.

[12] Source: https://www.senato.it/documenti/repository/istituzione/costituzione_inglese.pdf (last accessed: December 1, 2023).

The rights of man (and woman, we should add) are legally proclaimed to be inviolable, but they are not suggested to be "sacred" and, least of all, "natural." The *professorini* were not at all proposing a return to premodern legal thinking: they were applying Christian philosophy within the parameters of the modern episteme. As a matter of fact, the *dossettiani* agreed with the other founding fathers that meta-positive rights, that is, those based on natural law, should be excluded.[13] Interpreters of the Italian Constitution cannot escape the often-neglected fact that Part I of the Constitution outlines the "Rights and Duties of Citizens." This formulation is much more similar to the Weimar Constitution of August 11, 1919 (*Grundrechte und Grundpflichten der Deutschen*), than the French Declaration of the Rights of Man and of the Citizen of August 26, 1789. Additionally, it is clear that the "rights" are directly related to the social level and to the *duties* involved in bringing about social *solidarity*. Using anachronistic language, the wording is communitarian rather than liberal.

Article 3, in turn, stated—and still states—that "[i]t is the duty of the Republic to remove those obstacles of an economic or social nature which constrain the freedom and equality of citizens, thereby impeding the full development of the human person [. . .]." The conclusive words of Article 3, "and the effective participation of all workers in the political, economic and social organization of the country," confirmed the will of the *dossettiani* to collaborate with the Socialists and Communists to steer away from liberal individualism.[14] Importantly, the term "person" implies a completely different value from that of "individual" as employed in liberal thought, which penetrates most democratic constitutions. It is this worldview that emanates from the core, from the founding principles that hold up the edifice.

7.6 The *Dossettiani* between the State and the Church

The cultural and pedagogical concerns that had accompanied the first steps of the group around Dossetti were the prime and strongest motivation for its commitment to the constitutional project. In other words, the *professorini* rapidly grasped that the foundational process of Italian democracy required a firm and powerful ability to educate and guide a mass that had come physically, morally, and intellectually exhausted out of Fascism and the war. Likewise, they understood that the church was approaching the new situation by continuing the same confessional instances that it had previously entrusted to the regime and Mussolini.

[13] See the meeting of the first subcommittee of the Constituent Assembly (September 9, 1946) and, in particular, the contributions of Dossetti and Togliatti; Atti 1946: 21–2. See also Pace 2013.
[14] Source: https://www.senato.it/documenti/repository/istituzione/costituzione_inglese.pdf (last accessed: December 1, 2023).

Bearing such a situation in mind, it is possible to fully understand and value one of the most crucial aspects of Dossetti's constitutional work: Article 7, which regulates the relationship between the church and the state and included a mention of the Lateran Pact. On one hand, Dossetti knew that it was crucial to nip the potential re-emergence of the Roman question in the bud (see Chapters 1 and 2), which was also a concern of the Communist leader Palmiro Togliatti who, in fact, voted in favor of the inclusion of the Lateran Pact in Article 7, thus snatching a perfect polemical weapon away from the church and the DC, as the election was approaching (Agosti 1996: 336; see also R. Moro 2007). On the other hand, in the given historical and religious conditions of Italy, it was important to create the premises for Catholicism—which in a century had gone through the *non expedit*, the modernist crisis, and clerical Fascism—to eventually accept the idea of a democracy founded on the existence of spaces of mutual non-intrusiveness.

At the heart of Dossetti's political vision, there was the realistic acknowledgment of the cultural, civic, and democratic immaturity of Catholicism: "[T]he Italian church had largely failed in its mission in recent decades" (in Pombeni 1980: 246). However, there was also the commitment, from a position that was objectively a minority one, to work toward overcoming—or at least governing—such immaturity. The intense relationship that he established with the Vatican secretary of state was instrumental and aimed at combining the anachronistic, intransigent proposal advanced by the Holy See, which imagined and wanted a Constitution that would sacralize the Catholic confessionality of the Italian State (Sale 2008), with the need to clearly separate the state from the church (Elia 2009).

7.7 Freedom and Responsibility: The Letter and the Spirit of the Constitution

Thanks to Dossetti's efforts, and also to his will and skills to develop a dialogue with the Socialists and Communists, the Constitution enshrined not only the primacy of the human person as part of a social union (including a spiritual union) but also the principle of freedom as a *responsibility*. The Catholic view of freedom was alternative, if not opposed, to the idea of freedom as elaborated by most currents of modern constitutionalism. Freedom could only be accepted as the positive freedom to uphold the common good. In close affinity with Togliatti and the Communists, Moro declared—in a debate of the Constituent Assembly on October 2, 1946 (at the first subcommittee meeting for the preparatory text of the Constitution)—that "liberty in a democratic system aims not to permit individual free will to be attained, but to allow the full expression of a person's values as well as a positive collaboration among individuals to achieve the common good."[15] The debate concerned an article for the Constitution proposed by La Pira, which explicitly aimed at "endowing liberty with a different meaning than the one underlying the 1789 Declaration," which stated:

> The liberties guaranteed by this Constitution must be implemented to perfect the human person, in tune with the demands of social solidarity and toward the improvement of democracy by means of increasingly active and conscious participation of all for the common good. Hence liberty is the foundation of responsibility. (October 1, 1946)[16]

This article was not included in the final draft of the Constitution, despite Moro's and Dossetti's strong defense. Still, it is evident that the activism of Dossetti and the *professorini*—even if unsuccessful—strongly influenced the discussions by the committee for the Constitution's preparatory text. There was much debate, for instance, over whether the right to "resistance" should be included in the text. The draft, indeed, included an article that read as follows: "[T]he individual and collective resistance to oppression is a right and a duty of the citizen when the public powers violate the rights and fundamental liberties guaranteed by the Constitution." This proposal followed a suggestion by Dossetti and was met with strong opposition (see the debate in Atti 1946: 450–2). Throughout the debate, the view that it was impossible to legally regulate something that was by its very nature removed from the sphere of positive law prevailed, and the article was not approved.[17]

Liberty and equality, far from being tools for identifying rival ideologies, are mutually reconciled in light of the "full development of the human person" enshrined in Article 3, which is the cutting edge of constitutional principles. Civil, political, social, and economic rights are recognized and granted accordingly. The rights of the individual are granted within communities such as families, schools, unions, parties, and churches. Social and political pluralism becomes part of the constitutional landscape, grounded in what one might call a "communitarian personalism."

---

[15] Atti 1946: 171. The meeting was held over two days, on October 1 and 2.

[16] Atti 1946: 165. On the same occasion, Togliatti said that "our democratic regime differs from the previous century's individualist liberal regime . . . . The Christian Democrats will give [the] principle [of liberty] one expression, the social-communists another, but a point of convergence may be reached, namely the reading that for us, liberty is to be guaranteed by the state in order for certain aims to be achieved: perfecting the human person; strengthening and developing the democratic regime; constantly increasing social solidarity. Three objectives that we declare to maintain" (Atti 1946: 167).

[17] The opposite conclusion was reached in a country facing many of the same debates, and where Catholics equally sought to leave an imprint: the German Federal Republic. In its Constitution, there is an article (20) that unequivocally legalizes the right of resistance, stating that "against anyone who attempts to abolish [the democratic Constitution], all Germans have a right of resistance, if no other remedies are possible."

The pluralistic philosophy expressed here shines through in other parts of the document. For example, the second part of the Constitution—on the Republic's institutional framework—defines public power as shared both among diverse institutions at the central level (i.e. in parliament and government, by the president of the Republic, through referendums or the judiciary and Constitutional court) and among the state and local authorities, including regions, provinces, and municipalities. This definition is more sophisticated than Montesquieu's separation of powers, reflecting not only the need to grant citizens liberties but also a fundamentally pluralistic view of democracy.

The wordings of the Constitution represented small but significant results of a battle over values and visions of modernity won by the *dossettiani*. It was certainly a symbolic victory for the *professorini*, which had a lasting effect. The *professorini* had sought and contributed, with their "political spirituality," to building a post-liberal democracy with distinct spiritual foundations. Moreover, the writing of the Constitution was the first political-cultural operation led by Catholic lay intellectuals and politicians without the Vatican's support. Christian Democracy managed to do what political Catholicism had, until then, only been dreaming of: to regain a leading role in the modern world. Throughout the post-World War II period, the Constitution remained the fundament from where democracy could be consolidated.

8

Consolidating Democracy

This chapter focuses on the consolidation of Christian Democracy between the late 1940s and the late 1960s. The chapter also examines how after the death of De Gasperi and Dossetti's retirement from politics, Amintore Fanfani and Aldo Moro, representative of the "second generation" of Christian Democrats, worked to create a more structured party (less dependent from the Vatican's organizational support) and a governmental alliance with the Socialists (the "opening to the Left"), which was profoundly opposed by the Church's hierarchy. Finally, the chapter will also deal with the consequence of the Second Vatican Council on Italian politics.

Alcide De Gasperi's death in 1954 signaled the end of a crucial political era for Italy's Christian Democracy and the entire country. The immediate postwar period, dominated by reconstructions, had ended. Italy was a stable and effective—albeit fragile—democracy. Its position in the Western world was by now incontestable. The governments led by De Gasperi had launched important social reforms, such as a public housing plan (known as the Fanfani law), the Cassa per il Mezzogiorno (investements for the South), the agrarian reform, and a fiscal law based on progressive taxation (the Vanoni law). Italy was slowly changing. New values, morals, individual behaviors, and lifestyles inspired by the American way of life were challenging traditions and customs (including religion) but without completely erasing the "old Italy," rather blending in but mixing with it in a variety of ways. By the end of the 1950s, the Italian economic miracle known also as the economic "boom" was in full swing. In reality, this was not a sudden outburst but the culmination of trends, changes, and developments that had incubated in the preceding decade (Crainz 1996). The PCI had taken root in several geographical areas and different sectors of Italian society. However, the most intense period of the Cold War—after the end of the Korean War and Stalin's death, and despite the crisis of 1956 in Hungary—seemed to have passed. The Socialists were slowly moving away from the Communists. The rapid transformation of Italian society demanded new political moves and the inclusion of new forces in the system of power and government. The most important concerns about De Gasperi's successors Amintore Fanfani and Aldo Moro—later famously defined as *cavalli di razza* ("purebred horses") by their party fellow Carlo Donat Cattin—were the search for a new political figuration in which changes and transformations would be incorporated without breaking the fragile and

Italy's Christian Democracy: The Catholic Encounter with Political Modernity. Rosario Forlenza and Bjørn Thomassen,
Oxford University Press. © Rosario Forlenza and Bjørn Thomassen 2024. DOI: 10.1093/oso/9780198859864.003.0009

complicated balance of forces and powers of Italian politics and society, which obviously included the Catholic Church.

This complex historical and political transition, known as the "opening to the Left," took off with the party's 1954 congress in Naples. It ended in 1962, when Fanfani formed a government with the benevolent abstention of the Socialists. Only in 1963, the first "organic" center-left government, led by Moro and which included Socialist ministries, would come into office. The historical process that culminated in the center-left government was anything but smooth and, as Catholic historian Pietro Scoppola put it, "resembles more an agony than a birth" (Scoppola 1997: 361; see also Di Loreto 1993). The search for a new political figuration meant not only the elaboration of new governmental alliances but also a reconsideration of the role of Christian Democracy in the political, socioeconomic, and cultural context of a rapidly changing Italy.

8.1 From De Gasperi to Fanfani

At the party's June 1954 congress, a few weeks before he died, De Gasperi gave his farewell speech to politics, which in many ways reads as a sort of political testament. The old leader had suffered his most excoriating defeat at the 1953 political election. A new electoral law that he had wanted—against the stubborn resistance of and opposition from leftist and rightist parties, but also from politicians and intellectuals of the "centrist" area (i.e. republicans, liberals, and Social Democrats)—would give two-thirds of the seats to the party, or the grouping of parties, that won more than 50 percent of the votes. De Gasperi wanted to institutionalize *centrismo*, reinforcing the government and its potential for action to the detriment of the parties, including Christian Democracy, and their power of conditioning. The "swindle law," as opponents dubbed it, did not work out (Piretti 2003; Quagliariello 2003). The DC and the other parties of the center got 49.8 percent of the vote: 57,000 fewer votes than needed to obtain the majority bonus of seats. The DC and its allies lost 10 percent of the vote compared to the 1948 elections. De Gasperi formed a government that lasted less than a month; then, after seven and a half years in power, he resigned from office. The time was ripe for a change within the party and the search for a new political landscape and a renewed role for Christian Democracy.

At the Naples party congress, De Gasperi reflected deeply on the recent history and the condition of the young and fledgling Italian democracy, and he outlined a vision of the DC's role in the future. After a detailed analysis of the nation's election body and its manifold and fragmented articulation from a geographical and socioeconomic point of view, he highlighted that in a country like Italy, the only viable democratic politics could not be based but on "interclassism," and not on "class antagonism":

A valid democratic policy cannot fail to protect the poorest, first of all, including the owners of small infertile lands, the workers, but also the middle classes, the true nursery of private initiative and framework of democracy, linked to the development of the human person.

Thus, the DC inevitably had to anchor itself and its politics in the principle of social solidarity and assume the role of protector of pluralism in society. De Gasperi argued that in 1948, the DC had been able to grasp and represent the demands of wider sectors of the Italian people; however, in the following five years, while the government was taking fundamental historical choices and adopting a politics of bold reform, the party had failed to communicate promptly and effectively what was being done. Moreover, it proved unable to listen to and gather the demands that Italians advanced as a consequence of the transformation that the governmental policies and reforms had generated. In short, the DC had closed in on itself, reducing its role to a trite repetition of anti-Communist rhetoric. It had chosen a defensive approach, rejecting a much needed and more positive attitude based on initiatives, actions, and the elaboration of new ways of dealing with a changing society. What Italy needed was a party that could help the government to implement a social market economy, following the model of West Germany led by Konrad Adenauer, which meant "neither capitalism nor Communism, but the solidarity of the people, in which labor and capital are associated with the increasing prevalence of work, under the control and where necessary with the propulsion of the democratic state."

De Gasperi still thought that the propulsive center of the state should be the government and not the majority party. However, he wanted a more dynamic party, closer to the needs and demands of society and more determined to confront the problem of unemployment. He had asked Ezio Vanoni—then minister of budget, and minister of finance in his cabinets from 1948 to 1954—to draw up a ten-year development plan aimed at full employment. The plan, which Vanoni presented in draft form at the Naples congress, stressed that the state must stimulate and possibly coordinate private economic initiatives and enterprises (Vanoni 1977: 321–38).

De Gasperi also dealt with the issue of collaboration with other political forces, claiming that it was crucial to drive and lead the alliance—hence reaffirming the DC's centrality in the Italian political system and the principle of the political unity of Catholics in the party—while warning of the danger of being driven and led by the alliances. In other European countries, Christian Democrats already collaborated with the Socialists. This would inevitably happen in Italy, too, De Gasperi realistically thought. He warned:

We have already seen that this could only happen if we have the guarantee that it is a democratic form of Socialism, which has definitively accepted political freedom and renounced the Marxist dictatorship. But a second condition of this eventuality is that Christian Democracy is a united body, aware of its popular character, convinced of its national mission, anchored in a solid ideological basis, [and] suggestive in its driving force, so that present and future alliances do not appear to be combined with our internal centrifugal and disintegrating tendencies, but a conscious, disciplined cooperation reached by the governing bodies for the common purpose of weighted and decisive responsibility.

At the end of his speech, De Gasperi passionately recapped his concerns for the future of the party, and that of Italy: the thorny relationship with the church and the entire Catholic world, the risk of losing autonomy, the laity, the a-confessional character of a party that still took inspiration from Christian values, and the need to continue and enhance a politics of social and economic reforms (De Gasperi 1954).

The debate that followed De Gasperi's speech was intense. Ezio Vanoni presented his plan. Others, from Giorgio La Pira to the old *popolare* Giovanni Gronchi, from the Catholic union leader Giulio Pastore via Giulio Andreotti to Prime Minister Mario Scelba, tackled sensitive issues that related to the party's present and future. Symbolically, the final speech was by Amintore Fanfani, the emerging man whom the party's national council elected, only a few weeks later, as the new secretary (what follows is based on Malgeri 1989; Pombeni 1997; Craveri 2009; see also the memories by Rumor 1991).

8.2 The Advent of the "Second Generation"

Fanfani was a man of the "second generation," that is, one of those young Catholic intellectuals who had been educated under Fascism and, for a long time, endorsed the policies of the regime (see Chapter 4). As we have already indicated, this reference to generations was common among Christian Democrats. The first generation referred to the men who had been activists in the pre-Fascist era and members of the PPI. The second generation of the Catholic movements included the *dossettiani* and those who had been formed under Fascism. It was to be followed by a third generation, which was the new generation that succeeded the *dossettiani* and which would be profoundly influenced by the charismatic figure of Dossetti himself. Being one of the *professorini* at the Constituent Assembly (see Chapter 7), Fanfani had collaborated closely with Dossetti and was widely perceived as his heir. At the party's 1949 congress in Venice, Dossetti and his followers once again denounced the shortcomings of *degasperismo* and claimed that the time was ripe for a *terzo tempo sociale*: a social third phase, a season of radical social reform that came after the institutional and constitutional reconstruction of Italy and the political stability that followed the elections of April 18, 1948. In his speech, Dossetti talked of the "need to free a significant part of the working class from the Communist Party" in order "to include in the house of the state what is, in a certain way, the most dynamic part of the Italian people." To do so, it was urgent to "develop the construction of the new democratic state that we have just sketched out with the constitutional charter" through the "concrete and substantial development of some principles set out by the constitution," the "coordination of social reforms," and an "economic policy developed around a unitary will" (quoted in Baget Bozzo 1974: 283–4). More importantly, Dossetti added, the government and the ministries had to be liberated from the eccentricities of bureaucracy (Baget Bozzo 1974: 290). Dossetti's comprehensive geometric vision clearly considered social and economic reforms—a quintessential topic of Catholic social teaching—ineffective and difficult to implement without political, institutional, and bureaucratic reform, an unusual theme for Catholic social thought. In this reformist vision, the DC must become a party of "political designers" (*progettisti politici*).

In 1951, Dossetti announced his retirement from politics in two meetings at Rossena, on the Apennines. He was skeptical about the reformist politics of Christian Democracy. The Korean War had reignited the Cold War at the international level, shrinking the space of neutralism also within the country (Tassani 1988: 37–62; Villa 2008; Galavotti 2011b). Italian politics was unreformable, Dossetti thought: or, more precisely, Italian politics could be reformed only within the wider frame of the reform of the church. He started a new life, which would bring him to play a central role in the Second Vatican Council, as *peritus* ("expert," or "consultant") of the "progressive" Cardinal Giacomo Lercaro.

Fanfani took the baton passed on by Dossetti. He was the undisputed leader of *Iniziativa Democratica*, the *corrente* ("faction") within the party that gathered the former *dossettiani*, now orphans of their charismatic leader. Fanfani was the result and the most natural consequence of the challenge that Dossetti had posed to De Gasperi and the politics of *centrismo*. He was an intellectual and a man of great culture, but also a politician who thought that politics was a vocation in a Weberian sense. Sure, he was a "professional" politician, but politics always must involve a holistic meaning. It meant creating, forming, and educating political elites and subsequently controlling positions of power and vital functions of the life of a society. It also meant forging a comprehensive plan to deal with the conjunctures and fluctuations during an age of transformation. He had wider interests and skills that were not common among Italian politicians. These included knowledge of the emerging geopolitical spaces, such as the Middle East and, more generally, the Third World. He had made a precise cultural choice in favor of the industrial society, which he thought was the inevitable horizon that Catholics and Catholicism had to deal with and steer for the better. In this view, a political party was, for him, the key tool for the constitutional life of a modern state and not simply a feeble and vague movement of ideas linked to the social presence of Catholicism and Christianity.

The other members of the second generation, but also the younger members of the third generation, endorsed Fanfani's actions and ideas. They saw in him the creativity and the energy that would ensure more space for action for a Catholic political culture ready to cope with and steer the socioeconomic transformation of the present. By the mid-1950s, and more decidedly in the following years, the Italian economy rapidly expanded and culture and social behavior changed. Significantly, in 1954, Italian television started broadcasting. In fact, beyond the Italian context, Fanfani's ascent to power could be seen as part of a wider cultural and ideological transformation. In those years, the cultural debate focused on the "end of ideology," as in the title of the final chapter of Raymond Aron's essay "The Opium of the Intellectuals" (first published in 1955). It was time to overcome the eternal controversy about whether there was any truth in Marxism and its prediction of the contradiction of capitalism, late liberal arguments about the primacy of the freedom of competition, or one of the various "third-way" alternatives. The Western world had entered a stage of what was already then defined as "neo-capitalism." Progress and wealth for everyone could be achieved only by governing neo-capitalism, maximizing its advantages and minimizing its injustice, and not by condemning the industrial society and its way of life while waiting for a regenerative, apocalyptical crisis that would guarantee the return to a reassuring Golden Age.

8.3 Fanfani in Power

In his speech at the Naples congress, Fanfani argued for a firmly progressive strategy to make the party the primary agent for public intervention in the economy and the transformation of society. The party had to revitalize its organization and local branches (*sezioni*) and strengthen its autonomy and power, becoming independent from the church and economic and financial stakeholders, especially Confindustria (the Italian employers' organization). A new political elite was to become a ruling class firmly holding the reins of the economy, to be led and directed—with a Keynesian approach—through public investments and careful planning. Fanfani's strategy thus combined two fundamental aspects. On one hand, he appropriated De Gasperi's ideas on the lay, secular, and national role of the party to avoid being squeezed into the state–church alternative. On the other hand, he envisioned a political action in which an enlightened political, technical, and cultural elite—freed from the influence of external authorities—would be able to seize and manage positions of power and outline a technical-political project with which to steer the country's social reality. Emilio Colombo, a friend of Fanfani, gave political and cultural substance to the proposal of *Iniziativa Democratica*:

The DC has made reforms but in a paternalistic way; the party as a protagonist of the reform has been absent, so people have felt extraneous, [and] they have not appreciated the role of social promotion. (quoted in Radi 2005: 132)

In his speech, Fanfani insisted on the need to reconsider the DC's organization and structure, turning it into a force able to act as a bridge that constantly connected the parliament, the government, and the electorate:

Up to now, the DC has lacked a kind of center of experts to elaborate concrete solutions deriving from our principles. [The DC] must put [the creation of] a center of experts at the top of its agenda, a center that elaborates concrete solutions deriving from our principles...it must put the continuous, permanent, disinterested, and effective connection with the world of culture and experience at the top of its agenda.

Fanfani proposed the creation of an efficient structure directed not only by democratically elected leaders but also by intellectuals and experts specifically prepared to elaborate and implement initiatives and projects that could generate democratic advancement and wider citizen participation in politics. He continued: "Above all, we need to create active, efficient offices and organizations in southern Italy if we want to replace the propaganda of agitation and pasta with the propaganda of ideas and facts" (see also Fanfani 1954).

Fanfani presented a program that included, among other things, administrative decentralization, the reorganization of the IRI, the *Istituto per la Ricostruzione Industriale* (see Chapter 4), and the enhancement of the National Hydrocarbon Agency (Ente Nazionale Idrocarburi or ENI), founded in 1953 to facilitate the research, exploration, and commercialization of oil. Fanfani's program also included the extension of welfare, a public urbanism measure, and an intervention in climate policy. He insisted that only the active and responsible participation of workers and professionals in the growth and development of productive firms and the service industry could provide Italy with a much-needed "social" democracy. Fanfani recalled that in the five preceding years, Christian Democracy's concern had been the protection and the progress of a political democracy. This had been an important achievement—one that was crucial after Fascism and war. Yet, Fanfani argued, Christian Democracy had not attempted to implement "a veritable economic democracy" in line with the social doctrine of the church.[1] While the classic formula of European constitutional thought was the "party of government" based on the parliamentary majority, he had in mind a "government of the party" and a "monocratic" approach to power as the only way to effectively govern a modern society (Craveri 2009: 61). Already in 1949, he had

[1] Fanfani's speech in Naples and other useful documentation relating to this important congress can be found in Archivio Storico del Senato, Fondo Amintore Fanfani.

sensed that the Italian political and institutional system generated problems in terms of efficiency and rapidity of decisions (Baget Bozzo 1974: 2.242). A "governing" democracy—that is, one able to make clear decisions—implied the centrality of the government, in social terms and in the sense of the actions to be taken, which had to be controlled and steered by a hegemonic party: Christian Democracy (Craveri 2009: 67). Endorsed also by De Gasperi (see the letter that he wrote to Fanfani on August 11, 1954, eight days before he died, in De Gasperi 1974: 335), Fanfani put great efforts into implementing his progressive vision for the party, the government, and Italy.

From 1954 onward, Fanfani worked hard to implement his progressive renovation project. The party's leadership had changed, and the power was now firmly in the hands of the second generation. The cadres, the intermediate levels, and the base were changing, too. The party was revitalized at the local level and translated the internal political debate to this level. The attempt worked out also because the party was internally diverse and fragmented into various *correnti* with different political ideas; the competition between these factions, which started at the level of the parliamentary groups, pervaded the entire party structure. Membership grew, nourished also by the initiatives of the *correnti*. Fanfani carefully took care of the formation of the cadres, activities, and communication tools within and outside the party. He assumed an authoritarian and resolute manner and was known for his decisiveness. He was aware of the importance of political communication, propaganda, and the party's press. He considered public television (RAI) the crucial instrument for public competition. He decentralized the debate and, at the same time, centralized the process of decision-making and exercised a party discipline that was much more intense and effective than in the past.

In fact, the party did not change its organizational and associative structure but reinforced and disciplined it, establishing an organic link with society and its intermediate bodies. For example, it had a strong relationship with Coldiretti, the powerful organization of farmers founded and led by Paolo Bonomi. This was something different from traditional Catholic *collateralismo* with social associations, a quintessential element of Catholic social tradition since the time of Leo XIII. Its main feature was the organic relationship that such associations and organizations established, through the party, with the public system of economy, which was increasingly controlled by the state, that is, by Christian Democracy. The same happened with other associations, unions, and organizations of professional categories (e.g. teachers, doctors, artisans, and workers). Relationships of trust and collaboration were established between the party and such professional organizations. Small groups of Christian Democrats emerged within these associations, which allowed the party to enter into professional categories and gather their demands. The demands considered reasonable were selected and forwarded to the government or presented in parliament through the parliamentary groups. In this way, the DC functioned as a transmission belt between the center and the periphery. Complaints and requests were sent upward, while benefits such as state-directed infrastructures and works were provided downward.

In January 1955, the southern Italian provincial secretaries of the DC met at Castelgandolfo, near Rome (what follows draws on Forlenza 2010). Various comments and demands were voiced with respect to local and sectoral problems, which were addressed to whoever might be in a position to take action, whether in the party, the government, or an institution: the province of Caserta inquired with the minister for agriculture about the production of hemp. Caltanissetta raised the problem of sulfur mining with the undersecretary of state for industry; the minister for transport received complaints about the railway between Regalbuto and Nicosia in Sicily, and about suburban transport in Rome; the chairman of the agency that was implementing the agrarian reform in Sardinia was warned that the head of a colonization project in Nuoro was a Communist and that something needed to be done right away. All ministers, undersecretaries, and heads of collateral organizations had their responses, clarifications, explanations, interventions, and requests for future information ready.[2]

Apart from the nature of the requests and the promptness of the responses, it is interesting to note how this correspondence between the center and the periphery blurred the distinction between the government and the DC. In fact, the two were inextricably linked, as if forms of expression and responses from society at large had shaped the political system as well. The masses were becoming involved in the political life of the republic via the party. New loyalties and affinities, which still had a whiff of feudalism about them, were creating a link between ideological or religious conviction and material self-interest.

Thanks to this new social involvement and the ability to take root in the local, social context, the DC could free itself from the control and tutelage of the church and of the *Comitati Civici* (see Chapter 6). The relationship with the lay organizations of the church was no longer one of dependence: it had become an osmotic relationship. The same can be said for the parishes. The relationship with the ecclesiastical hierarchy remained strong at every level. The parishes had been—and largely still were, at the time—fundamental tools for gathering consensus. Now, though, it was no longer the party that asked them for help. Rather, the social and organizational problems of the parishes emerged through the party's local network.

At the same time, and in view of the party's reorganization, Fanfani and the new Christian democratic elites worked to reinforce the role of the state in the Italian economy. IRI left Confindustria. In 1957, the Ministry for State Holdings *Partecipazioni Statali* was created. The Cassa per il Mezzogiorno and the agrarian reform were crucial instruments that allowed the party to extend its network in the South and

---

[2] ASILS, Democrazia Cristiana, Segreteria Politica, sc. 69, f. 5.

colonize the state sector. The DC increasingly extended its power in the South, taking root in a geo-political area where the Catholic social movement had been traditionally weak or entirely absent, and reducing the influence of monarchist, neo-Fascist, and other local rightist forces that—until the end of the 1950s—still competed with the DC, at least at the local level (see again Forlenza 2010). In a seminal article, Aldo Moro identified the key feature of the "party for the *Mezzogiorno*" as the hope and confidence that the DC had distilled from "the former silent despair" of Italian southerners, and the now indissoluble union between the party and the government:

> The DC in the *Mezzogiorno* has cast off ignoble traditions and burdening clientelism and is now a liberated, living, [and] effective instrument of political action that can truly and energetically push forward the renewal of the Italian south. And despite the grave difficulties arising from the uncertain political situation, the government has continued to work efficiently on both the institutional and economic and the structural planes, to remedy the structural deficiencies of the *Mezzogiorno* and contribute, through uncompromising action and independently of private interest, to the social improvement of the masses and the creation of a genuine political initiative for the south. (Moro 1955; also quoted in Forlenza 2010: 339)

This state intervention, unprecedented both in scale and speed, was not politically neutral: the responsible politicians nailed their Christian Democrat colors firmly to the mast. The DC shaped itself as a federation of local leaders who directed the torrents of public largesse from Rome, and who also recorded local demands and passed them on to the relevant central authorities. Moreover, the electoral system required a strong local presence and encouraged politicians to attend to local priorities rather than forging a general ideological stance, even if the latter existed de facto in the form of anti-Communism. The party representatives could not simply be equated to the notables of the time of liberalism. Their approach to economic problems and public governance was neither rhetorical nor paternalist but based on hands-on experience and new ways of analyzing and interpreting local problems. Personal contacts and clientelism did not disappear but were combined with more modern political structures and forms of mass patronage: the party and its affiliated organizations (Forlenza 2010: 347–9).

8.4 Toward the Opening to the Left

In a few years, Fanfani succeeded in making the party independent from the financial support of Confindustria and the electoral support of the church and Catholic Action. In doing so, he rooted Christian Democracy into Italian society and economy and made it the prime agent of social and economic reform that, Fanfani thought, was crucial for the stabilization and progress of Italy.

After having given a clear shape to his party, Fanfani took a further step, which he considered necessary for the country's political stability. At the national council of Vallombrosa, in 1957, he addressed the problem of political alliances. He advanced the idea of collaboration with the Socialists through a governmental alliance without the liberals that was open to them. It was clear to Fanfani that the politics of *centrismo* was in crisis and that it was time to move toward a new parliamentary majority. The "state party," namely the DC that he had forged, could not be constrained in the parliamentary morass. To make democracy effective, DC had to be a hegemonic force, freed from the power of the party's parliamentary groups divided into factions. DC had the duty and responsibility to stabilize the entire political system. For De Gasperi, *centrismo* was a binding formula that reflected and made the political equilibrium of his time manifest. At that moment, the socioeconomic reality of the nation was in changing and a more stable and representative majority was necessary. This meant that the DC had to indicate the political force with which it wanted an alliance.

At Vallombrosa, Fanfani was cautious and prudent (the speech can be found in Fanfani 1959a). But the message for the Socialists and Italian politics at large was clear. After all, fundamental changes had occurred within the Italian and the European Left. The most heated time of the Cold War was behind, at least in Europe, whereas it flared up elsewhere in the world. Stalin's death, the Hungarian crisis of 1956, the advent of Khrushchev, and the Thaw opened the way for a relative easing of the Cold War tensions in Italy and other European countries. The PSI moved away from the Communists and elaborated, albeit in a confused, uncertain, and ambiguous way, independent and autonomous politics. Unlike the German SPD—who at the 1959 convention of Bad Godesberg embraced the basic tenet of liberal democracy—the Italian Socialists still did not reject Marxism and its revolutionary aim. However, something was nevertheless changing and collaboration appeared more and more viable.

For the 1958 political elections, the DC presented one of the most ambitious and progressive programs of the entire republican history; it increased its share of votes compared to the 1953 elections (from 40.1 percent to 42.3 percent), as the Socialists did (from 12.7 percent to 14.2 percent), while the rightist forces decreased remarkably. Fanfani decided to accelerate the implementation of his project (see his speech at the DC's national council of June 10, 1958; Fanfani 1959b). He remained party secretary while taking the offices of prime minister and foreign affairs minister. At the beginning of 1959, though, he met insuperable resistance and his project came to a halt. First, the enormous power he had acquired was intolerable for the different factions within the DC, whose suffocating and divisive struggle grew progressively, and many Christian Democrats and the church did not appreciate most of his plans. Already when Fanfani had stepped in as secretary of the party and leader of the second generation, the old guard—reunited in a group called Concentrazione, which included Giuseppe Pella, Guido Gonella, and Giovanni Gronchi, as well as the young Giulio Andreotti and about one hundred senators and deputies—decided to oppose Fanfani's project, remaining loyal to *centrismo*. Fanfani was acutely aware of the political dynamics both within Italy and his own party. Thus, although he had a wider plan in mind, he tried to please other sectors of the party as well as sectors of Catholicism that were not necessarily in line with his thinking. Time and again, he highlighted anti-Communism and embraced aspects of official, more conservative Catholic culture.

After 1959, his concentration of power and his move toward the Socialists provoked the hostile reaction of many other Christian Democrats, including his old friends from *Iniziativa Democratica*. Some of them (Mariano Rumor, Paolo Emilio Taviani, Emilio Colombo, and Antonio Segni) left the faction and created a new faction: the *dorotei*, after the convent of Santa Dorotea in Rome where the group first met. They were concerned not so much with the opening to the Left as such, but with the modality and the timing chosen by Fanfani. They did not want to lose contact with the bishops, productive forces and Confindustria, and the conservative Italian provinces that formed their electoral base. By joining forces with other factions in opposition to Fanfani, the *dorotei* voted Aldo Moro as the new party secretary. A few months earlier, Fanfani had resigned from his role as prime minister, hoping to be reappointed and gain a stronger position. His era had ended. At the party congress of October 1959, he presented a new faction, *Nuove Cronache* ("New Chronicles"), whose name paid homage to Dossetti and the Dossettian periodical *Cronache Sociali*. Moro continued the plan for the opening to the Left despite having been elected by the *dorotei*, who were hostile to such a political move, but his initiative was more prudent and cautious than Fanfani's strategy. More importantly, Moro had to cope with a crucial challenge: the church's opposition to the opening to the Left and, more generally, to the opening of the governmental area to forces that did not belong to the governmental parties of the first and second legislature.

8.5 Moro, the Opening to the Left, and the Opposition of the Church

With Moro, the historical process of the opening to the Left did not come to an end. In fact, Moro resumed Fanfani's project precisely where the predecessor had left it. However, Moro moved in a more cautious direction. He was convinced that Italy was still a fragile democracy. While the opening to the Left would certainly reinforce the democracy, the path to reach such a stage should be walked carefully and by reconciling the different, fragmented, and often competing forces that "made" the country in its complexity—including Catholicism and the Vatican, as well as Christian Democracy and its various factions.[3] The various social and political forces and the diverse identities that Italy consisted of raised positive, real, legitimate, and meaningful demands, but they were not integrated into a common vision of democracy: some of these forces were not even convinced of the value of democracy, while others—including important sectors of Catholicism and factions of Christian Democracy—were not convinced of, or frankly opposed, the opening to the Left. Yet, all these demands and forces were necessary to reinforce and consolidate the still fledgling democracy and fragile structure of the Italian state. All these demands and forces needed to be included in and incorporated into the process toward the opening to the Left.

This is why Moro adopted a careful, slow, and prudent approach; it was meant to convince the variety of subjects that made up the Italian body politic of the fact that the opening to the Left was not simply the creation of a new parliamentary and governmental majority but a process that concerned the fundamental tenets of Italian democracy itself. The opening to the Left was, therefore, a fundamental step in the slow, lengthy, and strenuous path toward the political education of the still young Italian democracy (Scoppola 1997: 357-8). It was a process that required Moro to work hard in order to convince the church to accept the transformation of the political system while, at the same time, preserving the unity of the party. In his mind, Christian Democracy was still the only force that could steer the democratic process.

It took a few more years for a center-left government to became a reality; it was a painful and slow delivery, marked by a sudden acceleration and sharp slowdown, dramatic events, and at least one delicate and crucial incident. At the beginning of 1960, the liberal party, fearing an alliance between the DC and the Socialists, provoked a government crisis, giving breath to those sectors of the DC that opposed the opening to the Left. As the system had reached a stalemate, a way out was found by Fernando Tambroni, a Christian Democrat who formed a government and obtained the majority in parliament with the support of the neo-Fascist MSI. Popular demonstrations and reactions, which to some extent slipped out of the Socialists' and Communists' hands, burst out in many cities and were violently suppressed. The demonstrations were particularly strong in Genoa, which had been awarded a gold medal for the Resistance: here, the neo-Fascists had been allowed to hold its congress in exchange for its support to Tambroni, but it was eventually canceled. Catholic and Christian Democratic intellectuals and politicians expressed serious concerns for the government's embrace of rightist forces. Tambroni resigned; a systemic alliance with the Right was unsustainable and it

---

[3] The following two sections are based on Baget Bozzo 1977: 270-5, 331-2; Baget Bozzo and Tassani 1983: 59-63, 98-100; Zizola 1988: 126-54; D'Angelo 2005; Totaro 2005; Marchi 2006, 2008.

became clear that the only alternative to *centrismo* was the opening to the Left and that anti-Fascism was the political culture on which republican Italy had to be based. Moro lost neither control of nor faith in his plan and continued to weave its comprehensive web. His action was accompanied by reflections, ideas, and discussions put forward by intellectuals who supported Moro's efforts.

The theoretical, ideological, and strategic basis for the alliance with the Socialists was presented at the San Pellegrino Terme conference in 1961. The sociologist and former *dossettiano* Achille Ardigò warned that Italy's rapid industrialization and the drastically diminishing number of peasants and rural middle classes meant that the Christian Democrats had to look for a "new synthesis." The latter was to take two forms: at a sociological level, the understanding and eventual political leadership of a new urban social class; at a governmental level, a new relationship with the Socialists. The economist Pasquale Saraceno (one of the participants in the Camaldoli meetings in 1943) explained how a market left to its own devices could not resolve—indeed, exacerbated—the geographical, social, and productive disequilibrium that characterized modern Italy; he believed steps had to be taken to remedy the deformations, inequalities, and imbalances specific to the Italian model of economic development. Meanwhile, Moro proceeded with local experiments of center-left government, for example in Milan, which provoked the negative reaction of the church's hierarchy.[4] In February 1962, Fanfani formed a government without the liberals and with the "external" support of the PSI (see Fanfani 1963). Finally, in December 1963, Moro formed the first "organic" center-left government. Moro himself was appointed prime minister and the Socialist leader Pietro Nenni his deputy.[5]

8.6 Moro between Religion and Politics

As we have seen in Chapters 4 and 5, Moro was one of those young Catholics who, between Fascism and the war had converted to democracy. In the late 1950s and early 1960s, by incorporating the lessons of Maritain, Moro's political culture remained consistently based on the firm belief in the progressive nature of political Christianity, and anchored in a constellation of political meanings tied to an underpinning "political spirituality." In a 1963 (March 24) speech, he made the following declaration:

---

[4] For example, in a letter to Moro, the Archbishop of Milan Montini asked that, in the context of Milan, "the DC act more in keeping with the interests and methods of the Catholic cause and its very function"; ACS, Fondo Moro, b. 65, f. 1, sf. 2 (first arrangement).

[5] The most important reforms linked to the DC's opening to the Left were the nationalization of electricity supply and the establishment of compulsory secondary (middle) schooling until the age of 14.

Bound as we are to traditions, for what they have that [is] essential and…human, we do not want to be men of the past but of the future. Tomorrow does not belong to conservatives or tyrants; it belongs to attentive and serious innovators, without rhetoric. And that tomorrow in civil society largely belongs, also for this reason, to the revolutionary and redeeming force of Christianity. Let us therefore leave the dead to bury the dead. We are different and we want to be different from the tired supporters of a world that is passing. (Moro 1979: 250)

Maritain's influence on Moro, together with the lessons of Sturzo and De Gasperi, proved crucial in what was still the most sensitive issue of postwar Italian politics: the relationship between Christian Democracy and the Vatican—in other words, the autonomy of the laity in politics. The question was all the more open at a time when Christian Democrats were looking for new alliances that included the Socialists, when influential sectors of the church were still trapped in what the historian Steven White has called "Pacellian populism" (White 2003) and in an "integralist" view that still considered Salazar and Franco as the political models to follow. Until the early 1960s, the Vatican and significant sectors of the local clergy were at the forefront of the attacks against Moro, Fanfani, and other Christian Democrats who, since the mid-1950s and in different ways, had been working in favor of the opening to the Left.

In May 1960, the *Osservatore Romano* issued an explicit condemnation of the opening to the Left in a famous article titled *Punti Fermi* ("Firm Points"), which has been attributed to powerful and influential cardinals such as Siri and Ottaviani. The article reaffirmed the hierarchy's right and duty to issue commands in the political and social spheres. The bishops alone were competent to judge the legitimacy of "coalitions" or "alliances." This moral judgment could not be left to the whim of the faithful. "Punti Fermi" recalled that there was "an unsurmountable opposition between Christian dogma and the Marxist system" and forbade Catholics to "belong to, support, or in any way collaborate with those who adopt and follow Marxist ideology and its applications."

Moro's resistance to the Vatican's positions and his constant call for a distinction between the political and religious spheres were strong. He believed that Christianity was the inspiring force for Catholic political and social action. Yet, Christian Democracy had to operate in the political realm with autonomy from the church hierarchy and its more contentious policy demands. If Christian Democrats were not allowed to make up their own minds about alliances and coalitions, then they would remain tied to the episcopal apron strings and never attain the political maturity that the DC had been fighting for ever since its creation. As early as 1950, Moro had published an article in *Church and Democracy* that drew heavily on Maritain's *Christianisme et démocratie*, which was translated into Italian in that year (Moro 1950), and where he showed how the church can effectively contribute to the establishment and consolidation of democracy.

Moro distinguished between the anti-democratic "methods" of the church (i.e. the hierarchical structure, the dogma, and the idea of a divine mission) and its "inner life" (i.e. the attention to human dignity, justice, the spiritual dimension, truth, and people's welfare), which gave a substantial and effective meaning to the otherwise empty concepts of democracy and liberty. He concluded, extolling the power of the "Christian conception of Man and world," as follows:

> Precisely because it is not purely technical, not merely a method, but has a spirit that expresses human dignity and the complex demands of life, such inspiration may facilitate the construction of democratic structures in which not only free opinions flow but a legal order is established that may respond to those demands. (Moro 1950)

Moro built a direct relationship with sectors of the Vatican that were more receptive to the idea of opening to the Left and the possibility that the historical juncture could fundamentally change the relationship between religion and politics; at the beginning of the 1960s, with the incipient Council, the latter started to appear hard to manage by the church. In other words, Moro launched a proper "ecclesiastical politics," as Achille Ardigò invited him to do, which could overcome the resistance and opposition to Moro's design.[6] Moro's most important "contact" in the Vatican was the substitute Secretary of State of the Holy See Angelo Dell'Acqua, who acted as a channel between Moro and Pope John XXIII (Galavotti 2004). In fact, even within some of the Vatican's most influential sectors, it became increasingly clear that Moro's intervention was to be supported. This happened for two reasons: one ideological, the other political. As far as the first reason is concerned, Moro wanted the DC to be detached from the church and the hierarchy, but his attempt started from a position of firm Christian faith; he was in favor of secularization in praxis, but he did not want to deprive politics of Catholic inspiration. As far as the second reason, many sectors of the Vatican understood that to support the conservative factions of the DC vis-à-vis the transformation of Italian society could mean condemning Christian Democracy to a breakup. Consequently, the DC would lose its connotation of interclassism and moderatism, which allowed it to remain the party of the relative majority in the country.

At the Eighth party congress in Naples (January 27–31, 1962), Moro explained Italy's need for a union between the DC and the Socialists and again tackled the burning question of religion and politics. As an example of Moro's continued concern about the situation in the Vatican, it is important to note that a few days before the congress, he sent a note directly to the pope explaining what was happening in Naples (Zizola 1988: 272–4). It is here that Moro outlined the most updated and advanced platform for the doctrine that affirmed the political

---

[6] The note is in ACS, Fondo Moro, b. 63, f. 7, sf. 1 (first arrangement).

autonomy of Catholics. This speech might be considered a sound response to the aforementioned article in the *Osservatore Romano, Punti Fermi*. Catholic politicians—Moro claimed—were not indifferent to Christianity and, in fact, found inspiration from the principles of Christianity. These principles, however, needed to be translated into a political and historical reality (the "ground of contingency," in Moro's words), depending on the circumstances and with extreme gradualness. In the historical, national context of the early 1960s, it was necessary to collaborate with parties of different inspirations and engage with other ideologies "in an encounter without discrimination." Such an alliance did not imply the betrayal and surrender of Christian inspiration and principles; it was simply an operational agreement on concrete, tactical, and immediate problems. The crucial question was: who is entitled to choose and decide whether such collaboration is necessary, appropriate, and timely? Moro's answer was crystal clear: the Catholics who operate in politics—that is, Christian Democracy—must work in a condition of autonomy. "Autonomy," Moro said, "is our assumption of responsibility. It means to run our own risks; it is our personal, unique way to render a service and possibly bear witness to Christian values and ideals in social and civic life."[7]

Moro's real objective in the wider project of opening to the Left was the end of the church's function as a political substitute and, therefore, the resolution of the alternative between Catholic action and political action (*azione cattolica* and *azione politica*, according to the title of a 1948 article by the *dossettiano* Giuseppe Lazzati) that had marked the history of the Catholic social movement and that still dominated the Christian Democratic debate in the late 1940s and 1950s (Lazzati 1948). The opening to the Left, in Moro's project, came to represent the autonomy of the Catholic believer who was committed to politics. It was a paradigmatic shift, or a Copernican revolution, aimed at the redefinition of a new Christian Democratic political elite that could perceive itself as free, autonomous, and independent from the duties, obligations, and restrictions that the hierarchy pretended to impose. Fanfani had not been able to fully elaborate on the political plan of the party's religious qualification and chose to substitute it with the internal organization and the transformation of the party into a modern political machine. Moro, instead, decided to regulate, once and for all, the relationship between politics and religion that was becoming difficult to manage for the Vatican and Christian Democrats, with important consequences for Italian politics and society.

8.7 Gendered Christian Democracy

In preceding chapters, we have talked about the "men" of Christian Democracy. Men were indeed leading the political movement from the outset. But not

[7] The speech, titled "The party and the fundamental choices of national politics," is published in Moro 1982b: 996–1098.

without the strong influence of women. Women's entry into politics was one of the more remarkable transformations of post-World War II Italian history (Rossi-Doria 2000). In June 1944, the Central Committee of the fledgling Christian Democracy decided to admit women into the party (Atti 1959: 82). In 1945, DC in collaboration with the other parties signed a decree that granted women to right to vote, which they exercised for the first time at the local elections in March 1946 and then at the institutional referendum and at the elections for the Constituent Assembly of 1946 (Gaiotti De Biase 1996; Forlenza 2008: 14–22; Gabrielli 2009). The proposal for the decree came from De Gasperi and Togliatti. The enfranchisement of women in 1945 was the direct outcome of the social revolution triggered by the war and its consequences for equality. Christian Democracy as well as all other parties started to appeal to women, who now constituted the largest part of the electorate, by adopting a particular language and rhetoric that depicted women as the bearers of peace, pragmatism, and care for the family and therefore the country (Forlenza 2019b: 192–5). Subsequently, the 1948 Constitution not only declared Italy to be a republic based on labor; it also guaranteed equality before the law to all, regardless of race, language, religion, political opinion, personal and social condition, and sex.

Although women were the largest part of Italy's body politics and despite the significant high number of women who soon became members of the party (from 1946 to 1963 one-third of the members of DC were women), there were very few women within the cadres and the leadership of the party (respectively 2–3 percent and 0.4 percent) (Maria Weber 1977: 26; Bizzarri 1980: 41–4). Within the party's candidates running for the June 1946 elections only twenty-nine were women, and only nine were elected. The numbers did not significantly change in the decades to come and only in 1951 a women entered a DC-led government: Angela Maria Guidi Cingolani, as an undersecretary (vice-ministry).

Yet, in Christian Democracy, as in other party, the role of women was not negligible. The first women to enter the party's leadership and then the Constituent Assembly and the parliament had been typically active in Catholic Action in the 1930s (such as Maria Federici and Laura Bianchini, who had been president of the women branch of the FUCI in her town, Brescia) or involved in a series of social and cultural activities carried by other Catholic movements or at the level of the parishes. Others (such as the already mentioned Guidi Cingolani) had been active before Fascism and collaborated with Sturzo and the PPI, having therefore experienced the tough confrontation between the Italian State and the Catholic Church. Some of them had joined the Resistance, sometimes in leading role, such as in the cases of Federici, Bianchini, Tina Anselmi, or Angela Gotelli. Others again entered the party in 1944–5 at very young age, such as Franca Falcucci, at the age of 18. Within the ranks of the women movement of Christian Democracy, from the pages of their magazine *Azione Femminile*, and as members of the

Constituent Assembly and of the Parliament, these women contributed to the life of the party, which could then develop a political discourse around women, and more generally to the reconstruction of the Italian democracy (Dau Novelli 1988; Di Maio 2009; Noce 2014; in a comparative vein see also Di Maio and Dau Novelli 2023). Their concerns often belonged to rather traditional spheres of women interests. For example, writing in 1944 in support of the enfranchisement of women, Angela Guidi highlighted that they had the rights to participate to the building of the new Italian democracy. However, she continued, they must be prepared to support with their political activity "those men" and "those parties" that "will ensure them the integrity, sanity, and development of families, allowing the full exercise of their educational mission" (Guidi 1944), where the reference to Christian Democracy was more than obvious. In the years to come, Christian Democratic women engaged especially with themes such as school and education, welfare for veterans and migrant workers, the promotion of laws for women's access to the labor market, childhood, and above all family, considered as the primary subject for the social and political reconstruction of the nation (Dau Novelli 1997).

The participation of women in the life of Christian Democracy did not lead to any open or vocal criticism of the predominantly male leadership of the party. Christian Democratic women did not engage with issues of gender equality, as we would understand them today. Roles within the party continued to be highly gendered and despite women's involvement in politics there was no trace of what one could call a feminist agenda connected to their activities and engagement. Yet, at the same time, participation in the politics of the immediate post-World War II Italy reinforced the signs of change that had emerged during the Resistance and the final years of the war. Such a participation sowed the seeds for the widespread emergence of a genuine political and social consciousness among women, also *as* women. It activated a process of emancipation in which Italian political Catholicism came to accept the organized presence of women in the public sphere, much beyond the private dimension and the traditional themes of welfare and family. The implications and consequences of this process on the history of female citizenship and gender identity were huge, even though the fruits of such a transformation would only ripe decades later. As Piccio (2014) has shown, from the 1960s onwards DC turned to a more "modern" conception of women, in particular after the emergence of the Italian feminist movement. Christian Democratic women shared many concerns and ideas of the leftist feminist movements that saw the day from the 1960s onwards, but they also disagreed on fundamental issues. Rather than passively disagreeing, they actively sought to reformulate the feminist core symbols—such as self-determination, autonomy, and personal realization—reincorporating them into their own more family-oriented vision of culture and society, with the aim of representing the moderate sectors of Italian women.

8.8 The Second Vatican Council (1962–5)

The changing relationship between religion and politics did not come only from within Christian Democracy but also from within the church. The Second Vatican Council—opened by Pope John XXIII and, after his death, presided over and concluded by Paul VI—reconciled the church with the modern world and recognized the moral superiority of democratic government and the value of human rights (on the Council see Alberigo 1995–2001, 2005; Formigoni 2008a: 141–60). The church no longer claimed to possess a monopoly over truth, and Catholics were encouraged to engage in dialogue with their fellow, non-Catholic citizens. The Council served to shape a new self-image of the church as an interpreter of the "sign of the times": as a companion traveler, partner, or guide of modernity. In hindsight, it was a quite remarkable discontinuity. The church now recognized the freedom of religion and human rights as central elements of the church's doctrines. Instead of rejecting modernity as a dark and godless force, it expressed the hope—in particular the final pastoral document, *Gaudium et Spes*—that the church and the good forces of the modern world would together be able to build a common house for all people.[8] In the closing address of December 8, 1965, Paul VI defined science and faith as "mutual servants of one another in the one truth." The Council initiated a new period, as discussed also by Bill McSweeney (1980: xiii–xv, 236–9).

Yet, scholars have taken that event for granted for too long. Catholic writers, in particular, have seen it—implicitly or explicitly—as the moment when the Catholic Church finally accepted a changed world, shaking off a reactionary past and the integralism embodied most clearly by the long pontificate of Pius XII (Schloesser 2006; Wicks 2018). This "internal" shift allegedly marked a decisive caesura in Catholic politics, but matters were more complex than that. First, already in the 1950s, there were reflections within the church on what a genuine Catholic modernity could and should look like. A key figure of transition was Giovambattista Montini, one of those thinkers insisting on a Catholic modernity. He had done so also during the years leading to the Council. At the Catholic Jurists' meeting in 1954, Montini refused the alleged incompatibility between the word "Catholic" and "this new, dynamic modernity, so abounding with new creations." The very fact of being Catholic, Montini continued, "is conducive to the probability of coinciding with the most significant and lively trajectories of the modern world." He claimed that:

---

[8] The *Gaudium et spes* ("Joy and Hope") stated that the church "is bound to no particular form of human culture, nor to any political, economic, or social system .... The church and the political community in their own fields are autonomous and independent from each other." The document added that all should "participate freely and actively in establishing the constitutional bases of a political community, governing the state, determining the scope and purpose of various institutions, and choosing leaders."

[i]f the modern world aspires to become unified, and if I am a Catholic, not only am I modern but in the vanguard of the modern world. I precede the others; I can enlighten the others; I have the brilliance of the progress of the modern word in my Catholicism; I can be proud and content; I can thank God for having given me this, not only to experience and carry forward but to enjoy, magnify, and spread around me. (quoted in Ambrosini et al. 1954: 156–8)

For Montini, the creation of sovereign national states belonged to the trajectories of modernity that should no longer be opposed. Catholic modernity also meant to acknowledge the nation as a foundation upon which to build the future international, European, and universal order.

Second, the rupture provoked by the Council was also to some extent the consequences of pressure from lay Catholics. In fact, many changes were essentially the result of the accession to positions of formal and informal influence of a new cohort of Catholics. They saw political Catholicism as an intellectual and cultural project and felt that the church should choose the right side with regard to the many pressing issues of the age: social justice, the welfare of citizens, the dignity of the person, peace, and democracy. In Italy, the redefinition of Catholicism as a modern intellectual and cultural project advanced by Christian Democracy as a basis for new politics and practices—reinforced by the wider social, economic, and cultural transformations of the 1950s—impinged upon the church's attitude to democracy and modernity. The Council encouraged Catholics to enter the stage of pluralism and democracy; in reality, Italian (and European) Christian Democrats had engaged in the political realm and embraced the cause of democracy at least from 1943. In sum, they were already democratic and ready to engage in pluralism and in what Moro called the "ground of contingency."

In addition to this, in the 1950s many dissenting voices were raised against the church and its difficult relationship with contemporary society. Critical voices (such as Father Primo Mazzolari and Father Lorenzo Milani, members of the Catholic Action, sectors of the Catholic press, local clergy) shared a commitment to concrete action in social issues and peace. Going against conservative currents of the DC and against the Vatican, they called for a profound revision of themes such as the relationship between the lay population and the church hierarchy, the autonomy of the laity, and the collaboration between believers and non-believers (Vecchio 2001: 190–5; Pollard 2008: 140–3).

Through the Council, the Vatican eventually endorsed democracy in an unequivocal manner only after many decades of "democratic" practices and programs advocated by the DC, often with unwanted consequences for the Vatican. The DC's political culture and its policies were not always controlled from above, and its programs often veered away from positions approved by the Holy See. Undoubtedly, not every Catholic was a democrat in post-war Italy, but Christian Democrats and Italian Catholics did not turn to democracy as a consequence of the

Vatican's binding statements: they were already democrats. It might even be argued that Christian Democracy's embrace of modern national politics—based on philosophical reflections on the compatibility of religion and politics that developed outside, and sometimes in opposition to, the church—eventually influenced the Vatican in its attempt to come to terms with democracy and political modernity.

Many lay Catholics and Christian Democrats directly influenced the debates at the Vatican Council. Dossetti, for example, acted as a *peritus* for the progressive and innovative Cardinal Giacomo Lercaro (Bologna), presenting the vision of a church that is less an introverted "society" than an organic "community," whose mission centered on preaching the gospel to the poor. Referring to Rosmini, Dossetti had come to define the church as "the people of God." He made many efforts to support the decree on ecumenism, which opened the way to the idea that Roman Catholicism did not necessarily have the monopoly over Christian truth, and the *Dignitatis humanae* declaration on religious freedom, which concerned the relationship between authority and freedom.[9] One of the aspects that Dossetti considered central was the fact that the Council, following the encyclical *Pacem in terris*, should explicitly reject any form of conflict and war. In this regard, he disagreed with the American bishops who considered such a declaration inappropriate as it would reduce support for US foreign policy.

Maritain also played a crucial role in the Second Council Vatican, together with the neo-Thomist Jesuit John Courtney Murray and other lay intellectuals.[10] The notions of human rights, pluralism in religion and politics, the acceptance of non-confessional states, the distinction between the religious and the political sphere, the centrality of the laity as the prime Christian actor in society, and religious and political freedom based on the dignity of the human person—all these ideas inspired John XXIII's most famous encyclical, *Pacem in terris*.[11] They were incorporated by the pastoral constitution *Gaudium and spes* and by the declaration of religious liberty *Dignitatis humanae*.

Maritain's role, in particular, cannot be stressed enough.[12] Symbolically, Pope Paul VI presented Maritain with the message "to the men of thought and science,"

---

[9] However, the Council did not satisfy Dossetti's lifelong quest for an authentic evangelical community. He was disappointed with the hasty flurry of decrees and constitutions whose mix of theology and anthropology blurred the Council's definition of the church in the modern world; see Alberigo 1998.

[10] According to Cardinal Giuseppe Siri, the Council would not have dealt with "certain topics" had Maritain not been so influential (Chenaux 1994: 64). The American Jesuit and theologian John Murray Courtney was another central figure of the Council. Notably, the individuals who were most influential in the Council (Maritain and Courtney) came from the two homelands of modern democracy: France and the United States.

[11] The *Pacem in terris* ("Peace on Earth") is a moving plea for international conciliation, based on the neutrality of the church and its refusal to accept Cold War divisions. It was addressed to "all men of good will," not just Catholics, and argued for the need for cooperation between people of different ideological beliefs.

[12] However, Maritain believed that the church was going too far in its modernism. After his wife's death, he moved to a monastic order, the Little Brothers of Jesus near Toulouse. His criticism of the church's more liberal position in a short volume titled *The Peasant of the Garonne* (1967) was greeted with anger by many of his followers.

at the closing of the Council (December 1965). There is no doubt that Paul VI was profoundly influenced by his reading of Maritain. This influence shines through, for example, in his encyclical on the "Development of Peoples" (*Populorum progressio*, 1967). Here, Pope Paul refers explicitly to Maritain's writings (notes 17 and 44 of the encyclical). Several central passages are literally transcribed versions of Maritain's "integral humanism" and draw on his image of "modern man":

> If further development calls for the work of more and more technicians, even more necessary is the deep thought and reflection of wise men in search of a new humanism that will enable modern man to find himself anew by embracing the higher values of love and friendship, of prayer and contemplation.[13]

Fittingly, as we have seen in previous chapters, the pope had been translator and interpreter of Maritain's works, mentor and teacher of many Christian Democrats, and supporter of De Gasperi's political action in the late 1940s, in his capacity as Vatican secretary of state.

8.9 Post-Conciliar Catholic Dissent

Until the late 1960s, Christian Democracy had been the most advanced Catholic driving force behind the modernization and transformation of Italian politics and society. Ironically, one of the most crucial consequences of the Second Vatican Council was that it ended up impoverishing the debate within the party. The Catholic movement, which had hitherto fueled the DC's political culture, was entirely absorbed by the internal clash within the church between "traditionalists" and "innovators," or between "conservatives" and "progressives"—even though these "secular" terms do not really apply to the internal life of the church. Politics ceased to be an exciting field for the new generation of Catholics and the party lost the "stimulus" and "sting" of intellectuals, as De Gasperi once said about Dossetti, turning more and more into a party of dull professional politicians devoted to pragmatism and power politics.

The rejection of authoritarianism spread within ever more ample sectors of Catholicism, particularly in the new generations, who were dissatisfied with Christian Democracy's conversion into a mere party of power. They were increasingly attracted toward the imperatives of social justice and driven by palingenetic visions of social and ecclesiastical renewal. Young Catholics preferred social activities in the impoverished peripheries of big cities or among the workers of

---

[13] Giovambattista Montini extensively invoked Maritain's humanism in his presentation for the commission preparing for the Council (1960), when he was archbishop of Milan, and in other encyclicals he wrote, such as *Ecclesiam suam* (August 1964), *Humanae vitae* (1968), and *Evangelii nuntiandi* (1975); see Montini 1997.

the industrial triangle, or they became important actors in the student and other revolutionary movements (including terrorist groups) that arose throughout the country in the late 1960s and into the 1970s, trying to combine Marxism with Catholicism, Jesus with Lenin. The Catholic element was also present in the Red Brigades, whose leaders, Renato Curcio and Mara Cagol, were young militants of Catholic Action before they became sociology students at the University of Trento. The first Italian university where the conflict flared up was the Cattolica in Milan (1967), followed precisely by the Faculty of Sociology at the University of Trento, which had been established by Christian Democratic leaders in order to educate and form a new Catholic elite able to understand and steer the transformation of the country. Many young Catholic students drifted toward the New Left and committed to spreading the gospel in factories and peripheries, living a life of a "Christian witness," or "social justice." One of the most read books by the student movement was *Lettera a una professoressa* ("Letter to a Teacher"), first published in 1967, in which the poor students of Don Milani's school (in the rural parish of Barbiana) effectively and unsparingly exposed the classism, injustice, and individualism supporting the Italian education system and Italian society writ large.

The period witnessed a profusion of groups (e.g. *Movimento dei Focolari, Comunità di Sant'Egidio, Rinnovamento dello Spirito,* and *Comunione e Liberazione,* to cite just a few), which were devoted to ecclesiastical and liturgical renewal, worship, commitment, and action in universities or factories, communal life, and social activities. For these groups and the young Catholics, the crucial point was the return to the spirit of the gospel, as the Council had invited them to do, which time and again became the rejection of the hierarchical structure of the official church and the increasingly secularized attitude of Christian Democracy. The tradition of dissident priests and worker priests, already present in Italy since the late 1940s, became even more important and widespread. In Italy more than anywhere else, so-called Christian base communities (*comunità di base,* known also as "ecclesial" or "spontaneous" groups) emerged out of the blue—a feature of radical Catholicism that is usually considered typical of South America and, more generally, of the Third World. Members of the base communities, such as priests and lay persons, who sometimes practiced communal forms of living, focused on a variety of activities: from ecclesial action to forms of social assistance for the poor and disadvantaged classes and neighborhoods, from spiritual and intellectual reflections to social services or political work. Members of the base communities might hail from more traditional associations within the Catholic movements and simultaneously be members of Christian Democracy or even other parties, but normally a community base operated largely independently from the traditional structures of Catholic organizational life.

Crucially, Catholic Action took the path of the "religious choice" and decided to abandon any form of "collateralism" with Christian Democracy and indeed to any party whatsoever. While still absorbed in a social dimension, Catholic Action decided to rediscover its religious origins through the commitment to the announcement of the gospel and the education to faith. In 1969, the Associazione Cattolica dei Lavoratori Italiani (ACLI, Association of Christian Italian Workers), founded in 1944 to halt the influence of Communists in the world of work, gave its members the freedom to vote; in 1970, it supported the "Socialist hypothesis" and then also decided to create a second, "left-wing" Catholic party.[14]

For many young Catholics, the shadow of the "old" by now pervaded Christian Democracy in contrast with the news of the "spring" represented by the Council. The DC was the compromise with power that had forgotten the gospel. Giuseppe Alberigo, a student of Dossetti, defined the DC as a "theological monster." The Christian democratic way and approach to politics, culture, language, and the mediation of the party were considered outdated for large sectors of Catholicism. To be a Christian democrat assumed a negative connotation: no longer a sign of modernism but rather a sign of conservation and the betrayal of Christian principles. The political unity of Catholics started to crumble.

8.10 Christian Democracy and the Challenge of Post-Conciliar Catholicism

The DC made an attempt to update itself and respond to the Council and the transformation that it had impressed on Catholic activism by organizing a conference in Lucca in 1967, called *I cattolici italiani nei tempi nuovi della cristianità* ("Italian Catholics in the new time of Christianity"). The conference was the first, partial attempt at elaborating a political and cultural response to the political, civil, and religious ferment that was passing through Italian society. It was a group of Catholic intellectuals who asked the DC to retrieve its original and ideal inspiration, blurred and impoverished—as they wrote in a document directly addressed to the DC—by power and its management. To overcome its "cold and technocratic neo-reformism," Vittore Branca, Sergio Cotta, Gabriele De Rosa, Cornelio Fabro, and Vittorino Veronese called for a political renewal based on the "political and cultural heritage" that had been built on the willingness "to serve the country with love for justice and thirst for truth." More specifically, the historian De Rosa invited to rediscover the party's original inspiration and do away with bureaucratization and "political professionalism."

In his talk, the secretary Mariano Rumor focused on finding an institutional and technical response to the challenge of the present, completely missing the more cultural and spiritual dimensions of what was happening in Italian society.

---

[14] For a further discussion of Catholic "dissent," see Cuminetti 1983; Verrucci 2002; Saresella 2004, 2019: ch. 4; Formigoni 2008a: 161–87; Horn 2015: 71–82, 111–72; Forlenza and Thomassen 2016: 209–45.

As we will see in the following chapter, Augusto Del Noce put this dimension forward in an insightful way (all documentation of the Lucca conference has been published in Rossini 1967).

Within the party, perhaps only Aldo Moro was able to propose a careful and perceptive analysis of what was happening in Italian society, the anxieties of youth, the emergence of new political subjectivities, the women's question, and the unrest and protest that were sweeping the country. At the national council of November 1968, he invited the party to put in motion a "politics for the new times" to seize the "irresistible move of history," turning it into a "peaceful evolution that unfolds with the law and with the innovative instruments of a truly open democracy." To this end, Moro invited the party to express self-criticism and take sides with "the things that are born, even if they have vague outlines" and not "the things that die, even if they are noticeable and seemingly very useful" (the speech can be found in Moro 1968). A few months later, in January 1969, Moro invited leftist factions of the DC to join forces with him and work toward the aim of "eventually opening the window of this caste in which we shelter, and letting the wind of life come inside, around us" (Moro 1988: 2642–3). Yet, the party was clinging more and more to power; it was a closed castle, which was in favor of "the things that die" and not the new things that were being born, to use Moro's expression.

This was also the consequence of generational changes and systemic factors. What was changing was the party leadership's awareness of the relationship between its political action and the comprehensive horizon of the project of Christianity, or a new Christianity, in the sense of Maritain. The second generation had been profoundly influenced by their education and formation in the various organizations of Catholic Action, which had also involved a direct link with the church hierarchy—a link that had been almost internalized. In the late 1960s and in the 1970s, the leadership of the party was taken over by the men of the third generation, whose formative path had been entirely political and certainly much less ecclesiastical, hence less sensitive to religious and moral dimensions (Tassani 1988).

The DC was becoming an increasingly clientelist and middle-class party, and its electoral center of gravity steadily shifted from the heartlands of Catholic subcultures in northern and eastern Italy to the South and the islands. In a way, this was also a direct consequence of the Cold War: the Communists were permanently excluded from power, and the DC was permanently installed in office. Italy, after all, was a "special," or "difficult," democracy, as many leaders, including Moro, repeated again and again. A Communist coming to power would have meant the end of democracy itself. The lack of alternation and the need to stay in power to keep the Communists out of government was a strong motivation for keeping together the various factions; however, it also prevented the DC from elaborating reformist policies and refining comprehensive strategies that might win over popular consensus. The DC was reduced to maintaining the existing system and its dominant role in Italian society; power had become an end in itself. Unsurprisingly, corruption and clientelism steadily increased. Although this process became common throughout Italy, it was most pronounced in the poor and job-hungry regions of the South, where the system of patronage and the degree of fusion between the state and the party grew extraordinarily (Masala 2004: 109). This, however, did not mean that Catholic intellectuals and Christian Democratic politicians renounced any attempt to propose their ideas and plans for the party's and the nation's present and future. Toward such attempts toward ideological and spiritual renewal we can now turn.

9

The Secular Challenge

This chapter examines how the force of secularism dramatically affected Italian political Catholicism from the late 1960s until the late 1980s. As acutely perceived by Augusto Del Noce, but also by the eclectic and heretic Marxist intellectual Pier Paolo Pasolini, Italy was changing under the pressure of secularization, consumerism, and sexual modernization. The referendum of 1974 on divorce and of 1981 on abortion were a clear sign that Italy was rapidly changing, as also confirmed by the so-called "second economic miracle" of the 1980s.

By the end of the 1960s, it had become increasingly clear that the opening to the Left had not overcome the limits of a democracy without a turnover. The weakness of the center-left government was, in the end, the weakness of the political road that Italian democracy took after the failure of De Gasperi's project of electoral reform and strengthening of the government at the expense of the parties. No effective and coherent government action was possible as the parties were the only political subjects. The coalitions to form a majority reflected the contradictions and tensions that were internal to the parties that formed such coalitions. The lack of an alternative to the DC, with the PCI having been denied access to power as a consequence of the Cold War, contributed to reinforcing the weakness of Italian democracy. Christian Democracy increasingly turned into a party of gray politicians that, after the Council, progressively lost the reservoir of ideas, cultures, and activism of a Catholic milieu that had entered a phase of self-assessment and re-thinking of its mission in Italian society. In the 1970s and 1980s, a growing gap opened between Christian Democracy and Catholicism. Meanwhile, against the backdrop of the immobility of the political system, Italian society had entered—starting in the 1960s—a time of profound transformation, marked by social conflicts, the terrorist threat, and a pervasive process of secularization; then, in the 1980s, it experienced a time of hedonism and a new economic miracle, which permanently pushed Italian culture away from traditional values and lifestyles. How did Christian Democracy respond to this complex situation? Aldo Moro (in the mid-1970s) and, in a much less effective way, Ciriaco De Mita—a representative of the third generation of Christian Democrats—attempted to reform the party, but their projects failed. The chapter Indeed, the chapter is also a story about the progressive decline of Christian Democracy as the "Italian party" (Giovagnoli 1996), even if it remained the biggest political party throughout the entire period.

Italy's Christian Democracy: The Catholic Encounter with Political Modernity. Rosario Forlenza and Bjørn Thomassen, Oxford University Press. © Rosario Forlenza and Bjørn Thomassen 2024. DOI: 10.1093/oso/9780198859864.003.0010

9.1 The End of Catholic Italy?

By the end of the 1960s, as Italian society was entering an intense and effervescent time of mobilization and social conflicts, the Italian political system and Christian Democracy remained trapped in a condition of immobilism. The opening to the Left and the center-left governments did not live up to the expectations (Scoppola 1997: 373–80). For the elections of 1963, the results were not favorable to the DC–PSI alliance. Christian Democracy lost a few percentage points. The liberal party, which had objected to the opening to the Left and asked for a center-right government, increased its votes, finding support in the quarrelsome circles of the monarchists. Moro's attempt at changing the setting of Italian democracy encountered the resistance of several opposing forces. Some of these forces threatened the very essence of democracy. In the summer of 1964, soon after the Socialists had entered the first government of the "organic" center-left (December 1963), the Commander of the Carabinieri and head of the Italian secret services (SIFAR) Giovanni De Lorenzo attempted a coup d'état (*Piano Solo*); recent research has revealed that the President of the Republic Antonio Segni was not unaware of the intent. De Lorenzo's coup d'état also found the support of Banca d'Italia, Confindustria, members of the DC, and experts of the CIA and Gladio, the codename for clandestine stay-behind operations of armed resistance planned by Washington and NATO for a potential Warsaw Pact invasion and conquest of Europe (see Franzinelli 2014). This time, the church—deeply involved in the Council—did not support the opponents to the opening to the Left. The collaboration between Christian Democracy and the PSI continued throughout the 1960s. However, the reformist drive that had supported the opening to the Left slowed down remarkably as a consequence of the limits and ties that the crisis of the mid-1960s had imposed on the Italian political system. This, much more than a supposed willingness to maintain political immobilism that was inscribed in the character and personality of Moro—as some ideological, biased, and unimaginative historians have argued—was the prime reason for the failure of the reformist attempts.[1] After all, the governments led by Moro from 1964 until 1968 maintained strong dynamism in international politics, thanks also to the skillful activity of Fanfani (then foreign minister), who became president of the UN Assembly in 1965 (see Fanfani 2010).

What was particularly important for Christian Democracy in this historical juncture was not only the fact that the party progressively lost contact with the vibrant pluralism that was emerging in Italian society; it also increasingly detached itself from the reservoir of ideas, activism, and organization of social

---

[1] For example, Ginsborg defined Moro "no more a committed reformist than the Dorotei were" and a "political tactician, but with little sense of the real needs of a rapidly changing country" (Ginsborg 1990: 282).

Catholicism. As we have seen in Chapter 8, the Council was fundamental in this respect, a real turning point that changed the relationship between the church and the party, between religion and politics. The post-conciliar era opened a new space and horizon for action between the political and the religious. The church and the wider world of Catholicism now approached politics in a different way. This was also the consequence of the awareness that Italy was changing. As a matter of fact, at the end of the 1960s, the idea of Italy as a "naturally" Catholic nation that had pervaded many sectors of Italian Catholicism started to crumble (Formigoni 2010: 181–2). Within the groups, associations, and journals of grassroots Catholicism, which had been revitalized by the Council, this idea was profoundly and widely discussed and reconsidered. In 1966, Luigi Pedrazzi, who had been a collaborator of Dossetti, defined this image as "an illusion naively clerical or progressively integralist" (Pedrazzi 1966). These convictions were, in fact, widespread also within the church hierarchy. In the 1970s, it became clear to many bishops that Italy was undergoing a deep process of secularization, which had to be opposed by a proper mission of re-evangelization that could not be based exclusively on an appeal to traditional practices and principles, or to the ideological struggle against hostile and anti-Christian ideologies: in another word, anti-Communism.

The church's new pastoral line manifested itself with a program of evangelization for a country that—it was felt—was heading toward secularization. It was a line of action that counted among its most important representatives and promoters the bishop Enrico Bartoletti, from 1972 general secretary of the Italian Bishops' Conference (Conferenza Episcopale Italiana, CEI), founded in 1952 (see Un vescovo 1988; Faggioli 2001). In a 1971 pastoral document titled *Vivere la fede oggi* ("Living one's faith today"), written by Bartoletti and approved by the Italian bishops, the challenge of the moment was the passage from mass Christianity to the secularization of public and private life:

> [T]he current process of transformation, which involves the religious life of our time, if well considered and courageously faced, does not endanger true faith in the living God; it can make it purer and more effective. If there are men enlightened and enlivened by this faith, God will not appear absent from the "city" that man is building for himself. (Evangelizzazione 1979: 347–8)

In 1973, the CEI launched a multi-year plan devoted to the theme of *Evangelizzazione e sacramenti* ("Evangelization and Sacraments"). Two years later, *Evangelizzazione e promozione umana* ("Evangelization and Human Promotion," the preparatory document for a 1976 conference) highlighted that "it does not seem exaggerated to say that Italy is a country that must be evangelized" (Evangelizzazione 1973, 1975). In December 1975, Paul VI published the encyclical *Evangelii nuntiandi*, which started with these words: "There is no doubt that the effort to proclaim the Gospel to the people of today, who are buoyed up by hope but at the same time often oppressed by fear and distress, is a service rendered to the Christian community and also to the whole of humanity."

The post-conciliar Italian church moved in the direction that Catholic Action had first indicated: the "religious choice" (see Chapter 8 and the various texts and documents in Cananzi 1988). The "religious choice" was a reshaping as well as the rebirth of the association. At the basis of the choice, there was not the detachment from politics but, rather, the awareness among Catholic Action's leadership— Vittorio Bachelet and Don Franco Costa, the latter very close to Montini's line— that the association must insert itself into the dynamic activated by the Council and embrace the stimulus coming from the Council itself. As the official document of Catholic Action said, the "religious choice" was to:

> rediscover the centrality of the proclamation of Christ, the proclamation of the faith from which everything else takes its meaning. This means that the proclamation of Christ can become a leaven of civilization, culture, [and] social commitment. (ACI 1988: 499, emphasis in original)

In the context of post-conciliar religious renewal, this "religious" choice extended to other sectors of Catholicism. In the end, the "religious choice" was reflecting the change in Italian society and became the premise for a new wave of evangelization in a country in which the sign of secularization was more and more evident. Sectors of Catholicism indeed considered the "religious choice" a consequence of the DC's losing its grip on Italian society, but this means to mistake change for effects. During Paul VI's pontificate, important changes altered the relationship between religion and politics, between the party and its social, cultural, and organizational Catholic background. Catholics thought that the time had come to put in motion a pastoral strategy that had to be based on the liturgical and participatory reform of the catechism proposed by the Council, as a way of giving new meanings and vitality to the evangelical presence of Catholicism in the fabric of Italian society (Formigoni 2008a: 161–87). The "religious choice" was an attempt at distancing Catholic social action from the use of politics as an instrument of religion. This, however, did not mean that politics was underestimated or dismissed as an unimportant sphere of life; rather, politics was entrusted to the responsibility and autonomy of lay Catholics and understood as "a demanding way of living the Christian commitment at the service of others."[2]

There was a differentiation within the Catholic world on the political plan. Such articulation led to the "social hypothesis" of the ACLI), the defeat of the

---

[2] This quote is from Paul VI's apostolic letter *Octogesima adveniens* of 1971 (n. 46). The letter celebrated the eightieth anniversary of the *Rerum novarum*.

Movimento Politico dei Lavoratori (Political Movement of Workers) at the elections of 1972 (which wanted to create a new, alternative Catholic party), the candidacy of important Catholic figures in the PCI's electoral lists in 1976, and—more importantly—the experience of the *Cattolici per il NO* ("Catholics for the No vote") movement at the 1974 referendum on divorce.

9.2 Debating Divorce

The history of Christian Democracy and the Catholic involvement in social and public life was profoundly marked by the law and the referendum on divorce (on which see Scirè 2007). In 1970, after a parliamentary debate that had isolated the Christian Democrats, a new law on divorce was introduced (*legge Fortuna-Baslini*) that was a major blow to Italian Catholicism. The law also involved canonical (or "concordatarian") marriage and could therefore not but generate frictions between the Vatican and the state, as the Holy See had explained through diplomatic channels since 1967, when the law was first put up for discussion. Furthermore, the process that culminated with the coming into effect of the law demonstrated to the Vatican and the more conservative sectors of Italian Catholicism that they could no longer count on Christian Democracy to contrast the ongoing secularization of habits, behaviors, and customs. The institutional relationship between the church, the DC, and the state thus became quite problematic.

The introduction of the law triggered the reaction of the Vatican and other sections of conservative Catholicism, which still believed that the traditional vision of a deeply Catholic country must be mobilized against its (secular) elites—a repetition of the eighteenth-century idea of a "real Italy" as opposed to a "legal Italy." A group of Catholic intellectuals, guided by Gabrio Lombardi, decided to attempt to repeal the law by requesting an abrogative referendum. Christian Democratic leaders tried, by all means, to avoid a divide within the Italian and Catholic electorate on a theme that was not directly political; after all, it concerned the sphere of moral values and individual behavior. The referendum was called for on May 13, 1974. Having recently been re-elected secretary of the party in 1973, Amintore Fanfani launched an aggressive campaign against the divorce law. Fanfani likely decided to closely associate his name to the battle—even Paul VI was quite lukewarm about, if not frankly opposed to, the referendum—in an attempt to keep Catholics out of the contest for strictly political, and not moral, reasons. On one hand, a victory of the "yes" campaign (i.e. the abrogation of the law) would demonstrate the endurance, resistance, and unity of the DC and allow Fanfani to ward off the rivalry of PCI, whose electoral results were coming close to those of the DC. In fact, the PCI was unenthusiastic about the theme of divorce. Following a Togliattian line, the PCI hesitated and refused to fully embrace a struggle that—the party's leadership thought—was too advanced for the Italian masses, Catholic or not. On the other hand, Fanfani wanted to settle accounts within the party, against the other factions that had obstructed his plan in the late 1950s. A triumph of the referendum would have been a triumph for Fanfani against his opponents, in as much as outside the party.

However, many Christian Democrats and also Catholics outside the party opposed the official line of Fanfani. The main Catholic trade unions (including CISL and the Italian Confederation of Trade Unions) gave their members freedom of choice. The youth section of the ACLI took a clear stance in favor of divorce. A few months before the referendum, a group of Catholic intellectuals formed a pro-divorce committee and the group came to be known as the *Cattolici per il NO* (Seymour 2006: 216).

The turnout was very high (88.1 percent of Italians who had the right to vote) and the "no" vote prevailed with 59.1 percent. The church, the DC, and Fanfani in person suffered a hitherto unimaginable defeat. The result was the final manifestation of the crisis of Catholic Italy. The referendum was the revealing moment, not the cause, of the transformation and secularization that had affected Italian society since the end of World War II. The appeal to defend Catholic Italy presupposed a society still imbued with Christian values. Although Christianity had not disappeared, it no longer had the force of the past.

The Italians' active participation in the referendum demonstrated the willingness and desire to radically change politics and intervene directly in matters of public, moral, and civil importance. In a way, Italians demonstrated that they were even more mature than what parties and observers believed. The result showed that Fanfani, the Vatican, and the PCI—anxious about the result and careful to conduct a campaign that would not "disturb" the supposedly Catholic masses—had wrongly judged the Italian people.[3] However, there were also other readings. Pier Paolo Pasolini argued that the prevailing "no" vote did not reflect the "miraculous" triumph of laicism, progress, and democracy but, rather, the anthropological transformation of the middle class, now dominated by a "hedonist ideology of consumerism" and the disappearance of peasant Italy, of which the church's traditional values were the symbol (Pasolini 1974a). In this assessment, Pasolini actually came close to the thought of Del Noce.

---

[3] As Mark Seymour has argued, "nearly all Italy's politicians approached the referendum from the point of view of its political rather than moral implications. This was certainly not the case among those who were ultimately to settle the controversy—the Italian people. The fact that the referendum was delayed by three and a half years after the introduction of the law was undoubtedly very significant for its outcome. The delays gave the law time to prove itself and to take its place in the mental landscape of the Italians. As a result, the familiar correspondence between political and moral stances, one that would have seen the Italian people vote according to the directives of their preferred political parties, had time to be eroded" (Seymour 2006: 216).

9.3 Catholic Neo-Intransigentism

The divorce issue had many consequences. For several sectors of Italian Catholicism, the outcome clearly demonstrated the already perceived need to re-evangelize Italian society as the best Catholic response vis-à-vis the open sea of modernity. On the more strictly political plan, the outcome of the referendum led to a weakening of the centrality of Christian Democracy in the political system and its status as a national party in Italian society. The official stance in favor of divorce contradicted the party's traditional position as the cornerstone of any aggregation at the center. Even more importantly, both the *Cattolici per il SI* and the *Cattolici per il NO* withdrew their political mandate to Christian Democracy. The promoters of the referendum, first, and then their opponents, claimed their right to express their stances and positions directly, rejecting the party's media-tion. For the first time after World War II, Catholics seriously put their political unity under strain, which was the essence and the basis of the DC's "centrality"— the hinge of the entire political system. In addition to the crucial cultural and societal aspect, the referendum on divorce therefore had a fundamental impact on the political life of Christian Democracy and Italian democracy altogether.

The most attentive sectors of Christian Democracy considered the referen-dum's result the seed of possible positive developments. At the party's national council, which was held after the referendum, Moro saw in the new times and development a possibility to defend Christian values and principles "outside insti-tutions and law" and within the "open and lively texture of our social life" (quoted in Moro 1979: 286–7, 294).

Other Catholic groups accepted the idea that the official Catholic position was a minority in the country and consequently developed new lines of action that renewed and revitalized the traditional intransigent approach. One of the most innovative, effective, and aggregating forms in which this neo-intransigentism expressed itself was the movement *Comunione e Liberazione* ((CL, Communion and Liberation). CL challenged the established distinction between religious experience and political experience (Abbruzzese 1991).

The first leader of CL was Don Luigi Giussani, who had initiated his work in Milan in the 1950s. He aimed at the mobilization of a cohesive, ideologically and culturally aggressive, equipped minority, able to respond to the challenge of secu-larization. For Don Giussani, secularization was the product of a hostile and adverse, cultural and social hegemony, and not the consequence of a molecular cultural and social process that had affected the whole society. In this vision, Italy was no longer a Catholic nation. Rather, there were two competing, contrasting Italies, struggling for hegemony; in this view, democracy appeared as the need to ensure the pluralism of institutions (see Giussani 1972: 234).

After the 1974 referendum, CL posed the problem of building anew a visible and organic social space for Catholics in Italy rather than reviving the improbable traditional myth of the anthropologically Catholic nation. As written in one of the movements' documents, CL wanted to act as a "Christian popular subject," historically rooted in the identity of a "cultural, ethnic, and social group" (L'Uomo 1976: 12). Such a subject structured itself along the modern and dynamic lines of the social movements that were so common and popular in those years among youth groups of every cultural and ideological background. This ensured the CL's success among young people. In a secularized and secularizing society, the tendency was to accentuate a Christian identity, not only for educational and personal growth but also as a social and political commitment. This position was diametrically opposed to the "religious choice" of Catholic Action, which had become common among wider sectors of Catholicism. Going against the "line of mediation" of the "religious choice," seen negatively as political disengagement, and refusing to claim its principles in the name of excessive mediation and compromise, CL proposed the position of "presence," that is, it claimed a strong presence and activism of Catholicism as a social group in public life. In the following years and especially in the 1980s, CL urged Catholics—with increasing emphasis—to focus on identitarian and religious themes, dismissing more "dialogical" themes such as the common good, civil life, and republican democracy. CL accused the DC of not really defending a truly Catholic identity and being too feeble about their values and principles (Camisasca 2006). Not surprisingly, Augusto Del Noce would soon become one of CL's main reference points.

9.4 Augusto Del Noce: Confronting Secularism and The Opulent Society

It is necessary to engage with Augusto Del Noce in some more details, both because his work points to the philosophical depth of Catholic thought in postwar Italy and because his trajectory evidences the difficulties of translating his penetrating critique of modernity into lived politics (Thomassen and Forlenza 2015, 2016b). Del Noce was one of the most original and incisive voices of post-World War II Italian culture. Del Noce attacked Marxism at the level of thought. His works on Marx were part of a lifelong interest in the role of atheism in modern philosophy, which culminated in his *magnum opus*, published in 1964, *Il problema dell'ateismo* ("The Problem of Atheism"). Positioning himself against mainstream modernity, defined as the "age of secularization" and immanentism, in his philosophical works Del Noce attempted to outline an alternative concept of modernity, open to transcendence (Del Noce 1970, 1990, 2014, 2017).

The framework of modern thought for which Del Noce tried to find an alternative was the scheme codified by Hegel and idealism, subsequently taken over by Marxism, with tenets shared even by Thomist neo-Scholasticism. According to this dominant narrative, modernity was a period of secularization in which the emancipation and freedom of the human being moved in tandem with the estrangement from God and faith. Against the French-German line of thought (i.e. Descartes-Hegel-Marx-Nietzsche), Del Noce retrieved an alternative French-Italian line of interpretation, the line of "ontologism." Del Noce understood this alternative as the theory according to which "the knowledge of God, through an a priori intuition, is the condition that makes possible any knowledge" (Del Noce 2006: 8147) that, alone, can guarantee the safeguarding of divine transcendence and the establishment of a Christian philosophy. Elaborating upon Maritain, Del Noce saw the possibility of a different "Cartesianism," that is, an Augustinian, Christian-modern position that passes from Pascal, Malebranche, and Vico to Gioberti, culminating in Antonio Rosmini, the thinker who represents the synthesis of freedom for Catholics and, for Del Noce, the very zenith of Italian philosophy (Del Noce 1991; see also Maritain 1944; 1953). By retracing such a different modernity Del Noce openly sought to make the modern project compatible with a Catholic-religious vision of politics and history.

Del Noce's intellectual trajectory intersected, often in a conflictual way and at various points, with larger political and intellectual debates in post-war Italy and within Christian Democracy. He constantly tried to reconcile philosophical reflection and political vocation, as he believed that "rethinking philosophy is the first problem of contemporary politics, so that the political becomes politics in a Platonic sense, correcting an imperfect world" (Del Noce 1978: 337). The red thread in Del Noce's work was the ideological and political problem of Catholics, that is, to understand how Catholics could participate and act in politics without being subordinate to other political-cultural positions—bringing into politics, society, and history the identity, novelty, and specificity of Catholicism (Del Noce 1964; see also Borghesi 1993).

Compared to a politician like Dossetti, with whom he was in constant dialogue and sometimes open conflict, Del Noce remained at the margins of the mainstream secular scene of Italian contemporary philosophy, but in the end also became a relatively isolated figure within Catholic politics. Large sectors of the Catholic and Christian Democratic intellectual milieu endorsed in the 1960s the opening to the Left, and in the 1970s the collaboration between the DC and the PCI (see below).

Del Noce felt that, in this process, Christian Democracy lost its religious-ideological character more and more, becoming a democratic party without an adjective: an "Americanized" DC. In short, Catholics and Christian Democrats had accepted modernity on their own terms, therefore also embracing an interpretative framework based on the false dichotomies of progress/conservation, revolution/reaction, or Left/Right. A political interpretation of history had replaced a religious interpretation of history based on the traditional category of Truth/Falsehood (or Good/Evil). "Il Santo" had turned into the "Progressist," whereas the "sinner" had become the "reactionary." Catholics had accepted a category of the modern void of religious substance. To the average Catholic, the enemy was no longer irreligion, atheism, or the blasphemous, but the "integralist": a Catholic who wants to be Catholic until the end, living faith as a perspective and guide for their life, and not as a weak and vague feeling. As such, the DC failed to understand that its ideal mission had to be defined against its third and perhaps more insidious enemy after Fascism and Communism: the "opulent society," or Western irreligion, which—just like Fascism and Communism—remained the product, if not the culmination, of modernity. It was against this enemy that the defense of a religious spirit and the rediscovery of Catholic tradition as a way of interpreting the present would represent a litmus test.

At the philosophical level, Del Noce attempted to install a theoretical platform for modern society, opposing the main competing "-isms," among which Catholic anti-modern fundamentalism and the ghosts of twentieth-century totalitarianism, in all its shades. In doing so, he helped to launch Christian Democracy, understood as a new liberalism of Christian inspiration (or, in Del Noce's words, *degasperismo*), into the second half of the twentieth century.

To Del Noce's great disappointment, by the end of the 1950s, the political culture of Christian Democracy had taken a rather different turn, as it became much more influenced by the leftist currents within Catholic thought and Dossetti's interpretation of the role of the church and Christian ethics within this-worldly politics. After De Gasperi's death in 1954, Christian Democrats had increasingly drifted away from *degasperismo*. What Del Noce defined as "Catholic progressivism," flourishing under the banner of the Christian Left or *catto-comunismo*, was re-emerging as a powerful alternative and heir to De Gasperi's DC. According to Del Noce, "Catholic progressivism" aimed at accepting some elements and features of Marxism, judging them "true" in undesirable ways. For Del Noce, Marxism could not be partitioned into healthy and rotten components but had to be wholly rejected.

The "progressive Catholic," Del Noce argued, absorbed and assumed—more or less consciously—the typical attitudes of revolutionary thought: the devaluation of the principles of liberty in favor of the principle of equality; the devaluation of the past (hence the detachment from tradition) and the divinization of the future; the need to consider the original sin as a disposable residue; and the reduction of the individual to their social relationships. Del Noce's critique of "Catholic progressivism" was primarily a critique of the concept and practice of the Revolution and its anthropological and moral repercussions. He contrasted the concept of Reform, or better, the concept of *Risorgimento*, which implies a completely different attitude toward reality, to the concept of Revolution. Whereas the latter dictated a never-ending transmutation of values and a complete destruction of tradition, the *Risorgimento* departed from the belief that there were permanent principles and values that, when faced with new problems and enemies, must be brought to life again and developed appropriately.

At the party and institutional level, as already mentioned, Del Noce was rather skeptical of the opening to the Left. Undoubtedly, Italian Socialism had freed itself from the yoke of Leninism and begun a revision of Marxism. Yet, Socialism still seemed a populist void to Del Noce, a government formula without ideal cohesiveness. An alliance between Christian Democracy and Socialism would be dominated by politics of public expenditure and weakness vis-à-vis corporativist pressures. A political constellation not founded on ideological clarity would always end up in demagogy and functionalism (Del Noce 1957: 485, 1960).

Italian Socialism was moved by an ideological perspective that Del Noce defined as "positivistic." The cultural backdrop of the opening of the Left, he argued, would not be Christian and religious but radically secular. The likely consequence of all this would be a wild modernization of habits, customs, and culture that would endanger traditional values (Del Noce 1959).

In the 1963 congress of San Pellegrino, the third of a series of meetings where Christian Democratic intellectuals and politicians met and discussed the opening to the Left (again, see Chapter 8), Del Noce gave a talk, "The ideological power of Marxism." He argued that the alliance between Socialists and Catholics had affirmed Socialist values at the expense of liberal ones, leading to an irreversible dissociation from the original ideas of Don Sturzo and De Gasperi (Del Noce 1994).

By the mid-1960s, however, Del Noce's philosophical trajectory started to evolve in different directions outside the primary battlefield of political ideologies. Del Noce realized that a new society was gaining momentum, a society that no longer needed religious forces to oppose Communism: a "post-Marxist" era, when the relativization of every ideal would blend with a technocratic vision of the world. The end of totalitarianism, as well as the crisis and the fall of Marxism and its Soviet embodiment, marked the end of the "sacral" period of secularization, when politics would become sacred and absorb the ideal of otherworldly redemption.

Del Noce argued that the twentieth century had now entered a new, "profane" period of secularization, marked by *irreligiosità naturale* ("natural irreligiosity") and a new form of totalitarianism: the *società opulenta* ("opulent society"). To Del Noce, opulent society was technocratic, nihilist, scientist, relativist, individualist, and marked by the primacy of instrumental reason. It was *more irreligious* than Communist atheism, and victorious on the very battleground of Communism itself—that of materialism. The "opulent society" was the triumph of Western irreligion:

> a society that accepts every Marxist negation regarding the denial of religion, metaphysics, and contemplative thought; that therefore accepts the Marxist reduction of ideas to an instrument of production; but that, on the other hand, refutes Marxism [and] its messianic, revolutionary aspects, namely the only religious remnant of the revolutionary idea... [the opulent society] represents

the Bourgeois spirit in its pure state, the Bourgeois spirit that has triumphed over its traditional opponents, transcendent religion, and revolutionary thought. (Del Noce 1970: 14)

In the end, Marxism served nihilism and the bourgeois spirit. Marxism broke all links with tradition but had no means of affirming a new dimension of reality that could replace tradition. The ultimate effect of Marxism was, then, the bourgeois society: opulent, rich, and "fat," a society that inhibited questioning and the search for meaning.

Within an "opulent" society, democracy risked becoming another form of relativism: being a democrat meant not believing in the existence of truth. In this sense, democracy confronted Marxist Gnosticism with its own agnosticism; it still equaled a frightening loss of standards and an existential loss of meaning, a negation not only of the human person in its integrity but also of the very Socratic-Platonic idea of *politics* as the glue tying together human beings in a meaningful order.

Contrary to an "opulent society" in opposition to Marxism (an economic and technical opposition), religious opposition to Marxism was based on the recognition of the dignity of the human person and did not renounce the idea of truth but remained rooted in it. The respect for human conscience and freedom was an absolute truth on which democracy could and must be based. By fearing and excluding the force of truth and rights, the agnostic form of democracy ended up recognizing only the truth and the right of force. In this way, Western irreligion went beyond Gnostic Marxism (Del Noce here drew on Voegelin's famous analysis of modernity as Gnosticism; see Voegelin 2000; Armellini 2011) because it is more radically irreligious and supersedes the incomplete materialism of Marxism by denying the idea of salvation and liberation altogether. This led to a new form of totalitarianism—the domination of opinion and the whims of the strong—that would need no form of legitimation or cover-up of power with ideology, because the only difference between opinions would depend on the strength or popularity of their advocates. The relativity of Western irreligion, which prepared the way for a form of totalitarianism that he saw as more powerful and consistent than Communism—a form of Marxism without any promise of future revolution— would end up in the suicide of democracy.

This was the dramatic situation for Italian and European culture as diagnosed by Del Noce. The crisis of Marxism, which experienced a revival after 1968, posited a conceptual return of the *pari*, or Pascal's wager: at the very moment in which atheism was losing its scientific guise, the possibility of a revival of the religious option looked relevant. Perhaps, Del Noce argued, the crisis of Italian and European culture could only be overcome by a renewal: a *Risorgimento* based on Christian philosophy and a conception of nature and human being open to transcendence.

However, Del Noce was disillusioned, and his hope for the resurrection of culture remained a possibility, not necessarily an actuality. Del Noce glimpsed possibilities for such renovation without being able to indicate positive outlets or clear-cut alternatives. Within the political realm, he ultimately found little reason for hope, as Christian Democracy had abandoned the potentiality of its endogenous principles only to surrender to the lure of the contrasting ideologies of Socialism and liberalism and the unlikely blending of both under the protective umbrella of an impoverished "Christian Democracy." Political Catholicism had abandoned its principles and was now indistinguishable from other political cultures. The triumph of the opulent society, hence of Western irreligion, was taking the wind out of any possible religious revival.

9.5 Moro and Crisis of Italian Democracy

By the mid-1970s, the crisis of Christian Democracy was evident not only to Del Noce. The crisis was not only a philosophical one, but was manifested in the party's difficulties to cope with ongoing challenges and transformations. The party, like the entire political system, was unable to respond to the intense mobilization and wave of radicalism that had affected Italian society, the factories, and the students since the mid-1960s. Italian democracy was under attack by both "red" (i.e. leftist and Communist) and "black" (i.e. neo-Fascist) terrorism. The country was hit by the so-called "strategy of tension," which led to a series of bombings and other obscure events whose main actors were neo-Fascist activists supported by sections of the secret services, the CIA, and Italian politicians. This situation was meant to sow the seeds of fear and uncertainty, hence favoring the conditions for an authoritarian turn (Cento Bull 2007). It was the same strategy that the colonels had successfully employed in Greece, in 1967.

After the referendum on divorce, the "Catholic question"—also known as the "demo-Christian question"—was discussed more and more frequently; even though Christian Democracy continued to be voted and confirmed as the party of the relative majority, it had lost its role as a Catholic guide of society. For many observers, the country's modernization and transformation rendered the Catholic hegemony over society culturally and morally illegitimate as it was no longer an expression of the popular will. Pier Paolo Pasolini talked about this illegitimacy but placed it in a different frame. He did not glorify consumerist modernization; quite the opposite, he denounced the inadequacy and unsuitableness of the DC vis-à-vis the anthropological transformation of Italy. In a country where fireflies—considered the epitome of rural, pre-industrial, genuine, and uncorrupted Italy—had disappeared, he wished for the church to lead an anti-consumerist crusade (Pasolini 1974b).

However, since the late 1960s, the DC's role was seriously put in question and the party experienced increasing cultural and political isolation. The internal debate on how to deal with this situation and imagine a future for the party and the country at large did not produce any particular solutions. After all, the reservoir of ideas that the Catholic milieu had always offered the DC had moved in a different direction after the Second Vatican Council and could not re-energize the party (see Chapter 8). The exception was once again Aldo Moro, who courageously attempted to reform the party, Italian politics, and Italian democracy—an attempt that cost him his life.

In November 1968, the center-left experience was considered over. Moro announced that he wanted to play an autonomous role within the party and detach himself from the majority group by aiming at changing the internal balance of power. In a speech to the party's national council, he said that "new times" were coming, a "new way of being in the human condition." Although these were difficult times, they were pregnant with opportunities and unexpected evolutions (Moro 1979: 223–4).

This was the beginning of a positive interpretation of the youth movement and the mobilization of Italian society, in which he saw the opportunity for an uncertain but crucial path of liberation. By confronting such a situation, Moro added, the DC should—to a certain extent—transform itself into a force of opposition and question itself, and its role in society, to grasp and nurture novel possibilities. Moro's speech was misunderstood; it was seen as the umpteenth episode of *transformismo*, the attempt at incorporating a perspective coming from the outside only to keep everything as it was, fixed in the traditional equilibrium of Christian Democracy. In fact, Moro wanted to govern the crisis. This meant viewing the mobilization of Italian society as the premise for a different approach to the Communist question, also in a wider, international perspective. The Thaw in the icy Cold War relationship between the US and the USSR had put social, cultural, and political processes in motion that could go well beyond the intentions of the superpowers. The Thaw had been initiated by the US and USSR leadership as a way to control the social, economic, and international effects of modernization, and prevented such effects from contrasting with the leading position of the superpowers. Yet, the Thaw could produce more profound changes in the social fabric, which would valorize the emergent subjectivity of youth, workers, and popular classes in a radically different social and political setting.

This was only the beginning of a reflection that would continue throughout the 1970s, coinciding with the final decade of Moro's life. The central question for him was the political reform, and hence the reform of Christian Democracy, which for Moro necessarily had to be the axis of Italian politics. In this context, Moro rejected any suggestions for presidential systems or the reinforcement of the executive at the parties' expense. Inspired by Sturzo, he believed that the parties were to be the center of the system, a vehicle and tool for collecting social demands and offering political answers.

The party system had to be the central core of the democratic system; even though "the future is not, at least partially, entirely in our own hands," as Moro admitted in 1975 (Moro 1990: 3345), the DC had to be at the center of the party system. However, parties—and especially the DC—had to reform themselves, go back to society, and reject their oligarchy and fragmentation into factions. At the party's congress of 1969, he said that the DC must be the "most important and significative link with popular conscience" as well as the "stable base of free institutions" (Moro 1979: 214). The DC's centrality had to be conserved, but at the same time, it had to relaunch the party's innovative thrust. When, in 1972, the DC formed a "neo-centrist" government with the liberals (guided by Andreotti), Moro defined it as a "substitute for an unpleasant fascism" (quoted in Baget Bozzo and Tassani 1983: 518 and 525). At the congress of 1973, Moro expressed his idea of a party that cannot occupy the conservative side in a bipolar scheme precisely in the name of Christian inspiration, understood as a force of human liberation and transformation. This meant adding further motivations for the DC's need to govern, from the center, a democracy conditioned by the presence of the neo-Fascist and Communist oppositions.

9.6 Moro and the "Third Phase"

From the mid-1970s, Moro continued his attempts of reform of Italian democracy and the role of Christian Democrats in it, and advanced the idea of a "third difficult phase of our experience," following the foundational moment of the birth of the republic and the enlargement and consolidation of the democratic state with the opening to the Left. The central problem of what was to be this "third phase" of the Italian democratic experience (on this see Scoppola 1997: 391–9; Formigoni 2008a: 189–202, 2016: 283–336), was the relationship with the PCI and its electoral advancement. At the local elections of 1975, the DC suffered a relative defeat and obtained 35.3 percent of the votes, while the PCI obtained 33.4 percent of the votes. In many important cities, including Rome, Milan, Genoa, Florence, and Naples, leftist councils and Communist mayors were elected. Yet, Moro's reflection also involved more radical questions pertaining to the nature of Italian democracy. Moro thought that the DC should draw the PCI close to the governmental majority. The reason for the collaboration was exclusively connected to the need and the contingency of the moment: the emergency of the Italian situation and the fact that there were no alternative solutions, given the Socialists' position. In other words, Moro did not fully accept the proposal of a "historic compromise" that the Communist leader Enrico Berlinguer advanced in 1973, inspired by the Catholic-Communist intellectual Franco Rodano.

The PCI had embraced—Berlinguer said during the party's congress in 1972—"reformist" politics, rejecting revolutionary methods and transmitting a reassuring and bourgeois image. In October 1973, in a series of three articles published by *Rinascita*, Berlinguer launched the concept of the "historic compromise" between the PCI and the DC as a way to solve the crisis of Italian democracy.[4] Berlinguer started with a reflection on the recent events in Chile, where a coup d'état by General Augusto Pinochet and the army had overthrown the democratically elected Socialist government of Salvador Allende. Berlinguer argued that these events showed that the Marxist Left could not govern in a democratic country without establishing alliances with moderate forces. To counter "reactionary forces" that favored "a climate of exasperated tension" aimed at stimulating an authoritarian turn, an alternative politics based on 51 percent of the vote was not enough. Berlinguer therefore proposed a return to the Great Coalition of the immediate post-World War II years, that is, the politics of collaboration among anti-Fascist forces that had allowed the democratic reconstruction of the country. Other than this initial, defensive concern, Berlinguer added more complex motivations. The encounter between the Communists and the Catholic world had to be the condition for the elaboration of a response to the country's moral degradation, the crisis of Italian democracy, under attack by both red and black terrorism, and the individualism and consumerism that affected Italian society. In Berlinguer's mind, the historic compromise assumed a moral value and became an exit strategy from capitalism for the achievement of a revolutionary, non-violent process: a third way, different from Soviet Communism, which had not incorporated the values of Western democracy, and from Western social-democracy, which had remained attached to the logic of capitalism. In the end, Berlinguer thought of the construction of a new society generated by the encounter between the Catholic and the Communist worlds.

For Moro, matters were completely different. He did not envision an enduring, strategic pact for the government. Collaboration with the Communists was an emergency due to the economic situation and the spread of terrorism. Owing to their persistent link with the Soviet Union and the revolutionary tradition, at least at the symbolic level and despite the Communist claim of detachment from Moscow, the Communists could not but be excluded from the government. Thus, allowing Communists to get "close to" the political majority was understood, by Moro, as a way to actively involve a popular force that could help Italy exit the crisis.

The need to involve a popular force in the government was how Moro defined the notion of "national solidarity," which was established after the 1976 elections and until 1979, when the Communists once again came extremely close to the

---

[4] The three articles were titled "Imperialismo e coesistena alla luce dei fatti cileni" (*Rinascita*, September 28, 1973, 3–4), "Via democratica e violenza rivoluzionaria" (*Rinascita*, October 5, 1973, 3–4), and "Alleanze sociali e schieramenti politici" (*Rinascita*, October 12, 1973, 3–5).

DC (34.4 percent and 38.7 percent of the vote, respectively), and still in the name of the "emergency." National solidarity was not a political coalition or a government program. In fact, it was the abstention of all parties of the "constitutional arc," including the Communists, from a *monocolore* government guided by Giulio Andreotti and composed only of DC ministers. In January 1978, the Communists opened a new crisis in the hope of being inserted into the government and participating directly in the executive. Although Moro rejected this option, he still thought that the collaboration with the Communists in the name of the emergency must continue. Only Moro's kidnapping convinced Berlinguer to accept a solution that was similar to the previous one. There were no Communist ministers in the government, even though this time, the PCI voted in favor of the new government on the same day of Moro's kidnapping.

However, Moro's *terza fase* was even more ambitious than the project of national solidarity as an urgency in the medium run. Its aim was to achieve increasing democratic legitimization of the PCI, stimulating its internal evolution toward a culture of democracy. It is difficult to understand what Moro had in mind after this initial step. In an interview with Eugenio Scalfari, published only a few months after his death, Moro discussed the idea of a bipolar evolution of the Italian political system, no longer based on an emergency but on the alternation (*alternanza*) of two competing and contrasting forces: in short, the shift from a politics of emergence (*emergenza*) to one of *alternanza*. For this to function, in a difficult democracy and in the wider historical and political context of the time, both forces had to be united in convergent democratic convictions, moving beyond the systemic rivalry of the Cold War. This would, and should, happen slowly, step by step.

> The DC will instantly benefit from the PCI's entry into the majority. But then I believe there must be a second phase, not too far ahead, in which the PCI joins the government. I know perfectly well that it will be a "tight" moment to overcome, but it must be overcome.... Only after we have governed together and both have given the country proof of our responsibility and skills can we launch the third phase, that of alternations in government. (Scalfari 1978)

Moro's final reflections contain an important intuition, although it is not an entirely clear and fully defined plan: the involvement and solidarity of all democratic forces that had built democracy were needed to confront the tumultuous changes that had affected Italian society in the 1960s and the 1970s. As the historian Gabriele De Rosa said in a paper titled "From Liberal Catholicism to Christian Democracy between the 1960s and the 1970s," presented at a conference that was held a few months after Moro's death, a large part of the Italian population did not recognize itself in the post-war state born from anti-Fascism and the Resistance. De Rosa argued that the mass parties appeared as alien bodies, incapable of playing a positive role and transforming reality. Moro, instead, had well understood this dramatic situation (De Rosa 1978: 42).

9.7   George Mosse on Moro

The year after Moro's death, the influential historian of Nazism and totalitarianism George Mosse advanced an important interpretation of Moro's thought. This interpretation did not gain much traction, neither in Italy nor abroad, and was at best considered the superficial analysis of a foreign scholar, unfamiliar with Italian dynamics and unable to grasp the intricacies of Italian politics. Moro was generally seen as the epitome of a Byzantine politician, the master of compromise and deferment, the *grande tessitore* ("the big weaver," i.e, "the brain behind") or, as Paul Ginsborg put it, an "unparalleled mediator...excessively meticulous and incapable of making decisions swiftly" (Ginsborg 1990: 255).[5]

Younger generations of Italian historians have rightfully taken Mosse's analysis much more seriously. Mosse understood Moro, his endeavor, his culture, and his politics in an interpretative framework that went far beyond the Italian scene. He understood Moro within the more general context of a deeper transformation of Western parliamentary democracy in the twentieth century. He perceived Moro as a statesman whose political career had a more general significance because he had sought to deal with a parliamentary crisis that was not unfamiliar to other democracies—quite the contrary. Moro confronted the crisis of post-war democracy in the 1970s, a crucial time of social and economic stress and mass politics, when powerful myths and symbols were used to mobilize people to subvert and challenge parliamentary democracy rather than support it.

Mosse thought that Moro approached the question in an original way, trying to broaden the basis of parliamentary governments and thoroughly rethinking the very nature of mass politics. Mosse argued that Moro always listened to the aspiration and desires of the people in order to further integrate them and promote their participation in the democratic process. This was particularly important for those masses that felt they were on the fringe of the political system and in dire need of a sense and possibility of representation. Moro—Mosse said—understood the state as an ongoing process, not a fixed outcome that could secure stability through its sheer presence. The democratic state was, therefore, exactly the opposite of the "coarse rigidity" (*rozza chiusura*) of totalitarianism.

The democratic state must be flexible enough to play the role of liberator. It was not an external order to be established, nor a power to be preserved or developed:

---

[5] Mosse advanced his interpretation in an interview with Alfonso Alfonsi in 1979, titled "L'opera di Aldo Moro nella crisi della democrazia parlamentare in Occidente" (published in Moro 1979: ix–lxxv). The interview has been republished in Mosse 2015.

it was a moral progress of society, the only true progress that needed to be secured. The democratic state could only function as a permanent process, constantly fueled and inspired by new forces to overcome the alienation of groups and broaden the basis of the system. In Mosse's opinion, Moro had understood this better than most others, but he had also paid the price for it.

For Moro, in the political passage toward the *terza fase*, Christian Democracy had to remain the crucial actor, the driver of the passage itself. The party therefore had to be defended against any attacks, including those related to the rising "moral question," concerning the ethical behavior of politicians within a system increasingly plagued by corruption. As Moro said in a speech at the Chamber on March 9, 1977, "there must be no scapegoats, no human sacrifice.... The DC closes ranks around its men.... You will not judge us in the public square, we won't let you put us on trial" (Moro 1979: 350–5). From Moro's point of view, this choice was inevitable. The DC was at the center of the entire political system, and the political system existed and functioned because the DC was at its center. In other words, Moro was bounded to a "strong" vision based on the primacy of politics. Such a vision contained several stagnant aspects. It was indeed a quite problematic vision, full of tensions and internal contradictions. It risked leading to the protection and defense of the status quo, the undervaluation of the moral question, and the illegal trafficking that had been built around and within Christian Democracy, rejecting any radical rupture with the party's historical and political continuity. It is true that Moro, when he regained control of the party in 1975, pushed for the renewal and reconsideration of the DC. He openly talked of the need for a moral refoundation of the party and the necessity to open the political process up to external contributions.

A politician working close with Moro was Benigno Zaccagnini, who was elected the new secretary (a position he kept until 1980). Known as "the honest Zac," Zaccagnini was not a man of faction but a truly reformist politician. He wanted to increase the degree of elite turnover in the party, parliament, and executive so as to encourage generational change. He wanted to prevent elected politicians from holding permanent party posts and, like Moro, open the party to outside forces. However, the resistance of the party's internal factions undermined Zaccagnini's courageous attempts at reform. As a result, even more Catholics who were committed to politics moved away from the party, which had not responded to the hopes of internal change. This was perhaps the most evident manifestation of Moro's internal and political tragedy.

The tragic end of Moro's life put an end to his reformist perspective. In his writings (the letters and the *Memoriale*) from the prison where the Red Brigades kept him for fifty-five days, many important aspects deserve to be underlined (Moro 2008; Gotor 2011). There are surprising judgments and reflections, considering his previous position on maintaining the status quo within the party in the name of a gradual and prudent evolution guided from above and within. The writings contain deep and scathing criticism, if not an outright accusation, of the link between the party's fellow men and its controversial milieu; indeed, they convey a deeply critical consideration of the moral question. Some fragments allude to the "secret history" of the Italian Republic, including acute observations on the "strategy of tension" and the logic to destabilize in order to stabilize, as well as the almost incestuous relationship between international political and military circles and national, internal political problems. Having reached the end of the line, perhaps Moro had become aware of the limits of his battle. In other words, he had reached the conclusion that it was impossible to keep together—in the medium run—his strong concern for the impoverishment of politics and his likewise firm logic of conservation of the unity of the DC. When Moro died, the third phase of Italian democracy remained an interrupted project, with profound historical consequences.

9.8 Christian Democracy Loses Its Centrality

From the late 1970s onward, the DC's "centrality" was no longer a given, far from it. The crisis of the party's centrality had emerged already in the early 1970s, and Moro had tried to respond to this crisis, but it assumed a definitive and irreversible character only in the following decade. The discontinuity between the 1970s and the 1980s appears, in retrospect, very evident. It is difficult to pin down the specific event that marked this discontinuity, whether it was Moro's death in 1978, the end of "national solidarity" in 1979, the PCI's decision to abandon any form of collaboration with the DC in 1980 (the so-called second "turning point of Salerno"),[6] or the DC's national congress in 1980 and the proposal of the line of the *preambolo* (an agreement between four internal factions that wanted to end the idea of national solidarity and collaboration with the Communists and, instead, re-establish an organic relationship with the Socialists). In 1980, on the occasion of the last important trade union action and at the end of over a decade of workers' protests, a dramatic situation emerged as a strike halted the production of the biggest Italian factory: the FIAT. Forty thousand cadres and white-collar workers took to the streets of Turin to protest against the workers' strike

[6] After returning to Italy from Moscow in March 1944, in the midst of World War II, the Communist leader Palmiro Togliatti proposed that the Communists should set aside their resentment of the monarchy, suppress any revolutionary ambition, and collaborate with the other anti-Fascist forces in defeating Germany and Fascism. This view would become known as "la svolta di Salerno" (turning point of Salerno) in reference to the city where Togliatti advanced his proposal. On the night of March 3, 1944 (i.e. the very eve of Togliatti's departure from Moscow), Togliatti and Stalin had secretly agreed upon this "politics of national unity" and collaboration that re-evoked and re-enacted the popular front policy introduced by the Seventh Congress of the Comintern (Moscow 1935).

and demand the right to work.[7] The 40,000 broke the pickets and re-entered the factory. The trade unions acknowledged their defeat and signed an agreement with the FIAT management. The so-called "march of the 40,000" was, therefore, "a watershed of national significance," as the balance of power between capital and labor "swung decisively back to the employers" (Ginsborg 1990: 407; Golden 1997: 58–9). The new culture of work that emerged from this situation puzzled not only the trade unions but also parties and politicians.

In addition to all these events, which were internal to the Italian horizon, wider developments invested the world. The 1980s were the beginning of the process of globalization that would lead to the collapse of European Communism and, at a structural level, the declining power of national states and traditional political parties and movements. In this general context, the Italian economy was also invested by another crucial change that came from abroad. Margaret Thatcher in the United Kingdom and Ronald Reagan in the US introduced harsh neo-liberal measures. At the same time, the American president assumed a strong and extremely aggressive anti-Communist and anti-Soviet rhetoric that revamped the Cold War. All this meant that the DC's political role and space for maneuver were dramatically reduced. The party entered a time of strategic confusion from which it would never recover. The changes of the beginning of the 1980s introduced a neo-liberal orientation that stood in contrast to the historically established convergence and agreement between the productive bourgeoisie and the popular classes. This new orientation also threatened the politics of aggregation at the center of the political spectrum and the progressive inclusion of marginal social groups on which the DC's politics had been based. The call for the abandonment of the old convergence manifested itself in many ways, including the emphasis on the moral question (evoked in an anti-Christian Democratic spirit), the proposal to create governments of technicians who were independent of parties, and the invitation to the PCI coming from different sectors of public opinion to move away from the *solidarietà nazionale*.

In the 1980s, the *questione democristiana*, which had not been solved in the 1970s, assumed a concrete political significance that was visible to everyone. It was precisely at this historical juncture that the project of the second generation came to an end. All these different threads converged in 1981 when the DC was forced to face a particularly delicate passage: the abortion referendum. The question involved "not negotiable principles," to use an anachronistic expression, and therefore opened the way for contrasts and conflicts between believers and non-believers that were not easy to solve and recompose, weakening the common ground of secular politics built on religious peace.

---

[7] The strike had been called after the FIAT had discharged 24,000 workers, including a huge number of union activists.

9.9 The Referendum on Abortion and the "Recomposition"

In 1978, a law (no. 194) was introduced that allowed women to terminate, under certain conditions, a pregnancy. A proposal to repeal the law became the object of a referendum in 1981: the referendum for the abrogation of law no. 194, proposed by the Movement for Life, a Catholic association led by the Christian Democrat MP Carlo Casini. More than 70 percent of Italians voted against the abrogation, and many observers saw in this result yet another confirmation of the secularization of Italian society and the increasing detachment of Italian people from Christian principles—most certainly from the church's directives and the DC's control of society, contrasted by the increasing awareness of the importance of civil rights (Scirè 2008; Pollard 2008: 152–5; Bracke 2017). However, the Catholic historian Pietro Scoppola offered a slightly different interpretation of the vote. The referendum was composed of five parts, which—in addition to abortion—included matters regarding public order, life sentences, and gun licenses. The referendum, called by the Radical Party, asked voters to reject life imprisonment as the highest punishment for crimes; a clear majority of Italians voted "against" (77.4 percent). Hence, if Italians had voted to maintain the law on abortion for civil and cultural motivations, why had they rejected the abolition of life imprisonment? Life imprisonment ruled out the idea that prisons and punishment can, and must, have a re-educational function: civil, moral, and cultural motivations should also have worked in this way. The contradiction disappears—Scoppola further argued—if the two votes are seen in a different light. Both the possibility to interrupt a pregnancy and the deterrent effect of a life sentence must not be seen in the general context of the affirmation of civil rights. They should rather be seen as the expression of a less ideal request for certainty and security, that is, a plea for *not* being disturbed by moral and fundamental problems, not renouncing any possibility offered by the law to protect one's safety and security. In this sense, the combined result of the 1981 referendum might instead be seen as the revelation of an "ethical void" toward which the process of secularization had pushed the country (Scoppola 1997: 419–20).

Ironically, one of the unexpected consequences of the referendum was the re-aggregation, or recomposition, of the Catholic world, even though the term "recomposition" had already been introduced at the end of the 1970s, by the Jesuit Bartolomeo Sorge (1979, 1981). This recomposition was based on moral and cultural foundations and occurred outside party politics, strictly speaking, manifesting itself through a series of meetings between ecclesial associations and movements. And yet, such recomposition once again seemed to benefit Christian Democracy, reverting—if only temporarily—the process that had seen Catholics progressively move away from Christian Democracy after the Council (see Chapter 8). The Communist threat was now much less real than in the past. The new challenge was secularization and value relativism, as Del Noce so vividly had pointed out. To confront this enemy, a new political unity started to form around Christian Democracy. New forces and energies coming from Catholicism were inserted into the party. The DC leadership recognized the need to initiate a new dialogue with the party's social and cultural background, hence with the Catholic milieu. To this end, in November 1981, the party convened a meeting open to non-members (*assemblea degli esterni*), which focused on the DC's role in the country, the party's identity, its organization, and its relationship with Catholic associationism. Ultimately, though, the party did not manage to revitalize the relationship with its social and cultural background, and more generally with the entire civil society. Its defensive reaction was of little effect. The 1981 referendum had, in fact, confirmed that the Catholic presence in Italian society was minor and that, especially in moral matters, Italian society was moving in directions that differed from the Vatican's indications. Direct democracy, or the parliamentary action of a party of Christian inspiration, could not guarantee the defense and promotion of Catholic and Christian principles in society. The diffused presence and participation of Catholics in many political parties would have been more effective and could have influenced such parties from within. Most of the Italian bishops did not perceive the problem. For them, the revision in 1984 of the 1929 Concordat, which confirmed the teaching of Catholicism in public schools— albeit on a voluntary and not compulsory basis—and the role of the ecclesiastical authorities in the organization of teaching (i.e. programs, the appointment of teachers, textbooks; Pertici 2009: 581–5), demonstrated that Italian society was still a predominantly Catholic society. However, as Scoppola explained, this was just an illusion.

9.10 Ciriaco De Mita: Reforming the Party, Reforming the System

One last attempt to reform the DC took place against the backdrop of the party's recomposition. In reality, the entire Italian political system was changing. In May 1982, De Mita was elected secretary of the party. This was the culmination of the transition from the second to the third generation. De Mita had already tried to alter the party's internal balance of power in 1969, when he sealed a deal with Arnaldo Forlani and other *quarantenni* (forty-somethings), known as the "pact of San Ginesio." The older generation, however, reversed the situation in the 1973 with the "pact of Palazzo Giustiniani," sealed by Moro and Fanfani—elected to the secretary—and signed by all leaders of the internal factions. Once in power, in the early 1980s. De Mita aimed at a wider institutional reform of the Italian political system and the reform of his party. He invited the party to discuss this institutional reform at a 1983 conference, where he also presented his proposal (De Mita 1984; Le istituzioni 1984).

The debate over institutional reforms had started in the late 1970s in reaction to a system that was deemed incapable of decision-making. The first initiative had come from the Socialists (Amato 1980). The debate culminated in the early 1980s, with the institution of the Commissione Bozzi (1983–5), derived from the name of Aldo Bozzi, the liberal MP who was called to preside over the commission. De Mita solicited the party to commit to institutional reform and he chose Roberto Ruffilli as his consultant. Ruffilli would later be assassinated by the Red Brigades (Scoppola 1997: 439–49). De Mita invited him to lead a "department concerning problems related to the state," namely the DC's internal commission. Ruffilli then entered into the Commissione Bozzi as the DC's expert on institutional matters.

De Mita had an electoral system in mind that was based on the principle that the parties must declare their government alliances *before* the elections. Citizens would thus have the power to choose not only their parliamentary representatives but, to a certain extent, also the government. At the DC's national council of September 12–13, 1984, Ruffilli said that the reference to the electoral law was by no means an attempt to propose "surreptitiously the perspective of an absolute primacy" of the government over the parliament. A year before, writing in the party's daily *Il Popolo*, Ruffilli had already raised the need to introduce a reform that was meant to give citizens the power to choose their representatives, political programs, and a government. In May 1984, De Mita—while talking before the Commissione Bozzi—once again advanced the idea of coalition pacts with a majority prize that would guarantee a political majority in parliament. The proposal was included in the DC's electoral program in 1987 (all these documents are in Ruffilli and Capotosti 1988).

In this way, De Mita responded to the challenge of the "alternative": the Socialists would be forced to choose, before the elections, whether to ally themselves with Christian Democracy for the government or with the Communists for the opposition. Essentially, the Communists were legitimized as an alternative pole to the DC, in a move that also valorized the experience of national solidarity. De Mita considered this move as a first step to unlock Italian democracy, overcoming the so-called *conventio ad excludendum* aimed against the Communists (i.e. their impossibility, in the frame of Cold War dichotomies, to govern the country), moving toward a bipolar model that would allow not simply a turnover of forces in guiding the executive branch but a proper alternative composed of competing political forces to govern the country. At the same time, the proposal also reopened the perspective of the center-left government (DC–PSI), though in a frame of stability and guaranteed majority, as the pre-eminent role of the party of the relative majority was guaranteed. For De Mita, the alliance with the Socialists was a necessity. He wanted to tie the Socialists to a coalition pact, claiming the role of majority party for the DC. However, De Mita's real aim was to involve the Communists, not simply in terms of collaborating with the government but at the institutional level. The role of the PCI was crucial, he thought, to the forging of a widely shared political and institutional reform. In perspective, his idea was that of a bipolar system based on a governmental *alternanza* between the DC and the PCI (or a leftist pole led by the Communists).

However, the line proposed by De Mita encountered strong resistance within and outside the party. On one hand, the idea of a bipolar system in which the DC would occupy a position alternative to the Left unleashed the opposition of the leftist factions within the party. On the other hand, the idea that the Socialists— and the other lay parties of the center—had a duty to declare their alliances and political positions before the elections provoked the reaction of the Socialists, and it was opposed by the supporters of the *preambolo*, the abovementioned agreement between four internal factions within the DC that had put an end to the national solidarity project, aiming for a new organic relationship with the PSI. The supporters of the *preambolo* thought that forcing the Socialists to choose alliances before the elections could hamper their effectiveness and weaken their willingness to collaborate. In addition to this, the PSI openly obstructed De Mita's plan, which it saw as a way to legitimize the Communists and put the Socialists at the margins of the system.

With very few exceptions, the PCI also declared its opposition to the institutional reforms. This happened for two reasons: first, Communist culture was traditionally not very sensitive to the theme of institutional reform, giving priority to social and economic aspects; second, the *alternanza* as understood by the Communists was not simply a governmental alternation in a Western democratic sense but an alternative to the liberal and capitalist system tout court. Sectors of public opinion in Italy shared with De Mita the idea that the PCI could be "recovered" and inserted into (Western and liberal) democracy and the democratic game in a substantial position of equality with other forces. After all, in 1981, after the Soviet invasion of Afghanistan and the introduction of martial law in Poland to crush the opposition of the Solidarity movement, party secretary Berlinguer said that the "propulsive drive of the October revolution" had come to an end. However, despite the struggle internal to the PCI, the party's leadership and base never broke completely with the Soviet Union nor abandoned the very idea of revolution, convinced that the real aim was to overcome capitalism. The idea of the "diversity" of Italian Communists with respect to Soviet Communists received little consideration at the international level, and John Paul II considered it unfounded. Perhaps De Mita and those who looked favorably at his plan undervalued such resistance. In the context of the still intense East–West contrast, the perspective advanced by De Mita could not have immediate political consequences. His project was not completely clear, as he confessed years later, and in any event, it could not be brought to completion.

Like most other Christian Democrats of the third generation, De Mita was less sensitive to the theme of Christian inspiration. His "new deal" of removal and comprehensive modernization hinged on overcoming the fragmentation of the quarrelsome factions in a new dialogue with the urban social classes that were becoming the main drivers of the new Italian miracle of the 1980s (Crainz 2012: 184–94). He wanted to abandon the traditional rural image of the DC and develop a new relationship with the cultural *milieu*.

The DC partially abandoned its physiognomy of a "national" and "Italian" party and sought to construct a new relationship with a rapidly changing civil society. De Mita aspired to establish a new party model in which the traditional interclassist system of representation turned into a new, flexible tool that could give a prompt and effective response to the solicitation of civil society. Fundamental aspects of this plan included the process of moralization of all sectors of the party, the renovation of the cadres, and the opening to cultural and ideological currents that were different from the Catholic tradition. At the level of economic politics, he tried to abandon the DC's laxness, embracing the policy of "fair strictness" (*rigore solidale*) sustained by the Catholic economist Beniamino Andreatta. In other words, he tried to counter the criticism of those who sustained the *questione democristiana*, that is, those who affirmed the moral illegitimacy of the DC's governing and leading role.

De Mita's idea was to transform the old Catholic party into a deft and modern centrist party, able to represent the productive classes in competition with the Socialists who, under Bettino Craxi's direction, presented themselves as the manifestation of the new modernization that the country was experiencing in the 1980s. Interviewed by Eugenio Scalfari—the editor of the influential daily *La Repubblica*—on April 11, 1983, De Mita proposed to overcome the "deceiving scheme" of the Left and the Right through a "new dialectics" between "old and new." The people, he said, "want government...innovation...and a modern and efficient administration of power," otherwise "they will reject politics" (Scalfari 1983).

De Mita's political project raised expectations within and outside the party and among those sectors of public opinion that understood the need for renewal. The 1983 elections were to be a crucial test for the new deal made by De Mita. At the elections, however, the DC suffered a serious defeat: votes decreased from 38.3 percent in 1979 to 32.9 percent. At the European elections of 1984, the DC was, for the first and only time, surpassed by the PCI. The result of the elections put the brakes on De Mita's plan for reform. Sectors internal to the party connected the defeat to the secretary's political move. The result was the end of a long political and democratic history, marked by an aggregation of political forces toward the center of the system, occupied and organized by Christian Democracy, and the final stage of a process that had started at least a decade before. De Mita said that the roots of the crisis dated back to the late 1960s and that the party had waited too long to take the road of reform and transformation. The defeat, he added, was the price paid for an innovative proposal that had not been fully understood but went in the right direction. It was necessary to insist, and Italians would eventually understand. To him, the result meant that the contradictions of the Italian system had to be confronted at the institutional level, introducing an electoral reform that would correct the problems tied to the proportional system.

In any event, the elections of 1983 made the idea that the DC could govern in the name of everybody more and more impossible. It was the end of the DC's centrality in the Italian political system but also the end of the search for a serious reconsideration of this system. The electoral result also confirmed that Italian society was emancipating from the tutelage of a Catholic party, which was Catholic and Christian only in name and on the surface. The DC of the second generation was history. The third generation, to which De Mita belonged, did not consider the question of the party's Christian inspiration politically relevant. As indicated above, a certain "recomposition" of Italian Catholicism had benefited Christian Democracy. It is also true that De Mita decided to present "external" Catholic intellectuals at the elections of 1983, who had been the main actors in the debate on the party's renewal, such as Scoppola, Ruffilli, and Del Noce. It was the recognition of the importance of the religious, cultural, and associative areas that they represented, but it did not suffice to reconnect the party with the church and Catholicism. Meanwhile, with the newly elected Pope John Paul II, the church itself had entered a time of profound transformation.

9.11 Moving Away from the DC: Catholicism between Presence and Mediation

The death of Paul VI in 1978, a few months after Moro's assassination, coincided with the end of a historical process that had taken off in the late 1930s in Italy as well as Europe, in which Montini played a central role. The process had laid the basis for the political commitment of Catholics in the post-war period, resulting in the "political unity of Catholics" through a party: Christian Democracy.

Between the two wars, in the context of evolving mass politics and the double challenge of pagan Fascism and atheistic Communism, the perception that Catholics had become a minority living through a temporary crisis of civilization forced the Catholics to deeply rethink Catholic presence in contemporary society. Especially after Pius XI condemned Action Française, the elaboration of a new Catholic project was forged in an anti-totalitarian perspective by intellectuals and politicians such as Jacques Maritain, Montini, De Gasperi, Dossetti, Fanfani, Moro, and many others. From the late 1970s to the early 1980s, this project had come to an end and "Maritainism" entered a crisis.

The pontificate of John Paul II turned a new page in the history of the entire world. In the 1980s, the consequences of the new pontificate started to be felt in Italy, too. After his election, the pope focused on the crisis that Western Catholicism was undergoing; in doing so, he paid close attention to the church in

Italy. John Paul II aimed at reinforcing the Italian Catholic ecclesiastical milieu to reaffirm its role as a guide, overcoming the anti-institutional and contesting winds of the 1970s (Acerbi 2003: 487–90). He was alien to the specificity of Italian politics and what the DC had been, and still was. Montini had paid close attention to Italian politics, of which he had profound knowledge. With the new pope, the gap between secular Rome and sacred Rome became bigger. "The Tiber became wider," as the republican Prime Minister Giovanni Spadolini (June 28, 1981–August 23, 1982, the first prime minister not to be a member of the DC since De Gasperi in 1945) famously said. At the same time, the pontificate opened itself to a new course in Italian Catholicism, marked less by the connection with party politics and projected toward a more active presence in society to counter the effect of secularization. At a famous conference in Loreto in 1985 (April 9–13), rightly seen as the great turn that marked the "Wojtylization of Italian Catholicism" (Scornajenghi 2012: 100), the pope urged the Italian church to become a new and active social force (the speech is reproduced on the Vatican's official website; see also Allocuzione 1985; Indicazioni 1986: 951–73).

This was not a proposal to relaunch the DC or any other Catholic party project. Yet, Wojtyla rejected the marginalization of the Christian tradition in Italian society that many Catholics had taken for granted. Thus, Catholics were invited to enter the public sphere actively and directly as Catholics and on their own, without the mediation of a party. John Paul had already appealed for a more active and direct, unmediated presence of the Catholics in society in a speech to the bishops given in Assisi in 1982. On this occasion, the pope seemed to ascribe the lack of such commitment to the CEI and its embracement of the line of mediation of Catholic Action (Giovanni Paolo II 1982: 824–5).

Through his speech at Assisi—which was followed by the official recognition of the fraternity of CL (opposed by the CEI)—and, even more, the speech at Loreto, the pope expressed his strong preference for the line of Catholic presence at the expense of the line of mediation. The debate between the latter, which was certainly majoritarian within the Italian church and the official position of the CEI and Catholic Action, and the former, sustained by CL and a few bishops, became intense after Assisi. In many ways, the Loreto conference was the showdown of the struggle between the two lines or, to put it differently, between *riconquista* and *discernimento* ("reconquest" and "discernment"), and their attempts at reconciling what was in reality irreconcilable. The debate had been intense already during the months preceding the Loreto conference. In a meeting of the preparatory committee, the different views came to the fore, especially regarding the meaning given to the pastoral dimension (see, for example, the president of Catholic Action, Alberto Monticone, and Don Massimo Camisasca of CL, as quoted in Prezzi 1985). Other controversies emerged after the publication of a collected book by circles within CL, in which the "religious choice" of Catholic Action was accused of "neo-Protestantism" (Riconciliazione 1984). The line of *mediazione* and that of *presenza* may not seem irreconcilable, but in many ways they were. While the supporters of *mediazione* continued to feel the importance of commitment at the political, social, and civil levels, the supporters of *presenza* did not consider it important to contribute to the building and consolidation of the state and democracy; for them, it was crucial to be present in the Italian public arena on their own. Significantly, neither of the two perspectives believed in the centrality of the DC and did not follow the logic of "collateralism." Both implicitly presupposed that the reference to a Christian tradition was still shared and important within Italian society as a whole but had lost its power to attract different classes and sectors. As Francesco Traniello has noted, these different and contrasting lines produced converging outcomes: both concurred with the wider Catholic detachment from the DC and contributed to the ongoing rupture of the political unity among Catholics (Traniello 2009: 41). In fact, in many Catholic circles, the DC was by now considered the main actor for the secularization of Italian society, as intellectuals such as Baget Bozzo and Del Noce highlighted.[8]

Either way, with the *allocuzione* of the pope at Loreto, the balance shifted decisively toward the line of presence. Even before the publication of the conference's concluding remarks, this passage was seen as a moment of rupture and great discontinuity. Del Noce, for example, saw in the event a moment of Catholic restoration (Del Noce 1985). A few years later, Camillo Ruini—who played an important role in the Loreto meeting—said that it inaugurated a "new" and "more ambitious" phase for the Italian church. Concerning politics, the conference did not signal an immediate detachment of Italian Catholics from the DC; it could more likely be seen as an attempt, especially by CL, at "Catholicizing" the party. Until the DC's dissolution, the church insisted on the political unity of Catholics motivating it not by the need to defend the democratic system but by the duty to protect and promote fundamental ethical and anthropological values. In Italy, as elsewhere in the world, the Communist question declined, while the religious and ethical questions triggered by a consumerist revolution and globalization became more and more central. In any event, this attempt at Catholicizing the DC in the final years of its life did not have significant consequences. It did not put brakes on the party's loss of a national political perspective; rather, it increased the process of the DC's "meridionalization" both among the electorate and the leadership, which were less and less tied to the church and the state, linked to the party's previous centrality in the system, and progressively exposed to corruption and the dynamics of patronage.

---

[8] In this vein, the unprecedented and novel role played by Catholics in Italian political life after World War II, for the first time after the unification of Italy, was considered little relevant or frankly negative (Baget Bozzo 1994).

However, with the turning point of Loreto, the seeds for a new and original action and initiative of Italian bishops reflecting John Paul's wishes for a more active presence in society were sown, independently from party politics. Camillo Ruini's appointment in 1991 and the wider transformation of Italian politics and the dissolution of the DC made this evident. The Italian church was ready for a new cultural project aimed at the continuation of the Catholic project without a Catholic party. Next chapter will describe this project.

10

Orphaned Catholics

At the beginning of the 1990s, the Italian political system entered a period of dramatic transformation as the result of a series of international and domestic crises. The most important of these was undoubtedly the end of the Cold War; it radically changed the ideological horizon that had oriented the Italians' electoral and political choices for fifty years. At the domestic level, the emergence of regionalism and the rising disaffection with traditional politics and parties among Italians challenged the political system. Last but not least, judicial investigations into political corruption revealed a huge scandal known as *Tangentopoli* ("Bribesville"). In a short span of time, the founding elements of the entire Italian political system evaporated. Old parties changed names and underwent a radical transformation, or simply disappeared; new parties and movements filled the political vacuum. Christian Democracy terminated its existence in 1994, seeking to regroup in a new party that took the name of Sturzo's original party, the Partito Popolare Italiano. The end of Christian Democracy, after governing the country for fifty years, not only represented a profound discontinuity in the Italian political system; it was also the end of the Catholics' political unity (Scoppola 1997: 502–13; Malgeri 1999; Formigoni 2008a: 203–27; Bernardi 2014; Giovagnoli 2014; Saresella 2014). This, however, did not mean the end of Catholic participation in politics. Rather, the forms and modes of Catholic politics changed, while the Catholic Church launched a new political and cultural project that aimed at reaffirming the role of Catholicism in the public sphere without the mediation of a party. This transformation is the focus of the last chapter.

10.1 The End of a System

The fall of the Berlin Wall in 1989, the collapse of the Soviet Union in 1991, and the end of the international relations system based on the East–West bipolarity had profound effects on the internal politics of Italy and other European states. The Italian Communist Party changed its name and tried to distance itself from its Communist past and evolve—not without contradictions—into a post-Communist, social democratic party (Partito Democratico della Sinistra, PDS). However, some of its hardcore members, who were still attached to Soviet symbolism, formed a small secessionist party called Rifondazione Comunista (Kertzer 1998).

Italy's Christian Democracy: The Catholic Encounter with Political Modernity. Rosario Forlenza and Bjørn Thomassen, Oxford University Press. © Rosario Forlenza and Bjørn Thomassen 2024. DOI: 10.1093/oso/9780198859864.003.0011

With the end of anti-Communism and its function of providing an ideological glue, the Italians floated away from Christian Democracy. Many northern Italians moved toward a regionalist movement founded by Umberto Bossi: the Northern League. The League first emerged during the local elections of 1990 but became particularly visible at the 1992 national elections, when Christian Democracy suffered a significant defeat and votes dropped to below 30 percent for the first time in history. The Northern League, instead, became a leading political actor as it gained 8.7 percent of the vote on the national level; in the northern provinces, especially in the northeast, it obtained no less than 18 percent of the vote, becoming the second party after the DC. Until the early 1980s, the DC had been the hegemonic party of the northeast as a consequence of its organizational strength but also the long history of Catholic associational life in the area. The League shattered the preexisting balance of power between parties and, in the post-1992 political scene, became the most important recipient of political protests against the degeneration and immobilism of Italy's republic of the parties, which was increasingly perceived as unable to carry out reforms and reply to the demands emerging from a changing society. More specifically, the DC was considered incapable of representing the socioeconomic reality of the northeast, which relied on small and medium-sized businesses. With the rallying cry *Roma ladrona* ("Thieving Rome"), the League screamed out loud that the state—and particularly Christian Democracy—had broken the democratic pact with northerners, squandering and stealing the money that they had earned through hard work. The *questione settentrionale* ("northern question") had always been a part of Italian history, but in the 1970s and the late 1980s, it had come to represent a burning issue for the party; yet, the DC gave no clear answers to the question.[1] The League grew rapidly, starting precisely from the "white" settlement of northern Italy, which had been one of the most sociologically enduring and evident symbols of "Catholic" Italy (De Luna 1994; Diamanti 1995, 1996; Jori 2009; Formigoni 2010: 187–8).

The turmoil within civil society and the criticism of the party system (particularly Christian Democracy) also came from other sectors, even within the party itself. In 1991, Leoluca Orlando—the former mayor of Palermo who had led a strong opposition to the mafia in the mid-1980s, giving life to the so-called *primavera di Palermo* ("Palermo spring")—founded the movement *La Rete-Movimento per la Democrazia* ("The Network-Movement for Democracy"). Another Christian Democrat, Mario Segni, founded and led a movement for

---

[1] See, for example, Walter Tobagi's investigative report of April 29, 1975, on Bergamo, which would become a stronghold of the Northern League, published by *Il Corriere d'Informazione* under the titled "L'avvocato ha un debole per il cemento." Consider also what a DC leader in the Veneto region—Toni Bisaglia—said in a 1983 interview, following elections in which a regionalist movement called Liga (which then merged with other forces and movements to form the Northern League) obtained a remarkable success: "[T]he votes for Liga are all demo-christian votes" (Ceccarelli 1983).

electoral reform through a referendum: the idea of the electoral reformers was that Italy's electoral system stimulated corruption and ballot fraud and prevented citizens from exercising the fundamental right to choose their government. In 1991, a referendum was held that abolished the single preference. This was a problem for DC's division into factions, as would become clear at the 1992 elections. For the first time, members of the same faction were forced to compete against each other, thereby undermining their cooperation. No members of the DC's political elite seemed to take the turmoil seriously, with the exception of Francesco Cossiga, the president of the Republic (1985–92), who in the last two years of his mandate gave voice to radical criticism of the party system. In the speech with which he announced his resignation (three months before the natural end of his mandate), he said that the democratic system had developed into "an oligarchy" (Cossiga 1993: 34).

The situation for Christian Democracy worsened after the 1992 elections, not simply as a result of the electoral outcome but also because political corruption had become the main political issue of the time. The aforementioned *Tangentopoli* corruption scandal came to light. Virtually every day, episodes of corruption were announced. The so-called judicial operation *Mani Pulite*, "Operation Clean Hands," sought to tackle systemic economic and political corruption. The trials that followed turned into a public spectacle. The investigation revealed that a huge number of politicians—ministers, members of parliament, and local administrators—as well as bureaucrats and entrepreneurs were involved in the corruption system. Operation Clean Hands initially and primarily struck the PSI but soon started to affect an increasing number of Christian Democrats. The investigation led to a dramatic crisis in the political system. The PSI disappeared, and its leader Bettino Craxi—prime minister from 1983 to 1987—escaped to Tunisia to avoid prison. Meanwhile, the mafia frontally attacked the state with a devastating wave of murders (especially the prosecuting magistrates Giovanni Falcone and Paolo Borsellino) and bombings. Accusations of collusion with the mafia hit the most symbolic representation and embodiment of the DC's power: Giulio Andreotti, or "divine Giulio," the most enduring symbol of Italian politics, heading seven governments in the 1970s and then again in office between 1989 and 1992.[2] Trials for corruption and mafia merged and resulted in a political trial covering the full fifty years of DC power. In a sense, all of this was only the culmination of a public opinion and civil society movement that had started in the 1970s with the *questione democristiana* (see Chapter 9) and continued in the

---

[2] Andreotti was acquitted of all charges in a first moment, then again on appeal to the Court of Appeals, and finally on appeal to the Court of Cassation in 2004, partially due to the expiration of the statute of limitations. The Court had found evidence of Andreotti colluding with Cosa Nostra until the spring of 1980 but not later, and the crime therefore fell owing to statute-barred limitations.

1980s with the *questione morale* ("moral question"). Yet, no one could have foreseen that the ensuing drama would have reached such peaks.

Christian Democracy was confronted with increasing political and cultural
isolation. Reformist forces within the party tried to react and wipe out the image
of DC as a party of either bribers or corrupt politicians. The leftist faction of the
DC, with the Manifesto di Lavarone (September 1992), pushed for a moral
renewal of the party and encouraged the prosecuting magistrate of Milan to continue the investigations. Other Catholic and Christian Democratic intellectuals
and politicians formed an association called Carta '93, which aimed at redefining
the party's structure through the creation of an alternative leadership and rethinking its Christian foundations. Mario Segni continued his battle for the electoral
and political reform of the party system, leaving Christian Democracy and forming the Movimento dei Popolari per la Riforma. In an interview in January 1993,
Segni said that the movement's objective was to pour "alcohol on the wounds" of
the Italian Republic in order to "disinfect it" from the seeds of corruption and
self-referentiality, in favor of political transparency, correctness, and honesty
within democratic institutions and procedures (Fuccari 1993).

10.2 From the DC to the PPI

In October 1992, Mino Martinazzoli was elected new secretary of Christian
Democracy. He was called to the arduous task of reforming and reorganizing the
party. Being one of the most respected representatives of the party's internal left-
wing faction, Martinazzoli was elected—he himself admitted—"out of desperation."
As a member of the third generation, Martinazzoli felt the link between the DC's
"national" role and its Christian inspiration—a link that had been crucial for the
first and second generations—with much less intensity. He had not experienced
the DC of De Gasperi and had held important roles when the party was led by
Fanfani and Moro. Like other members of the third generation, his experience
was characterized by the "condemnation to govern," imposed on the DC by the
bipolar structure of the Cold War and the fact that the party colluded more and
more with the state.

Martinazzoli's attempt at relaunching the party hinged on the idea of deep
moral renewal. He did not defend DC members under investigation, nor did he
criticize the prosecuting magistrates, as Moro had done in the 1970s. On the contrary, he accepted their actions, which were accompanied by the violent media
"trials" against the DC. The public sphere was boiling with discontent and
Martinazzoli did what he could to take the situation seriously.

However, Martinazzoli's attempts seemed to be insufficient to deal with the
pressure for a radical resetting and turnover of the party's leadership. There was

much internal resistance to Martinazzoli's plans, which was linked to a sense of nostalgia, the defense of interests targeted by the investigations, and protests against what was perceived as the "excess" of the prosecuting magistrates and the anti-DC press campaigns. The resistance against Martinazzoli was also connected to the vitality that, all things considered, the party continued to possess, especially in the periphery. The DC still had thousands of mayors and local administrators, much more than any other party. Both local politicians and the party's leadership had serious reservations about the uncertainties unleashed by Martinazzoli's wish for radical change. Meanwhile, ample sectors of the Catholic world continued to move away from the DC, disillusioned by the daily revelations of the rising wave of corruption that had invested the party. The contestation of the Catholics' political unity within a single party became widespread. Martinazzoli tried to recover the relationships with the primal elements of the party, namely Catholicism and the church, but the deepening dissatisfaction in civil society with the party system made it an almost impossible battle.

In April 1993, a popular referendum repealed the existing norms of the electoral law for the Senate. The referendum's success was yet another proof of the Italians' wish for change and became a political constraint for the parliament that started to work on a more comprehensive electoral reform. In August 1993, a new and predominantly majoritarian, uninominal electoral system was introduced, replacing the proportional system that had been instrumental in the protection of the consociational nature of the Italian political system, in which the DC had been at the center. The reform's objective was the creation of a Westminster-style bipolar democracy, based on a more competitive party system and the alternation, in office, of two dominant and easily identifiable parties or coalitions of parties.

The discussion on the electoral reform, which in reality was a discussion on the reform of Italian democracy as a whole, urged Martinazzoli to hasten his attempt at reforming Christian Democracy. In July 1993, Christian Democracy held a specific meeting (*Assemblea programmatica costituente*) for the creation of a new, post-DC party. According to Martinazzoli, Christian Democracy had to change from a "party of membership cards" to a "party of programs," opening the way for a "third historical phase" in the Catholic democratic tradition (Documenti 1993). This move was meant to be a decisive rupture and discontinuity with the recent past but certainly not with the historical, cultural, and ideal roots of Catholic politics. The emblem of a shield with a white cross on a red background and the Latin word *libertas* ("freedom"), which had once symbolized the party's militant Catholic and anti-Communist spirit, was to remain. The new party was to be called Partito Popolare Italiano, the name that Sturzo had given to the first Catholic party in Italian politics. Martinazzoli explained this choice by saying that "this image of renewing without denying explicitly expresses the spirit of my reflection" (Martinazzoli 1993).

On January 18, 1994, the same day of Sturzo's appeal to the free and strong that had marked the PPI's birth in 1918, Martinazzoli announced the birth of the new Partito Popolare Italiano, insisting once again on the unity of Catholics: "[I]f we are united we are strong, if we are strong we are effective, and if we are divided we condemn ourselves" (Il nuovo 1994: 13). This was a critical juncture of political history, but for those involved, it was also a moment of deep existential crisis, similar to what had happened a few years before when the PCI had renounced its name and transformed itself into the PDS. An entire, established universe of symbolic meanings collapsed. This watershed was subtly captured and rendered by Gabriele De Rosa, who, on January 12, 1994, wrote in his diary about the "state of anxiety and confusion" that captured Martinazzoli and many other politicians, who were essentially living through "the collapse, the end of a world" (De Rosa 1997b: 80–1; see also Scotti 2004: 52–3).

On a more pragmatic and strategic level, the crucial point for the future of the new party was the question of political and electoral alliances, hence its political positioning in the changing political geography of Italy's political system. At the abovementioned meeting of July 1993, Martinazzoli had said nothing about future electoral and political alliances. At the local elections in the autumn of 1993, held with a majoritarian run-off electoral system and the direct election of the mayor, the DC collapsed gathering only 11 percent of the popular vote. A new bipolar system was emerging and in such a system, the DC, or any centrist party, risked finding itself in a marginal and subaltern position. The general elections were scheduled for March 1994. The bipolar system was not only a consequence of the new electoral system but also of the wider transformations that had affected Italian politics since the fall of the Berlin Wall. An important change in the political system, especially for the Catholics, was the transformation of the neo-Fascist Movimento Sociale Italiano. From 1992 onward, the MSI distanced itself from its Fascist past and transformed into a more generic right-wing party, Alleanza Nazionale (AN, National Alliance), officially created in January 1994 (Ignazi 1994). For the local elections of Rome (November–December 1993), the struggle in the second round was between the MSI's leader Gianfranco Fini and Francesco Rutelli, supported by a center-left coalition led by the PDS but without Rifondazione Comunista, who eventually prevailed. Christian Democracy was simply out of the contest. Notably, the media tycoon Silvio Berlusconi endorsed Fini, legitimizing the democratic credentials of the Italian extreme and neo-Fascist Right.

A few weeks later, on January 26, 1994, Berlusconi announced his decision to "enter the field" of politics (Orsina 2013). He presented his own political creature, Forza Italy, which focused on protecting Italy and the liberal and pro-Western free market policies from the "Communists," which in his opinion were embodied—after the fall of the Berlin Wall and the end of the Communist

Party—by the PDS and the center-left coalition. Berlusconi's objective was to convince ample sectors of the anti-Communist middle class, orphaned from the parties that had defended their demands until the early 1990s: the DC and the PSI. Two main coalitions were emerging, one from the Right and one from the Left, and both converged toward the center. This dramatically limited the space for a party that wanted to ward off two extreme wings and occupy the center of the system.

10.3 In Search of a Political Identity

In the entire historical process that culminated with the end of the DC and the birth of the new PPI, Christian Democrats never abstained from debates on the party's positioning, electoral alliances, and what would be the value of a political center in the future, bipolar system. This was a burning issue. From within and outside the party, various voices confronted each other. Some of the leaders favored an alliance with the Right; others wanted to embrace the center-left progressive coalition that was forming under the direction of the PDS. Already in September 1993, a breakaway group called the Cristiano-Sociali had been formed with the aim of injecting the emerging progressive front with the organized presence of social Catholicism. Martinazzoli had to deal with and combine different, often contrasting, views. At the assembly of January 1994, Martinazzoli said:

> The choice of our position in national political life has long been made and is part and parcel of a convinced inclination to moderation, which is anything but moderatism, neutrality, and conservatism. The term moderation knows the value and limits of politics and thus depicts a reforming vocation and capacity for tolerance, harmony, [and] equity. (Il nuovo 1994: 19)

For some of the leaders, this exercise of moderatism meant moving the new party toward the Left. Another breakaway group was formed, carrying the name of Centro Cristiano Democratico, on the very same day the DC turned into the PPI. Its leaders and supporters advocated an alliance with the center-right coalition that was emerging under the guidance of Silvio Berlusconi's Forza Italia. At the 1994 elections, the PPI decided to run as a "third pole," autonomously from the center-left led by the PDS (which included the Green Party and other leftist groups) and the center-right coalition formed by Forza Italia, the Northern League, AN, and the post-DC Centro Cristiano Democratico.

Despite forces pushing in different and opposing directions, the PPI remained anchored to the image of a centrist party, trying to keep an autonomous profile. However, the radicalization of the struggle, Berlusconi's entry into politics, and the bipolar logic crushed the PPI, belatedly and vainly supported once again by

Mario Segni. The PPI obtained 11 percent of the vote, while the Patto per l'Italia—
the pole formed by the PPI and the Patto Segni (a pact of national rebirth)—
obtained 15.7 percent of the vote. The elections marked the PPI's irrelevance and
the real end of the DC and what it had been for fifty years: the central axis of
the Italian political system. The center-right coalition prevailed but the weight of the
Centro Cristiano Democratico was minimal. Forza Italia obtained 21 percent of
the vote, becoming the first Italian party. Forza Italia's success was the eventual
manifestation of the separation of the moderate, anti-Communist vote—which
had traditionally been a vote for the DC—from the heir of Christian Democracy.
For the first time in the history of republican Italy, a political movement of the
center-right no longer guided by Catholics (and no longer rooted in the
Resistance) was able to conquer the relative majority of the vote. The formation of
a government led by Berlusconi, which included a regionalist party and the first
neo- or post-Fascist movement to participate in Italy's government since the end
of the war, was a watershed in national politics.

The elections of 1994 and the end of the DC also meant the end of the politi-
cal unity of Catholics. In subsequent years, the parties that descended from the
DC's diaspora sought a political collocation along the Left–Right divide
(Baccetti 2007). The PPI merged with other forces of the center and the Left,
becoming the Margherita (2002), which in turn merged with the post-
Communist Democratici di Sinistra (DS, formerly PDS) to form the Democratic
Party (2007). The Centro Cristiano Democratico and other post-DC conserva-
tive and right-wing groups supported the center-right governments led by
Berlusconi (1994–6, 2001–6, 2008–11) and entered into the Popolo delle
Libertà, the party born from the union of Forza Italia and AN, which lasted
from 2009 to 2013. Catholic politicians could be found, and can still be found
today, in virtually every party and movement of post-Cold War and post-DC
Italy. The post-DC popular vote went in the direction of many political forces,
well beyond the traditional perimeters of the post-DC area, including movements such as the Northern League. The League initially presented itself as a
non-Catholic movement, and often accusing the church of being complicit with
the moral crisis of the nation. Rather than a Christian symbolism, the League
built its historical narrative on Celtic mythology and pre-Christian tropes.
Forza Italia received strong support from CL. The Catholic world had suddenly
become politically splintered.

Christian Democracy did not end right after the end of Communism in
Europe, nor did it end merely as a consequence of it. De Gasperi founded
Christian Democracy before the onset of the Cold War and with wider objectives
than to halt Communism. These included the Catholic non-involvement in the
life of the unified state, the development of an answer to the crisis of liberal institutions vis-à-vis mass politics, and the protection of politics from the challenge of
totalitarian Fascism. Christian Democracy forged an original political proposal

that wanted to overcome the divide between religion and politics, build a new democratic political system based on mass parties, and create an alliance between the productive classes and the popular classes. Anti-Communism represented a crucial motive that added itself to already existing objectives. In fifty years, Christian Democracy managed to reach quite a number of its original objectives. However, for this very reason, and because of the DC's politics and policies, Italy changed: unprecedented issues challenged the party's reason to exist. Crucially, consumerism and globalization fractured the relationship between the popular classes and productive classes that had been mediated by Catholics and raised unprecedented and bewildering ethical and religious issues. Christian Democracy did not tune in to the changes within Catholicism and the wider civil society that resulted from the ongoing social, economic, and cultural transformations. The end of the Cold War and anti-Communism, previously a founding element of Italian politics, was not the single cause of the end of the DC, but rather removed a "cover" that had allowed the party to avoid coming to terms with crucial problems. With the end of its role as an anti-Communist dam, movements and processes that had existed since the 1970s and 1980s eventually affected Christian Democracy and the entire Italian political system, leading them to collapse.

The end of the DC was not simply the end of a long-lasting political experience. As Guido Formigoni argued, it was also "the end of a general model of political commitment of Catholic believers, the model of the so-called party of Christian inspiration," and thus the end of a "mediation" between faith and politics expressed in an "ideological-ideal synthesis" supported by the church (Formigoni 2008a: 226, italics in the original). Yet, the end of DC's did not mean the end of Catholic participation in politics. Catholic politics and Christian Democratic ideas survived, even though in different forms. In the end, the very idea of democracy accompanied by the adjective "Christian" was more than Christian Democracy. In other words, it was not simply a party or an electoral alliance: it was a worldview and a political culture. Essentially, the end of the political unity of Catholics actually opened the way for a new role of the Catholic Church in the public sphere.

10.4 Ruini and the "Cultural Project" of the Catholic Church

In a climate of sweeping political change and with the end of Christian Democracy and the political unity of Catholics, in the early 1990s, the church launched a new project for direct Catholic presence and activism in the public sphere—"direct" in the sense of not being mediated by a party. The project soon came to be associated with Cardinal Camillo Ruini. Appointed by John Paul II as president of the CEI in March 1991, Ruini profoundly shaped the relationship between Italian politics and the Catholic Church at least until his resignation from the CEI's presidency in 2007, following a pastoral line of action known as *ruinismo* (Galavotti 2011c; Santagata 2014; Livi 2016). *Ruinismo* was a consequence of the combination of the pastoral, cultural, and political developments internal to the church that had been unfolding since the early 1980s and the transformation of the Italian political system caused by the upheavals of the early 1990s.

Already in the 1980s and with the ecclesial conference in Loreto (1985), following the referendum on divorce (1974) and abortion (1981) and the DC's electoral losses in 1983, the church had sidelined the "religious choice" and the characterization of Catholics as a "yeast" of society in favor of the line of presence as advocated by groups like CL (see Chapter 9). The new times required the church to be actively present in the public sphere through "a direct commitment to the testimony of faith and the common good of the nation" (Garelli 2006: 57). To the pope and various sectors of Catholicism, the DC appeared increasingly unable to cope, from a Christian and Catholic perspective, with the radical character of the cultural processes that were affecting Italian society—and global society, for that sake. The "mediation" model on which the relationship between religion and politics, that is, the church and the DC, had been based since World War II (i.e. a model that relied on a Catholic party of Christian inspiration independent from the Vatican but entrusted by it to "mediate" its directives), now seemed inadequate. Ruini had, in fact, been one of the ghostwriters of the pope's speech in Loreto; he had drafted the sections that related to more political matters, especially the theme of the political unity of Catholics (Galavotti 2011c: 1229).

With the DC still present and officially embodying the political unity of Catholics, mediating between the political and the religious worlds, the line of presence could not fully unfold. A line of action based on a renewed political commitment to the defense of Christian values and a direct relationship between the religious and the political fields without the mediation of secular parties actually implied the demise of Christian Democracy. As the newly elected president of the CEI, Ruini manifested his intention to ensure the continuity of the Italian church's support to the DC but in forms that differed from those of the past. He wanted to turn the party into a lever in the hands of the bishops to protect fundamental (Catholic) values, condensed in the formula of the promotion of the church's social doctrine. The discontinuity with the DC's historical experience in post-World War II Italian history could not be greater. The new approach that Ruini advocated implied the permanent overcoming of the concept of a Christian or Catholic party—or of a party of Christian or Catholic inspiration—as the means through which Catholic laity attempted to mediate between the Catholic faith and the principles of political modernity embedded in the Constitution of 1948; it therefore implied an instrumental relationship between the church and the party. Ruini challenged the party's sectors, which had constantly and firmly advocated the distinction of roles. Arguing against the cardinal and archbishop of

Milan, Carlo Maria Martini (known to be "progressive"), Ruini claimed that the CEI had the task of providing citizens with a direction and orientation founded on an "ethical" base (Acerbi 2003: 500). Despite the deterioration of the DC's situation due to *Tangentopoli* and the Clean Hands investigation, Ruini remained convinced that the crisis that affected the DC was temporary and that the party possessed the necessary resources, means, and personnel to overcome it. In his speech at the general assembly of the CEI in May 1992, one month after the election that saw the DC's votes drop to less than 30 percent of the popular vote, Ruini expressed his awareness of the DC's difficult moment but still pointed to the lack of an alternative (Conferenza 1992: 429).

In a subsequent reconstruction, Ruini highlighted that in the final years of the DC's life, the CEI firmly insisted on the political unity of Catholics, motivating it "not so much with the need to defend the democratic system, but rather with the duty of safeguarding and promoting certain fundamental ethical and anthropological matters." Moreover, the invitation to unity was entrusted to the "free evolution of Christian consciences," referring to the formula already used by the pope at the Loreto meeting (Ruini 2004: 5). Italy's political landscape was dramatically changing during what would soon become known as the "earthquake years": 1992–4. Ruini and the CEI adapted to the new situation. In a prolusion to the CEI's permanent council in September 1994, a few months after the first elections without the DC and with Catholics spread across different parties and coalitions, he introduced the term "cultural project" to explain the need for Catholics and the church to rethink their actions in the public sphere, clarifying that the term "culture" was to be understood as a "common ground between the mission of the church and the more burning issues of the nation" (Ruini 1996).[3] The aim of such an action, in a nutshell, and echoing the discussion in Loreto in 1985, was the "enculturation of the Christian message" and the "evangelization of culture" in a society that was to rediscover its Christian soul (Ruini 1996: 262; see also Ruini 2005, 2010). As Ruini later recalled:

> [i]n 1994, it was becoming quite clear that a new and different approach would
> need to be chosen…considering not only the political changes, making it
> impossible to revive an experience that had just been concluded…but in particular,
> the social-cultural perspective, where the conceptions of life and ethos historically
> established through the decisive influence of Christianity were questioned in an
> increasingly radical manner. (Ruini 2004: 6)

---

[3] The emphasis on culture would become a central concern for global Catholicism in the twenty-first century. As Massimo Faggioli has explained, "in recent times, emphasis on culture has become the main concern of certain Catholic pastoral and intellectual leaders. For them, the *reculturation* of the West is needed to avoid the *exculturation* of Christianity from culture. It is no longer a matter of *inculturation*, as it used to be during the early post-Vatican II period" (Faggioli 2017: 129). On the concept of *exculturation* see Hervieu-Léger 2003.

In 1995, an ecclesiastical meeting in Palermo gave its approval to the project. More importantly, the pope's seal of approval made the project official. In Palermo, the pope declared the importance of a line of politics that was attentive to the demands of the church. In his speech, the pope outlined the repositioning of the church in the new political context: "[T]he church must not and will not be involved in any choice of political and party factions, in the same way as it does not express any preference for one or another institutional or constitutional solution, and it respects authentic democracy." He invited Catholics to avoid "a cultural diaspora corresponding to the political diaspora, as if all reference points had been lost." He recognized pluralism as a legitimate political option, but he also highlighted that Catholics:

> cannot consider every vision of the world compatible with faith or their easy adherence to political and social forces that are opposed to, or do not pay enough attention to, the principles of the church's social doctrine concerning human beings and the respect for human life, the family, freedom of education, solidarity, and the promotion of peace and justice. (CEI 1997: 62–3; see also Formigoni 2008a: 233–4)

In 1996, three seminars promoted by the CEI and the general assembly of the bishops outlined the motivations and precise contents of the new cultural project launched by Ruini. In 1997, the project was extensively explained in a foundational document published by the CEI, titled *Progetto culturale in senso cristiano. Una prima proposta di lavoro* ("A cultural project with a Christian direction. A first working plan").

The cultural project aimed to reshape the relationship between faith and secular culture and mediate between Catholic values and the problems that globalization and modernization had generated. The church acknowledged the weakening of the Christian faith in terms of affecting the mentality, behavior, and habits of individuals in technologically advanced societies, marked by the pluralism of values and cultures. As a response, the church invited Catholics to engage with the public sphere and fundamental questions in the socioeconomic, philosophical, ecological, and bioethical fields. It wanted to defend and actively affirm Catholic ethical values such as human dignity, family life, and the Catholic community, thus promoting a kind of Christian anthropological ideology. The church still accepted pluralism in the sphere of religion and culture. Yet, it acted toward the defense of human values imbued with Catholic principles and the protection of a Catholic Italy that had become a minority (Garelli 2007).

The direct public commitment of the church aimed at the recreation of a new unity of the Catholic world, no longer only on the confessional plan but also on the more cultural, ethical-rational plan, focusing on the new need to redefine a national identity still anchored in Catholic values (Formigoni 2010: 190–5).

In the long run, the project's final objective was essentially to forge a hegemonic front of Catholic values that would allow Catholics in different parties and coalitions to converge on important key points, such as the family, education, and the defense of life from conception to natural death. Although these values were crucial for the teachings of the church, in Ruini's view, they could also resonate very broadly within more secular landscapes. This also explains why Ruini, in laying the foundations of his project in Palermo, returned to a reflection that dated from the time of Loreto and focused on the importance of culture (Ruini 1985, 1992: 323, 1996: 278).

On the pragmatic and practical plan, *ruinismo* was based on a strategy that abandoned the "from the pulpit to the party" model (Kalyvas 1998; Diamanti and Ceccarini 2007) and moved in an opposite direction, from the party to the pulpit (Magister 2001). It thus favored direct intervention in the public debate through thematic forums and powerful media, such as the CEI's newspaper *Avvenire* and the television channel TV2000, which had been on air since 1998 and with a focus on "non-negotiable" values and principles (Santagata 2014: 444; Livi 2016: 403). First introduced in 2002 by the Congregation for the Defense of the Faith under Joseph Ratzinger, in the *Nota dottrinale circa alcune questioni riguardanti l'impegno e il comportamento dei cattolici nella vita politica* ("A doctrinal note on questions concerning the engagement and behavior of Catholics in political life") the expression "non-negotiable" primarily included bioethical themes that had been at the center of John Paul II's 1995 encyclical *Evangelium vitae*. It also covered issues such as the retention of the cross in public space and the defense of the church's special fiscal status, as well as the defense of private Catholic schooling. By picking up these themes, the church fully engaged with the most crucial debates in the social and life sciences as well as in the public sphere of a post-modern society, such as the role of religion in public life, the process of secularization, and the comeback of religion, or desecularization or even resacralization processes, and the inconsistency and self-contradictions of the Western neo-liberal system that had defeated atheistic Communism.[4] Catholic politicians were, therefore, invited to find points of convergence and unity not in a party or following the "mediation rules within the democratic process," but rather in themes and priorities established by the bishops (Melloni 2010: 116).

10.5 Ruini, the Church, and Italian Politics without the DC

At the elections of 1994, the CEI called for a "united and coherent presence" to support "a force of Christian inspiration" (Accattoli 1994; see also Brunelli 1995;

---

[4] The debates and publications on this topic are many: Casanova 1994; Berger 1999; Stark 1999; Habermas and Ratzinger 2006; Habermas 2006, 2008a, 2008b; Demerath 2007; Taylor 2007.

Magister 1996). This was an implicit endorsement of the PPI. Until the elections, the CEI had believed that the PPI would replace the DC as the house of the political unity of Catholics and that the church could maintain the same kind of relationship with the PPI as it had had with the DC. Already at the end of 1993, Ruini had said to the Italian bishops that the DC's end would not mean the end of the Italian episcopate's intervention in Italian politics. The church could not "renounce the proposal of its social and moral teaching" (Ruini 1996: 218–19). The pope had confirmed this approach in January 1994, in a letter addressed to the bishops. He first recalled the special status of Italy as a nation that had the "task of defending, for the whole of Europe, the religious and cultural legacy grafted in Rome by the disciples Peter and Paul." He then spoke in favor of the permanence of "a force of Christian inspiration" that, as Ruini had said earlier, was "needed to express the social and political plan of the Christian cultural tradition of Italian society" (Insegnamenti 1996: 45–52; see also Ruini 1996: 266).

Ruini initially turned his attention to the PPI as the force that could translate this mission into policies and politics. However, like the PPI's secretary Martinazzoli, Ruini did not immediately understand that the new majoritarian electoral system rendered the existence of a center acting as a "cockpit" of the Italian politcs almost impossible (Ruini 1996: 314). Silvio Berlusconi's triumph was, in many ways, the epitome and more evident representation of the end of the Italian Catholic movement. The new bipolar system that was established after 1994 gave the PPI a negligible role in the political system, forcing the CEI to a rapid repositioning and change of strategy. Soon after the elections, Ruini—generating discontent among several bishops—applauded the success of Berlusconi and his coalition and declared that the CEI was open to positively consider "consonances and agreements," even only partial but "real and effective" ones, on the themes of Christian social teaching (Ruini 1996: 263–3; Galavotti 2011c: 1230; see also Formigoni 2010: 191). This was much more than a pragmatic opening to the winning coalition. Rather, the Italian church legitimized a governmental alliance formed by parties that, for the first time in republican history, had not taken part in the writing of the Constitution, nor did they have any roots in the anti-Fascist Resistance. In other words, the church legitimized a coalition that had been formed in opposition to the PPI (sustained by the CEI) and that also included a party such as the Northern League, which the CEI and the Holy See had strongly reprimanded in the past.

Giuseppe Dossetti soon grasped the profound implications of the CEI's move toward Berlusconi, which he considered of inconceivable gravity. For Dossetti, the church's approval of Berlusconi's triumph was similar to its weak attitude toward, and embrace of, Fascism and Mussolini in the mid-1920s. It is for this very reason that Dossetti invited Italians and the anti-Fascist forces to defend the constitutional pact on which Italy had been founded after World War II. Dossetti devoted the two final years of his life to this struggle, which was systematically ignored if not openly opposed by Ruini. The president of the CEI feared not so much an assault on the Constitution but the contiguity of Catholics and former Communists on the same front line, as epitomized by the image of Dossetti and Nilde Jotti[5] jointly talking to the committees for the defense of the Constitution at the Abbazia di Monteveglio, in September 1994 (Allegretti 2007). In fact, Ruini launched reassuring messages, as he was convinced that Italian democracy had "firm roots" and that it was quite difficult for anyone to tamper with "our constitutional rights" (Ruini 1996: 263).

In March 1995, the PPI was again split over future electoral and political alliances, facing fundamental disagreements about joining the center-left or the center-right coalition. The party secretary Rocco Buttiglione—who was inclined to join Berlusconi—left the PPI forming the Cristiani Democratici Uniti (United Democratic Christians). Buttiglione was a student of Del Noce and a counselor of John Paul II, and he was close to CL. The new split in the party permanently convinced Ruini that the experience of the Catholics' political unity had come to an end (Ruini 1996: 314–15). It was another critical passage in the PPI's history and, more generally, the Catholic involvement in politics. De Rosa exposed Ruini's heavy responsibilities and mistakes in this passage. In his diary, he wrote: "The clergy first meddled in the affairs of the PPI and now retire, exhibiting their white robe and pretending impartiality" (De Rosa 1997b: 167–8).

In the following years, the CEI and the Italian church were decidedly inclined toward the center-right coalition. From 1995 onward, the position of Italian bishops vis-à-vis Italian politics was officially one of "active neutrality," which obviously implied "voting for those who follow the ideas of the church" (Accattoli 2001), especially on matters of life, marriage, and education. It was Berlusconi and his center-right coalition that, despite their secular stances on many issues, ended up backing the CEI's wish list (Gibelli 2011). *Ruinismo* and *berlusconismo* therefore made an improbable yet effective deal and worked in synergy (Santagata 2014: 443–6; Bolzonar 2016: 451–3; Livi 2016). For Ruini, Berlusconi was the political barrier against the biopolitics of the Italian post-Communist Left—the alleged champion of same-sex marriage and euthanasia—and the guarantor of a fiscal system that was favorable to the church. As Massimiliano Livi argued:

> considering that Berlusconi explicitly supported the bishops' program from the April 1996 elections onward, and in particular considering the economic payback that he granted the Catholic Church for the whole of the subsequent decade (including the exemption from local taxes and public funding for Catholic schools), it is highly likely that it was not Ruini who chose Berlusconi,

---

[5] Nilde Jotti had been a Communist partisan at the time of the Resistance and had then a long relationship with the Communist leader Palmiro Togliatti. She was the first woman to become president of the Chamber of Deputies (1979–1992).

but rather Berlusconi who sought the (in Italy indispensable) legitimization of the Catholic Church. (Livi 2016: 404; see also Santagata 2014: 445)[6]

The center-left coalition also included an important Catholic component; the leader of the coalition was a Catholic, Romano Prodi, whose wedding had been celebrated decades before by a young priest called Ruini. However, Ruini and wide sectors of the Italian bishops did not approve of the link between Catholics and the post-Communist Left, nor did they appreciate their claim of independence from the hierarchy.

Crucially, the real "bridgehead" of the CEI and the Berlusconi coalition was CL: the movement that, as Del Noce wrote in the mid-1980s, had understood and tried to counter the de-Christianization of society and the crisis that modernity was undergoing, insisting on the relevance of a Catholic restoration (Del Noce 1985). Indeed, CL filled the "almost empty political room" (Livi 2016: 405) of Forza Italia with its own key themes, especially subsidiarity and the *più società, meno Stato* ("more society, less state") policy,[7] which became a cultural and ideological driver of Forza Italia and the priority of the center-right coalition, "among other priorities promoted by other actors, like the federalist issue promoted by the Northern League" (Giorgi and Polizzi 2015: 135; Livi 2016: 405). Moreover, the link between CL and Berlusconi was partly due "to an evident (and financial) continuity between the CL leaders and Silvio Berlusconi himself" that could be traced back to 1977, when the tycoon had started to finance the CL's weekly *Il Sabato*. Finally, the CL's founder, Luigi Giussani, endorsed the link between CL and Forza Italia because of Berlusconi's "liberalist alignment" with the movement's political mission and his "antagonism" with Romano Prodi, whom CL deemed "guilty, in particular of making compromises with the Left" (Livi 2016: 405) that CL considered the end of the Catholics' political identity (Baget Bozzo 2006).

Between 2001 and 2006, coinciding with Ruini's third mandate and Berlusconi's second and third cabinets, the marriage between *ruinismo* and *berlusconismo*

[6] See the pamphlet titled *I frutti e l'albero* ("the fruits and the tree") that Forza Italia sent to all Italian parishes in 2006; the policies of Berlusconi's second government were correlated with the church's social doctrine (Garagnani and Palmieri 2006).

[7] A central concept of CL's political commitment was the idea that private actors should be given an important role in providing public services to citizens without the interference of the state and public institutions, hence giving these a merely subsidiary role. The role of private actors in the public sector was indeed extended in the 1990s as a consequence of the crisis of the political legitimization of the party system, and subsidiarity was incorporated into the Italian Constitution in 2001; this occurred following a constitutional revision process that supported decentralization and federalist measures conducted by the center-left coalition, also as a way to deprive the Northern League of arguments and votes. Along with the *Fondazione per la Sussidiarietà* and the *Compagnia delle Opere* (a CL network of more than thirty thousand enterprises, associations, and not-for-profit organizations), CL was the main actor in the process of translating subsidiarity into practice (Giorgi and Polizzi 2015; Livi 2016: 413, no. 9).

"reached an all-time high," to the point of playing "a decisive role in holding together the coalition led by Berlusconi," also generating discontent among progressive and leftist-oriented bishops (Livi 2016: 406). In addition to provisions and measures taken by the center-right coalition—at both the national and the regional levels—in favor of the church, in matters of fiscal policy and private (i.e. Catholic) schools, it was in terms of specific moral issues that the alliance between the CEI and Berlusconi worked effectively. Combing a skillful use of the media with a clever strategy of mobilization on the ground through various grassroots movements, the CEI argued for and proactively defended its points of view on moral issues in the Italian public debate. For example, in 2005, Italians were called to a referendum on medically assisted reproduction, to repeal (or not) Law 40 introduced in 2004 by Berlusconi's government. Law 40 had imposed strong limitations on artificial insemination and stem cell research, thus backing the Catholic principle of the protection of the rights of the embryo over scientific reasoning. However, the referendum result was declared invalid, as not enough voters went to the poll. This was a very telling case of the "demobilization" of voters, which led to the failure of the objectives sought by those who had promoted the referendum. The CEI and CL were also successful in their battle against the project of the center-left government guided by Prodi that had succeeded Berlusconi to create a legal status for same-sex couples—a kind of civil union. The project was given the awkward name of DICO (Diritti e doveri delle persone stabilmente conviventi, "Rights and duties of stable cohabitants"). The CEI staged a demonstration in Rome, known as "family day," in defense of the traditional family and "healthy" (i.e. Christian) sexuality, which was joined by two Catholic ministers of Prodi's fractious cabinet. The proposal never became law, also because early elections were called in 2008, dissolving the incumbent parliament. The pending legislation died, and the center-left coalition disintegrated. The country went back to the poll and Berlusconi returned to government in 2008.

However, by 2008, *ruinismo* was over. On March 7, 2007, Pope Benedict XV accepted Ruini's resignation, on the grounds of age, and replaced him with Cardinal Angelo Bagnasco. In the final years of his "reign," Ruini and his policy, so attentive to politics and current affairs but less so to spiritual and pastoral matters, had aroused growing discontent among the clergy and the bishops (Galavotti 2011c: 1236; Santagata 2014: 446). It was the beginning of the church's gradual departure from deep involvement in Italian political life. This departure would eventually accelerate in the years of Pope Francis. Interviewed by the editor-in-chief of *Corriere della Sera*, Ferruccio De Bortoli, Francis explicitly distanced himself from the expression "non-negotiable values" (De Bortoli 2014) and called for a revision of CEI's role. In 2011, a "Forum of Catholic Associations" was held in Todi, on the theme of *La buona politica per il bene comune* ("Good politics for the common good"). The aim was to engage in a critical reflection and rethink the role of Catholics in politics as an alternative to the bipolar Italian system, following Aldo Moro's lesson to *scomporre per ricomporre*, to decompose in order to recompose. The participants in the meeting did not propose a clear political program, nor did they want to create a new party or a political movement inspired by Christianity. Rather, the Todi movement wanted "to play the role of a network of interest groups" (Diotallevi 2016: 493), rejecting Ruini's line of presence and alliance with Berlusconi aimed at the formation and launch of new Catholic elites for the moral and civil renovation of politics (Santagata 2014: 447; Bailey and Driessen 2016: 421–42; Bolzonar 2016: 453–4; Livi 2016: 410).

10.6 After Ruini

Several leading participants of the Todi initiative took part in the technocratic government of Mario Monti, which was appointed to succeed Berlusconi in November 2011 (a month after the Todi meeting). The governments that followed Monti were guided by self-declared Catholics: from Enrico Letta to Paolo Gentiloni, from Matteo Renzi to Giuseppe Conte, a follower of Padre Pio. Many ministers of these governments from across the political spectrum declared themselves Catholics, and some of them had been participants in the Todi meeting. After the demise of *ruinismo*, Catholic and Christian Democratic ideas did not disappear from Italian politics, and it is highly unlikely that they will disappear anytime soon. As in the 1990s, after the end of Christian Democracy, and during the first decade of the 2000s, Christian Democratic ideology and symbols continued, and continue, to "fertilize" other political families—from the Right to the Left, from the liberal to the social democratic camps—and Catholic political ideas still influence political parties and movements that emerged from outside the Christian Democratic tradition (Bolzonar 2016; Ozzano 2016). Time and again, political leaders from all over the political and ideological spectrum kept referring to Catholicism and its values and symbols. Moreover, *ruinismo* seems to have left a certain legacy. The basic idea of the "Catholicism as culture" project was that religious freedom is worthy and meaningful only if and when it represents a chance for a human being to point individuals to the ultimate truth. Catholicism must become culture if it is to lead society and state in the "right" direction. This view was not, and still is not, confined to CL. It was and remains advocated by circles broadly known as "Italian neo-conservatism": the so-called *teo-con*, which broadly follows the American model, arguing—also from a nonbeliever perspective—for the need for a traditional anchorage in Catholicism as a form of civil religion. More surprisingly perhaps, this "cultural" view of Catholicism has been appropriated also by politicians and intellectuals of the atheistic Left, who consider the church and the pope the only point of reference in a world in deep moral and spiritual crisis (Quagliariello 2006; Gentile 2007b; Pera 2008; Formigoni 2010: 193–4; Barcellona et al. 2012; Garelli 2014; Tronti 2019).

Undoubtedly, the birth of a new Catholic party like the DC seems improbable today. The pluralism and differentiation of Italian society and politics limit "the possibility of the Catholic world speaking with one voice, let alone it being united in one political party" (Bailey and Driessen 2016: 422). However, Catholic ideals and values have not disappeared from the public sphere. We might be witnessing a process of de-institutionalization (detachment from religious institutions) or a "subjectivization and pulverization" of beliefs, as Hervieu-Léger (2003) has argued in her analysis of the French case. Undoubtedly, participation in Catholic rituals in Italy has dramatically decreased in the last decades, and the Italians' observance of the church's teaching in terms of sexual behavior, marriage, and morality is lax (Garelli 2006; Cartocci 2011; Marzano 2012; Forlenza and Turner 2016). In Italy as in other countries, Catholicism is also transforming into a "low-intensity religion," or a religion that "demands little of practitioners, is related more to commercialism than commitment, and has little potential to affect social worlds or culture" (B. Turner 2011: 149–50; see also Diotallevi 2016). Sociologically speaking, the Catholic world is—on many accounts—not very different from a "Protestant world" (Marzano and Urbinati 2013: 40–56). Yet, Catholicism is still present in various forms in Italian politics.

10.7 The Catholic Narrative of the Northern League

The case of the Northern League offers further insight into the role and place of Catholicism in Italian politics. Starting in the 1980s, and particularly in the northeast of the country, the Northern League emerged as a political subculture and a movement ready to challenge and replace Christian Democracy. The party presented itself as a political "entrepreneur" in the midst of the vast and deep institutional and societal crisis. It thrived on the collapse of trust in the traditional party system and the "parasite" central state that had allegedly marginalized the northern provinces in favor of the South. In the 1990s, the Northern League became the representative and the interpreter of moral and social conservatism, industriousness, and local traditions of what had hitherto been the so-called "white" (i.e. Catholic) subculture of the northeast. There were important Catholic representatives within the Northern League, such as its "ideologue," Gianfranco Miglio, or Irene Pivetti, who became president of the House of Representatives following the 1994 elections. However, Catholicism, and religious inspiration in general, was not an important aspect of the movement's ideology, language, and policy in the first years of its existence. Rather, the movement promoted neo-pagan "Celtic" feasts and rituals that were alternative to Catholic liturgy and sacraments. This culminated in the deification of the river Po, whose waters reputedly allowed the people of northern Italy to be "reborn" (McDonnell 2016: 17–18), in opposition to *Roma ladrona*, the epitome of the old system.

At the beginning of the 2000s, though, the League started to turn to religion, a conversion that went hand in hand with the embrace of its anti-migration, anti-Muslim, and anti-Islamic agenda. The Northern League shifted its focus from the lazy (Italian) "southerners" and thieving secular elite in Rome (the central government)—profiteers of the productive and hard-working northerners—to Muslim immigrants, seen as "dangerous others" (McDonnell 2016: 27). In addition to this, the League's electoral and political platform started to include themes and principles that resembled statements of the CEI under Ruini. Indeed, some of those statements were directly inspired by papal documents, such as the defense and support of the family, the natural community founded on the marriage between a man and a woman, the cultural and anthropological supremacy of the heterosexual family, the freedom of education, and the principle of subsidiarity; in a sense, the League was "simply" presenting well-known Catholic values but with a strong identity and discriminatory character (Bolzonar 2016: 458).

The League's requests to place crucifixes in public schools and limit the construction of mosques started in the late 1990s and early 2000s, but it was not until recently that the religious discourse gained a central place in the political and ideological constellation of the League. Like other European right-wing movements, the League largely recurred to the past by evoking historical events such as the battle of Lepanto (1571), when Christian Europe pushed Islam "back to where it came from, on the other side of the Mediterranean," pitting "the cross against the crescent" (quoted in Betz and Meret 2009: 334). Furthermore, its popular leader Matteo Salvini time and again called for the defense of the "Christian roots" of Europe, threatened not only by immigration from Muslim countries but also by the secular attitude of a technocratic European Union. On several public occasions, Salvini—who was minister of the interior from June 2018 to September 2019—has been seen clutching a rosary and invoking the Virgin Mary.

The questions are: Is it genuine religious inspiration? Is it mere rhetoric? Is it only a cosmetic veneer and a cover for liberal or conservative policies? Pertinent questions for understanding the role of religion in contemporary politics in Italy and beyond still remain.

11

Conclusion

The Futures of Christian Democratic Politics

This book has discussed how Catholic ideas have framed hermeneutics of democracy and political modernity in Italy, tracing continuities and changes in the tension between religion and secularity in the country's history from the French Revolution to today's post-secular era. The Church and Italian Catholics have since the middle of the nineteenth century engaged with democracy and political modernity in a plurality of ways, moving towards what we termed a "critical co-articulation" of the modern project that took decisive shape in the immediate post-World War II period.

Elaborations of a distinctively Catholic vision of the modern took place both within and outside the Church proper, involving clergy, lay intellectuals, movements, associations and politicians. From different angles, and in different periods, alternatives to the singular narrative of an Enlightenment-based secular version of political modernity, based on pure reason and autonomy, were articulated; alternatives that reincorporated transcendence as a legitimate perspective of truth and reason, and that sought to re-anchor democracy, justice and freedom in a religiously argued ethos. The final and irreversible Catholic conversion to democracy happened between the 1930s and the 1950s and was then sanctioned by the Second Vatican Council. This development did not just unfold within the realm of ideas; it was eventually institutionalized in a series of ways influencing constitutional formulations and party politics. The rapid establishment of Christian Democracy after World War II played a huge role in the emergence and consolidation of this alternative political spirituality. At the same time, Christian Democracy did not emerge out of nowhere. It was in many ways a culmination of a dialogue between Christian ideas and modern politics that had begun in the nineteenth century.

Seen in a wider perspective, the worldwide establishment of Christian Democratic parties during the twentieth century was perhaps *the* most important political transformation in modern European politics since the French Revolution—one that had huge consequences on politics in many parts of the world.

In each of the chapters of this book we have sought to give importance to an aspect that is problematically absent in much of the existing work on Christian Democracy and political Catholicism, as already alluded to in the Introduction.

Italy's Christian Democracy: The Catholic Encounter with Political Modernity. Rosario Forlenza and Bjørn Thomassen, Oxford University Press. © Rosario Forlenza and Bjørn Thomassen 2024. DOI: 10.1093/oso/9780198859864.003.0012

This fundamentally involves the importance of transcendence and spirituality for the articulation of a political vision. In his famous *Zwischenbetrachtung*, Max Weber claimed that a religious ethic "receives its stamp, primarily, from religious sources, starting from 'the content of its annunciation and its promise.'" In this spirit we have attempted to take seriously how Christianity influenced the political vision and action of Catholic politicians in several generations. Importantly, however, in the same essay Weber went on to explain:

> Frequently the very next generation reinterprets these annunciations and promises in a fundamental fashion. Such reinterpretations adjust the revelations to the needs of the religious community. If this occurs, then it is at least usual that religious doctrines are adjusted to *religious needs*.

It is *usual* or typical that this is so, but Weber also reminded that "other spheres of interest could have only a secondary influence; often, however, such influence is very obvious and sometimes it is decisive" (Weber 1958: 270). In other words, specific social strata may seek to seize a religious ethic, reinterpret it according to its needs and desires in shifting historical figurations. Weber pointed to a fundamental dynamic here. For, as Weber goes on to say, once a religion is stamped, it usually exerts a far-reaching influence upon the life-conduct of very heterogenous strata. Significantly, a religious worldview can have lasting effects outside of its own immediate sphere, influencing a person's life-conduct and practical orientations of people (Szakolczai 2003: 27). The historical analysis we have tried to put on offer in this book has in this spirit highlighted the ways in which a religious ethic was indeed "seized" by historical personalities, and with a "stamping effect" on the political community that took shape during pivotal moments of transformation in Italy's political history. Following Weber, we have not approached religion as a particular faith or a set of doctrines, but rather focused on the practical, political, non religious effects of religious worldviews, especially in times of crisis and transition.

Christian Democracy as it developed throughout the twentieth century was never simply a cosmetic operation which translated a pre-packaged liberal language and made it digestible to a southern European population for whom Christianity and religion still played a huge role. Catholic politicians embraced democracy and liberal principles in the political realm; but they did not embrace liberalism as a grounding ideology or point of orientation—quite the contrary. Christian Democracy developed as a reflection of the Fascist experience, but it also developed *against* liberalism (as much as Socialism) by insisting on a completely different set of grounding values and ideas. It developed by re-substantiating the modern call to freedom *from within* a classical and Christian tradition, opening the way for an "integral" and "spiritual" post-liberal democracy. Such wording may sound vague and inherently open to interpretation, and questions surely abounded concerning its actual political realization. But may not the same be said about liberal formulas?

We are not here simply dealing with a thinly veiled liberalism, mere jargon which did not alter a quintessential liberal substance or revamped conservatism re-emerging triumphantly after the "parenthesis" of Fascism; we are dealing indeed with an alternative vision and political model, one that developed as a reflection on the misadventures of Fascism *and* as a critique of classical liberalism. Indeed, as we have insisted throughout, Christian Democracy can in this vein be conceptualized as a distinct "political spirituality", where political thought and action are animated by religious concerns and values. At the deepest level, this involves, pace Foucault, the search for new foundations and a regime of truth and government of both oneself and of the body politic (Forlenza and Thomassen 2022). It is true, as we have discussed in the two previous chapters, that the politics Christian Democracy from the late 1960s and increasingly during 1970s and 1980s became less and less directly inspired by a Christian ethos. This was particularly clear among the so-called third generation of Christian democrats, for whom the "spiritual dimension" of politics was much less present. Following our proposed framework of thinking through the question of generations as linked to transformative experiences of crisis, this is anything but surprising. However, the Christian element never disappeared, not even with the demise of the DC.

11.1   Further Theoretical Perspectives

The historical reconstruction and the argument advanced in this book prompts a series of concluding remarks pertaining to the question of how to understand the general relationship between modernity and secularity and how the Italian case may inform our thinking more broadly.

First, and to begin with, what we have argued above carries relevance for social theoretical and historically informed attempts to capture the meanings and modalities of "modernity" and for a wider reflection on the role of religion in the modern political project. It is becoming increasingly clear to everyone that "secularity" did not triumph in the way that mainstream modernization theories had predicted during most of the twentieth century. Modernization can no longer be taken to equal secularization, and that is well known by now. Social developments force us to rethink our theories and concepts we used to invoke to explain modernizing societies and the direction in which they are going and should be going in the future. Within such a larger picture, "Catholic modernity" is of course just one answer to the situation, but also an incredibly important one, and for two obvious reasons: the Catholic Church is, after all, the world's biggest religious organization, and the dominant Church in Europe's historical experience; and Christian Democracy is one of the most influential political movements in twentieth century Europe. Given the salience of current debates on the limits and possibilities of "Islamic" or "Muslim Democracy," the question of how other sets of religious ideas were adapted to national politics in particular historical circumstances turns out to be of utmost relevance (Nasr 2005). We cannot theorize the tension between religion and secularity in the unfolding of multiple modernities (Eisenstadt 2000) if we do not bring Europe itself into the discussion.

The Italian case carries its own intrinsic value here. Italy was *the* one state which territorially came to embody a millennia-old universalistic Church structure, representing a huge part of Europe's cultural and intellectual luggage (*how* huge is of course open to interpretation). Unlike Turkey, which deprived Islam of its organizing, institutional center, this structure remained. Italian state formation and nation-building was greatly influenced by this, and this is well known. What is less well known is the fact that Italian thinkers, partly due to this particular setting, made a series of contributions to alternative articulations of the modern which preceded by decades current efforts to conceptualize the multiple forms of the modern. Indeed, the Italian narrative is evidently not only an Italian story. The centrality of the "person," a "social" view of the economy, the defense of non-statal entities, from the family to the Church, and the valorization of forms of organization which were both political (parties) and corporative (trade unions): these were principles introduced, via Christian Democracy, not only in the Italian Constitution but also in European core countries, including France and West Germany. This serves to underline that the received wisdom about Christian Democracy, that it should not be taken very seriously as a distinctive political philosophy with real-world agency, simply does not stand up to scrutiny.

Second, and in addition to this, the general situation of what we have termed a Catholic "critical co-articulation" of political modernity, that to such an extent shaped post-World War II Italy, is not just of historical interest. Rather, it is a basic position that in many ways still reigns today. It has become incorporated within the still existing Christian-inspired political parties in Italy and beyond, to an extent that we don't even recognize that co-existence as an "issue." As is well known, it was a largely similar position that animated not a few of the founders of the European community in the post-war period, another legacy so evident that we sometimes forget it (Forlenza 2017a). But it has also remained the basic position of official Church doctrine and the so-called social doctrines of the Catholic Church. Here we need only point to the repeated attempts made by recent popes to articulate and defend a vision for science, politics and faith, reason, truth, and religion, where the autonomy of those spheres is defended, without giving up on the ethical foundations laid down in the teachings of the gospel. This has been most profoundly elaborated in the rich authorship of Pope Benedict XVI. This, of course, is a universalistic discussion that goes much beyond Italy, but that nonetheless has a specific resonance for Italian debates. Moreover, it is exactly by revisiting the tormented trajectories of Catholic thought within Italy, and the way it opened up toward modernity, that one is better able to appreciate the underpinning rationale of someone like Pope Benedict's philosophy. This is not just a matter of debate for Catholics. It should not be forgotten that the one theoretician—and staunch defender—of modernity to recognize the significance of Benedict's philosophy of modernity was Habermas. The debate with Ratzinger was one important inspiration behind Habermas's understanding of post-secularity, and his recognition of the role of religion within the modern (Habermas 2006, 2008a, 2008b).

Third, and in continuation, the more particular Italian discussion has a universal appeal in more than one way. It is noteworthy that the mature project of one of the most important contemporary political philosophers, Charles Taylor, has been to seek a convergence between post-liberal thought, communitarianism, and Catholicism. In *Varieties of Religion Today* (2003) and in *A Catholic Modernity* (1996), Taylor has insisted that a religious dimension gives shape to how we experience and make an image of the world. Here Taylor is not just aligning Catholicism with democracy: he is situating Catholicism as a foundational platform for recognizing and accepting pluralism and difference, within the context of today's multi-cultural society. Or, we might say, within today's multiple, global modernities. He does that on the basis of a genealogy of thought unfolding within Western modernity that needs recognition.

As we have argued in our previous book (Forlenza and Thomassen 2016) the substantiality of Italian contributions to the formation of modern ideas cannot be overlooked or drowned in moral and political rhetoric which systematically dumps Italy as a latecomer to modernity desperately trying to catch up. The Italian debate works as a reminder that rather than insisting on the single validity of secular Enlightenment rationality, and the modernization built onto it, alternative modernities do exist and with a different set of genealogies of values. In short, what emerges from a critical understanding of Italy's roads to modernity should not simply serve as an adjustment of the Italian picture; it must relate to a revision of the very discourse of "modernity," and the tension between religion and secularity as it unfolded so differently within Europe itself.

11.2 Christian Democracy, the Populist Challenge

Seen in a global perspective, Christian Democracy has become much less influential and much less coherent in the last decades. At the same time, more and more movements and political parties in all of Europe and beyond—typically right-wing or far-right parties—explicitly refer to Christianity and to the defense of Christian Europe to articulate their political platforms, often in an anti-liberal key (Marzouki et al. 2016). In Italy, it has been particularly the Northern

League—now the League for Salvini premier, from the name of its leader Matteo Salvini—that have appropriated such a "religious" narrative (McDonnell 2016). As we see it, this instrumental use of religion is in many ways a product of the disappearance of Christian Democracy.

For the vast majority of scholars, the Northern League as well as other European right-wing and populist parties, movements, and their leaders (including Fratelli d'Italia guided by Giorgia Meloni, nominated prime minister in October 2022) have purposely hijacked religion for political and electoral purposes (Marzouki et al. 2016). In other words, they are seen as not genuinely Christian. In this reading, their references to religion are considered a political-electoral, vote-maximizing strategy, a tool to stir up anti-immigrant sentiment and legitimize claims for the restriction of immigration. By appealing to Christianity, they are cynically and instrumentally seizing upon the Europeans' fear of Islam.

For this scholarship, the League's religious narrative can be better understood as a form of secular identity politics based on nostalgia for an imagined Christian past and a virulent hatred and fear of Islam. It is a secular movement interested in religion only because it considers religion a core component of national identity. Hence, Christianity as invoked by the League is not a substantive type of Christianity but rather a series of shared values that have nothing to do with religion and religious beliefs and practices (Bolzonar 2016: 459; Ozzano 2016). It is a thoroughly secularized Christian culture or a civilizational and identitarian Christianity: a matter of belonging rather than believing and a way of defining "us" versus "them." Such "identitarian" Christianity and the definition of the Other in civilizational terms implies the characterization of the self along the same line. The concern about Islam calls forth a corresponding and explicit concern about Christianity, understood not as a religion but as a civilization that is coextensive with Europe, or what was once called Christendom. In short, we are—and must be—Christian because they are Muslim but without implying that "we" must be religious (Brubaker 2017; Roy 2016b). All of this happens without suggesting or forging a complete alignment with the Catholic Church and Christian churches, but rather by creating an ambivalent if not antagonist relationship between populists and religious leaders and institutions (in Italy the Lega have for example continued to attack the Catholic Church for its stance on immigration). This "culturalization" is considered one of the consequences of "the ongoing erosion of Christianity as doctrine, organization, and ritual" that "makes it easy to invoke Christianity as a cultural and civilization identity" (Brubaker 2017: 1199). Hence, the different paradoxes associated with current right-wing populism can be summed up as follows: a secular posture, a philosemitic stance, the adoption of liberal rhetoric by parties often characterized as "illiberal," and the increasing salience of Christian identity in what is considered the most secularized region of the world—a place where religious practices are dramatically declining.

Thus, the reigning scholarship on populism tends to read the current use of religion in a clearly instrumental key, forming part of a strategic identity politics: a matter of belonging and not of believing (McDonnell 2016: 23–7; Roy 2016). There are undoubtedly grains of truth in this interpretation. However, in our view this scholarship ultimately ends on a fairly reductionistic, simplistic, and thus highly unsatisfactory stance that is not so different from the ways in which mainstream political theory downplayed the uniqueness of Christian democratic ideas. Indeed, from such a stance it becomes difficult to really grasp the resilience of religion in politics and why the religious narratives and symbolisms resonate through multiple constituencies in Italy's (and Europe's) social fabric, fostering the appeal and success of the League and other right-wing movements and party politics.

The problems of this dominant view, which thrive in the media as well, are many. Let us here highlight just four of these. First of all, it simply downplays the significant fact that the appeal to religion is used. Even if the transmitter of the message might be exercising nothing but manipulation, it still says something about an appeal that has not completely disappeared.

Second, it assumes a clear-cut and simplistic division between active producers and generators of images and narratives (the leaders) and passive common people, recipients of a discourse that inevitably comes from above. Consequently, it assumes that there is nothing genuinely Christian or religious or Catholic about the religious politics of the League, Fratelli d'Italia, or other right-wing movements, seeing the religious appeal merely as an instrumentalization. But how are we actually to decide when a religious attachment is for "real"? Normative positions aside, the analytical point is that we cannot simply reduce right-wing religious politics to an electoral strategy, or to a propaganda tool that superficially injected political mobilization with religious symbolism, disregarding the meanings of such a politics and the historical context in which it emerges.

Thirdly, and related to this, a problematic aspect of the dominant approaches on right-wing religious politics is an arbitrary and top-down understanding of what counts as "religion." This leads to an artificially rigid separation of religion from culture, as if a "true" religion ever existed out there. This becomes even more relevant in the current age of post-secularism, seeing a return of religion in the public sphere. To frame the belief aspect of religion as the only legitimate version of religion simply because it is the version supported by religious elites is problematic. Rather than understanding religion as a set of beliefs and institutional practices, social scientists and particularly anthropologists have always examined the way such practices and beliefs are constitutive of each other via a broad range of representations, embodiments, and ethical, socio-cultural, and political practices—in short, through lived religion. These everyday practices are constituted of manifold aspects of life, including gender, desire, performance, politics, and power. Christianity and religion are indeed two crucial aspects of European cultural memory (Forlenza 2017a, 2018). In other words, religion is a thoroughly social practice linked to cultural patterns—it has always been about cultural identity and belonging as much as sincerity of belief.

Fourth, and finally, the League and right-wing religious politics and narratives of a Catholic Italy need to be historically problematized by putting them in the context of the demise of a democratic religious politics as embodied in post-World War II Europe by Christian Democracy. In fact, Christian Democracy is quite relevant for the discussion of contemporary right-wing religious politics and helps frame it—against the presentism and a-historical perspectives often offered by the recent scholarship on the topic—in a more appropriate temporal and historical dimension. With Christian Democracy reigning or playing a much stronger role, the kind of "direct" political use of Christianity was either off the table or at least very marginal. The post-totalitarian political culture of Christian Democracy, with a sincere commitment to democracy and human dignity silenced and tamed the no longer acceptable, exclusionary, and reactionary components of religion, or the potentially anti-democratic aspects of Catholicism. With the end or demise of Christian Democracy, "religious politics," deprived of a political force sincerely committed to democracy and human rights, could drift freely as a floating signifier and be seized by other, not always so democratic, forces. Ironically, it is today becoming more and more clear that Christian Democracy functioned as a bulwark against the political use of religion.

In a situation of political and socio economic crisis, religion can indeed serve to mark Europe as an imagined community. The temptation remains to invoke Italy's incompatibility with the "non-European" and to recreate new symbolic borders based on religion and religious identities. This is evidently highly problematic—and in fact repeatedly identified as such also by Pope Francis.

The original Christian Democratic project as developed in the aftermath of World War II provided a genuine alternative not only to Fascism, but also to Socialism, liberalism, and conservatism, the reigning political ideologies that crystallized in the aftermath of the French Revolution. Today Christian Democratic political movements are presented with an enormous challenge of retaining their own political space in many parts of the world. In Hungary, Viktor Orbàn is claiming to have taken over Christian Democracy (Lamour 2021; Wolkenstein 2023), even scolding the European People's Party for "secularism" and having abandoned the defense of Christian Europe. Political theorist Carlo Invernizzi Accetti has argued that the real values and principles of Christian Democracy might be a better reference point for the social and political demands of religious and conservative constituencies. In this view, Christian Democracy, a force more committed to the health and stability of democracy, could and should actually compete for support with far-right populist movements. This, however, would mean that Christian Democracy should claim back and re-appropriate its language and symbolism, recovering its history. Seen in such a perspective,

Dossetti's attempt at delineating a Christian Democratic political space in the threshold moment of 1945, in the letter he sent to the priests of the Apennines in March 1945, might indeed resonate equally well today:

> Christian Democracy does not want to nor can it be a conservative movement, but one imbued with the certainty that between the ideology and experience of capitalistic Liberalism and the experience, if not the ideology, of massive anti-Capitalist movements, *the most radically anti-Christian is not the latter, but the former*; therefore Christians, hitherto firm and fervent critics and opponents of every socialist revolutionary position (because materialist, atheist, and violent), must likewise become as never before firm and fervent critics and opponents of any reactionary position, that under the veneer of legality and justice may cover violent illegality and injustice no less grave, albeit better concealed, than any committed by the desperate and the marginalized. (Dossetti 1995a, italics added)

We are not in 1945 and the likelihood of the rebirth of a strong and hegemonic Christian Democracy is minimal. Yet, Dossetti's understanding of the need of a political thought transcending liberalism and socialism without succumbing to problematic forms of populism could be argued to be as relevant today as never before.

11.3 What Future for Christian Democracy?

The question left on the table is this: is there a relevance of a Catholic-inspired Christian Democracy today, in Europe and beyond? In terms of current tendencies, one can look at it from two perspectives. On one hand, one can still see politicians and technocrats, from all sides of the political spectrum, that in Italy and elsewhere define themselves as Catholics or Christian. The largest coalition in the European Parliament is still the European People's Party, a force that is the direct heir of Christian Democracy. On the other hand, we might also ask: when and where do we actually find a strong Catholic voice in politics? The claim that Christian Democracy is just a conservative cover for liberalism may be more relevant and truer today than it was throughout the entire post-war period. Sure, the Catholic Church is there, and Pope Francis time and again raises his voice on social and environmental issues—but it is a voice that politicians can ignore at their will, and they often do, not least in Italy.

Indeed, the question needs to be posed: is Christian Democracy a dead-end, a project of the past, no longer possible to revive and revitalize in a post-secular, multicultural society, in a world driven by global capitalism and populist anti-globalization? Or is it instead this very global condition which forces us to revisit the relevance of Christian Democracy in the twenty-first century, also in light of the transformations Catholic thought went through in the short but dramatic twentieth century? Was there ever a historical moment when we needed alternative visions of the social than the empty shell of "neo-liberalism" to give direction to society, economy, and politics? We ought to give that question more consideration, for the future of European and global politics hinges on the answers given to it. At least to some extent.

References

A colloquio. 2003. A colloquio con Dossetti e Lazzati. Intervista di Leopoldo Elia e Pietro Scoppola. Bologna: Il Mulino.

Abbruzzese, Salvatore. 1991. Comunione e liberazione. Identità religiosa e disincanto laico. Rome and Bari: Laterza.

Acanfora, Paolo. 2007. "Myths and the Political Use of Religion in Christian Democratic Culture." Journal of Modern Italian Studies 12(3): pp. 307–38.

Acanfora, Paolo. 2013. Miti e ideologia nella politica estera DC. Nazione, Europa, Comunità atlantica (1943–1945). Bologna: Il Mulino.

Acanfora, Paolo. 2015. "Alcide De Gasperi." Aggiornamenti Sociali 66(1): pp. 83–6.

Accattoli, Luigi. 1994. "Ruini: cattolici al Centro, se potete." Corriere della Sera, March 15.

Accattoli, Luigi. 2001. "Votate per chi segue le idee della Chiesa." Corriere della Sera, March 27.

Acerbi, Antonio. 2003. "La Chiesa Italiana dalla conclusione del Concilio alla fine della Democrazia cristiana." In La Chiesa e l'Italia. Per una storia dei loro rapporti negli ultimi due secoli, edited by Antonio Acerbi, pp. 449–520. Milan: Vita e Pensiero.

ACI. 1988. Aci, scelta religiosa e politica. Documenti 1969–1988, edited by Raffaele Cananzi. Rome: AVE.

Agosti, Aldo. 1996. Palmiro Togliatti. Turin: UTET.

Alberigo, Giuseppe. 1964. Lo sviluppo della dottrina sui poteri della Chiesa universale. Momenti essenziali tra il XVI e il XIX secolo. Rome: Herder.

Alberigo, Giuseppe (ed.). 1995–2001. Storia del Concilio Vaticano II. 5 vols (Italian edition edited by A. Melloni). Bologna: Il Mulino.

Alberigo, Giuseppe. 1998. "Rinnovamento della Chiesa e partecipazione al Concilio Vaticano II." In Giuseppe Dossetti. Prime prospettive e ipotesi di ricerca, edited by Giuseppe Alberigo, pp. 41–82. Bologna: Il Mulino.

Alberigo, Giuseppe. 2005. Breve storia del Concilio Vaticano II. Bologna: Il Mulino.

Allegretti, Umberto. 2007. "Dossetti, difesa e sviluppo della Costituzione." In Giuseppe Dossetti: la fede e la storia. Studi nel decennale della morte, edited by Alberto Melloni, pp. 67–146. Bologna: Il Mulino.

Allocuzione. 1985. "Allocuzione del Santo Padre." In Riconciliazione cristiana e comunità degli uomini. Atti del secondo convegno ecclesiale, Loreto 9–13 Aprile 1985, edited by the Conferenza Episcopale Italiana, pp. 45–60. Rome: AVE.

Amato, Giuliano. 1980. Una repubblica da riformare. Bologna: Il Mulino.

Ambrosini, Gaspare, et al. 1954. Nazione e comunità internazionale. Rome: Studium.

Ambrosoli, Luigi. 1958. Il primo movimento democratico cristiano in Italia, 1897–1904. Rome: Cinque Lune.

Anderson, Margaret Lavinia. 1981. Windthorst: A Political Biography. Oxford: Oxford University Press.

Anderson, Margaret Lavinia. 1986. "The Kulturkampf and the Course of German History." Central European History 19(1): pp. 82–115.

Anderson, Margaret Lavinia. 1995. "The Limit of Secularization: On the Problem of Catholic Revival in Nineteenth-Century Germany." Historical Journal 38(3): pp. 647–70.

Andes, Stephen J. C. 2014. *The Vatican and Catholic Activism in Mexico and Chile: The Politics of Transnational Catholicism, 1920–1940*. Oxford: Oxford University Press.

Arata, Rodolfo. 1951. "18 Aprile." *Il Popolo*, April 18.

Ardigò, Achille. 1947. "Le due fasi dell'esperimento laburista." *Cronache Sociali* 1(2): pp. 9–11.

Ardigò, Achille. 1978. "Jacques Maritain e 'Cronache Sociali' (ovvero Maritain e il dossettismo)." In *Il pensiero politico di Jacques Maritain*, edited by Giancarlo Galeazzi, pp. 195–202. Milan: Editrice Massimo.

Are, Giuseppe. 1963. *I cattolici e la questione sociale in Italia, 1894–1904*. Milan: Feltrinelli.

Armellini, Paolo. 2011. "Del Noce lettore di Voegelin: la critica della modernità." In *Lo stato degli studi voegeliniani: a cinquant'anni da Ordine e Storia*, edited by Gian Franco Lami, pp. 215–48. Milan: Franco Angeli.

Arpaia, Luigi. 2015. "Luigi Federzoni and the Converging and Diverging Parallels of Fascism and Catholicism." In *Catholicism and Fascism in Europe: 1918–1945*, edited by Jan Nelis, Anne Morelli, and Danny Praet, pp. 237–54. Hildesheim: George Olms Verlag AG.

Asad, Talal. 2003. *Formations of the Secular: Christianity, Islam, Modernity*. Stanford: Stanford University Press.

Atti. 1946. *Atti dell'Assemblea Costituente. Prima sottocommissione. Resoconti Sommari*. Rome: Camera dei deputati.

Atti. 1959. *Atti e documenti della Democrazia cristiana: 1943–1959*. Rome: Cinque Lune.

Atti e Documenti. 1968. *Atti e documenti della Democrazia Cristiana: 1943–1967*, Vol. I, edited by Andrea Damilano. Rome: Cinque Lune.

Baccetti, Carlo. 2007. *I post-democristiani*. Bologna: Il Mulino.

Baget Bozzo, Gianni. 1974. *Il partito cristiano al potere. La DC di De Gasperi e di Dossetti, 1945–1954*. Florence: Vallecchi.

Baget Bozzo, Gianni. 1977. *Il partito cristiano e l'apertura a sinistra. La DC di Fanfani e Moro, 1954–1962*. Florence: Vallecchi.

Baget Bozzo, Gianni. 1994. *Cattolici e democristiani. Un'esperienza politica italiana*. Milan: Rizzoli.

Baget Bozzo, Gianni. 2006. "Prodi 'cattolico adulto'." *Il Giornale*, August 11.

Baget Bozzo, Gianni, and Giovanni Tassani. 1983. *Aldo Moro. Il politico nella crisi 1962–1973*. Florence: Sansoni.

Bailey, Tom, and Michael Driessen. 2016. "Mapping Contemporary Catholic Politics in Italy." *Journal of Modern Italian Studies* 21(3): pp. 419–25.

Banfield, Edward. 1958. *The Moral Basis of a Backward Society*. Glencoe, IL: Free Press.

Baragli, Matteo. 2015. "The *Centro Nazionale Italiano*: Profiles and Projects of Italian Clerico-Fascism (1924–1930)." In *Catholicism and Fascism in Europe: 1918–1945*, edited by Jan Nelis, Anne Morelli, and Danny Praet, pp. 277–92. Hildesheim: George Olms Verlag AG.

Barbanti, Marco. 1988. "Funzioni strategiche dell'anticomunismo nell'età del centrismo." *Italia Contemporanea* 170: pp. 39–69.

Barcellona, Pietro, Paolo Sorbi, Mario Tronti, and Giuseppe Vacca (eds). 2012. *Emergenza Antropologica. Per una nuova alleanza tra credenti e non credenti*. Milan: Guerini e Associati.

Barré, Jean-Luc. 1995. *Jacques et Raïssa Maritain: les mendiants du Ciel: biographies croisées*. Paris: Stock.

Battistacci, Giorgio. 1978. "Cattolici perugini tra Resistenza e impegno politico." In *Cattolici e fascisti in Umbria (1922–1945)*, edited by Alberto Monticone, pp. 465–9. Bologna; Il Mulino.

Bedeschi, Lorenzo. 1959. *Le origini della gioventù cattolica: dalla caduta del governo pontificio al primo congresso cattolico di Venezia su documenti inediti d'archivio*. Bologna: Cappelli.

Behr, Thomas C. 2019. *Social Justice and Subsidiarity: Luigi Taparelli and the Origins of Modern Catholic Social Thought*. Washington, DC: Catholic University of America Press.

Belardinelli, Sergio. 1990. "Die politische Philosophie des christlichen Personalismus." In *Politische Philosophie des 20. Jahrhunderts*, edited by Karl Graf Ballestrem and Henning Ottmann, pp. 243–62. Munich: De Gruyter.

Bell, David A. 2007. *The First Total War: Napoleon's Europe and the Birth of Warfare as We Know It*. Boston: Houghton Mifflin.

Bennette, Rebecca Ayako. 2012. *Fighting for the Soul of Germany: The Catholic Struggle for Inclusion after Unification*. Cambridge, MA: Harvard University Press.

Berger, Peter L. (ed.). 1999. *The Desecularization of the World: Resurgent Religions and World Politics*. Grand Rapids, MI: Eerdmans Publishing Company.

Bernardi, Emanuele. 2014. "La DC e la crisi del sistema politico. Temi e personaggi, 1989-1994." In *L'Italia contemporanea dagli anni Ottanta a oggi*, Vol. III: *Istituzioni e politica*, edited by Simona Colarizi, Agostino Giovagnoli, and Paolo Pombeni, pp. 227–37. Rome: Carocci.

Betz, Hans George, and Susi Meret. 2009. "Revisiting Lepanto: The Political Mobilization against Islam in Contemporary Western Europe." *Patterns of Prejudices* 43(3–4): pp. 313–34.

Biagini, Eugenio. 2007. "Keynesian Ideas and the Recasting of Italian Democracy." In *The Strange Survival of Liberal England: Political Leaders, Moral Values and the Reception of Economic Debate*, edited by Ewen H. H. Green and Duncan M. Tanner, pp. 212–44. Cambridge: Cambridge University Press.

Biaglioli, Ilaria, Alfonso Botti, and Rocco Cerrato (eds). 2004. *Romolo Murri e i murrismi in Italia e in Europa cent'anni dopo*. Urbino: Quattro Venti.

Bianchini, Laura. 1944a. "Il disarmo degli spiriti." *Il Ribelle* 8, July 25.

Bianchini, Laura. 1944b. "Democrazia." *Il Ribelle* 18, December 1.

Bizzarri, Elisa. 1980. *L'organizzazione del movimento femminile cattolico dal 1943 al 1948*. Rome: Quaderni della FIAP.

Blackbourn, David. 1991. "The Catholic Church in Europe since the French Revolution: A Review Article." *Comparative Studies in Society and History* 33(4): pp. 778–90.

Blackbourn, David. 1993. *Marpingen: Apparitions of the Virgin Mary in Bismarkian Germany*. Oxford: Oxford University Press.

Blessing, Werner K. 1988. "'Deutschland in Not, wir im Glauben...': Kirche und Kirchenvolk in einer katholischen Region, 1933-1949." In *Von Stalingrad zur Währungsreform. Zur Sozialgeschichte des Umbruchs in Deutschland*, edited by Martin Broszat, Klaus Dieter Henke, and Hans Woller, pp. 3–111. Munich: Oldenbourg.

Bobbio, Norberto. 1995. *Ideological Profile of Twentieth-Century Italy*, translated by L. G. Cochrane. Princeton: Princeton University Press.

Bocci, Maria. 1995. "Il gruppo della 'Cattolica'—Appunti sulla formazione di un alternativa al totalitarismo." *Civilta Ambrosiana* 4: pp. 273–94.

Bocci, Maria. 1999. *Oltre lo Stato liberale. Ipotesi su politica e società nel dibattito cattolico tra fascismo e democrazia*. Rome: Bulzoni.

Bocci, Maria. 2003. *Agostino Gemelli rettore e francescano. Chiesa, regime, democrazia*. Brescia: Morcelliana.

Bolzonar, Fabio. 2016. "A Christian Democratization of Politics: The New Influence of Catholicism on Italian Politics since the Demise of the Democrazia Cristiana." *Journal of Modern Italian Studies* 21(3): pp. 445–63.

Borghesi, Massimo. 1993. "Il problema politico dei cattolici." In *Filosofia e democrazia in Augusto Del Noce*, edited by Giuseppe Ceci and Lorella Cedroni. Rome: Cinque Lune.

Borutta, Manuel. 2003. "Enemies at the Gate: The Moabit *Klostersturm* and the *Kulturkampf*: Germany." In *Culture Wars: Secular-Catholic Conflict in Nineteenth-Century Europe*, edited by Christopher Clark and Wolfram Kaiser, pp. 227–54. Cambridge: Cambridge University Press.

Bracher, Karl Dietrich. 1984. *The Age of Ideologies: A History of Political Thought in the Twentieth Century*, translated by E. Osers. London: Weidenfeld and Nicolson.

Bracke, Maud Anne. 2017. "Feminism, the Sate, and the Centrality of Reproduction: Abortion Struggles in 1970s Italy." *Journal of Social History* 42(4): pp. 524–46.

Brodies, Thomas. 2017. "Religion and Germany's Twentieth Century." *English Historical Review* 132(559): pp. 1499–1518.

Brogi, Alessandro. 2011. *Confronting America: The Cold War between the United States and the Communists in France and in Italy*. Chapel Hill: University of North Carolina Press.

Brubaker, Roger. 2017. "Between Nationalism and Civilizationism: The European Populist Moment in Comparative Perspective." *Ethnic and Racial Studies* 40(8): pp. 1191–1226.

Brunelli, Gianfranco. 1995. "La scommessa perduta sul partito cattolico." *Il Mulino* 44(358): pp. 273–43.

Buchanan, Tom, and Martin Conway. 1996. *Political Catholicism in Europe, 1918–1965*. New York: Oxford University.

Burleigh, Michael. 2005. *Earthly Powers: The Clash of Religion and Politics in Europe from the French Revolution to the Great War*. New York: Harper and Collins.

Byrnes, Joseph F. 2005. *Catholic and French Forever: Religion and National Identity in Modern France*. University Park: Pennsylvania State University Press.

Caciagli, Mario. 2003. "Christian Democracy." In *The Cambridge History of Twentieth Century Political Thought*, edited by Terence Ball and Richard Bellamy, pp. 165–90. Cambridge: Cambridge University Press.

Camisasca, Massimo. 2006. *Comunione e Liberazione*, Vol. III: *Il riconoscimento (1976–1984)*. Cinisello Balsamo: San Paolo.

Campanini, Giorgio. 1997. "La Democrazia nel pensiero politico dei cattolici italiani." In *Cattolici, Chiesa, Resistenza*, edited by Gabriele De Rosa, pp. 491–511. Bologna: Il Mulino.

Campanini, Giorgio. 2006. "Dal Codice di Camaldoli alla Costituzione. I cattolici e la rinascita della democrazia." *Aggiornamenti Sociali* 57(5): pp. 399–410.

Cananzi, Raffaele (ed.). 1988. *ACI, scelta religiosa e scelta politica*. Rome: AVE.

Canavero, Alfredo. 1988. *Albertario e "l'Osservatore Cattolico."* Rome: Studium.

Canfora, Luciano. 2008. *Democracy in Europe: A History of an Ideology*, translated by Simon Jones. Malden, MA: Blackwell.

Cappellari, Bartolomeo. 1799. *Il trionfo della Santa Sede e della Chiesa contro gli assalti de' novatori respinti e combattuti colle stesse loro armi*. Rome: Pagliarini.

Capperucci, Vera. 2003. "La sinistra democristiana e la difficile integrazione tra Europa e America (1945–1958)." In *Atlantismo e Europeismo*, edited by Piero Craveri and Gaetano Quagliariello, pp. 71–93. Soveria Mannelli: Rubbettino.

Capperucci, Vera. 2004. "Le correnti della Democrazia Cristiana di fronte all'America. Tra differenziazione culturale ed integrazione politica, 1944–1954." In *L'anti-americanismo in Italia e in Europa nel secondo dopoguerra*, edited by Piero Craveri and Gaetano Quagliariello, pp. 249–89. Soveria Mannelli: Rubettino.

Capperucci, Vera. 2009. "Alcide De Gasperi and the Problem of Reconstruction." *Modern Italy* 14(4): pp. 445–57.

Caracciolo, Alberto. 1975. *Teresio Olivelli.* Brescia: La Scuola.

Cartocci, Roberto. 2011. *Geografia dell'Italia cattolica.* Bologna: Il Mulino.

Casanova, José. 1994. *Public Religions in the Modern World.* Chicago: University of Chicago Press.

Casanova, José. 1996. "Global Catholicism and the Politics of Civil Society." *Sociological Inquiry* 66(3): pp. 356–63.

Casella, Mario. 1984. *L'Azione Cattolica alla caduta del fascismo. Attività e progetti per il dopoguerra (1942–45).* Rome: Studium.

Casella, Mario. 1987. *Cattolici e Costituente. Orientamenti e iniziative del cattolicesimo organizzato (1945–1947).* Naples: Edizioni Scientifiche Italiane.

Casella, Mario. 1992. *L'Azione Cattolica nell'Italia contemporanea.* Rome: AVE.

Casula, Carlo Felice. 1988. *Domenico Tardini. L'azione della Santa Sede nella crisi fra le due guerre.* Rome: Studium.

Cavour, Camillo Benso. 1872. *Discorsi Parlamentari,* vol. XI. Rome: Eredi Botta.

Ceccarelli, Filippo. 1983. "La frana bianca." *Panorama,* July 25: p. 18.

Ceci, Lucia. 2008. "'Il fascismo manda l'Italia in rovina.' Le note inedite di monsignor Domenico Tardini (23 settembre-13 dicembre 1935)." *Rivista Storica Italiana* 120(1): pp. 323–46.

Ceci, Lucia. 2010. *Il papa non deve parlare. Chiesa, fascismo e guerra d'Etiopia.* Rome and Bari: Laterza.

Ceci, Lucia. 2014. *L'interesse superiore, Il Vaticano e l'Italia di Mussolini.* Rome and Bari: Laterza.

CEI. 1997. *Il Vangelo della carità per una nuova società in Italia—Atti del III Convegno ecclesiale (Palermo, 20–24 novembre 1995).* Rome: AVE.

Cento Bull, Anna. 2007. *Italian Neofascism: The Strategy of Tension and the Politics of Nonreconciliation.* New York and Oxford: Berghahn.

Chadwick, Owen. 1981. *The Popes and European Revolution.* Oxford: Clarendon Press.

Chadwick, Owen. 1998. *A History of Popes, 1830–1914.* Oxford: Oxford University Press.

Chamedes, Giuliana. 2013. "The Vatican and the Reshaping of the European International Order after the First World War." *Historical Journal* 56(4): pp. 955–76.

Chamedes, Giuliana. 2019. *A Twentieth-Century Crusade: The Vatican's Battle to Remake Christian Europe.* Cambridge, MA: Harvard University Press.

Chappel, James. 2011. "The Catholic Origins of Totalitarianism Theory in Interwar Europe." *Modern Intellectual History* 8(3): pp. 561–90.

Chappel, James. 2018. *Catholic Modern: The Challenge of Totalitarianism and the Remaking of the Church.* Cambridge, MA: Harvard University Press.

Chenaux, Philippe. 1994. *Paul VI et Maritain. Les rapports du "montinianisme" et du "maritanisme."* Rome: Studium.

Chiesa. 1983. *Chiesa, Azione Cattolica e fascismo nel 1931.* Rome: AVE.

Civitas. 2013. "Il Codice di Camaldoli e la riemergenza del cattolicesimo politico." *Civitas* 1–2 special issue.

Clark, Christopher, and Wolfram Kaiser. 2003. *Culture Wars: Secular-Catholic Conflict in Nineteenth-Century Europe.* Cambridge: Cambridge University Press.

Conferenza Episcopale Italiana. 1992. *Atti della XXXV Assemblea generale Roma 11–15 maggio 1992.* Rome: CEI.

Confessore, Ornella. 1999. *I cattolici e la "fede nella libertà." "Annali cattolici," "Rivista universale," "Rassegna nazionale."* Rome: Studium.

Congar, Yves. 1960. "L'ecclésiologie de la Révolution française au Councile du Vatican, sous le signe de l'affirmation de l'autorité." In *L'ecclésiologie au XIX Siècle*, edited by M. Nédoncelle, pp. 77–14. Paris: Cerf.

Conway, Martin. 1996. "Introduction." In *Political Catholicism in Europe, 1918–1965*, edited by Tom Buchanan and Martin Conway, pp. 1–33. New York: Oxford University.

Conway, Martin. 1997. *Catholic Politics in Europe, 1918–1945*. London and New York: Routledge.

Conway, Martin. 2003. "The Age of Christian Democracy: The Frontiers of Success and Failure." In *European Christian Democracy: Historical Legacies and Comparative Perspective*, edited by Thomas Kselman and Joseph A. Buttigieg, pp. 43–67. Notre Dame, IN: University of Notre Dame Press.

Conway, Martin. 2020. *Western Europe's Democratic Age, 1945–1968*. Princeton: Princeton University Press.

Coppa, Jr, Frank. 2013. *The Modern Papacy since 1789*. London and New York: Routledge.

Cossiga, Francesco. 1993. *Il torto e il diritto. Quasi un'antologia personale*, edited by Pasquale Chessa. Milan: Mondadori.

Costituzione e Costituente. 1946. *Costituzione e Costituente: La XIX Settimana Sociale dei cattolici d'Italia (Firenze 22–28 ottobre 1945)*. Rome: ICAS.

Cox, Jeffrey, Thomas Albert Howard, Thomas Kselman, and George S. Williamson. 2006. "Modern European Historiography Forum." *Church History* 75(1): pp. 120–62.

Craveri, Piero. 2006. *De Gasperi*. Bologna: Il Mulino.

Craveri, Piero. 2009. "Lo Stato e il partito nell'opera politica di Amintore Fanfani." *Annali dell'Università Suor Orsola Benincasa* 1: pp. 51–67.

Crainz, Guido. 1996. *Storia del miracolo italiano. Culture, identità, trasformazioni fra anni Cinquanta e Sessanta*. Rome: Donzelli.

Crainz, Guido. 2012. *Il paese reale. Dall'assissinio di Moro all'Italia di oggi*. Rome: Donzelli.

Crivellin, Walter (ed.). 2000. *Cattolici, Chiesa, Resistenza. I testimoni*. Bologna: Il Mulino.

Crivellin, Walter (ed.). 2010. *Luigi Sturzo nella cultura politica del '900*. Special issue of *Storia e politica: Rivista Quadrimestrale* 2(1).

Cuminetti, Mario. 1983. *Il dissenso cattolico in Italia 1965–1980*. Milan: Rizzoli.

Dagnino, Jorge. 2007. "Catholic Modernities in Fascist Italy: The Intellectuals of Azione Cattolica." *Totalitarian Movement and Political Religion* 8(2): pp. 329–41.

Dagnino, Jorge. 2009. "Catholic Students at War: The Federazione Universitaria Cattolica Italiana, 1940–43." *Journal of Modern Italian Studies* 14(3): pp. 285–304.

Dagnino, Jorge. 2012. "The Intellectuals of Italian Catholic Action and the Sacralisation of Politics in 1930s Europe." *Contemporary European History* 21(2): pp. 215–33.

Dagnino, Jorge. 2017. *Faith and Fascism: Catholic Intellectuals in Italy, 1925–1943*. London: Routledge.

Daly, Gabriel. 1980. *Catholic Transcendence and Immanence: A Study in Catholic Modernism and Integralism*. New York and Oxford: Oxford University Press.

Daly, Gabriel. 1985. "Catholicism and Modernity." *Journal of the American Academy of Religion* 53(3): pp. 773–96.

D'Angelo Augusto. 2002. *De Gasperi, le destre e l'operazione Sturzo. Voto amministrativo del 1952 e progetti di riforma elettorale*. Rome: Studium.

D'Angelo, Augusto. 2005. *Moro, i vescovi e l'apertura a sinistra*. Rome: Studium.

Dau Novelli, Cecilia. 1988. "Il movimento femminile della Democrazia cristiana dal 1944 al 1964." In *Storia della Democrazia cristiana*, edited by Francesco Malgeri III, *Gli anni di transizione: Da Fanfani a Moro, 1954–1962*, pp. 331–68. Rome: Cinque Lune.

Dau Novelli, Cecilia. 1996. *Sorelle d'Italia. Casalinghe, militanti, impiegate nel Novecento*. Rome: AVE.

Dau Novelli, Cecilia. 1997. "La famiglia come soggetto della ricostruzione sociale (1942–1949)." In *Cattolici, Chiesa, Resistenza*, edited by Gabriele De Rosa, pp. 469–90. Bologna: Il Mulino.

Dawes, Helena. 2011. "The Catholic Church and the Woman Question: Catholic Feminism in Italy in the Early 1900s." *Catholic Historical Review* 97(3): pp. 484–526.

De Bortoli, Ferruccio. 2014. "'Benedetto XVI non è una statua'." *Corriere della Sera*, March 5.

De Felice, Renzo. 1974. *Mussolini Il Duce*, Vol. I: *Gli anni del consenso, 1929–1936*. Turin: Einaudi.

De Felice, Renzo. 1981. *Mussolini Il Duce*, Vol. II: *Lo Stato totalitario 1938–1940*. Turin: Einaudi.

De Gasperi, Alcide [Spectator]. 1934. "La quindicina internazionale." *L'Illustrazione Vaticana* 5, March 1: pp. 216–17.

De Gasperi, Alcide [Spectator]. 1935. "La quindicina internazionale." *L'Illustrazione Vaticana* 6, February 16: pp. 179–80.

De Gasperi, Alcide [Spectator]. 1936. "La quindicina internazionale." *L'Illustrazione Vaticana* 7, September 1: pp. 799–800.

De Gasperi, Alcide [Spectator]. 1937. "La quindicina internazionale." *L'Illustrazione Vaticana* 8, January 16: pp. 17–18.

De Gasperi, Alcide. 1947. *Non diserteremo il nostro posto!* Rome: SPES.

De Gasperi, Alcide. 1948. *Le basi morali della democrazia: conferenza tenuta dal Presidente del Consiglio Alcide De Gasperi al Palais des beaux-arts a Bruxelles il 20 novembre 1948*. Rome: SELI.

De Gasperi, Alcide. 1954. *Nella lotta per la democrazia*. Rome: Cinque Lune.

De Gasperi, Alcide. 1956. *Discorsi politici*, edited by Tommaso Bozza, preface by Amintore Fanfani. 2 vols. Rome: Cinque Lune.

De Gasperi, Alcide. 1974. *De Gasperi scrive. Corrispondenza con capi di stato, cardinali, uomini politici, giornalisti, diplomatici*, edited by Maria Romana De Gasperi. 2 vols. Brescia: Morcelliana.

De Gasperi, Alcide. 1985. *Discorsi Parlamentari*, Vol. I: *1921–1949*. Rome: Camera dei Deputati.

De Gasperi, Alcide. 1990. *Discorsi politici, 1923–1954*, edited by Giovanni Allara and Angelo Gatti. Rome: Cinque Lune.

De Gasperi, Alcide. 2008. *Scritti e discorsi politici*, Vol. III: *Alcide De Gasperi e la Fondazione della democrazia italiana (1943–1948)*, edited by Vera Capperucci and Sara Lorenzini, t. 2. Bologna: Il Mulino.

De Gasperi, Alcide. 2009. *Scritti e discorsi politici*, Vol. IV: *Alcide Gasperi e la stabilizzazione della Repubblica (1948–1954)*, edited by Sara Lorenzini and Barbara Taverni, t. 2. Bologna: Il Mulino.

De Giorgi, Fulvio. 1999. *Cattolici e educazione tra Risorgimento e Restaurazione. Ordini religiosi, antigesuitismo e pedagogia nei processi di modernizzazione*. Milan: ISU—Università Cattolica.

De Giorgi, Fulvio. 2003. *Rosmini e il suo tempo. L'educazione dell'uomo moderno tra riforma della filosofia e rinnovamento della Chiesa (1797–1833)*. Brescia: Morcelliana.

De Luna, Giovanni (ed.). 1994. *Figli di un benessere minore. La Lega, 1979–1993*. Florence: La Nuova Italia.

De Mita, Ciriaco. 1984. *Ragionando di politica. Le prospettive della democrazia italiana negli anni Ottanta*. Milan: Rusconi.

De Rosa, Gabriele. 1966. *Storia del movimento cattolico in Italia. Dalla Restaurazione all'età giolittiana*. Bari: Laterza.

De Rosa, Gabriele. 1973. "Luigi Sturzo nella Storia d'Italia." In *Luigi Sturzo nella Storia d'Italia. Atti del convegno di Studi internazionali promosso dall'Assemblea Regionale Siciliana (Palermo-Caltagirone, 26–28 novembre 1971)*, Vol. I: *Relazioni e dibattiti*, pp. 43–107. Rome: Edizioni di Storia e Letteratura.

De Rosa, Gabriele. 1977. *Sturzo*. Turin: Utet.

De Rosa, Gabriele. 1978. *Dal cattolicesimo liberale alla Democrazia Cristiana del secondo dopoguerra*. Turin: Fondazione G. Agnelli.

De Rosa, Gabriele (ed.). 1997a. *Cattolici, Chiesa, Resistenza*. Bologna: Il Mulino.

De Rosa, Gabriele. 1997b. *La transizione infinita. Diario politico, 1990–1996*. Rome and Bari: Laterza.

De Rosa, Luigi. 1993. *Luigi Taparelli. L'altro D'Azeglio*. Milan: Cisalpino.

Del Noce, Augusto. 1957. "Fine o crisi del degasperismo?" *Il Mulino* 6(7–8): pp. 479–85.

Del Noce, Augusto. 1959. "Ideologia socialista e fronte popolare." *L'Ordine Civile* 1(3), July 25: pp. 1–3.

Del Noce, Augusto. 1960. "Fanfani: il politico dell'Università Cattolica." *Il Mulino* 9(2): pp. 81–9.

Del Noce, Augusto. 1964. *Il problema ideologico dei cattolici italiani*. Turin: Bottega d'Erasmo.

Del Noce, Augusto. 1970. *L'epoca della secolarizzazione*. Milan: Giuffrè.

Del Noce, Augusto. 1978. *Il suicidio della rivoluzione*. Milan: Rusconi.

Del Noce, Augusto. 1983. "Rosmini e la categoria filosofica-politica di Risorgimento." www.cattedrarosmini.org (last accessed: June 2, 2023).

Del Noce, Augusto. 1985. "Risposte alla scristianità. Il S. Padre a Loreto." *Il Sabato*, June 1.

Del Noce, Augusto. 1990. *Il problema dell'ateismo* (1964), with an introduction by Nicola Matteucci. Bologna: Il Mulino.

Del Noce, Augusto. 1991. *Da Cartesio a Rosmini. Scritti vari, anche inediti, di filosofia e storia della filosofia*, edited by Francesco Mercadante and Bernardino Casadei. Milan: Giuffrè.

Del Noce, Augusto. 1994. "La potenza ideologica del marxismo e la possibilità del successo del comunismo in Italia per via democratica." In *I cattolici e il progressismo*, edited by Bernardino Casadei, preface by Rocco Buttiglione, pp. 45–92. Milan: Mondadori.

Del Noce, Augusto. 2006. "Ontologismo" (1968–1969). In *Enciclopedia Filosofica*, vol. VIII, pp. 8147–53. Milan: Bompiani.

Del Noce, Augusto. 2014. *The Crisis of Modernity*, edited and translated by Carlo Lancellotti. Montreal & Kingston: McGill-Queen's University Press.

Del Noce, Augusto. 2017. *The Age of Secularization*, edited and translated by Carlo Lancellotti. Montreal & Kingston: McGill-Queen's University Press.

Del Pero, Mario. 2001. *L'alleato scomodo. Gli USA e la DC negli anni del centrismo, 1948–1955*. Rome: Carocci.

Delbreil, Jean Claude. 2001. "The French Catholic Left and the Political Parties." In *Left Catholicism 1943–1955: Catholics and Society in Western Europe at the Point of Liberation*, edited by Gerd-Rainer Horn and Emmanuel Gerard, pp. 45–63. Leuven: Leuven University Press.

Della Missione. 1998. *Della Missione a Roma di Antonio Rosmini-Serbati negli anni 1848–49. Commentario*, edited by L. Malusa, G. Bergamaschi, E. Botto, L. Mauro, D. Preda, I. Senino, and D. Veneruso. Stresa: Edizione Rosminiane.

Demerath, N. J., III. 2007. "Secularization and Sacralization Deconstructed and Reconstructed." In *The SAGE Handbook of the Sociology of Religion*, edited by Jameas A. Beckford and N. J. Demerath III, pp. 57–80. London: SAGE.

Di Loreto, Pietro. 1993. *La difficile transizione. Dalla fine del centrismo al centro-sinistra, 1953-1960*. Bologna: Il Mulino.

Di Maio, Tiziana (ed.). 2009. *Le democristiane. Le donne cattoliche nella costruzione della democrazia repubblicana*. Soveria Mannelli: Rubbettino.

Di Maio, Tiziana, and Cecilia Dau Novelli (eds). 2023. *Female Activism and Christian Democratic Parties in Europe*. Leuven: Leuven University Press.

Diamanti, Ilvo. 1995. *La Lega. Geografia, storia e sociologia di un nuovo soggetto politico*. Rome: Donzelli.

Diamanti, Ilvo. 1996. *Il male del Nord. Lega, localismo, secessione*. Rome: Donzelli.

Diamanti, Ilvo, and Luigi Ceccarini. 2007. "Catholics and Politics after the Christian Democrats: The Influential Minority." *Journal of Modern Italian Studies* 12(1): pp. 37–59.

Dichiarazioni. 1949. "Dichiarazioni di Dossetti." *Il Popolo*, March 9.

DiJoseph, John. 1996. *Jacques Maritain and the Moral Foundation of Democracy*. Lanham, MD: Rowman and Littlefield.

Diotallevi, Luca. 2016. "On the Current Absence and Future Improbability of Political Catholicism in Italy." *Journal of Modern Italian Studies* 21(3): pp. 485–510.

Discorsi. 1961. *Discorsi di Pio XI*, Vol. III, edited by Domenico Bertetto. Turin: SEI.

Documenti. 1993. "Documenti della 'Costituente DC'." *Il Popolo*, June 24.

Doering, Bernard. 1983. *Jacques Maritain and the French Catholic Intellectuals*. Notre Dame, IN: University of Notre Dame Press.

Domenidò, Francesco Maria. 1948. "Democrazia nazionale." *Il Popolo*, April 27.

Dossetti, Giuseppe. 1947. "Fine del Tripartito?" *Cronache Sociali* 1(2): pp. 1–2.

Dossetti, Giuseppe. 1948. "Unità della politica: connessione fra la politica interna e la politica estera italiana." *Cronache Sociali* 2(31): pp. 1–4.

Dossetti, Giuseppe. 1951. "Tattica elettorale." *Cronache Sociali* 5(7/8): pp. 1–7.

Dossetti, Giuseppe. 1982. *Scritti reggiani, 1944-1948*. Rome: Cinque Lune.

Dossetti, Giuseppe. 1988. *Ho imparato a guardare lontano*, edited by Salvatore Fanfareggi. Cavriago: Pozzi.

Dossetti, Giuseppe. 1994. *La ricerca costituente, 1945-1952*, edited by Alberto Melloni. Bologna: Il Mulino.

Dossetti, Giuseppe. 1995a. "Il Movimento Democratico Cristiano (27 March 1945)." in *Scritti Politici, 1943-1951*, edited by Giuseppe Trotta, pp. 20–1. Genoa: Marietti.

Dossetti, Giuseppe. 1995b. "Lettera a Piccioni (23 February 1948)." In *Scritti politici, 1943-1951*, edited by Giuseppe Trotta. Genoa: Marietti.

Dossetti, Giuseppe. 2008. "La coscienza del partito." In *Dossetti a Rossena. I piani e i tempi dell'impegno politico*, edited by Roberto Villa, pp. 187–98. Reggio Emilia: Aliberti.

Dossier Lazzati. 1993. *Dossier Lazzati 4. Lazzati, il Lager, il Regno*. Rome: AVE.

Durand, Jean-Dominique. 1984. "Alcide De Gasperi ovvero la politica ispirata." *Storia Contemporanea* 15(4): pp. 545–91.

Durand, Jean-Dominique. 1995. *L'Europe de le Démocraties chrétienne*. Paris: Éditions Complexe.

Durand, Jean-Dominique. 1996. "Jacques Maritain et l'Italie." In *Jacques Maritain en Europe: la réception de sa pensée*, edited by Bernard Hubert, pp. 13–85. Paris: Éditions Beauchesne.

Eickelman, Dale. 2000. "Islam and the Languages of Modernity." *Daedalus* 129(1): pp. 119–35.

Eickelman, Dale, and James Piscatori. 2004 [1996]. *Muslim Politics*. Princeton: Princeton University Press.

Eisenstadt, Sh'muel N. 2000. "Multiple Modernities." *Daedalus* 129(1): pp. 1–29.

Elia, Leopoldo. 2009. "Giuseppe Dossetti e l'art. 7." In *La storia, il dialogo, il rispetto della persona. Scritti in onore del cardinale Achille Silvestrini*, edited by Luca Monteferrante and Damiano Nocillla, pp. 433–51. Rome: Studium.

Evangelizzazione. 1973. *Evangelizzazione e sacramenti: documento pastorale dell'episcopato italiano*. Milan: OR.

Evangelizzazione. 1975. *Evangelizzazione e promozione umana: documento base n. 1 a cura del Comitato Preparatiorio del Convegno 1976 e Traccia per la riflessione*. Milan: OR.

Evangelizzazione. 1979. *Evangelizzazione, sacramenti, promozione umana. Le scelte pastorali della Chiesa in Italia*. Rome: AVE.

Faggioli, Massimo. 2001. "Enrico Bartoletti tra concilio e post-concilio: il primate dell'evangelizzazione e la 'commissione donna'." *Rivista di Storia della Chiesa in Italia* 55(2): pp. 471–500.

Faggioli, Massimo. 2014. *Sorting Out Catholicism: A Brief History of the New Ecclesial Movements*, translated by Demetrio S. Yocum. Collegeville, MN: Liturgical Press.

Faggioli, Massimo. 2017. *Catholicism and Citizenship: Political Cultures of the Church in the Twenty First Century*. Collegeville, MN: Liturgical Press.

Fanfani, Amintore. 1936. "Da Soli!" *Rivista Internazionale di Scienze Sociali* 44(3): pp. 229–31.

Fanfani, Amintore. 1937. *Il significato del corporativismo; testo ad uso dei licei e degli istituti magistrali*. Como: Cavalleri.

Fanfani, Amintore. 1939. "L'impulso politico all'economia." *Rivista Internazionale di Scienze Sociali* 47(3): pp. 247–460.

Fanfani, Amintore. 1945. *Persona, beni, società in una rinnovata civiltà cristiana*. Milan: Giuffrè.

Fanfani, Amintore. 1946. "Partiti di ispirazione cristiana e Chiesa cattolica." *Humanitas* 1(2): pp. 381–5.

Fanfani, Amintore. 1948. "Politica economica italiana: problemi residui e problemi futuri." *Cronache Sociali* 2(8): pp. 7–8.

Fanfani, Amintore. 1954. *Problemi italiani e impegno cristiano. Discorso pronunciato a Firenze il 28 marzo 1954*. Florence: Palagi.

Fanfani, Amintore. 1959a. "La DC di fronte al problema socialista." In *Da Napoli a Firenze, 1954–1959*, pp. 177–207. Milan: Garzanti.

Fanfani, Amintore. 1959b. "La vittoria del 25 maggio (Relazione al CN della DC di Roma, 10 giugno 1958)." In *Da Napoli a Firenze, 1954–1959*. Milan: Garzanti.

Fanfani, Amintore. 1963. *Centrosinistra*. Milan: Garzanti.

Fanfani, Amintore. 2010. *Amintore Fanfani e la politica estera italiana*, edited by Agostino Giovagnoli and Luciano Tosi. Venice: Marsilio.

Fanfani e la casa. 2002. *Fanfani e la casa: gli anni Cinquanta e il modello italiano di welfare state: il piano INA-Casa*. Soveria Mannelli: Rubbettino.

Felice, Costantino. 1993. *Guerra, Resistenza, Dopoguerra in Abruzzo. Uomini, economie, istituzioni*. Milan: Franco Angeli.

Foa, Anna. 2011. "Le leggi razziste." In *Cristiani d'Italia. Chiese, Società, Stato, 1861–2011*, Vol. 1, edited by Alberto Melloni, pp. 261–8. Rome: Istituto della Enciclopedia Italiana.

Fontaine, Darcie. 2016. *Decolonizing Christianity: Religion and the End of Empire in France and Algeria*. New York: Cambridge University Press.

Forlenza, Rosario. 2002. "Le elezioni politiche e amministrative a Roma del 1948 al 1953." *Clio* 38(3): pp. 511–44.

Forlenza, Rosario. 2008. *Le elezioni amministrative della Prima Repubblica. Politica e propaganda locale nell'Italia del secondo dopoguerra, 1946–1956*. Rome: Donzelli.

Forlenza, Rosario. 2010. "A Party for the Mezzogiorno: The Christian Democratic Party, Agrarian Reform and the Government of Italy." *Contemporary European History* 19(4): pp. 331–49.

Forlenza, Rosario. 2012. "Sacrificial Memory and Political Legitimacy in Post-War Italy: Reliving and Remembering World War II." *History & Memory* 24(2): pp. 73–116.

Forlenza, Rosario. 2017a. "The Politics of the *Abendland*: Christian Democracy and the Idea of Europe after the Second World War." *Contemporary European History* 26(2): pp. 261–86.

Forlenza, Rosario. 2017b. "The Enemy Within: Catholic Anti-Communism in Cold War Italy." *Past & Present* 235: pp. 207–42.

Forlenza, Rosario. 2018. "Populism and Religion in Contemporary European Politics." In *Populism and the Crisis of Democracy*, Vol. 3: *Migration, Gender and Religion*, edited by Gregor Fitzi, Jürgen Mackert, and Bryan S. Turner, pp. 133–49. London: Routledge.

Forlenza, Rosario. 2019a. "New Perspectives on Twentieth Century Catholicism." *Contemporary European History* 28(4): pp. 581–95.

Forlenza, Rosario. 2019b. *On the Edge of Democracy: Italy, 1943–1948*. Oxford: Oxford University Press.

Forlenza, Rosario. 2020. "In Search of Order: Portrayal of Communists in Cold War Italy." *Journal of Cold War Studies* 22(2): pp. 94–132.

Forlenza, Rosario, and Bjørn Thomassen. 2011. "From Myth to Reality and Back Again: The Fascist and Post-Fascist Reading of Garibaldi and the Risorgimento." *Bulletin of Italian Politics* 3(2): pp. 263–81.

Forlenza, Rosario, and Bjørn Thomassen. 2016. *Italian Modernities: Competing Narratives of Nationhood*. New York: Palgrave Macmillan.

Forlenza, Rosario, and Bjørn Thomassen. 2017. "Resurrections and Rebirths: How the Risorgimento Shaped Modern Italian Politics." *Journal of Modern Italian Studies* 22(3): pp. 291–313.

Forlenza, Rosario, and Bjørn Thomassen. 2020. "Social Dramas and Memory Formation: Resistance and Resurgence in the Italian Politics of Memory, 1943–1948." *History and Anthropology* 32(5): pp. 527–48.

Forlenza, Rosario, and Bjørn Thomassen. 2022. "The Globalization of Christian Democracy: Religious Entanglements in the Making of Modern Poltics." *Religions* 13: 659, https://www.mdpi.com/2077-1444/13/7/659 (last accessed: November 7, 2023).

Forlenza, Rosario, and Bryan S. Turner. 2016. "The Last Frontier: The Struggle over Sex and Marriage under Pope Francis." *Rassegna Italiana di Sociologia* 57(4): pp. 689–710.

Formigoni, Guido. 1996. *La Democrazia Cristiana e l'alleanza occidentale, 1943–1953*. Bologna: Il Mulino.

Formigoni, Guido. 2003. "De Gasperi e la crisi politica italiana del maggio 1947. Documenti e Reinterpretazioni." *Richerche di Storia Politica* 6(3): pp. 361–88.

Formigoni, Guido. 2008a. *Alla prova della democrazia. Chiesa, cattolici e modernità nell'Italia del Novecento*. Trento: Il Margine.

Formigoni, Guido. 2008b. "Alcide De Gasperi 1943–1948. Il politico vincente alla guida della transizione." In *Alcide De Gasperi. Scritti e discorsi politici. Edizione critica*, Vol. III: *Alcide De Gasperi e la fondazione della democrazia italiana, 1943–1948*, edited by Vera Capperucci and Sara Lorenzini, pp. 11–34. Bologna: Il Mulino.

Formigoni, Guido. 2010. *L'Italia dei cattolici. Dal Risorgimento ad oggi*. Bologna: Il Mulino.

Formigoni, Guido. 2016. *Aldo Moro. Lo statista e il suo dramma*. Bologna: Il Mulino.

Foucault, Michel. 1991. "Questions of Method." In *The Foucault Effect: Studies in Governmentality*, edited by Graham Burchell, Colin Gordin, and Peter Miller, pp. 73–86. Chicago: University of Chicago Press.

Foucault, Michel. 1998. *Taccuino Persiano*, edited by Renzo Guolo and Pierluigi Panza. Milan: Guerini e Associati.

Franceschini, Ezio. 1983. "Il mio 'no' al fascismo." In *Uomini liberi—Scritti sulla Resistenza*, edited by Francesco Minuto Peri, pp. 7–8. Casale Monferrato: Piemme.

Francia, Enrico. 1948. "L'Italia ha detto no." *Il Popolo*, April 22.

Franzinelli, Mimmo. 2014. *Il piano Solo, I servizi segreti, il centro-sinistra e il "golpe" del 1964*. Milan: Mondadori.

Fuccari, Lorenzo. 1993. "Alcol sulle ferite, la ricetta di Segni." *Corriere della Sera*, January 21.

Furlong, Paul, and David Curtis (eds). 1994. *The Church Faces the Modern World: Rerum Novarum and Its Impact*. Scunthorpe: Earlsgate.

Gabrielli, Patrizia. 2009. *Il 1946, le donne, la Repubblica*. Rome: Donzelli.

Gaiotti De Biase, Paola. 1996. *I cattolici e il voto alle donne*. Turin: SEI.

Gaiotti De Biase, Paola. 2002. *Le origini del movimento cattolico femminile*. Brescia: Morcelliana.

Galavotti, Enrico. 2004. "Dell'Acqua sostituto e la politica italiana, 1953–1967." In *Angelo Dall'Acqua. Prete, diplomatico e cardinale al cuore della politica italiana (1903–1972)*, pp. 119–60. Bologna: Il Mulino.

Galavotti, Enrico. 2006. *Il giovani Dossetti. Gli anni della formazione, 1913–1939*. Bologna: Il Mulino.

Galavotti, Enrico. 2011a. "Le riunoni di scioglimento della corrente dossettiana nei reso-conti dei partecipanti (agosto-settembre 1951)." *Cristianesimo nella Storia* 32(2): pp. 563–731.

Galavotti, Enrico. 2011b. "Il ruinismo. Visione e pressi politica del presidente della Conferenza Episcopale Italiana, 1991–2007." In *Cristiani d'Italia. Chiese, società Stato, 1861–2011*, Vol. II, edited by Alberto Melloni, pp. 1219–38. Rome: Istituto della Enciclopedia Italiana.

Galavotti, Enrico. 2011c. "Il dossettismo. Dinamismi, prospettive e damnation memoriae di un'esperienza politica e culturale." In *Cristiani d'Italia. Chiese, società Stato 1861–2011*, Vol. II, edited by Alberto Melloni, pp. 1367–87. Rome: Istituto della Enciclopedia Italiana.

Galavotti, Enrico. 2013. *Il professorino. Giuseppe Dossetti tra la crisi del fascismo e la costruzione della democrazia, 1940–1948*. Bologna: Il Mulino.

Galli, Giorgio. 1977. *Fanfani*. Milan: Feltrinelli.

Gambasin, Angelo. 1958. *Il movimento sociale nell'Opera dei Congressi (1874–1904). Contributo per la storia del cattolicesimo in Italia*. Rome: Pontificia Università Gregoriana.

Garagnani, Fabio, and Antonio Palmieri. 2006. *I frutti e l'albero. Cinque anni di governo Berlusconi letti alla luce della dottrina sociale della Chiesa*. Rome: Gruppo Parlamentare di Forza Italia.

Garelli, Franco. 2006. *L'Italia cattolica ai tempi del pluralismo*. Bologna: Il Mulino.

Garelli, Franco. 2007. *La Chiesa in Italia*. Bologna: Il Mulino.

Garelli, Franco. 2014. "Religione e politica in Italia: I nuovi sviluppi." *Quaderni di Sociologia* 66: pp. 9–26.

Gedda, Luigi. 1951. *Risposta a Togliatti*. Rome: Editrice Domani.

Gedda, Luigi. 1998. *18 Aprile 1948: Memorie inedite dell'artefice della sconfitta del Fronte Popolare*. Milan: Mondadori.

Gehler, Michael, and Wolfram Kaiser. 2004. *Christian Democracy in Europe since 1945*. London: Routledge.

Gemelli, Agostino. 1918. *Principio di nazionalità e amor di patria nella dottrina cattolica*. Turin: Libreria Editrice Internazionale.

Gemelli, Agostino. 1929. "La missione dell'Università Cattolica nell'ora presente." *Vita e Pensiero* 15(1): pp. 8–25.

Gemelli, Agostino. 1939. *Un grande chirurgo medievale. Guglielmo da Saliceto*. Bologna: Tip. Compositori.

Gentile, Emilio. 1990. "Fascism as Political Religion." *Journal of Contemporary History* 25(2–3): pp. 229–51.

Gentile, Emilio. 1996. *The Sacralization of Political in Fascist Italy*, translated by Keith Botsford. Cambridge, MA: Harvard University Press.

Gentile, Emilio. 2007a. *Fascismo di Pietra*. Rome and Bari: Laterza.

Gentile, Emilio. 2007b. *La democrazia di Dio. La religione americana nell'era dell'impero e del terrore*. Rome and Bari: Laterza.

Gentile, Emilio. 2009. *La Grande Italia: The Myth of the Nation in the Twentieth Century Italy*, translated by S. Dingee and J. Pudney. Madison: University of Wisconsin Press.

Gentile, Emilio. 2010. *Contro Cesare. Cristianesimo e totalitarismo nell'epoca dei fascismi*. Milan: Feltrinelli.

Gibelli, Antonio. 2001. *La Grande Guerra degli italiani 1915–1918*. Milan: Sansoni.

Gibelli, Antonio. 2007. *L'officina della Guerra. La Grande Guerra e la trasformazione del mondo mentale*. Turin: Bollati Boringhieri.

Gibelli, Antonio. 2011. "Il berlusconismo nella Chiesa Cattolica." In *Berlusconismo. Analisi di un sistema di potere*, edited by Paul Ginsborg and Enrica Asquer, pp. 68–82. Rome: Laterza.

Gibelli, Antonio, and Carlo Stiaccini. 2006. "Il miracolo della guerra: Appunti su religione e superstizione nei soldati della Grande Guerra." In *Il soldato, la guerra, e il rischio di morire*, pp. 125–36. Milan: Unicopli.

Gilette, Aaron. 2002. *Racial Theories in Fascist Italy*. London: Routledge.

Ginsborg, Paul. 1990. *A History of Contemporary Italy; Society and Politics, 1943–1948*. London: Penguin.

Gioberti, Vincenzo. 1846. *Del Primato Morale e Civile degli Italiani*, Vol. 2. Lausanne: S. Bonamici e Compagnia Tipografi Editori.

Gioberti, Vincenzo. 1969 [1851]. *Del Rinnovamento civile dell'Italia*, edited by Luigi Quattrocchi. Rome: Abete.

Giordani, Igino (ed.). 1948. *Le encicliche sociali dei papi da Pio IX a Pio XII (1846–1946)*. Rome: Studium.

Giordani, Igino, and Luigi Sturzo. 1987. *Igino Giordani-Luigi Sturzo. Un ponte tra due generazioni: carteggio 1924–1958*, preface by Gabriele De Rosa, introduction by Paolo Piccoli. Milan–Bari: Laterza–Cariplo.

Giorgi, Luigi (ed.). 2002. "La sinistra e Dossetti: l'Unità, 1946–1951." *Bailamme* 28(5): pp. 231–66.

Giorgi, Luigi. 2007. *Una vicenda politica. Giuseppe Dossetti, 1943–1958*. Milan: Scriptorium.

Giorgi, Alberta, and Emanuela Polizzi. 2015. "Communion and Liberation: A Catholic Movement in a Multilevel Governance Perspective." *Religion, State and Society* 43(2): pp. 133–49.

Giovagnoli, Agostino. 1982. *Le premesse della ricostruzione. Tradizione e modernità nella classe dirigente cattolica del secondo dopoguerra*. Milan: Nuovo Istituto Editoriale Italiano.

Giovagnoli, Agostino. 1985. "Chiesa, assistenza e società a Roma fra il 1943 e il 1945." In *L'altro dopoguerra. Roma e il sud 1943–1945*, edited by Nicola Gallerano, pp. 213–24; Milan: Franco Angeli.

Giovagnoli, Agostino. 1991. *La cultura democristiana. Tra Chiesa cattolica e identità italiana, 1918–1948*. Rome and Bari: Laterza.

Giovagnoli, Agostino. 1996. *Il partito italiano. La Democrazia Cristiana dal 1942 al 1994*. Rome and Bari: Laterza.

Giovagnoli, Agostino. 2014. "Cattolici e politica dalla prima alla seconda fase della storia repubblicana." In *L'Italia contemporanea dagli anni Ottanta a oggi*, Vol. III: *Istituzioni e politica*, edited by Simona Colarizi, Agostino Giovagnoli, and Paolo Pombeni, pp. 185–204. Rome: Carocci.

Giovanni Paolo II. 1982. "Giovanni Paolo II ad Assisi. Atto di pellegrinaggio e di comunione." In *Insegnamenti di Giovanni Paolo II, V/1: 1982 (gennaio aprile)*. Rome: Libreria Editrice Vaticana.

Giovannini, Claudio. 1981. "Lega democratica nazionale." In *Dizionario del movimento cattolico in Italia 1860–1980*, Vol. I: *I fatti e le idee*, edited by Francesco Traniello and Giorgio Campanini, pp. 304–9. Casale Monferrato: Marietti.

Giuntella, Maria Cristina. 1975. "I fatti del 1931 e la formazione della seconda generazione." In *I cattolici fra fascismo e democrazia*, edited by Pietro Scoppola and Francesco Traniello, pp. 183–223. Bologna: Il Mulino.

Giuntella, Vittorio Emanuele. 1979. *Il nazismo e i Lager*. Rome: Studium.

Giuntella, Vittorio Emanuele. 1981. "I cattolici nella Resistenza." In *Dizionario storico del movimento cattolico in Italia, 1860–1980*, edited by Francesco Traniello and Giorgio Campanini, I, 2, *I fatti e le idee*, pp. 112–28. Casale Monferrato: Marietti.

Giussani, Luigi. 1972. *Tracce di esperienze e appunti di metodo cristiano*. Milan: Jaca Book.

Golden, Miriam A. 1997. *Heroic Defeats: The Politics of Job Loss*. Cambridge: Cambridge University Press.

Goldstein Sepinwall, Alyssa. 2005. *The Abbé Grégoire and the French Revolution: The Making of Modern Universalism*. Berkeley: University of California Press.

Gonella Guido. 1935a. "Tra la vita e il libro: Individuo e persona." *Studium* 31(2): pp. 85–7.

Gonella, Guido. 1935b. "La dottrina della personalità ed alcuni suoi riflessi sociali." *Studium* 30(1): pp. 39–41.

Gonella, Guido. 1946a. "Il passato è sepolto." *Il Popolo*, June 9.

Gonella, Guido. 1946b. "Parole e preghiere." *Il Popolo*, May 21.

Gorrieri, Ermanno. 1966. *La Repubblica di Montefiorino. Per una storia della Resistenza in Emilia*. Bologna: Il Mulino.

Gotor, Miguel. 2011. *Il memoriale della Repubblica. Gli scritti di Aldo Moro dalla prigionia e l'anatomia del potere italiano*. Turin: Einaudi.

Griffin, Roger. 1991. *The Nature of Fascism*. London: Pinter.

Griffin, Roger. 2015. "An Unholy Alliance? The Convergence between Revealed Religion and Sacralized Politics in Interwar Europe." In *Catholicism and Fascism in Europe: 1918–1945*, edited by Jan Nelis, Anne Morelli, and Danny Praet, pp. 49–66. Hildesheim: George Olms Verlag AG.

Gross, Michael B. 2005. *The War against Catholicism: Liberalism and the Anti-Catholic Imagination in Nineteenth-Century Germany*. Ann Arbor, MI: University of Michigan Press.

Guasco, Maurilio. 1995. *Modernismo: i fatti, le idee, i personaggi*. Turin: San Paolo.

Gugelot, Fréderic. 1998. *La conversion des intellectuels au catholicisme en France, 1885–1935*. Paris: CNRS Éditions.

Guidi, Angela Maria. 1944. "Precisazioni." *Azione Femminile* 1(1): p. 1.

Habermas, Jürgen. 2006. "Religion in the Public Sphere." *European Journal of Philosophy* 14(1): pp. 1–25.

Habermas, Jürgen. 2008a. *Between Naturalism and Religion*. Malden, MA: Polity.

Habermas, Jürgen. 2008b. "Notes on Post-Secular Society." *New Perspectives Quarterly* 25(4): pp. 17–29.

Habermas, Jürgen, and Joseph Ratzinger. 2006. *The Dialectic of Secularization: On Reason and Religion*. San Francisco: Ignatius Press.

Hanley, David (ed.). 1994. *Christian Democracy in Europe: A Comparative Perspective*. London: Printer.

Hayek, Friedrich A. 1949. "The Intellectuals and Socialism." *University of Chicago Law Review* 16(3): pp. 417–33.

Hellemans, Staf. 2001. "From 'Catholicism against Modernity' to the Problematic 'Modernity of Catholicism'." *Ethical Perspective* 8(2): pp. 117–27.

Hellman, John. 1981. *Emmanuel Mounier and the New Catholic Left, 1930–1950*. Toronto: University of Toronto Press.

Hellman, John. 1997. *The Knight-Monks of Vichy France: Uriage, 1940–1945*. Montreal and Kingston: McGill-Queen's University Press.

Hervieu-Léger, Danièle. 2003. *Catholicisme, la fin d'un monde*. Paris: Bayard.

Hobsbawm, Eric J. 1994. *Age of Extremes: The Short Twentieth Century, 1914–1991*. New York: Pantheon Books.

Horn, Gerd-Rainer. 2015. *The Spirit of Vatican II: Western European Progressive Catholicism in the Long Sixties*. Oxford: Oxford University Press.

Houlihan, Patrick. 2015. *Catholicism and the Great War: Religion and Everyday Life in Germany and Austria–Hungary, 1914–1922*. Cambridge: Cambridge University Press.

Howard, Thomas Albert. 2003. "A 'Religious Turn' in Modern European Historiography?" *Historically Speaking* 4(5): pp. 24–6.

Howard, Thomas Albert. 2006. "Commentary—A 'Religious Turn' in Modern European Historiography." *Church History* 75(1): pp. 157–63.

Horvath, Agnes, Bjørn Thomassen, and Harald Wydra, eds. 2015. *Breaking Boundaries: Varieties of Liminality*. New York and Oxford: Berghahn Books.

I valori. 1995. *I valori della Costituzione. Giuseppe Dossetti e Nilde Iotti a Monteveglio (Monteveglio, 16 settembre 1994)*. Reggio Emilia: Pozzi.

Idee e programmi. 1984. *Idee e programmi della DC nella Resistenza*, edited by Giovanni Battista Varnier. Rome: Civitas.

Ignazi, Piero. 1994. *Postfascisti? Dal Movimento sociale italiano ad Alleanza Nazionale*. Bologna: Il Mulino.

Il nuovo. 1994. *Il Nuovo Partito Popolare, Roma 22 gennaio 1994*. Speeches by Mino Martinazzoli, Gabriele De Rosa, Gerardo Bianco, and Rosa Russo Jervolino. Rome: Gruppi Parlamentari del Partito Popolare Italiano.

Indicazioni. 1986. "Indicazioni per un cammino di Chiesa." In *Enchiridion della Conferenza Episcopale Italiana. Decreti dichiarazioni documenti pastorali per la chiesa italiana*, Vol. III: *1980–1985*. Bologna: Dehoniane.

Insegnamenti. 1996. *Insegnamenti di Giovanni Paolo II*, Vol. XVII/1: *1994*. Città del Vaticano: Libreria Editrice Vaticana.

Invernizzi Accetti, Carlo. 2019. *What Is Christian Democracy? Politics, Religion and Ideology*. New York: Cambridge University Press.

Isnenghi, Mario, and Giorgio Rochat. 2014. *La Grade Guerra, 1914–1918*. Bologna: Il Mulino.

Istituti di credito. 1998. "Istituti di credito cattolici. Santa Sede e Opera dei Congressi fra fine Ottocento e inizio Novecento: il caso del Banco di San Marco di Venezia." In *Atti dell'Istituto Veneto di Scienze, Lettere ed Arti. Classe di scienze morali, lettere, ed arti*, t. 156, f. 2: pp. 238–411. Venice: IVSLA.

Jodock, Darrel (ed.). 2000. *Catholicism Contending with Modernity: Roman Catholic Modernism and Anti-Modernism in Historical Context*. Cambridge: Cambridge University Press.

Jori, Francesco. 2009. *Dalla Liga alla Lega: storia, movimenti, protagonisti*, preface by Ilvo Diamanti. Venice: Marsilio.

Judt, Tony. 1992. *Past Imperfect: French Intellectuals, 1944–1956*. Berkeley: University of California Press.

Judt, Tony. 2005. *Postwar: A History of Europe since 1945*. London: Heinemann.

Kaiser, Wolfram. 2004. "Christian Democracy in Twentieth-Century Europe." *Journal of Contemporary History* 39(1): pp. 127–35.

Kaiser, Wolfram. 2007. *Christian Democracy and the Origins of European Union*. Cambridge: Cambridge University Press.

Kaiser, Wolfram, and Helmut Wohnout. 2004. *Political Catholicism in Europe, 1918–1945*. London: Routledge.

Kalyvas, Stathis N. 1996. *The Rise of Christian Democracy in Europe*. Ithaca and London: Cornell University Press.

Kalyvas, Stathis N. 1998. "From Pulpit to Party: Party Formation and the Christian Democratic Phenomenon." *Comparative Politics* 30(3): pp. 293–312.

Kertzer, David I. 1998. *Politics and Symbols: The Italian Communist Party and the Fall of Communism*. New Haven: Yale University Press.

Kertzer, David I. 2001. *The Popes against the Jews: the Vatican's Role in the Rise of Modern Anti-Semitism*. New York: Knopf.

Kertzer, David I. 2014. *The Pope and Mussolini: The Secret History of Pius XI and the Rise of Fascism in Europe*. Oxford: Oxford University Press.

Keyman, E. F. 2007. "Modernity, Secularism and Islam: The Case of Turkey." *Theory, Culture & Society* 24(2): pp. 215–34.

Koon, Tracy H. 1985. *Believe, Obey, Fight: Political Socialization of Youth in Fascist Italy*. Chapel Hill: University of North Carolina Press.

Korten, Christopher. 2016. "Il Trionfo? The Untold Story of Its Development and Pope Gregory XVI's Struggle with Orthodoxy." *Harvard Theological Review* 109(2): pp. 278–301.

Koselleck, Reinhart. 1985. "'Space of Experience' and 'Horizon of Expectation': Two Historical Categories." In *Futures Past: On the Semantics of Historical Time*, translated by Keith Tribe, pp. 267–88. Cambridge, MA: MIT Press.

Kosicki, Piotr H. 2018. *Catholics on the Barricades: Poland, France, and "Revolution," 1891–1956*. New Haven and London: Yale University Press.

Kraynak, Robert. 2007. "Pope Leo XIII and the Catholic Response to Modernity." *Modern Age* 49(4): pp. 527–36.

Kselman, Thomas, and Joseph A. Buttigieg (eds). 2003. *European Christian Democracy: Historical Legacies and Comparative Perspectives*. Notre Dame, IN: University of Notre Dame Press.

La Gioventù Cattolica. 1972. *La "Gioventù cattolica" dopo l'unità. 1868–1968*, edited by Luciano Osbat and Francesco Piva. Rome: Edizioni di Storia e Letteratura.

La Pira, Giorgio. 1948. "Il valore della Costituzione Italiana." *Cronache Sociali* 2(2): pp. 1–3.

La Pira, Giorgio. 1950a. "L'attesa della povera gente." *Cronache Sociali* 4(1): pp. 2–6.

La Pira, Giorgio. 1950b. "Difesa della povera gente." *Conache Sociali* 4(5–6): pp. 1–9.

La Pira Sindaco. 1988. *Giorgio La Pira Sindaco. Scritti, discorsi, e lettere*, Vol. I: *1951–1954*, edited by Ugo De Siervo, Gianni Giovannoni, and Giorgio Giovannoni. Florence: Cultura Nuova.

Lamour, Christian. 2021. "Orbàn Urbi et Orbi: Christianity as a Nodal Point of Radical-Right Populism." *Politics and Religion* 15(2): pp. 317–43.

Lanzardo, Liliana. 1989. *Personalità operaia e coscienza di classe. Comunisti e cattolici nelle fabbriche torinesi del dopoguerra*. Milan: Franco Angeli.

L'Azione cattolica bresciana. 1987. *L'Azione cattolica bresciana di ieri. Ricordi e testimonianze di militanti e dirigenti*. Brescia: Ce.Doc.

Lazzati, Giuseppe. 1948. "Azione cattolica e azione politica." *Cronache Sociali* 2(20): pp. 1–3.

Lazzati, Giuseppe. 1988. *Pensare politicamente*, Vol. I: *Il tempo dell'azione politica. Dal centrismo al centrosinistra*. Rome: AVE.

Lazzati, Giuseppe. 1989. "Il valore di un 'no' (1953)." In *Giuseppe Lazzati: gli anni del Lager (1943–1945)*, edited by Marilena Morini. Rome: AVE.

Lazzati, Giuseppe. 2009. "Trent'anni di Costituzione: contesto di pacifica libertà? (1978)." In *Laici e cristiani nella città dell'uomo. Scritti ecclesiali e politici 1945–1986*, edited by Guido Formigoni, pp. 245–60. Cinisello Balsamo: San Paolo.

Le Guillou, L. 1966. *L'evolution de la pensée religeuse de Félicité Lammennais*. Paris: Colin.

Le istituzioni. 1984. *Le istituzioni della democrazia pluralista. Convegno nazionale della Democrazia Cristiana, Roma 21–22- 23 aprile 1983*. Rome: Cinque Lune.

Leflon, Jean. 1958. *Pie VII. Des abbayes bénédictines à la papauté*. Paris: Plon.

Lefort, Claude. 1986. *Essais sur politique XIXe–XXe siècles*. Paris: Éditions du Seuil.

Linch, John. 1986. "The Catholic Church in Latin America, 1830–1930." In *The Cambridge History of Latin America*, Vol. 4: *c.1870 to 1930*, edited by Leslie Bethell, pp. 527–86. Cambridge: Cambridge University Press.

Livi, Massimiliano. 2016. "The Ruini System and 'Berlusconismo': Synergy and Transformation between the Catholic Church and Italian Politics in the 'Second Republic'." *Journal of Modern Italian Studies* 21(3): pp. 399–418.

L'uomo. 1976. *L'uomo, un popolo, la liberazione*. Milan: Strumenti di lavoro di Comunione e Liberazione per il Movimento Popolare.

Magister, Sandro. 1996. "La Chiesa e la fine del partito cattolico." In *Politica in Italia*, edited by Mario Caciagli and David I. Kertzer, pp. 237–56. Bologna: Il Mulino.

Magister, Sandro. 2001. *Chiesa extraparlamentare. Il trionfo del pulpito dell'età democristiana*. Naples: L'ancora del mediterraneo.

Magri, Enzo. 1984. "Noi comunistelli di sagrestia." *Europeo* 44(November 3): pp. 140–8.

Maier, Charles. 2000. "Consigning the Twentieth Century to History: Alternative Narratives for the Modern Era." *The American Historical Review* 105(3): pp. 807–31.

Mainwaring Scott, and Timothy E. Scully. 2003. *Christian Democracy in Latin America: Electoral Competition and Regime Conflicts*. Stanford: Stanford University Press.

Malgeri, Francesco. 1980. *La Chiesa italiana e la guerra, 1940–1945*. Rome: AVE.

Malgeri, Francesco (ed.). 1988. *Storia della Democrazia Cristiana*, Vol. II: *De Gasperi e l'età del centrismo, 1948–1954*. Rome: Cinque Lune.

Malgeri, Francesco (ed.). 1989. *Storia della Demorazia Cristiana*, Vol. III: *Gli anni di transizione: Da Fafani a Moro, 1954–1962*. Rome: Cinque Lune.

Malgeri, Francesco. 1994. "Chiesa cattolica e regime fascista." *Italia Contemporanea* 194: pp. 53–63.

Malgeri, Francesco. 1995. "La Chiesa, i cattolici e la prima guerra mondiale." In *Storia dell'Italia religiosa*, Vol. III: *L'età contemporanea*, pp. 189–222. Rome and Bari: Laterza.

Malgeri, Francesco. 1997. "La Democrazia Cristiana in Italia." In *Christian Democracy in the European Union 1945/1995*, edited by Emiel Lambert, pp. 93–104. Leuven: Leuven University Press.

Malgeri, Francesco (ed.). 1999. *Storia della Democrazia Cristiana*, Vol. VI: *Il tramonto della DC, 1989–1993*. Palermo: Éditore Mediterranea.

Malpensa, Marcello. 2010. "I vescovi davanti alla Guerra." In *Un paese in guerra: La mobilitazione civile in Italia (1914–1918)*, edited by Daniele Menozzi, Giovanna Procacci, and Simonetta Soldani, pp. 295–315. Milan: Unicopli.

Malusa, Luciano. 2011. *Antonio Rosmini per l'Unità d'Italia. Tra aspirazione nazionale e fede cristiana*. Milan: Franco Angeli.

Mannheim, Karl. 1952. "The Problem of Generations (1927–1928)". In *Essay on the Sociology of Knowledge*, edited by Paul Kecskemeti, pp. 276–322. London: Routledge.

Marchi, Michele. 2006. "Moro, i vescovi, e l'apertura a sinistra." *Ricerche di storia politica* 9(2): pp. 147–79.

Marchi, Michele. 2008. "La DC, la Chiesa e il centro-sinistra. Fanfani, Moro e 'l'asse vaticano', 1959–1962." *Mondo Contemporaneao* 4(2): pp. 41–90.

Maritain, Jacques. 1934. "Au sujet de la democratie et la revolution." *L'Aube*, January 25.

Maritain, Jacques. 1943. *Christianity and Democracy*, translated by Doris C. Anson. New York: Scribner's sons.

Maritain, Jacques. 1944. *The Dream of Descartes, Together with Some Other Essays*, translated by Mabelle L. Anderson. New York: Philosophical Library.

Maritain, Jacques. 1953. *The Range of Reason*. London: Geoffrey Bles.

Martin, Jean-Clément. 2014. *La guerre de Vendée, 1793–1800*. Paris: Éditions du Seuil.

Martinazzoli, Mino. 1993. "Vi chiedo unità e fiducia." *Il Popolo*, July 24.

Marzano, Marco. 2012. *Quel che resta dell'Italia dei cattolici*. Milan: Feltrinell.

Marzano, Marco, and Nadia Urbinati. 2013. *Missione impossibile. La riconquista cattolica della sfera pubblica*. Bologna: Il Mulino.

Marzouki, Nadia, Duncan McDonnell, and Olivier Roy. 2016. *Saving the People: How Populists Hijack Religion*. Oxford: Oxford University Press.

Masala, Carlo. 2004. "Born for Government: The Democrazia Cristiana in Italy." In *Christian Democracy in Europe since 1945*, edited by Michael Gehler and Wolfram Kaiser, pp. 88–117. London and New York: Routledge.

Mazower, Mark. 1999. *Dark Continent: Europe's Twentieth Century*. New York: Knopf.

Mazzini, Giuseppe. 1936. "The Duties of Man." In *The Duties of Man and Other Essays*, edited by Ernest Rhys. London: J. M. Dent and Company.

Mazzonis, Filippo. 1970. "L'Unione Romana e la partecipazione dei cattolici alle elezioni amministrative in Roma (1870–1881)." *Storia e politica* 9(2): pp. 216–58.

Mazzonis, Filippo. 1997. "La Chiesa e la Liberazione del Mezzogiorno (1943–44)." In *Italy and America, 1943–1944: Italian, American and Italian-American Experiences of the Liberation of the Italian Mezzogiorno*, edited by John A. Davis, pp. 1–37. Naples: La Citta del Sole.

McDonnell, Duncan. 2016. "The Lega Nord: The New Saviour of Northern Italy." In *Saving the People: How Populists Hijack Religion*, edited by Nadia Marzouki, Donald McDonnell, and Olivier Roy, pp. 11–28. New York: Oxford University Press.

McLeod, Hugh. 1981. *Religion and the People of Western Europe, 1789–1970*. Oxford: Oxford University Press.

McSweeney, Bill. 1983. *Roman Catholicism: The Search for Relevance*. New York: St Martin Press.

Mellano, Franca M. 1982. *Cattolici e voto politico in Italia: Il "non expedit" all'inzio del pontificato di Leone XIII*. Genoa: Marietti.

Melloni, Alberto. 1994. "L'utopia come utopia." Introduction to Giuseppe Dossetti, *La ricerca costituente, 1945-1952*, edited by Alberto Melloni, pp. 13–59. Bologna: Il Mulino.

Melloni, Alberto. 2010. "L'occasione perduta. Appunti sulla Chiesa italiana, 1979-2009." In *Il Vangelo basta. Sul disagio e sulla fede della Chiesa italiana*, edited by Alberto Melloni and Giuseppe Ruggieri, pp. 69-121. Bologna: Il Mulino.

Melloni, Alberto. 2013. *Dossetti e l'indicibile: Il quaderno scomparso di "Cronache Sociali": I cattolici per un nuovo partito a sinistra della DC (1948)*. Rome: Donzelli.

Menozzi, Daniele. 1993. *La Chiesa cattolica e la secolarizzazione*. Turin: Einaudi.

Menozzi, Daniele. 2007. "I gesuiti, Pio IX e la nazione italiana." In *Storia d'Italia. Annali 22. Il Risorgimento*, pp. 451-78. Turin: Einaudi.

Menozzi, Daniele. 2008a. *Chiesa, pace e guerra nel Novecento. Verso una delegittimazione religiosa dei conflitti*. Bologna: Il Mulino.

Menozzi, Daniele. 2008b. "La Chiesa e la Guerra: I cattolici italiani nel primo conflitto mondiale." *Humanitas* 63: pp. 900–91.

Menozzi, Daniele. 2010. "Chiesa e città." In *Un paese in guerra. La mobilitazione civile in Italia, 1914-1918*, edited by Daniele Menozzi, Giovanna Procacci, and Simonetta Soldani, pp. 269-74. Milan: Unicopli.

Menozzi, Daniele (ed.). 2015. *La Chiesa Italiana nella Grande Guerra*. Brescia: Morcelliana.

Miccoli, Giovanni. 1994. "La Chiesa di Pio XII nella società italiana nel secondo dopoguerra." In *Storia dell'Italia repubblicana*, Vol. I: *La costruzione della democrazia. Dalla caduta del fascism agli anni Cinquanta*, edited by Francesco Barbagallo, pp. 537-613. Turin: Einaudi.

Miccoli, Giovanni. 1997. "Santa Sede, questione ebraica e antisemitismo." In *Storia d'Italia, Annali, XI, 2, Gli ebrei in Italia. Dall'emancipazione a oggi*, edited by Corrado Vivanti, pp. 1371-1574. Turin: Einaudi.

Milback, Sylvain, and Richard Lebrun. 2018. *Lammenais: A Believer's Revolutionary Politics*. Leiden: Brill.

Misciattelli, Piero. 1924. *Fascisti e cattolici*. Milan: Imperia.

Misner, Paul. 1991. *Social Catholicism in Europe: From the Onset of the Industrialization to the First World War*. New York: Crossroad.

Mistry, Kaeten. 2014. *The United States, Italy and the Origins of the Cold War: Waging Political Warfare, 1945-1950*. Cambridge: Cambridge University Press.

Mitchell, Maria. 2012. *The Origins of Christian Democracy: Politics and Confession in Modern Germany*. Ann Arbor, MI: University of Michigan Press.

Molony, John M. 1977. *The Emergence of Political Catholicism in Italy: Partito Popolare, 1919-1926*. Totowa, NJ: Rowman & Littlefield.

Monticone, Alberto. 1984. "Alcide De Gasperi e la scelta politica per la democrazia occidentale." In *Konrad Adenauer e Alcide De Gasperi: due esperienze di rifondazione della democrazia*, edited by Umberto Corsini and Konrad Repgen, pp. 55-78. Bologna: Il Mulino.

Montini, Giovambattista. 1997. "Pareri e voti per la buona riuscita del Concilio." In *Discorsi e scritti milanesi: 1954-1963*, Vol. I, edited by Xenio Toscani, pp. 3582-8. Rome: Studium.

Montuclard, Maurice. 1965. *Conscience religieuse et démocratie. La deuxième démocratie chrétienne in France, 1891-1902*. Paris: Éditions du Seuil.

Moro, Aldo. 1941. "Vita militare." *Azione Fucina*, July 30.

Moro, Aldo. 1944. "Apologetica dell'amore." *Pensiero e vita*, August 5. Now in Moro, Aldo. 1982. *Scritti e discorsi*, Vol. I: *1940-1947*, edited by Giuseppe Rossini, pp. 48-9. Rome: Cinque Lune.

Moro, Aldo. 1947. "Democrazia Integrale." *Studium*. Now in Moro, Aldo. 1982. *Al di là della politica e altri scritti. "Studium" 1942-1952*, edited by Giorgio Campanini, introduction by Giovanni Battista Scaglia, pp. 124-7. Rome: Studium.

Moro, Aldo. 1950. "Chiesa e democrazia." *Studium*, December 1950. Now in Moro, Aldo. 1982. *Al di là della politica e altri scritti. "Studium" 1942-1952*, edited by Giorgio Campanini, introduction by Giovanni Battista Scaglia, pp. 197-208. Rome: Studium.

Moro, Aldo. 1955. "Un partito per il Mezzogiorno." *La discussione* 104(3): p. 1.

Moro, Aldo. 1968. *Una politica per i tempi nuovi (discorso al Consiglio nazionale DC del 21 novembre 1968)*. Rome: Agenzia Progetto.

Moro, Aldo. 1979. *L'intelligenza e gli avvenimenti: Testi 1959-1978*, edited by Giancarlo Quaranta, introduction by George L. Mosse. Milan: Garzanti.

Moro, Aldo. 1982a. *Scritti e discorsi politici*, Vol. I: *1940-1947*, edited by Giuseppe Rossini. Rome: Cinque Lune.

Moro, Aldo. 1982b. *Scritti e discorsi politici*, Vol. II: *1951-1963*, edited by Giuseppe Rossini. Rome: Cinque Lune.

Moro, Aldo. 1988. *Scritti e discorsi*, Vol. V: *1969-1973*, edited by Giuseppe Rossini. Rome: Cinque Lune.

Moro, Aldo. 1990. *Scritti e discorsi*, Vol. VI: *1974-1978*, edited by Giuseppe Rossini. Rome: Cinque Lune.

Moro, Aldo. 2008. *Lettere dalla prigionia*, edited by Miguel Gotor. Turin: Einaudi.

Moro, Renato. 1975. "Afascismo e antifascismo nei movimenti intellectuali di Azione Cattolica dopo il '31." *Storia Contemporanea* 6: pp. 733-99.

Moro, Renato. 1979a. *La formazione della classe dirigente cattolica 1929-1937*. Bologna: Il Mulino.

Moro, Renato. 1979b. "I movimenti intellettuali cattolici." In *Cultura politica e partiti nell'età della Costituente*, edited by Roberto Ruffilli, Vol. I, pp. 159-261. Bologna: Il Mulino.

Moro, Renato. 1980. "Azione Cattolica, clero e laicato durante il Fascismo." In *Storia del movimento cattolico in Italia*, edited by Francesco Malgeri, pp. 335-45. Rome: AVE.

Moro, Renato. 1992. "L'atteggiamento dei cattolici tra teologia e politica." In *Stato nazionale ed emancipazione ebraica*, edited by Francesca Sofia and Mario Toscano, pp. 311-49. Rome: Bonacci.

Moro, Renato. 1998. "I cattolici italiani di fronte alla guerra fascista." In *La cultura della pace dalla Resistenza al patto Atlantico*, edited by Massimo Pacetti, Massimo Papini, and Marisa Saracinelli, pp. 75-126. Bologna: Il Mulino.

Moro, Renato. 2005. "Religione del trascendente e religioni politiche: il cattolicesimo italiano di fronte alla sacralizzazione fascista della politica." *Mondo Contemporaneo* 1(1): pp. 9-67.

Moro, Renato. 2007. "Togliatti nel giudizio del mondo cattolico." In *Togliatti nel suo tempo*, edited by Roberto Gualtieri, Carlo Spagnolo, and Ermanno Taviani, pp. 337-93. Rome: Carocci.

Morozzo della Rocca, Roberto. 1980. *La fede e la guerra. Cappelani militari e preti-soldati (1915-1919)*. Rome: Studium.

Morozzo della Rocca, Roberto. 1995. "I cappellani militari cattolici nel 1915-1918." In *La spada e la croce: I cappellani militari nelle due guerre mondiali, atti del XXIV convegno di studi sulla Riforma e i movimenti religiosi in Italia*, pp. 61-71. Torre Pellice: Società di studi valdesi.

Morozzo della Rocca, Roberto. 2005. "Benedetto XV e la sacralizzazione della prima guerra mondiale." In *Chiesa e guerra. Dalla "Benedizione della armi" alla Pacem in terris*, edited by Mimmo Franzinelli and Riccardo Bottoni, pp. 165–81. Bologna: il Mulino.

Mosse, George L. 1975. *The Nazionalization of the Masses: Political Symbolism and Mass Movements in Germany from the Napoleonic Wars through the Third Reich*. New York: Howard Fertig.

Mosse, George L. 1978. *Toward the Final Solution. A History of European Racism*. New York: Howard Fertig.

Mosse, George L. 2015. *Intervista su Moro*, edited by Alfonso Alfonsi. Soveria Mannelli: Rubbettino.

Mounier, Emmanuel. 1963. *Oeuvres*, Vol. 4: *Recueils posthumes et correspondances*. Paris: Éditions du Seuil.

Moyn, Samuel. 2011. "Personalism, Community and the Origins of Human Rights." In *Human Rights in the Twentieth Century*, edited by Stefan-Ludwig Hoffmann, pp. 86–106. New York: Cambridge University Press.

Moyn, Samuel. 2014. "The Secret History of Constitutional Dignity." *Yale Human Rights and Development Journal* 17(1): pp. 39–73.

Moyn, Samuel. 2015. *Christian Human Rights*. Philadelphia: University of Pennsylvania Press.

Müller, Jan-Wener. 2008. "Die eigentlich katholische Entscharfung? Jacques Maritain und die Fluchtwege aus dem Zeitalter der Extreme." *Zeitschrift für Ideengeschichte* 2(3): pp. 40–54.

Müller, Jan-Werner. 2011. *Contesting Democracy: Political Ideas in Twentieth-Century Europe*. New Haven: Yale University Press.

Müller, Jan-Werner. 2013a. "The Paradoxes of Post-War Italian Political Thought." *History of European Ideas* 39(1): pp. 79–102.

Müller, Jan Werner. 2013b. "Towards a New History of Christian Democracy." *Journal of Political Ideologies* 18(2): pp. 243–55.

Murray, John Courtney. 1953. "Leo XIII: Two Concepts of Governments." *Theological Studies* 14(4): pp. 555–67.

Murri, Romolo. 1898. "La crisi del liberalismo in Italia." *Cultura Sociale* 1(12): p. 178.

Murri, Romolo. 1905. "Partiti e accordi." *Cultura Sociale* 8(187): pp. 305–6.

Nasr, Vali. 2005. "The Rise of Muslim Democracy." *Journal of Democracy* 16(2): pp. 13–27.

Nelis, Jan. 2011. "The Clerical Response to a Totalitarian Political Religion: *La Civiltà Cattolica* and Italian Fascism." *Journal of Contemporary History* 46(2): pp. 245–70.

Nelis, Jan. 2015. "Italian Catholic Opinion and the Advent of Fascism: l'Avvenire d'Italia." In *Catholicism and Fascism in Europe: 1918–1945*, edited by Jan Nelis, Anne Morelli, and Danny Praet, pp. 293–302. Hildesheim: George Olms Verlag AG.

Noce, Tiziana. 2014. *Donne di fede. Le democristiane nella secolarizzazione italiana*. Pisa: ETS.

Novacco, Domenico. 2000. *L'officina della Costituzione Italiana, 1943–1948*. Milan: Feltrinelli.

O'Connell, Marvin O. 1994. *Critics on Trial: An Introduction to the Catholic Modernist Crisis*. Washington, DC: Catholic University of America Press.

Olgiati, Francesco. 1919a. "Gesù Cristo in soffitta." *Vita e Pensiero* 5(65): pp. 305–9.

Olgiati, Francesco. 1919b. *Il programma del partito popolare. Come non è e come dovrebbe essere*. Milan: Vita e Pensiero.

Ornaghi, Lorenzo. 2011. "La concezione corporativa di Amintore Fanfani e il corporativismo dell'età fascista." *Bollettino dell'Archivio per la Storia del Movimento Sociale Cattolico in Italia* 46(1/2): pp. 171–88.

Orsina, Giovanni. 2013. *Il berlusconismo nella storia d'Italia*. Venice: Marsilio.

Ozzano, Luca. 2016. "Two Forms of Catholicism in Twenty-First-Century Italian Public Debate: An Analysis of Positions on Same Sex Marriage and Muslim Dress Code." *Journal of Modern Italian Studies* 21(3): pp. 464–84.

Pace, Alessandro. 2013. "From the Rights of the Citizen to the Fundamental Rights of Man: The Italian Experience." In *The Universalisism of Human Rights*, edited by Rainer Arnold, pp. 269–86. Dordrecht and New York: Springer.

Papenheim, Martin. 2003. "Culture Wars in Italy." In *Secular-Catholic Conflict in Nineteenth Century Europe*, edited by Christopher Clark and Wolfram Kaiser, pp. 202–28. Cambridge: Cambridge University Press.

Papini, Roberto. 1997. *The Christian Democratic International*. Lanham, Boulder, New York, and London: Rowman & Littlefield Publishers.

Parisella, Antonio. 2001. "Christian Movements and Parties of the Left in Italy, 1938–1958." In *Left Catholicism 1943–1955: Catholics and Society in Western Europe at the Point of Liberation*, edited by Gerd-Rainer Horn and Emmanuel Gerard, pp. 142–73. Leuven: Leuven University Press.

Parola, Alessandro. 2007. "Pensare la ricostruzione: gli incontri di casa Padovani." In *Giuseppe Dossetti: la fede e la storia. Studi nel decennale della morte*, edited by Alberto Melloni, pp. 261–80. Bologna: Il Mulino.

Parola, Alessandro, and Marcello Malpensa. 2005. *Lazzati: una sentinella nella notte, 1909–1986*. Bologna: Il Mulino.

Pasolini, Pier Paolo. 1974a. "Gli italiani non sono più quelli." *Corriere della Sera*, June 10.

Pasolini, Pier Paolo. 1974b. "I dilemmi di un Papa oggi." *Corriere della Sera*, September, 22

Passelecq, Georges, and Bernard Sucheky. 1997. T*he Hidden Encyclical of Pius XI*. New York and London: Harcourt and Brace.

Passerin D'Entrèves, Ettore. 1981. "Cattolici liberali." In *Dizionario storico del Movimento cattolico in Italia*, edited by Francesco Traniello and Giorgio Campanini, vol. I/2, pp. 2–9. Casale Monferrato: Marietti.

Patch, William. 2010. "The Catholic Church, the Third Reich, and the Origins of the Cold War: On the Utility and Limitations of Historical Evidence." *Journal of Modern History* 82(2): pp. 396–433.

Pavone, Claudio. 1991. *Una Guerra civile. Saggio storico sulla moralità nella Resistenza*. Turin: Bollati Boringhieri.

Pedrazzi, Luigi. 1966. "Il rinnovamento religioso in Italia." *Il Mulino* 16(3): pp. 232–47.

Pellettier, Gérard. 2013. *Rome et la Révolution Française. La théologie politique et la politique du Saint-Siège devan la Révolution française*. Rome: Publications de l'École française de Rome.

Per la comunità. 1945. *Per la comunità cristiana. Principi dell'ordinamento sociale, a cura di un gruppo di studiosi amici di Camaldoli*. Rome: ICAS.

Pera, Marcello. 2008. *Perchè dobbiamo dirci cristiani*. Milan: Mondadori.

Pertici, Roberto. 2003. "Il vario anticomunismo italiano (1936–1960). Lineamenti di una storia." In *Due nazioni. Legittimazione e delegittimazione nella storia dell'Italia contemporanea*, edited by Loreto De Nucci and Ernesto Galli della Loggia, pp. 261–334. Bologna: Il Mulino.

Pertici, Roberto. 2009. *Chiesa e Stato in Italia. Dalla Grande Guerra al nuovo Concordato, 1914–1984*. Bologna: Il Mulino.

Piccio, Daniela R. 2014 "Party Feminisation from Below: Christian Democracy in Feminist Times." In *Gender, Conservatism and Womens' Political Representation*, edited by Karen Celis and Sarah Childs, pp. 63–82. Colchester: ECPR Press.

Piretti, Maria Serena. 2003. *La legge truffa. Il fallimento dell'ingegneria politica*. Bologna: Il Mulino.

Plongeron, Bernard. 1973. *Théologie et politique au siècle des lumières, 1770–1820*. Geneva: Droz.

Pollard, John. 1990. "Catholic Conservatives and Italian Fascism: The Clerico-Fascists." In *Fascists and Conservatives: The Radical Right and the Establishment in Twentieth Century Europe*, edited by Martin Blinkhorn, pp. 31–49. London: Unwin Hyman.

Pollard, John. 2005. *The Vatican and Italian Fascism, 1929–1932*. Cambridge: Cambridge University Press.

Pollard, John. 2007. "Clerical Fascism: Context, Overview and Conclusion." *Totalitarian Movements and Political Religions* 8(2): pp. 433–46.

Pollard, John. 2008. *Catholicism in Modern Italy: Religion, Society and Politics since 1861*. London and New York: Routledge.

Pollard, John. 2013. "Pius XI's Promotion of the Italian Model of Catholic Action in the World-Wide Church." *Journal of Ecclesiastic History* 63(4): pp. 758–84.

Pombeni, Paolo. 1976. *Le "Cronache Sociali" di Dossetti: Geografia di un movimento d'opinione*. Florence: Vallecchi.

Pombeni, Paolo. 1979a. *Il gruppo dossettiano e la fondazione della democrazia in Italia, 1943–1948*. Bologna: Il Mulino.

Pombeni, Paolo. 1979b. "Il gruppo dossettiano." In *Cultura, politica e partiti nell'età della Costituente*, Vol. I: *L'area liberal-democratica. Il mondo cattolico e la Democrazia Cristiana*, edited by Roberto Ruffili, pp. 425–92. Bologna: Il Mulino.

Pombeni, Paolo. 1980. "Alle origini della proposta culturale di Giuseppe Dossetti." *Cristianesimo nella storia* 1(1): pp. 251–72.

Pombeni, Paolo. 1995. *La Costituente. Un problema storico-politico*. Bologna: Il Mulino.

Pombeni, Paolo. 1996. "Individuo/persona nella Costituzione Italiana. Il contributo del Dossettismo." *Parola Chiave* 10–11: pp. 197–218.

Pombeni, Paolo. 1997. "I partiti e la politica dal 1948 al 1963." In *Storia d'Italia*, Vol. V: *La Repubblica*, edited by Giovanni Sabbatucci and Vittorio Vidotto, pp. 127–251. Rome and Bari: Laterza.

Pombeni, Paolo. 2000. "The Ideology of Christian Democracy." *Journal of Political Ideologies* 5: pp. 289–300.

Pombeni, Paolo. 2006. "Il contributo dei cattolici alla Costituente." In *Valori e principi del regime repubblicano*, Vol. I: *Sovranità e democrazia*, edited by Silvano Labriola, pp. 37–80. Rome and Bari: Larterza.

Pombeni, Paolo. 2008. "Anti-Liberalism and the Liberal Legacy in Post-War European Constitutionalism: Consideration on Some Case Studies." *European Journal of Political Theory* 7(1): pp. 31–44.

Pombeni, Paolo. 2013. *Giuseppe Dossetti. L'avventura politica di un riformatore cristiano*. Bologna: Il Mulino.

Pombeni, Paolo, Guido Formigoni, and Giorgio Vecchio. 2023. *Storia della Democrazia Cristiana, 1943–1993*. Bologna: Il Mulino.

Ponzio, Alessio. 2015. *Shaping the New Man: Youth Training Regimes in Fascist Italy and Nazi Germany*. Madison: University of Wisconsin Press.

Porter-Szücs, Brian. 2011. *Faith and Fatherland: Catholicism, Modernity, and Poland*. Oxford: Oxford University Press.

Portoghesi Tuzi, Telemaco, and Grazia Tuzi. 2010. *Quando si faceva la Costituzione. Storia e personaggi della Comunità del porcellino*. Milan: Il Saggiatore.

Poulat, Émile. 1969. *Intégrisme et Catholicisme Intégral. Un réseau secret international anti-moderniste: La "Sapinière" 1909–1921*. Paris: Casterman.

Poulat, Émile. 1996 [1962]. *Histoire, dogme et critique dans la crise moderniste*. Paris: Michel.

Preda, Daniela. 2004. *Alcide De Gasperi federalista europeo*. Bologna: Il Mulino.

Prelot, Marcel. 1969. *Le libéralisme catholique*. Paris: Colin.

Preston, Andrew. 2006. "Bridging the Gap between Church and State in the History of American Foreign Relations." *Diplomatic History* 30(5): pp. 783–812.

Prezzi, Lorenzo. 1985. "Le note di Loreto: maturità e 'parresia'." *Il Regno* 30(529): pp. 279–89.

Quagliariello, Gaetano. 2003. *La legge elettorale del 1953*. Bologna: Il Mulino.

Quagliariello, Gaetano. 2006. *Cattolici, pacifisti, teocon. Chiesa e politica in Italia dopo la caduta del muro*. Milan: Mondadori.

Radi, Luciano. 2005. *La DC da De Gasperi a Fanfani*. Soveria Mannelli: Rubbettino.

Rauch, Jr, Rufus W. 1972. *Politics and Beliefs in Contemporary France: Emmanuel Mounier and Christian Democracy, 1932–1950*. The Hague: Martinus Nijhoff.

Rawls, John. 1993. *Political Liberalism*. New York: Columbia University Press.

Riccardi, Andrea. 1979. *Roma "citta sacra"? Dalla Conciliazione all'operazione Sturzo*. Milan: Vita e Pensiero.

Riccardi, Andrea. 1981. "Il clerico-fascismo." In *Storia del movimento cattolico italiano*, Vol. 4: *I cattolici dal fascismo alla Resistenza*, edited by Francesco Malgeri, pp. 3–38. Rome: Il Poligono.

Riccardi, Andrea. 1983. *Il "partito romano" del secondo dopoguerra (1945–1954)*. Brescia: Morcelliana.

Riccardi, Andrea. 1998. "La 'nazione cattolica'." In *Interpretazioni della Repubblica*, edited by Agostino Giovagnoli, pp. 47–72. Bologna: Il Mulino.

Riccardi, Andrea. 2003. *Pio XII e Alcide De Gasperi. Una storia segreta*. Rome and Bari: Laterza.

Riconciliazione. 1984. *Riconciliazione cristiana e comunità degli uomini. Contributi per un dibattito*. Milan: EDIT.

Ricoeur, Paul. 1950. "Une philosophie personnaliste." *Esprit* 18(174): pp. 860–87.

Rinaldini, Emi. 1957. *Il sigillo del sangue*. Brescia: La Scuola.

Rosati, Massimo. 2012. "The Turkish Laboratory: Local Modernity and the Postsecular in Turkey." In *Multiple Modernities and Postsecular Societies*, edited by Massimo Rosati and Kristina Stoeckl, pp. 61–78. Farnham, Surrey, UK and Burlington, VT: Ashgate.

Rosmini, Antonio. 1848. *La Costituzione secondo la giustizia sociale*. Milan: Redaelli.

Rosmini, Antonio. 1892. *Epistolario Completo*, vol. X. Casale Monferrato: Giovanni Panne.

Rosmini, Antonio. 1985. *Filosofia della politica*, edited by Sergio Cotta. Milan: Rusconi.

Rossi, Mario G. 1977. *Le origini del partito cattolico. Movimento cattolico e lotta di classe nell'Italia liberale*. Rome: Editori Riuniti.

Rossi, Nicola, and Gianni Toniolo. 1992. "Catching Up or Falling Behind? Italy's Economic Growth, 1895–1947." *Economic History Review* 45(3): pp. 537–63.

Rossi, Nicola, and Gianni Toniolo. 1998. "Italy." In *Economic Growth in Europe since 1945*, edited by Nicholas Crafts and Gianni Toniolo, pp. 427–54. Cambridge: Cambridge University Press.

Rossi-Doria, Anna. 2000. "Italian Women Enter Politics." In *When the War Was Over: Women, War and Peace in Europe, 1940–1956*, edited by Claire Duchen and Irene Bandhauer-Schöffmann, pp. 89–102. London and New York: Leicester University Press.

Rossini, Giuseppe (ed.). 1967. *I cattolici nei tempi nuovi della cristianità*. Rome: Cinque Lune.

Roundtable. 2011. "Roundtable: Historians and the Question of Modernity." *American Historical Review* 116(3): pp. 577–751.

Roy, Olivier. 2016. "Beyond Populism: The Conservative Right, the Courts, the Churches and the Concept of Christian Europe." In *Saving the People: How Populists Hijack Religion*, edited by Nadia Marzouki, Duncan McDonnell, and Olivier Roy, pp. 185–201. New York: Oxford University Press.

Ruffilli, Roberto. 1980. "La formazione del progetto democratico cristiano nella società italiana dopo il fascismo." In *Democrazia Cristiana e Costituente*, Vol. I, edited by Giuseppe Rossini, pp. 29–106. Rome: Cinque Lune.

Ruffilli, Roberto, and Piero Alberto Capotosti (eds) 1988. *Il cittadino come arbitro. La DC e le riforme istituzionali*. Bologna: Il Mulino.

Ruini, Camillo. 1985. "Dalla Parola alla cultura." *Vita & Pensiero* 70(5): pp. 322–38.

Ruini, Camillo. 1992. "Evangelizzazione e testimonianza della carità nel ministero del Cardinale Giacomo Lercaro." In *L'eredità pastorale di Giacomo Lercaro. Studi e testimonianze*, edited by the Centro servizi generali dell'arcidiocesi di Bologna, pp. 299–324. Bologna: Dehoniane.

Ruini, Camillo. 1996. *Chiesa del nostro tempo. Prolusioni 1991-1996*. Casale Monferrato: Piemme.

Ruini, Camillo. 2004. "La Chiesa in Italia: Da Loreto ai compiti del presente." *Vita & Pensiero* 87(6): pp. 7–16.

Ruini, Camillo. 2005. *"Nuovi segni dei tempi." Le sorti della fede nell'età dei mutamenti*. Milan: Mondadori.

Ruini, Camillo. 2010. *Verità è libertà. Il ruolo della Chiesa in una società aperta*. Milan: Mondadori.

Rumor, Mariano. 1991. *Memorie, 1943-1970*, edited by Ermenegildo Russo and Francesco Malgeri. Vicenza: Neri Pozza.

Sala, Giorgio. 1945. "Mazzini vivo." *Il Popolo*, March 10.

Sale, Giovanni. 2005. *De Gasperi, gli Usa e il Vaticano all'inizio della guerra fredda*. Milan: Jaca Book.

Sale, Giovanni. 2008. *Il Vaticano e la Costituzione*. Milan: Jaca Book.

Sale, Giovanni. 2009. *Le leggi razziali in Italia e il Vaticano*. Milan: Jaca Book.

Salvadori, Massimo L. 2011. *Liberalismo italiano: I dilemmi della libertà*. Rome: Donzelli.

Sani, Roberto. 2004. *"La Civiltà Cattolica" e la politica italiana del secondo dopoguerra (1945-1958)*. Milano: Vita e Pensiero.

Santagata, Alessandro. 2014. *"Ruinismo*: The Catholic Church in Italy from 'Mediation Culture' to the Cultural Project." *Journal of Modern Italian Studies* 19(4): pp. 438–52.

Sarfatti, Michele. 2000. *Gli ebrei nell'Italia fascista. Vicende, identità, persecuzione*. Turin: Einaudi.

Saresella, Daniela. 1994. *Romolo Murri e il movimento socialista (1891-1907)*. Urbino: Quattro Venti.

Saresella, Daniela. 2004. "Il dissenso cattolico." In *La nazione cattolica. Chiesa e società in Italia dal 1958 ad oggi*, pp. 265–89. Milan: Guerini.

Saresella, Daniela. 2014. "I cattolici democratici e la fine dell'unità politica dei cattolici." In *L'Italia contemporanea dagli anni Ottanta a oggi*, Vol. III: *Istituzioni e politica*, edited by Simona Colarizi, Agostino Giovagnoli, and Paolo Pombeni, pp. 205–25. Rome: Carocci.

Saresella, Daniela. 2019. *Catholics and Communists in Twentieth-Century Italy: Between Conflict and Dialogue*. London and New York: Bloomsbury.

Scalfari, Eugenio. 1978. "Quel che Moro mi disse il 18 febbraio. L'ultima intervista del leader DC." *La Repubblica*, October 18.

Scalfari, Eugenio. 1983. "De Mita risponde a Craxi e Berlinguer." *La Repubblica*, April 11.

Scotti, Vincenzo. 2004. *Diario minimo. Un irregolare nel palazzo*. Rome: Memori.

Schloesser, Stephen. 2006. "Against Forgetting: Memory, History, Vatican II." *Theological Studies* 67(2): pp. 275–319.

Scirè, Giambattista. 2007. *Il divorzio in Italia. Partiti, Chiesa, società civile dalla legge al referendum (1965–1974)*. Milan: Mondadori.

Scirè, Giambattista. 2008. *L'aborto in Italia. Storia di una legge*. Milan: Mondadori

Scoppola, Pietro. 1961. *Crisi modernista e rinnovamento cattolico in Italia*. Bologna: Il Mulino.

Scoppola, Pietro. 1967. "I fatti del '31: verso il conflitto." In *Chiesa e fascismo. Documenti e interpretazioni*, pp. 255–81. Bari: Laterza.

Scoppola, Pietro. 1977. *La proposta politica di De Gasperi*. Bologna: Il Mulino.

Scoppola, Pietro. 1980. *Gli anni della Costituente fra politica e storia*. Bologna: Il Mulino.

Scoppola, Pietro. 1981. "La spiritualità sorgente interiore dell'azione." *La Discussione/ Storia* 13(13).

Scoppola, Pietro. 1997. *La repubblica dei partiti. Evoluzione e crisi di un sistema politico, 1945–1996*. Bologna: Il Mulino.

Scornajenghi, Antonio. 2012. *L'Italia di Giovanni Paolo II*. Cinisello Balsano: San Paolo.

Scultenover, David G. 1993. *A View from Rome: On the Eve of the Modernist Crisis*. New York: Fordham University Press.

Secondo congresso. 1875. *Secondo congresso cattolico italiano tenutosi in Firenze dal 22 al 26 novembre 1875*. Bologna: Tipografia Felsinea.

Setta, Sandro. 1995. *L'Uomo Qualunque, 1944–1948*. Rome and Bari: Laterza.

Seymour, Mark. 2006. *Debating Divorce in Italy: Marriage and the Making of Modern Italians, 1860–1974*. New York: Palgrave Macmillan.

Shah, Timothy Samuel, Alfred C. Stepan, and Monica Duffy Toft (eds). 2012. *Rethinking Religion and World Affairs*. New York: Oxford University Press.

Sheehan, Jonathan. 2003. "Enlightenment, Religion and the Enigma of Secularization." *American Historical Review* 108(4): pp. 1061–80.

Sigmund, Paul. 1987. "The Catholic Tradition and Democracy." *Review of Politics* 49(4): pp. 530–48.

Sorge, Bartolomeo. 1979. *La "ricomposizione" dell'area cattolica in Italia*. Rome: Città Nuova.

Sorge, Bartolomeo (ed.). 1981. *Il dibattito sulla "ricomposizione" dell'area cattolica in Italia*. Rome: Città Nuova.

Sorkin, David. 2008. *The Religious Enlightenment: Protestants, Jews, and Catholics from London to Vienna*. Princeton: Princeton University Press.

Spataro, Giuseppe. 1949. "La rinascita del Parlamento." *Il Popolo*, April 16.

Spreafico, Sandro. 1989. *I cattolici reggiani dallo Stato totalitario alla democrazia: la Resistenza come problema*, Vol. II: *Davide senza fionda: il laicato cattolico dalla opposizione bloccata al collateralismo conflittuale*. Reggio Emilia: Tecnograf.

Stark, Rodney. 1999. "Secularization R.I.P." *Sociology of Religion* 60(3): pp. 249–73.

Sternhell, Zeev. 1983. *Ni droite, ni gauche. L'idéologie fasciste en France*. Paris: Éditions du Seuil.

Stone, Marla. 2008. "The Changing Face of the Enemy in Fascist Italy." *Constellations* 15(3): pp. 332–50.

Stone, Marla. 2012. "Italian Fascism's Soviet Enemy and the Propaganda of Hate, 1941–1943." *Journal of Hate Studies* 10(1): 73–97.

Stow, Kenneth. 2006. *Jewish Dogs. An Image and Its Interpreters*. Stanford: Stanford University Press.

Sturzo, Luigi. 1898. "La Cultura sociale." *La Croce di Costantino*, February 6.

Sturzo, Luigi. 1902. "Cultura e azione." *La Croce di Costantino*, April 13.

Sturzo, Luigi. 1906. *I problemi della vita nazionale dei cattolici italiani*. Rome: Società nazionale di cultura.

Sturzo, Luigi. 1945a. "Chiesa cattolica e Democrazia Cristiana. Oggi e dopo la guerra." *La Libertà*, May 10.

Sturzo, Luigi. 1945b. "Has Fascism Ended with Mussolini?" *Review of Politics* 7(3): pp. 306–15.

Sturzo, Luigi. 1946. "La libertà nelle mani del popolo." *Il Popolo*, June 8.

Sturzo, Luigi. 1947. "The Philosopic Background of Christian Democracy." *Review of Politics* 9(1): pp. 3–15.

Sturzo, Luigi. 1951. *I discorsi politici*. Rome: Istituto Luigi Sturzo.

Sturzo, Luigi. 1956. *Il Partito Popolare Italiano*, Vol. I: *1919–1922*. Bologna: Il Mulino.

Sturzo, Luigi. 1957. "Il problema della libertà e la crisi italiana." In *Il Partito Popolare Italiano*, Vol. III: *1923–1926*, pp. 178–208. Bologna: Zanichelli.

Sturzo, Luigi. 1958. "Il Nostro Programma (1900)." In *La Croce di Costantino*. Rome: Edizioni di Storia e Letteratura.

Sturzo, Luigi. 1959. "Il pericolo dell'operazione Sturzo." *Il Giornale d'Italia*, February 21.

Sturzo, Luigi. 1960. *La società: sua natura e leggi (1935)*. Bologna: Zanichelli.

Sturzo, Luigi. 1961a. *Sintesi sociali. L'organizzazione di classi e le unioni professionali*. Bologna: Zanichelli.

Sturzo, Luigi. 1961b. "Costituzione, Finalità e Funzionamento del Partito Popolare Italiano (1919)." In *Opera Omnia*, Seconda Serie, Vol. III: *Il Partito Popolare Italiano*, pp. 74–87. Bologna: Zanichelli.

Sturzo, Luigi. 1971. "Democrazia cristiana (1936)." In *Nazionalismo e internazionalismo (1946)*. Bologna: Zanichelli.

Sturzo, Luigi. 1972. *Politica e morale (1938). Coscienza e politica (1953)*. Bologna: Zanichelli.

Sturzo, Luigi. 1974a. "Due papi e l'ora presente (1904)." In *Scritti inediti I, 1890–1924*, pp. 250–7. Rome: Cinque Lune.

Sturzo, Luigi. 1974b. "Giornalismo ed educazione nei seminari. (1902)." In *Scritti Inediti I, 1890–1924*, pp. 224–6. Rome: Cinque Lune.

Sturzo, Luigi. 1996. *Il manuale del buon politico*, edited by Gabriele De Rosa. Cinisello Balsamo: San Paolo.

Szakolczai, Arpad. 1998. *Max Weber and Michel Foucault: Parallel Life-Works*. London and New York: Routledge.

Szakolczai, Arpad. 2003. *The Genesis of Modernity*. London: Routledge.

Szakolczai, Arpad. 2007. *Sociology, Religion and Grace: A Quest for the Renaissance*. London: Routledge.

Szakolczai, Arpad. 2008. "Sinn aus Erfahrung." In *Erleben, Erleiden, Erfahren: Die Konstitution sozialen Sinns jenseits instrumenteller Vernunft*, edited by Kay Junge, Daniel Suber, and Gerold Gerber, pp. 63–99. Bielefeld: Transcript Verlag.

Szakolczai, Arpad. 2009. "Liminality and Experience: Structuring Transitory Situations and Transformative Events." *International Political Anthropology* 2(1): 141–72.

Taccolini, Mario, and Pietro Cafaro. 1996. *Il banco Ambrosiano. Una banca cattolica negli anni dell'ascesa economica lombarda*. Rome and Bari: Laterza.

Tassani, Giovanni. 1988. *La terza generazione. Da Dossetti a De Gasperi, tra Stato e rivoluzione*. Rome: Edizioni Lavoro.

Taviani, Paolo Emilio. 1949. "Al di là dell'inquietudine." *Il Popolo*, December 4.

Taviani, Paolo Emilio. 1988. "Il contributo dei cattolici." *Civitas* 2: pp. 71–81.

Taviani, Paolo Emilio. 2002. *Politica a memoria d'uomo*. Bologna: Il Mulino.

Taylor, Charles. 1996. *A Catholic Modernity? Charles Taylor's Marianist Award Lecture*, edited and introduced by James L. Heft. Oxford: Oxford University Press.

Taylor, Charles. 2003. *Varieties of Religion Today: William James Revisited.* Cambridge, MA: Harvard University Press.

Taylor, Charles. 2007. *A Secular Age.* Cambridge, MA: Harvard University Press.

The Persistence. 2010. "The Persistence of Religion in Modern Europe." Special issue of *Journal of Modern History* 82(2): pp. 255–517.

Thomas, Scott M. 2005. *The Global Resurgence of Religion in the Transformation of International Relations: The Struggle for the Soul of the Twentieth-First Century.* New York: Palgrave Macmillan.

Thomassen, Bjørn. 2001. *The Borders and Boundaries of the Julian Region: Narrating Self and Nation from the Fringes of the Italo-Slav Border,* PhD dissertation, European University Institute, Florence.

Thomassen, Bjørn. 2006. "Italy from Below and from the Outside-In: An Istrian Life Story across the Italo-Yugoslav Border." *Acta Histriae* 14(1): pp. 155–78.

Thomassen, Bjørn. 2009. "The Uses and Meaning of Liminality." *International Political Anthropology* 2(1): 5–28.

Thomassen, Bjørn. 2010. "Anthropology, Multiple Modernities, and the Axial Age Debate." *Anthropological Theory* 10(4): 321–42.

Thomassen, Bjørn. 2012a. "Notes Toward an Anthropology of Political Revolution." *Comparative Studies in Society and History* 54(3): pp. 679–706.

Thomassen, Bjørn. 2012b. "Reason and Religion in Rawls: Voegelin's Challenge." *Philosophia* 40(2): pp. 237–52.

Thomassen, Bjørn. 2014a. *Liminality and the Modern: Living Through the In-Between.* Farnham: Ashgate.

Thomassen, Bjørn. 2014b. "Debating Modernity as Secular Religion: Hans Kelsen's Futile Exchange with Eric Voegelin." *History and Theory* 53(3): 435–50.

Thomassen, Bjørn, and Rosario Forlenza. 2015. "Voegelin's Impact on the Italian Response to Modernity: The Parallel Life-Works of Augusto Del Noce and Eric Voegelin." *VoegelinView,* November 26, 2014, http://voegelinview.com/voegelins-impact-italian-response-modernity-parallel-life-works-augusto-del-noce-eric-voegelin/ (last accessed: June 6, 2023).

Thomassen, Bjørn, and Rosario Forlenza. 2016a. "Catholic Modernity and the Italian Constitution." *History Workshop Journal* 81: 231–51.

Thomassen, Bjørn, and Rosario Forlenza. 2016b. "Christianity and Political Thought: Augusto Del Noce and the Ideology of Christian Democracy in Post-War Italy." *Journal of Political Ideologies* 21(2): pp. 181–99.

Toniolo, Giuseppe. 1897. "Il concetto cristiano della democrazia." *Rivista Internazionale di Scienze Sociali e Discipline Ausiliare* 14: pp. 325–69.

Toniolo, Giuseppe. 1949. "Il concetto cristiano della democrazia (1897)." In *Democrazia cristiana. Concetti e indirizzi,* with a preface by Alcide De Gasperi, pp. 17–90. Città del Vaticano: Tip. Poliglotta Vaticana.

Tornielli, Andrea. 2011. *La fragile concordia. Stato e cattolici in centocinquant'anni di storia italiana.* Milan: Rizzoli.

Totaro, Pierluigi. 2005. "L'azione politica di Aldo Moro per l'autonomia e l'unità della DC nella crisi del 1960." *Studi Storici* 46(2): pp. 437–513.

Tramontin, Silvio. 1968. *La figura e l'opera sociale di Luigi Cerutti. Aspetti e momenti del movimento cattolico nel Veneto.* Brescia: Morcelliana.

Traniello, Francesco. 1966. *Società religiosa e società civile in Rosmini.* Bologna: Il Mulino.

Traniello, Francesco. 1970. *Cattolicesimo conciliarista. Religione e cultura nella tradizione rosminiana lombardo-piemontese (1825–1870).* Milan: Marzorati.

Traniello, Francesco. 1998. *Città dell'uomo. Cattolici, partito e Stato nella Storia d'Italia*. Bologna: Il Mulino.

Traniello, Francesco. 2007a. "Mondo cattolico e cultura popolare in Italia." In *Religione Cattolica e Stato nazionale. Dal Risorgimento al secondo dopoguerra*, pp. 193–263. Bologna: Il Mulino.

Traniello, Francesco. 2007b. "La nazione cattolica. Lineamenti di una storia." In *Religione cattolica e stato nazionale. Dal Risorgimento al secondo dopoguerra*, pp. 7–57. Bologna: Il Mulino.

Traniello, Francesco. 2007c. "Guerra e religione. L'Italia cattolica nella seconda guerra mondiale." In *Religione cattolica e stato nazionale. Dal Risorgimento al secondo dopoguerra*, pp. 265–97. Bologna: Il Mulino.

Traniello, Francesco. 2009. "Verso un nuovo profilo dei rapporti tra Stato e Chiesa in Italia." In *Stato e Chiesa in Italia. Le radici di una svolta*, edited by Francesco Traniello, Franco Bolgiani, and Francesco Margiotta Broglio, pp. 13–52. Bologna: Il Mulino.

Tronti, Mario. 2019. *Il popolo perduto. Per una critica della sinistra*. Rome: Nutrimenti.

Trotta, Giuseppe. 1996. *Giuseppe Dossetti. La rivoluzione nello Stato*. Florence: Camunia.

Turner, Bryan S. 2011. *Religion and Modern Society: Citizenship, Secularization and the State*. Cambridge: Cambridge University Press.

Turner, Victor W. 1967. "Betwixt and Between: The Liminal Period in Rites de Passage." In *The Forest of Symbols: Aspects of Ndembu Ritual*, pp. 93–111. Ithaca: Cornell University Press.

Turoldo, David Maria. 1948. "Meditazione sul voto del 18 aprile." *Cronache Sociali* 2(8): pp. 1–2.

Un vescovo. 1988. *Un vescovo italiano del Concilio, Enrico Bartoletti 1916–1976*. Genoa: Marietti.

Vaillancourt, Jean-Guy. 1980. *Papal Power: A Study of Vatican Control over Lay Catholic Elites*. Berkeley: University of California Press.

Van Gennep, Arnold. 1960. *The Rites of Passage*, translated by Monika B. Vizedom and Gabrielle L. Caffee. Chicago: University of Chicago Press (originally published in 1909 as *Les rites de passage*).

Van Hecke, Steven, and Emmanuel Gerard (eds). 2004. *Christian Democratic Parties in Europe since the End of the Cold War*. Leuven: Leuven University Press.

Van Kley, Dale K. 1996. *The Religious Origins of the French Revolution: From Calvin to the Civil Constitution, 1560–1791*. New Haven: Yale University Press.

Vanoni, Ezio. 1977. *La politica economica degli anni degasperiani. Scritti e discorsi politici ed economici*, edited by Piero Barucci. Florence: Le Monnier.

Vecchio, Giorgio. 1997. "Il laicato cattolico italiano di fronte alla Guerra e alla Resistenza: scelte personali e appartenenza ecclesiale." In *Cattolici, Chiesa, Resistenza*, edited by Gabriele De Rosa, pp. 251–98. Bologna: Il Mulino.

Vecchio, Giorgio. 2001. "Left Catholicism and the Experiences on the Frontier of the Church and Italian Society (1939–1958)." In *Left Catholicism: Catholics and Society in Western Europe at the Point of Liberation*, edited by Gerd-Rainer Horn and Emmanuel Gerard, pp. 174–95. Leuven: Leuven University Press.

Vecchio, Giorgio. 2009. " 'Esule in patria': gli anni del fascismo." In *Alcide De Gasperi. Dal Trentino all'esilio in patria (1881–1943)*, edited by Alfredo Canavero, Paolo Pombeni, Giovanni Battista Re, and Giorgio Vecchio, pp. 422–722. Soveria Mannelli: Rubbettino.

Vecchio, Giorgio. 2011. "Guerra e resistenza." *Cristiani d'Italia*, Vol. 1, edited by Alberto Melloni, pp. 733–46. Rome: Istituto della Enciclopedia Italiana.

Verucci, Guido. 1967. *L'"Avenir."* *Antologia degli articoli*. Rome: Edizioni di Storia e Letteratura.

Verucci, Guido. 2002. "Il dissenso cattolico in Italia." *Studi Storici* 43(1): pp. 215–33.

Vezzosi, Elisabetta. 1986. "La sinistra democristiana tra neutralismo e Patto Atlantico (1947–1949)." In *L'Italia e la politica di potenza in Europa*, edited by Ennio Di Nolfo, Roman H. Rainero, and Brunello Vigezzi, pp. 195–221. Milan: Marzorati.

Viaene, Vincent. 2000. *Belgium and the Holy See from Gregory XVI to Pius IX (1831–1859): Catholic Revival, Society and Politics in Nineteenth-Century Europe*. Leuven: Leuven University Press.

Viaene, Vincent. 2008. "International History, Religious History, Catholic History: Perspectives for Cross-Fertilization (1830–1914)." *European History Quarterly* 38(4): pp. 568–607.

Villa, Roberto (ed.). 2008. *Dossetti a Rossena. I piani e i tempi dell'impegno politico*. Reggio Emilia: Aliberti.

Vincent, Mary. 1996. *Catholicism in the Second Spanish Republic: Religion and Politics in Salamanca, 1930–1936*. Oxford: Oxford University Press.

Violi, Roberto P. 1997. "Il Sud." In *Cattolici, Chiesa, Resistenza*, edited by Gabriele De Rosa, pp. 109–46. Bologna: Il Mulino.

Voegelin, Eric. 1952. *The New Science of Politics: An Introduction*. Chicago: University of Chicago Press.

Voegelin, Eric. 1987. "Equivalences of Experiences and Symbolization in History (1970)." In *The Collected Works*, Vol. 12: *Published Essays, 1966–1985*, edited by E. Sandoz, pp. 115–33. Baton Rouge: Louisiana State University Press.

Voegelin, Eric. 1999. *Collected Works*, Vol. 4: *The Authoritarian State: An Essay on the Problem of the Austrian State (1936)*, edited by Gilbert Weiss. Columbia: University of Missouri Press.

Voegelin, Eric. 2000. "Gnostic Politics (1952)." In *The Collected Works of Eric Voegelin*, Vol. 10: *Published Essays, 1940–1952*, edited by Ellis Sandoz, pp. 223–40. Columbia and London: University of Missouri Press.

Wagner, Peter. 2012. *Modernity: Understanding the Present*. Cambridge and Malden, MA: Polity Press.

Warner, Carolyn M. 2000. *Confessions of an Interest Group: The Catholic Church and Political Parties in Europe*. Princeton: Princeton University Press.

Weber, Maria. 1977. *Il voto alle donne*. Turin: Quaderni di Biblioteca della Libertà.

Weber, Max. 1920-1. *Gesammelte Aufsätze zur Religionssoziologie*, edited by Marianne Wever. Tübingen: Mohr.

Weber, Max. 1958. "The Social Psychology of the World Religions (1922–1923)." In *From Max Weber: Essays in Sociology*, edited and translated by Hans H. Gerth and C. Wright Mills, pp. 267–301. New York: Oxford University Press.

White, Steven A. 2003. "Christian Democracy or Pacellian Populism? Rival Forms of Postwar Italian Catholicism." In *European Christian Democracy: Historical Legacies and Comparative Perspectives*, edited by Thomas Kselman and Joseph A. Buttigieg, pp. 199–228. Notre Dame, IN: University of Notre Dame Press.

Wicks, Jared. 2018. *Investigating Vatican II: Its Theologians, Ecumenical Turn, and Biblical Commitment*. Washington, DC: Catholic University of America Press.

Williams, Olivier F., and John W. Houch (eds). 1993. *Catholic Social Thought and the New World Order: Building on One Hundred Years*. Notre Dame, IN: University of Notre Dame Press.

Wolkenstein, Fabio. 2023. "Christian Europe Redux." *Journal of Common Market Studies* 61(3): pp. 636–52, https://doi.org/10.1111/jcms.13400 (last accessed: October 18, 2022).

Wydra, Harald. 2007. *Communism and the Emergence of Democracy*. Cambridge: Cambridge University Press.

Wydra, Harald. 2015. *Politics and the Sacred*. Cambridge: Cambridge University Press.

Wydra, Harald. 2018. "Generations of Memory: Elements of a Conceptual Framework." *Comparative Studies in Society and History* 60(1): 5–34.

Zaccagnini, Begnino. 1975. "La partecipazione dei cattolici al C.L.N." In *Cattolici nella Resistenza ravennate*, pp. 35–50. Ravenna: Edizioni del Centro studi Giuseppe Donati.

Zaccaria, Francesco Maria. 1790. *Le dottrine del preteso secolo illuminato XVIII. Intorno la gerarchia e la disciplina ecclesiastica confrontata colle dottrine del tenebroso secolo XVI*. Faenza: G. Archi.

Zampetti, Enrico. 1992. *Dal lager. Lettera a Marisa*, edited by Olindo Orlando and Claudio Sommaruga. Rome: Studium.

Zizola, Giancarlo. 1988. *Giovanni XXIII. La fede e la politica*. Rome-Bari: Laterza.

Index

For the benefit of digital users, indexed terms that span two pages (e.g., 52–53) may, on occasion, appear on only one of those pages.